CHINA
IN
LIFE'S
FOREGROUND

Also by Audrey Donnithorne

China's Economic System (Allen & Unwin, 1967)

British Rubber Manufacturing (Duckworth, 1958)

With G.C. Allen, *Western Enterprise in Indonesia and Malaya* (Allen & Unwin, 1957)

With G.C. Allen, *Western Enterprise in the Development of China and Japan* (Allen & Unwin, 1954)

'Is the World Heading to Starvation?' (The Catholic Social Guild, 1953)

Also, many articles and papers

CHINA
IN
LIFE'S
FOREGROUND

AUDREY G. DONNITHORNE

Australian Scholarly

© 2019,2020 Audrey G. Donnithorne
First published 2019 by
Australian Scholarly Publishing Pty Ltd
7 Lt Lothian St Nth, North Melbourne, Vic 3051

Tel: 03 9329 6963 / Fax: 03 9329 5452
enquiry@scholarly.info / www.scholarly.info

ISBN 978-1-925984-41-5

Cover: Anxian, early 1920s. Photograph by V. H. Donnithorne

Cover design: Wayne Saunders

Acknowledgements

I have many debts of thanks to pay in presenting these memoirs of a life, and first to the huge throng of persons who have contributed to my experiences in a journey of many decades. Limitations of space and time prevent me from mentioning them all, but this does not diminish my gratitude to each of them.

Mention must be made, however, of those who have helped me compose and publish this volume. With kindness and generosity Ilyas and Mara Khan have sponsored the preparation of these memoirs for publication while the expertise, skill and endless patience of Martin Alexander, the editor of the *Asia Literary Review*, have made a great contribution. I am also grateful to Terry and Bernadette Tobin for advice on publishers.

At an earlier stage, Brother Nicholas Koss OSB and Roy Peachey both gave me valuable assistance, while Leo F. Goodstadt read the whole manuscript with care and made many useful suggestions as did other kind friends including Father Jean Charbonnier, Francesca Currie, Grace Goodell, Father Pierre Jeanne, Robert and Parvine Merrillees, and Richard Rigby, to whom I am also most grateful for the Foreword that follows this note.

My cousin Philippa Ingram and other members of my family have given me constant encouragement and advice while Theodore Kwok and Martin Hui have shown great patience and kindness in frequently helping me overcome my digital incompetence.

I should like to give special thanks to my good friends who generously and with every consideration provide a support network through my old age in Hong Kong, especially Jimmy and Teresa Lai and their family, Dr

Helen Tinsley, Dr Kenneth Tsang, the Salesian clergy across the road and my wonderful helpers Johnette Rabanal and Editha Alacar; and, in earlier years, Leo and Rose Goodstadt, and also Dr Irene Osmund and Dr Ramon Ruiz. If I have overlooked anyone, I hope they will accept my deep apologies.

None of those mentioned, of course, is responsible for any of the opinions expressed in this book, or for any errors that may inadvertently have been included: these are all mine.

Audrey G. Donnithorne
Hong Kong
August 2018

Foreword

Anyone who has been in a Hong Kong taxi with Audrey Donnithorne and noted the reaction of the unsuspecting driver to her directions issued in a fluent stream of Sichuan-accented Mandarin, with just a dash of Oxford, will know that this is no ordinary woman. She is, indeed, in the very best sense, a woman with a past. And what a past! In the following pages she sets out in fascinating detail – except where an appropriate reticence is applied to some matters of continuing sensitivity – a most variegated life, lived and observed to the full in a range of countries, milieux and, indeed, eras: from late Imperial Britain through war and revolution, in England, in India, post-war Germany, cold-war Poland, Japan, America, Australia and, of course, most of all in China.

Dong Yude, to give Audrey the name by which her many Chinese friends have known her throughout a long life, is, in her own words, "an overseas Brit and a Sichuan country girl". She knew China, the land of her birth, well before she knew Britain (or the India that forms another fascinating family *leitmotiv* – of particular interest to me as a keen horseman, given her direct links to Skinner of the eponymous Skinner's Horse!). What is more, it was rural, inland China that formed the background to her childhood, the realities of which have continued to inform her subsequent approach to that country whether as a student, as a path-breaking scholar of the post-1949 Chinese economy, or as one who, to this day, continues a close and intimate involvement in that country.

Not the least intriguing aspect of this involvement is that of religion, in particular her engagement with the Catholic Church in China, through its many trials, triumphs and tragedies. This involvement, as she herself reveals, has included at times acting as a channel between the Chinese church and the Holy See – a matter of renewed topicality as I write these lines. This is, of course, one of those areas where discretion must, for the moment, apply, but she is still able to give enough of the story to engage and fascinate.

Overseas Brit and Sichuan country girl she may well be, but as an Australian I take particular pride in the knowledge that she did much of her best academic work and, as a scholar, spent some of her most productive years at the Australian National University. China scholars continue to benefit from her legacy to this day (although, sadly, not as much as some of us may wish). Her years at the ANU coincided with what was in many ways the Golden Age of this institution, and she met and interacted with many other outstanding scholars during this period, including the then relatively unknown Pierre Ryckmans/Simon Leys (she quotes a most poignant passage from one of his letters). Outside the field of China studies she engaged particularly with those working on countries of the socialist bloc (including my father, a Soviet specialist, and thus became a family friend); and was also a moving light behind a more vibrant and intellectually engaged Catholicism on the campus and in Canberra. Not perhaps surprising for one who had heard Ronald Knox preaching in Oxford, but much needed then, as it is now.

Speaking of times, and places, Audrey has an almost *Zelig*-like[1] quality of being present at crucial events and places – wartime Chongqing, London at the time of the flying bombs, Israel during the Yom Kippur War, and Cultural Revolution Macau and Hong Kong, to name but a few. This too adds to the interest of her story, but in particular because of her acute perception and the record she provides of these events, and the people associated with them. And although this is a serious book about serious issues, it is far from lacking in humour, a quality Audrey has never lacked and which has I am sure, together with her faith (and the two may well be related) stood her in good stead in more than a few tricky moments. One might mention as a good example of her eye for the

---

1 Woody Allen, 1983 – if you haven't, see the movie!

absurd her noting the slogan 'Down with Running Dogs' adjacent to the Macau Canidrome.

This eye for the absurd, however, should come with a health warning in the present era. Audrey is a person of strong and consistent principles, not all of which sit well with current orthodoxies. This applies just as much to contemporary intellectual and social life, and in particular to the university world, as it does to the behaviour of the Chinese Communist Party. When she was two and a half, and she and her family were kidnapped by bandits, her father wrote in his diary that she "has begun to realise the real character of our guards and is full of indignation at what she calls these 'naughty men'." The reader will soon learn that during the intervening years this aspect of Audrey's character, to her great credit, has not changed.

The only thing lacking from this volume is an account of some of Audrey's more recent involvement with matters Chinese; in particular, but not only, ecclesiastical. Towards the end of the memoir she intimates that, at a more propitious time, perhaps long after her death, a second volume might appear. One may only hope that it will. Audrey: *ad multos annos*!

Emeritus Professor Richard Rigby
Founding Director ANU China Institute
ANU College of Asia and the Pacific
Canberra
August 2018

Contents

Part One: Early Life: 1922–45

1. Childhood in China: 1922–27 3

2. Childhood in England: 1927–35 16

3. Secondary Schooling: 1935–39 – Parents' Furlough:
   1935–36 – My Return to China: 1940 39

4. Wartime in Sichuan: 1940–43........................57

5. A Wartime Journey and Life in Britain: 1943–45.............85

Part Two: University Life in Britain: 1945–68

6. Studying in Post-War Oxford: 1945–48 107

7. University College London,
   and South-East Asia Research: 1948–52 129

8. University College London – Turning to
   Contemporary China Research: 1953–60...................... 143

9. China Studies in London and Elsewhere: 1961–68......... 167

10. Extra-Mural Interests –
    Civic, Religious and Social: 1948–54............................ 198

11. More Extra-Mural Interests – Personal, Newman
    Demographic Survey, Culture Wars and
    Malta Interlude: 1954–68..213

Part Three: Life in Australia

12. Australia, and the Australian
    National University: 1969...241

13. Contemporary China Studies in
    Canberra: 1969–72..255

14. Life in Canberra, and the Culture Wars: 1969–73.........263

15. The Australian National University's
    First China Visit: 1973..278

16. Interlude – Israel and the Yom Kippur War: 1973 287

17. More Culture Warfare, China Studies, Australian
    Journeyings, Family and Friends: 1973–79....................295

18. Back to China on My Own –
    In Sichuan Again: 1980 325

19. Family and Friends, and Another Visit
    to China: 1980–82 339

20. More China Visits, American
    and UK Interludes: 1983–84 362

21. Retirement to Hong Kong: 1985.................................387

22. Interim Final Chapter..400

Appendix:
V. H. Donnithorne's Account of His Conversion 417

Index 424

PART ONE

Early Life: 1922–45

The kidnapped group just after release in August 1925. L–r: the Donnithornes, Major Iles, the Misses Armfield, Carleton and Settle (I do not know which is which), Mrs Mowll, Bishop Howard Mowll (later Anglican Archbishop of Sydney), and the Mowlls' servant, Ho Sze

CHAPTER 1

Childhood in China: 1922–27

I am an Overseas Brit and a Sichuan country girl. My grandparents were born in four different countries on three different continents, but all were intensely British, especially, perhaps, the duskier among them.

My parents were missionaries in Sichuan Province, China, where they were sent by the Church Missionary Society, an evangelical Anglican body with its headquarters in London, founded in 1799 by members of the "Clapham Sect",[1] with William Wilberforce, the great emancipator, as its vice president. My father, Vyvyan[2] Henry Donnithorne, as a young man in the first decade of the twentieth century, had been an engineer, the technical manager of a firm making early X-ray machines. He had lapsed into agnosticism from his childhood Anglicanism until, around the age of twenty-three, he experienced a conversion to evangelical Christianity. He determined to be a missionary to China, as a result of a friendship with a young man, Quincy Wong, who led a delegation to the missionary conference at Edinburgh in 1910, which my father attended as an usher.[3]

---

1 The 'Clapham Sect' (active from around the years 1780–1840) was a group of mainly Church of England social reformers, based at Clapham, London, and described as a "network of a friends and families in England with William Wilberforce as its centre of gravity, who were powerfully bound by their shared moral and spiritual values, by their religious mission and social activism, by their love for each other and by marriage." Stephen M. Tomkins, *The Clapham Sect: How Wilberforce's Circle Changed Britain*, 2010 (ref. from Wikipedia).

2 The Cornish version of this name. It is that of a Cornish family to which we are distantly related.

3 See Appendix: V. H. Donnithorne's account of his conversion.

To prepare himself, he decided, with the help of a timely legacy, to study Chinese at Cambridge University, which had just introduced a degree in classical Chinese language and culture. In the autumn of 1911 he went up to Clare College where he was told, on his arrival, that there was no such thing as a tripos in Chinese. He convinced them to the contrary and went on to take a first-class degree. Some of his papers had to be sent to the Netherlands to be read by an external examiner because of the shortage of scholars of Chinese in Britain. Vyvyan was active in the Cambridge Inter-Collegiate Christian Union (CICCU) which was in schism with the Student Christian Movement which espoused a more modernist theology. Since the 1880s and "the Cambridge Seven",[4] Cambridge had been a centre of enthusiasm for foreign missions, particularly to China.

In 1884, seven notable young Cambridge graduates joined the China Inland Mission. One of the seven was D. E. Hoste, whose help had enabled Vyvyan to attend the Edinburgh Conference as an usher; another was William Cassels, later Anglican Bishop in Sichuan, who baptised me, while one of the two Polhill brothers became the grandfather of Victor Funnell, many years later my student in London.

The First World War interrupted my father's plans. He was wounded in Belgium, where he won the MC. In September 1919, he married Gladys Ingram, three of whose siblings had already married into his family. Gladys, the seventh daughter and tenth child of Thomas Lewis and Victoria (née Skinner) Ingram, had been born in India, where her mother had inherited a large estate near Delhi from her great-grandfather, James Skinner, an Anglo-Indian military adventurer and founder of a regiment, Skinner's Horse, which was eventually incorporated into the Indian Army. Victoria's husband, a barrister, had managed the estate, which became the scene of early experiments in rural development. He had been born in the Gambia, at that time a small British colony consisting of narrow strips of land along the banks of the eponymous river, where his father was, at various times, a trader and a government servant, rising in 1847 to be governor.[5]

---

4 Marcus Loane, *Archbishop Mowll*, Hodder & Stoughton, London, 1960, p. 84.

5 See *Journal of a Mission to the Kings and Chiefs on the Banks of the River Gambia in*

Soon after their wedding, Vyvyan and Gladys left for China. First, they had a couple of year's study of spoken Chinese (not part of the Cambridge syllabus at that time) and were based at Mianzhu, a small county town and a traditional haunt of artists. On 27 November 1922, I was born in another town, Santai (previously known as Tongchuan), in the Mianyang Prefecture, where my parents had friends at the Quaker mission hospital.[6]

About three weeks after my birth we went by boat to Mianzhu but, before long, my parents moved to Anxian, another small county town north-west of the provincial capital, Chengdu. My earliest memories are of Anxian, where the Chengdu plain meets the foothills of Central Asia, of the compound where we lived and of the mountainous countryside around the town.

I was baptized the following February, at Mianyang, by Bishop Cassels, during a conference of local missionaries. For general convenience, he baptized me in the conference room, which was some distance from the church.

The times were turbulent. Sichuan was riven by conflicts between warlords and by the ravages of bandits. The provincial authorities, much less the central government, could exercise scant control. In 1923, two clergy colleagues of my father in Sichuan, F. J. Watt and R. A. Whiteside, were killed by brigands.[7] In May 1925, anti-foreign feeling on the coast and in big cities had been inflamed by the Shanghai incident, later known as the May Thirtieth Movement, when British police in the International Settlement in Shanghai had fired on a Chinese crowd.

December 1842 and January 1843 by Acting Governor Thomas Lewis Ingram. This Journal tells of the commercial treaties with Britain which T. L. Ingram went around getting signed by the "kings and chiefs", with a clause stipulating "agreement for the suppression of the slave trade", pp. 13, 27 and 31. The parchment document, signed "Victoria R", dated 1847, appointing her "trusty and well-beloved" T. L. Ingram as Lieutenant-Governor of the Gambia, is still in the possession of my family.

6 On 22 May 1921, a son had been born to my parents, and named David Vyvyan. He died within hours or minutes of his birth and was buried in the foreigners' cemetery adjoining the campus of the West China Union University, Chengdu, where I sometimes visited his grave.

7 Years later, some of the Watt children were fellow pupils of mine at St Michael's School, Limpsfield, where Mr Whiteside's daughter was my piano teacher.

In the summer of 1925, we had been staying at a small place in the hills, in Mianzhu county, where the missionary community had built a couple of bungalows to escape from the summer heat. In addition to my parents, there were six other adult foreigners staying there that August, including Bishop Howard Mowll, later the Anglican Archbishop of Sydney. Early one morning we were disturbed by a band of brigands who took us off with them on a twenty-four-day trek through wild mountainous country. Our captors were members of the Red Lamp bandits, with Triad affiliations.

I cannot remember anything of this adventure, although I have other memories of that summer, notably perching on my father's back as he swam in a mountain pool (this may of course have been during the brigand escapade).

My father later wrote a long account, based on diary entries, of our trip with the brigands:[8]

"It was at daybreak on the morning of August 6 that we were aroused from our beds by an outburst of rifle firing under our windows, accompanied by wild yelling ... and almost simultaneously we heard the doors burst open and a rush of shouting men inside and up the stairs...they were firing even inside the house."

"My wife bent over the cot where little Audrey, aged two and a half, was lying in half awakened amazement, and picked her up, saying quietly, 'Don't be afraid little girl; we are going for a walk now.' Instantly, the little one's fears were allayed, and she remained quiet in her mother's arms ... When they hurried us downstairs, they produced a long rope and proceeded to rope us all together with a halter round our necks; my wife persuaded her brigand to allow her to go free long enough to get half a dozen tins of condensed milk ... for the child and a sun hat for myself." ...

"Prodded on by our guards we then started out on our journey across the stream and up the mountain road to an unknown destination; we, shuffling along in Indian file with our necks in a halter and our feet

8 This was published, many years later, in the *Australian Review of Missions*, Vol. 2, No. 1, June 2008. The episode was also written up in Loane, *Archbishop Mowll*, p. 91 see the bishop's remark about Audrey "looking so sweet in her blue dressing gown".

in bedroom slippers ... and the little girl carried pick-a-back by an old mason, who had been doing our building and whom the robbers had now impressed to carry our goods ... The path now became steeper and as it became apparent that we could not proceed tied up as we were, they released our neck ropes and untied our thumbs." ...

"We could now ... take some stock of our captors. There appeared to be some twenty to thirty men in the gang, one half of whom were armed with rifles, and one half with long pikes ...The chief was an evil-looking man of some thirty-five years, naked to the waist and armed with two automatic pistols ... During that day, I had several conversations with him in which they informed me that the ransom they wanted was 200 automatic pistols ... I told him that missionaries did not carry arms and had no method of procuring them." ...

"We have often wondered since how we made that day's journey ... We were led up and down precipitous steeps by woodcutters' paths through the dense jungle, over a mountain range and down the other side. For her (Audrey), poor wee mite, it was especially difficult, awaked out of her sleep by the sudden terrifying inrush of armed men, kept all day without food except a biscuit or two, deprived of her midday sleep and carried in all sorts of uncomfortable positions on the backs of all kinds of people, all her routine of life hopelessly broken up. We feared her usual happy disposition would desert her under the strain, and yet, from that morning until the last of the twenty-four days we spent in these evil men's hands, Audrey was the one who set the best example for us all. All days she was bright and full of smiles, singing happily to herself even at the end of the day, as she clung with her arms around his neck, on the back of some unwashed coolie." ...

That night was spent in a semi-ruined fortress on the top of a high hill. "We found a place where the roof was sufficiently sound to enable us to spread our bedding under it and before long our loads of clothes and bedding arrived and were dumped down ... It was not a big room and the nine of us had to sleep in it as best we could. A big cupboard stood at the end, so we pulled it down and laid it face to the ground, and four of the ladies and the little girl laid down their bedding on the top and passed the night there. The rest of us lay as best we could on the dirty mud floor … one of the robbers came over and gave us a small piece of pork on the end of his bayonet and some cakes made of coarse maize. A cloud of mosquitoes swooped joyfully on the prey and from the mud floor an army of insects rose up to the spoil and, worn though we were from the fatigue of the day, few or none of us slept that night."

So it continued throughout the twenty-four days – many forced marches, interspersed with stays of a few days in some insalubrious lodging. Bundles of clothes and bedding, seized by the robbers from our bungalows, had been carried by porters impressed by the brigands, and dumped at the halting places where the captives then sorted through them – the brigands having already taken what they wanted. "And best of all (sc. in one of the bundles) we found a pocket New Testament with Psalms … which was handed from one to the other with a time ration allowed to each … The Psalms of David need to be read in the presence of imminent danger to give their real flavour." …

"It has rained all day and so we have been able to get washing water by catching the drip from the eaves. Little Audrey's spirits are unconquerable. She has again had a very disturbed night, for though now we have got our mosquito nets hung up, the fleas are still innumerable. But today she has recovered all her brightness, thinks it great fun to eat maize gruel from the saucepan and to catch the rain drops for washing… The place is full of short lengths of bamboo" which Audrey "finds capital material for building houses and bridges; and her trustful innocence as she runs in and out among the robbers, fetching this material and prattling away in Chinese in answer to their questions, is having an effect even on these hard men. Several of them are obviously already attached to her and treat us better in consequence."

We were taken deeper into the mountains. Crossing "streams on bridges consisting of a single log … we at length reached a little farmhouse." The brigands, "for themselves, commandeered the main house and put us into an outhouse … a shed with a roof made of bark, which leaks badly. It has two little rooms which are dark and horribly dirty; the fleas jump everywhere … and the smells are horrible, for just outside is the inevitable cesspit. … We found some rough planks and laid them down on the ground and spread our sleeping gear on that. To our relief, we found that having no fear of our escape from this place, our guards allowed us considerable liberty. We were by the banks of a river and we were soon enjoying a good bathe … the river is very swift and turbulent and full of rapids, but we found a place where an outcrop of rocks made a little bay … we had a great time washing clothes. … There are great stretches of white sand here which made an ideal beach for Audrey to play on, and it was good to see the delight she took in building in the sand and paddling in the water."

The next stage involved crossing a turbulent stream on a "rough raft of pine logs tied together with bamboo strips … it was manipulated by bamboo strips twisted together into a rope, one tied to each end of the raft, the other ends being held by men on the two banks. By this means, two by two, we got safely across… while here, by the riverside, a coolie sent by our friends in Mianzhu reached us with a basket of provisions… These people (in the farmhouses where the brigands took us), who are our unwilling hosts, show us every kindness when they have the opportunity to do so without attracting the robbers' attention … the old woman several times came stealthily … bringing with her little gifts of food, and asking if we had enough to eat … the simple old folk are very kind and indeed we are glad enough of the gifts of maize cakes they give us for our food is getting very scarce and we live chiefly on boiled cobs of maize."

Audrey "has begun to realise the real character of our guards and is full of indignation at what she calls these 'naughty men'. Passing their room today, she saw and recognized my pillow, which one of them was using as a cushion. Without a moment's hesitation, she marched straight into the midst of the brigands and laid hands on the pillow, calling out in Chinese, 'This is not yours, it's my daddy's; give it to me.' The man who had it of course would not let her take it, but she was not to be denied. At last the others, who were laughing at her audacity, said to him, 'Let her have it, then,' and he had grudgingly to comply and to yield to public opinion, whereupon little Audrey tucked the pillow under her arm and marched triumphantly out." It has always grieved me that the one noble deed of my life was done when I was too young to be responsible for my actions! (I have sometimes thought of including in my c.v. the fact that in 1925 I successfully negotiated the return of a stolen foreign asset in China.)

And so it continued. "Adjoining our room is a ruined house in which stand two coffins, each containing corpses of captives who had recently been killed when ransom was not forthcoming … the next two nights were miserable in the extreme, for rain fell heavily all night … our bedding was quickly soaked through." Then came a pleasanter experience. On 20 August "a very welcome load reached us … it contained bread and tinned foods, and best of all a number of letters and newspapers. Amongst the letters was one, which encouraged and helped us all. It was from the Christians of Anxian church, and it told how of their own accord they were meeting at five o'clock for prayer for us. Coming at a time when every Chinese newspaper was breathing out anti-foreign sentiments and hatred of the English, it came as a touching illustration of the truth that we are indeed 'all one in Christ Jesus.'" …

"The record of the next ten days would make a story very similar to the preceding. We were moved again four times, each time to a small farmhouse, and crossed the river by raft twice more. On 29 August came the happy news that the negotiations for our release had been effected and that we were to start off at once for Mianzhu and liberty. After we had gone not many *li* (sc. a measurement of length – about one third of a mile, but somewhat variable) we came in sight of a string of coolies coming towards us, who proved to be men sent by the officials to carry back any things which the robbers had allowed us to retain. On this our captors retired with no further ceremony and we went on a few *li* where we met with a detachment of militia waiting at this safe distance to receive us."

"The officer in charge greeted us very courteously … Light carrying chairs were provided … The next day, after having spent the night with them in a small temple, a hundred soldiers escorted us to the summit of a pass from which we could overlook Mianzhu city. Here we waited for an hour for the arrival of the major deputed by the mandarin to escort us into the city. The latter, when he arrived with 200 men, was accompanied by an official representing the mandarin and by the local headman, who was himself a notorious brigand chief and, as we heard later, had been chiefly instrumental in effecting our release."

"When we eventually reached the city, we had to go straight to the *yamen*, ragged and dirty and unkempt as we were. There the mandarin, who had been appointed subsequent to our capture, treated us with great courtesy and gave a feast to us next day which we shall long remember." A few days later, my parents and I returned to Anxian where "we found a great welcome prepared for us. … Some *li* out on the road we were met by the Christians, men and women and all the school children, the girls in their best flowery dresses and the boys in their clean white and blue uniforms. Here, our sedan chairs, even Audrey's little one, were draped with red silk and we were escorted in procession over the bridge and through the streets, while the crackers exploded with a horrible din and all the street people ran out to see what was happening."

"Anyone watching this welcome of Christians, so obviously warm and sincere, would find it hard to believe that for the two months past all the newspapers had been shrieking vituperations at the wicked foreigner." …

"Our continual prayer while we were in captivity there was that our experience might in some way be used to open these valleys to the message of the world's Saviour. In several conversations we found the country people there very friendly and ready to hear more of our message."

"In those happy days which will come, when the temples where these idolatrous brigands burn incense have given place to Christian churches, when instead of the reports of rifles will be heard the sound of church bells summoning a God-fearing people to worship, then these green and rich valleys will be indeed an earthly paradise."

Throughout our time with the brigands, a silver mug, specially made for me, had been carried by one or the other of my parents, hung by its handle on their belts, to collect drinking water from mountain streams. They always argued as to which of them had carried it – I suspect sometimes one, sometimes the other. I still have the mug; fortunately, it is dull, not shiny, which may have been why it escaped being seized by our captors.

The brigands demanded a ransom for us. It was the firm policy of the missionary society to which the group belonged that ransom demands should not be met, otherwise none of its personnel would be safe. Everyone accepted this as reasonable. The local county magistrate, the British consul and the captives' colleagues managed to negotiate with the brigands; but finally, in order to give our captors face, agreed to pay a little for "board and lodging", though less than the brigands had actually paid in bribes and tips during the episode, thus ensuring that they remained out of pocket and discouraged from trying to make profits by demanding ransoms.

This episode must have put a special strain on my father. His left leg was still weakened by the effect of a severe war wound and, as the only one of the three men in our party who spoke fluent Chinese, he must have been the chief person dealing directly with the brigands. Bishop Mowll was already sick before it began and had never really acclimatised himself to China; while the third man, always referred to by my parents as "Major Iles" (I do not know his Christian name nor even his initials), did not settle down to missionary life and soon returned to England. For myself, I probably found much of the trip fun, encountering so many new and strange things. Also, I must have enjoyed having more of my parents' attention than when they were engrossed with their work at Anxian.

It was probably in 1926 that my father and I stood one day at the gate of our compound in Anxian, watching a thief calmly walk off down the street with our cow; he had, presumably, "fixed" the local police. I must have seen a photo of my father in his First World War uniform because, in my three-year-old fury, I exclaimed "Daddy, why don't you go after him with a gun?" My father quietly replied, "I didn't come to China to do that."

My mother was busy with mission life and also suffered from ill health and several miscarriages. Much of my care devolved on our two amahs, kindly country women whom I remember as Wang Wang and Gu Gu. Like most Chinese women of their generation, they had bound feet, and I fear that I took advantage of this when, at my bedtime, they tried to catch me as I dashed furiously away from them in my little pedal car which someone, probably my father, had improvised from tin cans! Pots of geraniums stood in front of our house. One winter when I was very small, some water in these pots froze. It was the first time I had ever seen ice and I immediately tried to eat it, whereupon someone quickly picked me up and rinsed out my mouth!

Two Australian women missionaries also lived on the compound as did some Chinese church workers, including a catechist with a young son, a bit older than myself, with whom I used to play. Friendly grownups hid cigarette cards at various places around the compound, for which we then hunted. One of my pastimes was keeping silkworms in a drawer which had frequently to be opened to give them mulberry leaves to eat. When they developed to the chrysalis stage, they were taken away from my care to be used to produce silk.

Apart from our family and the two Australians, there were no other foreigners in the town. There was a Catholic mission in the county, but it was in a large market town some distance from the county town of Anxian where we lived, and I never even heard of its existence until some sixty years later. Whenever I went out on the street, other children – often chewing bits of sugar cane, the local substitute for candy – called out at the strange foreign child, but in a friendly manner. One thing I absorbed from my early childhood experience of being the only foreign child in a Chinese town may have been a feeling that being Chinese was the normal way of being human and that we foreigners were the odd ones out.

Among our Chinese friends, we were, of course, always known by our Chinese family name, Dong. My Chinese given name, Yude, selected no doubt by my father, sounds, in its Sichuan pronunciation, rather like Audrey, besides having a good traditional Chinese flavour. Usually, as a child, I was called Dong Mei-mei (younger sister Dong). Many of my friends in China have known me by no other name than Dong Yude.

Anxian at that time was encircled by a city wall within which old traditional houses were crowded together. My tin-can pedal car may have been the most modern form of transport the place had ever seen. Outside one of the city gates flowed a small river, down which logs from the nearby mountains were floated to market. In the hills, on whose slopes I was taken for walks, Aaron lilies (or some flowers which, at least in my memory, resemble them) grew. My father used to walk long distances, sometimes taking many days, to visit the mission outstations. My mother and I seldom went further than Mianyang, a larger city about thirty miles away, and we would go there by sedan chair. I had my own small sedan chair. On one occasion, going probably to Mianyang, my chair was delayed, and I arrived after dark, sometime later than my parents. I do not remember feeling in the least bit alarmed – the chair bearers were friendly and reliable, and I enjoyed the experience – I can recall the thrill of bright street stalls with the pomegranates cut in half and glistening, to attract buyers. To round off the evening, I arrived when the grownups were about to have their evening meal and, for the first time in my life, was allowed to stay up and join them.

There were no doctors or modern medical facilities in Anxian. Once, when I was seriously ill, my father's colleague, Dr John Lechler, made the long and dangerous journey from Mianzhu, where he ran the Church Missionary Society hospital, to Anxian on foot at night to treat me.

Our life in Anxian was suddenly interrupted by events in the wider world. When the Guomindang forces began pushing north in the spring of 1927, foreign consuls gave an order for their nationals to evacuate the interior and make for the coast. We were staying at another mission station when this news came. My parents left me in the care of our hosts while they returned home to pack up. The slow journey to Shanghai must have taken many days. First, we travelled on junks down one of Sichuan's rivers, joining the Yangtze at Chongqing. Then we went through the Gorges, which I can remember towering on either side of us while, in the recesses of the junk, I played with my dolls. At that time, the journey by junk was dangerous, with many of the wooden vessels coming to grief in the swift rapids. Going upriver, the problems were even greater. Gangs of trackers, linked together, pulled junks against the currents with ropes – a bitter and dangerous life.

At two more points on our downriver journey, we changed boats – probably at Yichang, from junk to steamer; and then to a larger steamer at Wuhan. I have dim memories of these occasions, usually at night – they were fun. On one steamer, our fellow passengers included a contingent of Scandinavian missionaries' children, having to evacuate their school. At one meal, we were served bananas, which most of us children had never seen before – small experimental first bites were followed by enthusiastic larger ones!

Shanghai was a new and strange experience. Like many others from the interior of China, it was here that I first met the modern world, with its trains and motor vehicles – with their noise and their smell. I was terrified by the sound of a train that rushed by, near where we were staying, while I took my afternoon rest. Because of the throngs of foreigners arriving from the interior, our family could not find lodgings together. My mother and I stayed at a White Russian guesthouse, while my father lodged elsewhere. It was some time before we could get passages to Britain.

The journey to England, by a P & O liner, took four or five weeks. It went smoothly, and as far as I can remember, quite enjoyably, except that a fall on some metal deck structures resulted in what was described as "a green-bone fracture", causing me to arrive at our destination with an arm in a sling. On the ship, my parents tried speaking Chinese to me, so that I should not forget this language in which up to then I had been bilingual. However, I had always spoken to them in English and, in any case, probably disliked their accent, so I refused to speak Chinese with them. As a result, I completely forgot my Chinese, to my subsequent great regret.

On that far-off voyage in 1927, all the ports where we stopped (Hong Kong, Singapore, Penang, Colombo, Aden, Port Said and Gibraltar) were marked red on the map, under the protection of Pax Britannica. I cannot remember anyone remarking on this or thinking it strange – it was just how things, providentially, happened to be.

CHAPTER 2

Childhood in England: 1927–35

Arriving "home" meant meeting my extended family. For my mother, home-coming must have been tinged with sadness, because her father had died during her seven years' absence. Other members of the family had married, and children had been born. I had suddenly to get to know, and be appraised by, many adult relatives, including my three godparents – my mother's siblings, Maud Crofts and Robert Ingram, and my father's favourite sister, Loveday. In addition, of course, I associated with numerous cousins of various ages.

On arrival, we stayed with one of my mother's sisters, Mabel Ingram (later, Lady Berry), a medical doctor who lived in Roehampton. When my Granny Ingram arrived back in England for the summer (every winter she spent camping in great "durbar tents" on her estate near Delhi), we moved for a while to her large house on Wimbledon Common, a mock Gothic mansion known as the Priory, next to King's College School.

The Priory was a house in which time stood still. My grandparents had bought it shortly before the First World War and had furnished it in contemporary taste, with added Indian touches. After my grandfather's death in 1921, nothing was permitted to be altered and it remained as it had been until 1938 when his widow died, and the place was sold. It was staffed partly by old retainers and partly by an ever-changing succession of younger domestics. The appropriately named Mrs Cook, always known as "Cookie", presided over the multi-racial servants' hall. She had joined the family in India in 1892, the year after my mother's birth. An Anglo-Indian, she made delicious curries and dal soup. An even older retainer was the kitchen maid, Cattie, a West African who had come with the family from the Gambia, where she may have been rescued from slavery. No one knew her age, but eventually, when it was felt that she really should retire, a small flat was found for her, with a pension. She was a devout member of an early charismatic religious body in London whose services she regularly attended. The third and only English long-term retainer was the stately parlour maid, Ball, whose serene welcome greeted arrivals at the house. These three had a secure, it could be said a "tenured", place in the household, treasured by all and great favourites with us grandchildren. Less fortunate were the young local housemaids, who constantly incurred my grandmother's displeasure and whose stays tended to be short and unhappy. Every morning, family prayers were held in the front hall, attended by all the household. The only heating in the Priory, as in almost all houses in England at that date, was that provided by coal fires in grates. I can remember being woken up early in the morning by the sound of a housemaid clearing the ashes and re-laying the fire in my bedroom.

A grand piano stood in one corner of the large drawing room. In the musically challenged Ingram family, I can never remember it being played but its top provided a site for family photos. Two especially I remember. One was of my Aunt Nell, the eldest daughter, in a Salvation Army bonnet; the other was of my Ingram grandfather, with his four sons, all in court dress when he presented them at a levée. No one ever remarked that the Ingram girls had never been presented. Court presentation for young ladies was a way of formally putting them on the marriage market, with mutual exchange of invitations to balls and other social events. In the social climate of that day the Ingram daughters might have been blackballed because of their racially mixed background; in any case, balls – and dancing in general – did not accord with the Ingrams' evangelical faith.

The front door of the house was approached by a drive, leading from Southside, the road bordering Wimbledon Common. The drive passed under an arch which joined two sides of a building, one side being a residence for a chauffeur and the other a garage sheltering Granny Ingram's ancient Rolls. This vehicle may have been capable of speeds up to thirty or forty miles an hour, but when Victoria was in it, the maximum permitted was twenty. The chauffeur, a wizened chap perhaps in his forties during my childhood, was said to have had a French mother and to have spent some years in the Foreign Legion. He was rather a favourite of Victoria's, perhaps because his name was Skinner; although I never heard a suggestion that he was a relative. During the winter when Victoria was in India, the car was not used, but he spent much time dismantling and examining the engine and then re-installing it before her return, around late April.

A well-tended garden of around three acres surrounded the Priory, under the care of the gardener, Brown, who occupied a cottage at the back end of the property where a drive led to the Ridgway. Opposite the front door lay a circular rose garden, with another flower bed with an herbaceous border of flowers, backing on to the wall with King's College School. Beyond the house stretched a tennis court and beyond that, shrubs and a monkey-puzzle tree, with prickle-covered bark and a tall trunk, topped by short, spiky branches; also a round bed of massed lilies of the valley. To one side of the tennis court, at a suitable distance, stood an overhanging cedar and, behind it, two large glass conservatories, with black and white grapes respectively; and beyond them, an extensive vegetable garden with strawberry and asparagus beds, fruit bushes and trees, including a peach splayed across a south-facing brick wall.

My grandmother, Victoria, I remember as a very secure and contented matriarch, a forceful but kind personality. Although we grandchildren were always on our best behaviour in her presence and were somewhat overawed by her, she was warm and affectionate, except for her short temper towards the young housemaids whose modern ways she disliked. On at least one occasion, too, she was harsh with a member of her family. Her third son, James, who at one time managed her Indian estate, was a good friend of the assistant manager, Parshadi Lal, whose father had also worked for our family. My grandmother insisted that at least one of the pair, either James or Parshadi, should always be present on the estate. This conflicted with their desire to go off together on a holiday to Kashmir. On their return from the holiday, Victoria was furious and dismissed her son from his post. (It is significant that, while also annoyed with Parshadi Lal, she did not sack him, which would have had more deleterious effects for him, as well as conflicting with the obligations which had grown up between the two families.) In any case, however, James was before long re-instated as estate manager. Victoria's anger soon cooled.[1]

Victoria married at sixteen. Thomas Lewis Ingram, then aged thirty-two, had had an earlier career in his father's administration in the Gambia. Due probably both to nepotism and to the difficulty of persuading Europeans to come and survive in the unhealthy climate of West Africa, he had, at a very young age, and apparently without any formal study of law, been appointed attorney general. In this post, his interest in legal matters deepened and he later went to London to read for the Bar at the Middle Temple. After that, perhaps finding life in England tame, he went out to teach law at a college in India, while also practising at the local bar. At that time, young Victoria Skinner's inheritance was threatened by kinsmen who became known to her descendants as "the wicked uncles". Ingram, according to what I heard from family sources, was briefed to take her case, won it and promptly married the heiress![2]

---

1 For more about the Ingram-Skinner Estate see the booklet by Parshadi Lal, *The Ingram Estate (1988–1944)*, revised edn. 1961, privately published.

2 While finishing these memoirs, I have been sent a lot of interesting material that I had never seen before, about Victoria's early life. According to one account, her father, George Skinner, had been killed in the events of 1857 (this I already knew), after Moslem soldiery ascertained he was a Christian. In 1859, at the age of three, Victoria had been baptized in St James' Church, Delhi, built by her great-grandfather, Colonel James Skinner. Victoria's mother, Helen, née Grant, and her paramour, John Thomas John, both became Moslems in order to contract a marriage which, as Christians, they could not do, as Mr John was already married. The young Victoria, now known as Nawshaba Begum, was for some years brought up in purdah as a Moslem. This led to a family lawsuit (Skinner v. Orde), that went up to the Privy Council in London, which decided it by putting young Victoria's person under the guardianship of Miss Scanlan, a schoolmistress in Mussoorie, a nearby hill station, and her fortune under that of Mr Bailey of the Agra Bank. I would like to add that, in her old age, the only time I knew her, Victoria showed no trace of the strains of her contested youth, seemingly being a model of contentment, stability and assurance. In the subconscious thoughts of some of her grandchildren, the image of our Victoria sometimes merged with that of her royal namesake – a young heiress who, early

19

Victoria and Lewis (as he was known in the family, probably to distinguish him from his father) were a perfect match, he – her senior by sixteen years – providing the father figure she had lacked, and they lived happily ever after. He devoted much of his time to the management and improvement of her estate and settled the contested division of the Skinner properties to the subsequent contentment of all. Lewis also continued to take some legal cases, including one on behalf of the Salvation Army, then in its early years. The Salvos wanted to establish themselves in India, but the Raj balked at their military nomenclature. Ingram won the case for them, legitimising their activities in the country. (This is the account I heard from my family; I have not authenticated it.) As a result, he and his wife became friends of the founder, General Booth, and his wife. I do not know if this episode was a cause or a result of the young couple's strengthened religious devotion and its evangelical direction. In the early years of their marriage, they were said to have been what some members of a later generation of the family would describe as "worldly", with an interest in horse racing.

As children, my cousins and I never thought of Granny Ingram as being of mixed race nor had we ever heard of her Indian ancestry. She was somewhat tanned, as was Colonel James Skinner in his portrait which hung in the Priory dining room, but that was to be expected of those who had lived long under the Indian sun.

The Ingram-Skinner Estate in Gurgaon near Delhi comprised, after 1925, some ten villages and twenty hamlets in the Punjab and a few in the United Provinces, with a population of around 20,000. A *chaprasi*, a uniformed estate employee, was stationed in each village, reporting to the manager. At the estate headquarters, near the Jumna River at a spot where the Moghal kings were said to break their journey when going from Delhi to Agra by river, a brick bungalow had been built for the manager, who

---

on, married an older man-of-the-world, was guided and mentored by him in the duties of her station and who, later in life, spent long years, in widow's weeds, mourning his memory. Our Victoria, too, had a whiff of "Empress of India" around her!

There is a continuing uncertainty on the point at which Thomas Lewis Ingram impinged on her life – I had heard that it was when he was briefed to take on her case at some court in India, but there is at least one other version.

would be there throughout the year; his assistant, for long a member of the Lal family, lived nearby.

When my grandparents visited in the winter they camped in big "durbar tents" at the estate headquarters. The estate office, staff quarters, clinic, dispensary and veterinary hospital (all in brick buildings), were also there and the home farm and garden were attached. The durbar tents were elaborate. They included a "purdah curtain" of long strings of heavy beads behind which my grandmother could interview her tenants, who might otherwise be embarrassed at speaking to a non-related woman. The tents were cooled by *punkah* fans, activated by *punkah-wallahs* pulling on ropes. My mother told me that when she was small, there was a special nursery tent where the five youngest children of the family (Mabel, Maud, Gladys, Tina and Robert), slept and lived. A governess taught the two eldest of these and a nursery nurse cared for the younger ones. Grandfather Ingram had an office tent where he worked on estate matters and kept regular office hours, including special times when anyone might come to see him. During the hot season, the family moved to a hill station such as Mussoorie or Simla or somewhere in Kashmir. During in-between seasons, they lived in a house with big rooms and surrounded by wide verandahs, at Muttra (now called Mathura), in Uttar Pradesh, south of Delhi. My mother remembered playing with "canal children" there and recalled an incident when she was riding a camel which suddenly bolted, while she desperately clung to its hump, until it stopped to eat some leaves and she was able to slip down off it.

After her husband's death in 1921, my grandmother made a practice of spending the summer months in England and going to the estate in India every autumn, where she would stay until the following spring. My grandmother was accompanied to India by her youngest daughter, my Aunt Tina (Evangeline) who took over as "home daughter" after her eldest sister Nell, sickened and died. I can remember going once with Granny Ingram and Tina to Victoria Station in London to see them on to the train for Southampton where they would embark on a P & O liner to Bombay. Tina trained as a midwife and went on pony from village to village on the estate to give modern training to the traditional midwives (*dais*).

When they settled at the Priory, St Mary's, Wimbledon Hill[3] became my grandparents' parish church and that is where family weddings thenceforward took place; while, on death, family members were buried in St Mary's churchyard, where their graves eventually occupied a considerable stretch. On my last visit to the graves, in the late twentieth century, I was distressed to see them overgrown with brambles and tried to arouse cousins to join in a party to clear them. This was deflected by the opposition of some of the older generation who disliked any discussion about graves. This shocked both my Christian and my Chinese sensibilities, but at that time I lived abroad and was about to leave England, so I could not follow it up. The same held true for the grave of my great-grandfather, Thomas Lewis Ingram of the Gambia, whose tomb in Brompton Cemetery was damaged in an air raid during the Second World War.

However, for ordinary weekly Sunday services, Granny Ingram always went, not to the parish church, but to Emmanuel Church at the corner of Lingfield Road and the Ridgeway. This was, indeed, nearer the Priory but the reason for her choice was that the Anglican evangelicals who clustered around Ridgeway Road and Wimbledon Common, were a rather cohesive group, almost, it might be said, in a semi-schismatic relationship with even the middle-of-the-road Anglicanism of St Mary's. My grandmother, with poor hearing, had a front row pew in Emmanuel and was in the habit of arriving somewhat late for eleven o'clock Sunday matins, so those of us with her had the embarrassment of following her down the aisle while the service was already in progress. In later years, my parents were adopted by the Emmanuel congregation as "our own missionaries", with their work at least partly supported by that church.

Both my grandfathers died before I was born, and I have always regretted not having known them. My Donnithorne grandmother lived in straitened circumstances as a result of the failure of the engineering business which my grandfather established after retiring from the army, in which he

3 Near the All-England Tennis Club where the Wimbledon tennis championships are played. The church supplemented its funds by using a field it owned as a car park during the tennis season.

had been Lieutenant Colonel of the Scots Greys; both his own and his wife's money was lost. This business, even before it failed, had strained relations with his wife's family, the Irish ascendancy Alexanders, and also his own, to whom "trade" was not something in which a gentleman should engage![4]

When, in 1927, we arrived from China, Granny Don, as we always called her, lived in a cottage in Alexandra Place, Wimbledon, in housing provided for widows of officers. Later, she moved to a flat in Wimbledon High Street. Her grandchildren (a number of whom were also grandchildren of Granny Ingram, because of the marriages of four siblings from each family, which gave me six double first cousins) were very fond of her and visiting her was always more informal and less strained than seeing Granny Ingram. Before we went to her house, she would carefully think out ways of occupying us and would go to great trouble to find the necessary objects and materials. Granny Don had weathered many changes in her life, beginning as the only daughter, with several brothers, in a prominent Irish Protestant Ascendancy family, descended from one of the original Scots raiders who had landed on the shores of Ulster – in 1617 or 1618, I think, in the case of Andrew Alexander, who was also a Presbyterian minister. Her father had been the MP for Carlow in the Westminster Parliament from 1853 until 1859 when he was defeated by John Acton, later the first Lord Acton. Young Harriet was well-versed in the family traditions and, in 1870, when news of the Italian Risorgimento and its onslaught on the Papacy gladdened the ears of her family and their co-religionists in Ireland, she donned a red blouse to show her support for Garibaldi. A few years later, she married an officer of the occupying British Army and settled in his family home in Twickenham, Middlesex, with its lawn sloping down to the Thames. There her two sons and three daughters were born. Then, after her husband's bankruptcy and his subsequent decline into depression and addiction, all this was lost and the family moved eventually to Kensington where they bought the cheap "end lease" of a house in Queensgate. On the expiry

---

4 My father was fifth cousin to Field Marshall Harold Alexander and also related, rather more distantly, to the husband of the hymn writer Fanny Alexander.

of such leases, the holder was obliged to pay the heavy cost of restoring the property to its former condition; thus, it provided a way of living temporarily at a socially acceptable address, at the cost of future stringency. Around 1910, after the death of their father, Harriet's five children each received a share in a legacy from some distant relative. I do not know on what the eldest son, Harold, used his share; my father, Vyvyan, used his to put himself through Cambridge while the two elder sisters, Lilian and Loveday, set up a select millinery business which, however, failed because the fine ladies who bought the hats did not pay their bills. The only share of the legacy that remained unspent was that falling to Edith, the youngest in the family and, in due course, she was pressured to put it towards fulfilling the obligations of the Queensgate house lease, something which she reasonably continued to resent all her life. Edith was the only one of her siblings who did not marry an Ingram, but Granny Ingram said that she always regarded her as one of the family.

Two of my mother's sisters were ever to loom large in my consciousness. One was Mabel, the doctor, with whom we stayed on our first arrival from China, and the other was Maud (Mrs Crofts). In the years before the World War they, and to some extent my mother too, were smitten, perhaps quite naturally, with the currently fashionable feminism. Mabel qualified in medicine. She interrupted her studies during the First World War to join a medical team, which one of her teachers at the Royal Free Hospital in London, James Berry, led to the war-torn small Balkan country of Montenegro where, I have heard, Mabel did good work. After she qualified she opened an early contraceptive clinic. The modern contraceptive movement, in its origins, was driven by that hydra-headed eugenic and racist movement which had shown itself among the British in India, to the detriment of our own Anglo-Indian forebears;[5] in the United States

5 A decree of 1792 of the Court of the East India Company laid down "that no person, the son of a native Indian, shall henceforth be appointed by this Court to appointments in the Civil, Military or Marine services of the country." This rule was later expanded or interpreted to mean that all officers of the Indian Army should be of pure European descent, thus debarring any descendent of James Skinner from serving in the regiment he founded. See Dennis Holmann, *Sikander Sahib – The Life of James Skinner 1778–1841*, Heinemann, 1961, p. 9.

in the black-white divide and the hostility shown to immigrants from Ireland and southern Europe, and in its worst manifestation, in the Nazi movement in Germany. In Britain, contraception (the word wrongly used as a synonym for birth control) was first prescribed as a way of keeping down the population of "undesirables", whether undesirability was defined by race, income level, class or presumed intelligence.

Maud took a law degree at Cambridge and then became the first woman in Britain to practise as a solicitor. She married a colleague, John Crofts and, with him and her brother, Robert Ingram, set up a firm, Crofts, Ingram Wyatt & Co. in Artillery Row, off Victoria St. in central London. Mabel and Maud both had strong racist views as well as domineering characters and they, even more than others in the family, were determined to hide their mixed origin. As I grew up, their influence made me put aside the idea of either medicine or law as careers, to avoid being patronised and mentored by one or other of the aunts. Of another aunt, Nell, my mother's eldest sister (and, also, her godmother) my memories are very different. Her activities in the Salvation Army may have been little more than symbolic – to show support for the Booths – and also because ill health dogged her. She was the "home daughter" who lived with and accompanied her mother to India and back in the years soon after her father's death, living a quiet life of devotion. When I was six, I can remember that she gave me my first Bible, after I had recited to her Psalm 23 (in the King James version), the "Shepherd's Psalm". She died soon afterwards and her duties, as the unmarried "home daughter", were taken over by the youngest sister, Tina.

Mary Ingram, one of my double first cousins who lived nearby, was the cousin nearest me in age and with whom I first became friends. Also, slightly older, was Ilsley Ingram, the only child of my maternal Uncle George and his wife May, at that time living in Wimbledon while on furlough from India where they were missionaries. On our first summer in England, my parents and Ilsley's parents, with the two children, Ilsley and myself, went for a summer holiday to Bacton in Norfolk. Ilsley was a delicate child, suffering from tuberculosis. For this reason, he and his mother spent a considerable time in Switzerland. In later years, when he had recovered, and his parents returned to India, he used to pass his school holidays with the same family, the Thompsons, where I lived when my parents went back to China. As a result, and because we were both only children, we seemed more like brother and sister than cousins. We had rather more intellectual tastes than the Thompson children and used to search together for fossils and prehistoric worked flints in a sandpit near Beeston Bump, a murrain hill near the sea cliff down which it was gradually crumbling as, we were told, had a conjoined hill in years past. Then we would take our findings to a museum in Norwich to have them assessed. At a later age, we both had an interest in modern poetry. Ilsley's father and my mother, although separated by a ten-year age gap, had always been close, sharing more deeply than some of their other siblings, a fervent evangelical faith.

Another summer holiday was spent at Hayling Island, on the south coast, where my Ingram grandmother had a seaside house, named Priory Lodge. Here, I particularly recall the presence of another double first cousin, Tom, the son of my father's eldest sister and of my mother's eldest brother who had been killed in France in the First World War. I always felt close to him but never saw nearly as much of him as of Ilsley.[6]

Four siblings from one family marrying four siblings from another, as happened with the Donnithornes and Ingrams, did not indicate any element of arranged marriages, but probably just the fact that the two families had complementary qualities, each being able to make up for what the other lacked. Socially, by the standards of that day, the Donnithornes were better positioned. For the Ingrams, our ancestor, the genial Anglo-Indian James Skinner, brought none of the positive feelings which he does to many in subsequent generations, but rather the stigma of "a touch of the tar brush". Financially, the Ingrams were far better off than the impoverished Donnithornes. However, the immediate cause of the first mutual acquaintance of the two families was religious, through the agency of the Cambridge Inter-Collegiate Christian Union (CICCU) of which my mother's brother, George Ingram, was an active member. In it he met Stuart

6 Tom's father, my uncle Dr Thomas Lewis Ingram DSO MC, had been a rural general practitioner in Northamptonshire. When war broke out he joined the RAMC and was last seen, in September 1917, tending wounded in no man's land. He is the family hero.

Donnithorne, a first cousin of my father Vyvyan. This friendship led to the two families getting to know each other at the Keswick Convention, the major annual gathering of evangelicals in Britain at that time. The Ingram family had superior practical abilities to the Donnithornes and were good at getting things done, but the Donnithornes were more sensitive, with better abstract intelligence.

Two or three of our relatives (including at first John and Maud Crofts), had houses in Lingfield Road, not far from the Priory, my Ingram grandmother's home. After staying for some time at the Priory after their arrival from China, my parents moved to a flat at Alford House, on Wimbledon High Street close to Lingfield Road. On 6 November 1927, half way through the autumn term, I began school at the kindergarten of Wimbledon High School where my cousin Mary Ingram was already a pupil. There, the admirable Miss Penny presided over the beginners' form and, under her, I quickly learned to read. Apart from that, the chief activity I remember from my term and a half there is a sand tray, with palm trees, camels and other objects to help us learn about the Middle East.

In those days of Christian England, the Lord Mayor of London used to give an annual children's party at the Guildhall in aid of the British and Foreign Bible Society. Probably because of our episode with the brigands, in March 1928 I was dressed in brocade Chinese clothes to cut the cake on the platform where the Lord Mayor and other dignitaries were seated.[7] The Lord Mayor addressed the children, offering information about China. I listened with patience for a bit, but when he said, "And if you went on to a street in China, you would see that most people wear black", it was really more than I could stand. Turning to the person next to me, I blurted out, "No, they wear blue." Unfortunately, there was a microphone near my chair, and my remark resounded across the hall!

Unable to return to China because of the disturbed situation there, my father became for a time chaplain at Downing College Cambridge while my mother and I continued to live in Wimbledon with occasional visits to Cambridge. In 1928, we moved to Slough in Buckinghamshire where

7 See photo in the *Daily Mirror,* 5 March 1928, p. 5.

my father had taken a curacy at All Saints, Stoke Poges. Early in 1929, conditions in the interior of China became easier, and my parents were able to return. At that time, there was a firm opinion among the British that Asia was no place for their school-age children, who consequently remained in, or were sent to, Britain to live with relatives or guardians or at boarding school. This meant that the children lost their early bilingualism which, in my case, I never regained. No doubt it also produced a considerable psychological impact on the children – which at that period was ignored but may now be over-exaggerated. It was something taken for granted in the families concerned and in the circles in which they moved, as well as in the wider society of the time. In my case, while it caused me unhappiness, both in my childhood and perhaps even more in later life, it also strengthened my psychological independence.

Shortly before my parents' departure, I dreamed that I was walking in a meadow picking flowers, with a dark wood on one side, and I saw Our Lord there – probably a common enough type of dream among Christian children. In my case, it made me confident that I had my own line to Our Lord and need not trouble myself about the demands of grown-ups' religion, notably the constant insistence, by the evangelicals who surrounded me, on the immediate need to "be saved" which I always found rather ridiculous, especially when I came to read that even St Paul asserted that in this life he could not be assured of salvation. I managed to remain immune to these demands, which might otherwise have put me off all religion.

It may be wondered why my parents did not leave me with some branch of our extended family. Probably, none, except possibly the Rawlences, were judged sufficiently devout, in the evangelical sense. Perhaps some disapproved of my parents leaving me in England and wanted my father to settle down in an English parish; or, perhaps, having firmly decided how many children of their own they would have, saw no reason for taking on another. The choice of the family with whom I was left was very likely due to Gurney Barclay, the East Asian Secretary of the Church Missionary Society, to which my parents belonged, and who was the brother-in-law of the Thompsons, who became my guardians. The intense atmosphere in which the evangelical missionary community and their associates lived must be kept in mind, sometimes leading to comic results as when a cult of conspicuous parsimony was combined with a rather affluent background, for instance in the report that a missionary aunt had a cardboard box, carefully labelled, "pieces of string, too short for use".

In any case, I was fortunate in the guardians, Hamlet and Dora Thompson, with whom my parents left me on their return to China. While I cannot say that I was always happy with them – I was conscious that I did not really belong there, but that was not through any fault of theirs – I may have had a better upbringing with them, in a family with a number of children, than if I had remained alone with my parents. The Thompsons were good and, in most things, sensible people and Dora, especially, was intelligent. Like my parents, the Thompsons had been missionaries in the province of Sichuan, but in a different missionary society, the China Inland Mission (CIM); and Hammy Thompson was, in fact, still a member of CIM's London Board.

The Thompsons had four children: three boys, older than me – John, Tom and David – and a girl, Janet, a year and a half my junior. Because of their children, they decided not to return to China but to settle in England and to provide a home for some of the children of missionaries abroad. Hammy was a clergyman, an evangelical Anglican. Dora had been a doctor who had originally gone out to China as a medical missionary, together with her sister Lily, also a doctor. Another of Dora's sisters, Gwen, married Gurney Barclay, a member of the prominent Barclay, Gurney and Buxton clan, originally Quaker but becoming Anglican as they rose in society, contributing greatly to British life, notably in supporting the anti-slavery movement, and also as bankers, in the nineteenth century. Gwen and her husband Gurney Barclay, had been missionaries in Japan with the CMS and, on his return to Britain, Gurney took over the oversight of its work in East Asia. So it is probable that he was the link that led to me being left with the Thompsons.

Hammy, like my paternal grandmother, came from an Anglo-Irish ascendancy family and his parental home had been in Dublin while Dora was born a Watney, whose doctor father, for religious reasons, had broken away from the family's brewing interests. She had been brought up with German governesses and spoke good German. There was a widespread feeling, especially among evangelicals, that the more Protestant civilization of north Europe was to be preferred to that of the Latin countries, where morals were considered to be looser. The Great War may have weakened this feeling but had not wholly dissipated it. In my teens, before war seemed imminent, I was told that, when I left school, it would be all right for me to go on my own for language study to Germany, but not to France. My mother had gone to Paris for six months to "finish", but in a chaperoned environment. She did not retain much French, but brought home a memory of having seen the Mona Lisa and also had some small editions of French classical literature which I now own.

When I joined the Thompsons, in March 1929, Hammy was a curate in Sevenoaks but soon afterwards accepted the living of All Saints, Beeston Regis,[8] between Sheringham and Cromer on the coast of north Norfolk. The rectory was a largish house, with outer walls of worked flint. Electricity did not reach that area until a few years after the Thompsons moved in; until then, we used kerosene oil lamps. Heating was by coal and peat fires in open grates in the main living rooms. Every year, a load of Irish peat would be delivered and stacked in the backyard. The north wall of the house was coated with tar to keep out the cold. There is no land between the north Norfolk coast and the North Pole and northerly winds make winters bitterly cold. We all suffered from chilblains; this was something taken for granted among all social classes in those days.

The rectory, about half a mile from the sea cliff, was set in a two-and-a-half-acre garden, rambling and varied. It included a front lawn, surrounded by lilac bushes, on which the parish sale of work was held every summer, a grass tennis court, an extensive vegetable garden with apple trees and soft fruit bushes and beds for strawberries and asparagus, an untidy piece of woodland, a large bed of daffodils and sundry other flower beds and a fig tree. Near the front door a tall hawthorn showered fragrance from

8 "Regis" presumably because the living was in the gift of the Duchy of Lancaster i.e. of the Crown.

white flowers in spring and brightness from red haws in the autumn. A Spanish chestnut hung spring lanterns and dropped autumnal conkers near the garden gate while sycamores provided easy climbing for children. A chicken run was soon installed, and Janet and I took part in feeding the chickens and collecting their eggs.

During school holidays, we passed a lot of time playing in the garden or reading in the perches clumsily constructed on trees where we enjoyed the advantage of being able to read undisturbed. Sometimes, the front lawn was laid out for croquet or the boys would kick a football around on it and I might, unwillingly, be pushed into joining them. My preference would be for reading indoors, but Dora Thompson was a great believer in the benefits of fresh air and would constantly interrupt my reading to tell me to go out into the garden to play.

The church of All Saints, Beeston Regis, of which my guardian, Hammy Thompson was rector, was about half a mile from the rectory. It stood alone in a rough grass field, with a square tower, the lower portion Norman, heightened, perhaps a couple of centuries later from which time the nave also dated; a simple, rather austere building, but with dignity and beauty and a prayerful atmosphere. At one time the field around the church was put up for sale and it was thought a developer might build on it and spoil the church's setting. The parish raised the funds to buy the field and instead of building on it, contented itself with the income from letting caravan sites during the summer. Indeed, during my parents' furlough in 1935–6 we rented a caravan for a week or two on the field.

A couple of hundred yards from the rectory, along the main road from Sheringham to Cromer which skirted the rectory garden, in a roadside cottage, lived an elderly brother and sister, Reginald and Rachel Mortimer. Reg had been a gardener and now lavished his skills on his front garden; he was also verger at the church. Opposite this cottage, shielded by a dark wood that housed a rookery and down a long drive, stood Beeston Hall, where Colonel Batt and his wife lived; he was at one time a churchwarden. The Batts' children were quite a bit younger than Janet and myself, but we were sometimes invited to their Christmas parties. The Batts kept stables with horses for hunting. When, hit by financial stringency in the depression of the 1930s, Mrs Batt sold her horse, her husband kept his. She henceforth attended hunts on foot, at least going to the pre-hunt gatherings at the mansions of her friends who might have been friends or relatives of her husband's family. Sometimes, she took the rectory children, Janet and myself, along on these trips. Colonel Batt's father possessed a manor house in another part of the county which his son would, in due course, inherit; meanwhile he rented Beeston Hall. They probably knew that Dora Thompson's mother had been a member of another Norfolk county family, the Spurrells, and this may have influenced them to include the rectory children in their circle.

About half a mile away from the rectory, in the opposite direction to the church, lay Beeston Common, where cottagers around had commoner rights to put out poultry; we were often chased by hissing geese when wandering on it. Near the Common stood the ruins of an ancient priory, with a farm house now attached. Several times we tried to go to see the ruins but were driven away by an angry farmer's wife.

Across the road from the Common lay Beeston Bog, famed for marsh flowers. There we went in gum boots, with mud oozing over their tops. A distance further inland from the bog stretched a line of low murrain hills, marking the edge of some Ice Age glacier. They were covered with bracken, the valleys and lanes between them harbouring excellent blackberries which we would sally out with baskets to pick. Later, they would be stewed or made into blackberry pies or jam.

Local farming was mostly arable, with both grain and root crops – wheat, barley, oats, sugar beet and mangel-wurzel, with hay on an occasional fallow field. Most ploughing was still by horses, although machines were being introduced. On the roads, horse carts were common but throughout my childhood they were being replaced by lorries and motor vans. Some of these horses, both farm and cart, were mighty beasts, beribboned and competing in championships. The countryside lost character with their replacement.

Usually on week days, Janet and I got up at 7 a.m. After breakfast, there were family prayers, with a reading of the Scripture Union daily portion of the Bible. Then we would be driven to the Bluebird School in Sheringham or, in later years, I would walk or cycle to Runton Hill School, which was nearer. After school, we would have a substantial afternoon tea at around 4:30 p.m. and then do homework, if any, until around 6 p.m., when we might listen to Children's Hour on the BBC and, after a light supper, have a bath and go to bed. We might also have had an hour or so of homework on Saturday mornings, but we were not allowed to do much more.

During school holidays, the Thompson family was swollen with several other children of missionaries, such as the Bruces, whose father was at one time headmaster of the China Inland Mission's School at Chefoo (now Yantai) in Shandong. Dora's nieces and nephews of the Watney and Barclay families were also sometimes there. Dora's sister, Dr Lily Watney, now retired from China and in declining health, used to spend long periods with the family. Once, she brought with her a paid companion who, unusually for our circle, was a Catholic, probably the first I had ever met. One day, at the age of six or seven, when speaking to Lily, I repeated some anti-Catholic allusion I had come across in a book I had read. Immediately the companion, whose name I have long forgotten, rose and left the room. No reference to this instance was later made but it stuck in my memory as a quiet and dignified protest. Another frequent comer to the family was my cousin, Ilsley Ingram, sometimes, in earlier days, accompanied by his mother who at times remained in England because of Ilsley's poor health, while her husband was in India.

To assist with the children, Dora Thompson usually had a resident mother's help. For some years this was Elisabeth Liechti, a Swiss lady, who later became a missionary in south India; I was very fond of her and she was my confidant and I clung to her. I was very sad when she left. Her father had been an engineer in Ukraine during the Stalin-provoked famine there and she told us of seeing skulls lying around the countryside. Elisabeth was succeeded by Charlotte Martin, a German Lutheran. Dora took the opportunity to use her fluent German in speaking to them and we heard a lot spoken although unfortunately we were not learning it at that time at school. I remember Fraulein Martin's anxiety, in the early 1930s, about the growing influence of the Communists in Germany and her alluding to another party, which she seemed to favour, which might provide resistance to them. I cannot remember more of what she said on the topic, but I fear that the alternative she mentioned may have been the Nazis.

Hammy Thompson, a good simple man, was assiduous in visiting all his parishioners, whether they attended church or not. One day he came home in puzzlement, having called on the only local fascist, whom he found quite incomprehensible. This gentleman could sometimes be seen walking around in a black shirt but otherwise did not seem to be of any note.

As the 1930s went on, we heard, of course, of the persecution of the Jews in Germany and grieved for it. A clause in a chorus we sang was changed to reflect this. It had run:

> *Jesus died to save the children: all the children of the world.*
> *Red and yellow, black and white: all are precious in His sight.*

This was changed so that the second line ran:

> *Jew and Gentile, black and white: all are precious in His sight ...*

There were few Jews in Norfolk and as a child I never knowingly met one. To us, Jews were people in the Bible. The establishment of a national home for the Jews in Palestine was strongly welcomed in our circle, the return of the Jewish people to their old homeland being taken as the fulfilment of a prophecy foretelling the Second Coming of Christ.

Two resident servants, a cook and a housemaid, shared a room next to that occupied by Janet and myself. Ivy, the cook, and her colleague Daisy, were both young locals and took part, in a friendly manner, in looking after Janet and myself. One disadvantage we had, however, was that no children were allowed in the kitchen when cooking was going on. This rule may have been understandable, considering the size to which the family sometimes swelled but it left a great gap in my upbringing which has been a permanent disadvantage. We undertook other chores, such as drying up, and also washing up when we were considered sufficiently responsible. Domestic science classes at secondary school centred on making cakes – much simpler for the teacher to arrange; my need in later life was to throw together basic meals in a hurry.

A small prefabricated house had been installed in the rectory back garden as overflow accommodation and during the holidays some of the older boys slept there. Friends brought their families to local lodgings during the summer and sometimes came to the rectory for meals or to play on the tennis court or to join parties going to the beach or elsewhere. It was a bustling and cheerful household. Sundays were quieter and rather more solemn. In the morning, we would walk to All Saints' Church for the 11 a.m. service and then come home to a cold lunch, on the remains of the Saturday roast, so the servants could take a day's rest. Games and secular reading, including newspapers, were forbidden on Sundays. On Sunday afternoons, we usually went for a family walk in the countryside and on Sunday evenings there would be hymn singing round the piano in the drawing room. On Sundays, too, I would write my weekly, rather dull, letter to my parents while theirs to me would arrive, as throughout my childhood, at irregular intervals sometimes of several months, as the internal situation in China occasioned. Usually, I remember, I wrote "via Siberia" on the envelopes to them; at one time, more specifically, "via Irkutsk".

Activities connected with the evangelical Children's Special Services Mission (CSSM) were a feature of our summer holidays. This body held beach services in many British seaside resorts, catering for the children of holiday makers. We would go every day to their morning service before bathing in the often-chilly waters of the North Sea and then perhaps having a picnic lunch on the beach, or buying locally caught fish, with chips, wrapped in newspapers and eating them with our fingers – which made the meal taste extra good! In the afternoons, we might participate in sports or other social programmes arranged by the CSSM. In the summer holidays, we would usually go for a family outing on the Norfolk Broads, swimming in the cold fresh water with mud squelching under our feet. Sometimes we would visit the Blakeney Point Bird Sanctuary, with its great expanses of sandy beaches.

The Thompsons' sons, in their teens, attended boarding school; John and Tom at Monkton Combe, near Bath, and the youngest, David, at Gresham School, Holt, in Norfolk, not far from where we lived and which I can remember visiting to watch him play Puck in *A Midsummer Night's Dream*. Janet and I attended the Bluebird School in Sheringham, a small private establishment run by two sisters, Grace and Joan Shilcock (known as "Miss G" and "Miss J") while their old mother organised our lunches. An assistant teacher, Violet O'Connell, was employed and various French ladies, visiting or locally resident, were co-opted to teach oral French. One afternoon a week we were taken out to nearby places for "nature walks", with Miss J, a keen naturalist, talking about the various flowers and trees we saw. Once or twice, I remember, she helped us plant bulbs of garden spring flowers – daffodils and others – in wild woodlands; I have always hoped these may have spread and still be flowering annually. Dora Thompson had a deep love of trees, derived from her parental home at Buckhurst, Berkshire and this love of trees she passed on to me. The beauty of the natural world in which I revelled in Norfolk and later in Limpsfield (with earlier memories, too, of mountains and rice fields in Sichuan) has provided treasured recollections which I can delve out of my childhood while passing most of my adult life in urban environments. Dew or frost on the grass and water dropping from leaves after a rainy night when the front door is opened first thing in the morning, are memories that embed the nearness of the natural world.

I do not know, or care, whether the Misses Shilcock had, or did not have, formal teacher training. They were good practical teachers and altogether I consider the Bluebird School the best educational institution with which I have ever been associated. There were probably never more than about thirty pupils, divided into four forms – Nestlings (the most junior), Explorers B, Explorers A and Pathfinders. With the very high teacher-to-pupil ratio, teaching could be informal and we were able largely to learn at our own pace and in our own way. It may have resembled the "dame schools" of earlier times. If ever a voucher system was introduced by which the government gave parents vouchers for their children by which the equivalent of the cost of educating a child of the relevant age in state schools might be spent on a private school of their choice, small schools of this type might multiply. This would have the additional benefit of giving more teachers the opportunity to set up and run their own schools and thus make teaching a much more attractive career.

One of my friends at the Bluebird School, Peggy Garnett, qualified as a doctor, became a Catholic and entered an Irish religious congregation, the Medical Missionaries of Mary. For many years she did good work in Tanzania and at one time held the position of Assistant Superior General of the MMMs. We met only once after childhood when, around forty years later, we were both in London at the same time, Peggy (Sister Margaret Garnett) temporarily back from Africa and myself on study leave from the Australian National University. Peggy lunched with me in the Senior Common Room at the London School of Economics where I was a visiting scholar.

The 1931 economic crisis and the subsequent general election were the first political events that I can remember. The crisis came in summer, when Sheringham and its district was crowded with visitors. A pervading air of anxiety hung over the country. Usually, adults around us did not discuss their troubles in the presence of children, but this time they did. The country's gold and foreign exchange reserves were running out, food imports were threatened and I recall someone saying that rationing might be introduced as in the Great War. No one knew what might happen and it was the first time I had seen a grown-up cry. Summer visitors, without access to radios (which at that time and for long afterwards were bulky objects, not portable), were bereft of news and the Sheringham stationmaster was offered a shilling for his penny newspaper. The King interrupted his holiday at Balmoral to return by the royal train to London.

In the subsequent general election, which returned a National Coalition government, still led by the former Labour Prime Minister

Ramsay MacDonald, the sitting Labour Member of Parliament for North Norfolk, Lady Noel-Buxton, was defeated by the Conservative Thomas Cook, of the travel firm which bore his name.[9] Most of our immediate circle quietly backed the conservatives, except that at school, Miss G (who doubled as the Hon Secretary of the local League of Nations Association), when giving us an explanation of the election process, mentioned the name of our present MP, commenting that it was hoped she would continue to be so. I thought she must have made an unintentional slip of the tongue. Miss G liked to brighten up the local League of Nations branch meetings with performances of country dancing by pupils of her school. For these, we had to practise during our mid-morning breaks, instilling in me an early aversion to the League!

Norfolk, which had little industry, was not severely hit by the depression of the 1930s, but it was brought to our attention by the steady stream of tramps from northern England coming south to look for jobs. Often, they made their way to the rectory where they would be asked to do some work in the garden, then given a good meal and some money and sent on their way. We also were provided, by some agency, with the name of an unemployed family in the Newcastle area to whom we sent provisions from time to time and seasonable presents at Christmas.

The 1931 depression, while it impinged even on a rectory in rural Norfolk, did not deeply unsettle our local society. As the 1930s coursed on, small indications of trouble abroad continued to appear. One summer, an international boys' camp was held locally and a German teenager who had undergone an emergency appendectomy stayed at the rectory to recover. He would not denote himself as either Lutheran or Catholic, insisting that for a German these labels were now outdated. It was clear that some influences had clouded his childhood Christian formation in a manner that my Thompson guardians found difficult to unravel. However, for us, life remained stable.

---

9 Sir Thomas Cook had bought a country house in Norfolk and became master of the local hunt, a rather expensive position, when the Depression dissuaded others from this role. His portrait on horseback was duly painted, at which I can remember one county lady acerbically remarking that it was probably the only time he had mounted a horse.

Audrey with her parents at Anxian, 1924

Left

The tin-can pedal car. Anxian,
1925–26

Below

Audrey, March 1928

Gladys and Vyvyan H. Donnithorne with Audrey, early 1929

The Rev Hamlet and Mrs Dora Thompson, 1930s

Beeston Regis Rectory, 1930s

Beeston Regis Church, Norfolk, 1930s

CHAPTER 3

Secondary Schooling: 1935–39
– Parents' Furlough: 1935–36
– My Return to China: 1940

By the summer of 1933, when I was ten, it was clear that I had outgrown the Bluebird School, excellent though it was. It was thought that my long-term secondary schooling should not be settled until my parents came back on furlough. This furlough was delayed by a year because the Church Missionary Society had been hit financially by the depression, so it was the summer of 1935 before my parents returned to England.

As a temporary measure, I was sent to Runton Hill School, a private secondary school for girls, in the nearby village of West Runton, within walking or cycling distance from Beeston Rectory. As a general rule the school was solely for boarders and I was one of only two day-girls at the time. It had been founded by the high-minded and forceful Janet Vernon Harcourt who was still the principal. JVH (as she was generally known) was one of the last generation of the nineteenth and twentieth centuries who could believe in secular human progress. This influence still lingered on until Hitler and his contemporaries snuffed it out in the mid-1930s. In keeping with this opinion, she had great confidence in the League of Nations and also adhered to the Modernist wing of the Church of England which was apt to water down many traditional Christian teachings and place hope, not in the world to come – "a new Jerusalem coming down from heaven" – but in an assured secular improvement of the human condition. One of the hymns sung at school assembly ran:

> *These things shall be! A loftier race*
> *Than e'er the world has known shall rise*
> *With flame of freedom in their souls*
> *And light of science in their eyes.*

Around this time, the most scientific nation on earth elected Hitler as its leader.

JVH taught Divinity to each form at least once a week. She took religion seriously, but her beliefs were somewhat nebulous. She seemed to believe in an impersonal life force rather than the God of Christianity. For a time this influenced me, and I began to think of God in impersonal terms. However, before long I realised that an impersonal entity would be inferior to self-conscious human beings and therefore not God, the Supreme Being. So around the age of twelve, I drifted back to a belief and consciousness of God in the traditional Christian sense which has been with me ever since.

It was at Runton Hill that I received most of the formal science education I ever had. It may have been part of JVH's progressiveness which led her to provide a year's physics and a year's chemistry in the syllabus for the Lower and Upper Fourth forms. At that date (1933–35) these subjects were not often taught at girls' schools in England.[1] I am afraid that about all I can remember from my physics is the information that an atom is the smallest indivisible unit of matter. This may not have greatly benefitted my education in science, but it has helped my historical perspective. My poor manual dexterity hampered me in science. I was around two years younger than the class as a whole but had no difficulty in keeping up with the subject matter. In manual dexterity, however I may well have been two years behind my own age group. I was apt to fumble with equipment and break test tubes which made me feel that science was not for me.

---

1 Janet Vernon Harcourt's father had been a distinguished Oxford chemist and a Fellow of the Royal Society; a forebear had been one of the founders of the British Association for the Advancement of Science.

Also, at Runton Hill I had the best art education I ever had. At one time, JVH brought in a professional artist, Margaret Fisher Prout, perhaps a personal friend of hers, to teach us. On warm summer days, we could choose a spot in the school grounds to sit with our easels and paint what we wanted of our surroundings. The artist would go around from one to another, commentating and making suggestions.

By 1935, the Depression had largely lifted, enabling the nation to celebrate George V's Silver Jubilee in a cheerful mood. It was a memorable day, especially for children; in Sheringham pupils from state and private schools gathered together for a civic celebration. Bonfires were lit on the neighbouring hills, indeed all over the country. It was a culminating point in my childhood, but one I recall with a certain irony. That evening, the old king broadcast to the nation. One passage in his speech we later learned by heart: "To the children I have a special word: The King is speaking to you. In the years to come, you will be the citizens of a great empire ..." so we must deport ourselves to shoulder our future responsibilities.

My parents came back on furlough in the middle of the summer term of 1935 and I took the rest of the term off to be with them. I was twelve and had not seen them since I was six. However, I cannot remember any serious problems arising from our long separation. Their furlough was a happy time. We were based at my Ingram grandmother's house, the Priory, on Wimbledon Common, so we lived very comfortably. My parents were anxious to settle me at a long-term secondary school soon, so that autumn I went as a boarder to St Michael's School, Limpsfield, Surrey, a school founded to provide for the free education of the daughters, and junior-aged sons, of the missionaries of the Church Missionary Society. Here, again I had the advantage of being allowed to take the whole of the 1936 summer term off to enable me to spend more time with my parents.

Granny Ingram and Aunt Tina returned from India to the Priory every summer, so I saw a lot of them, more than on my parents' previous furlough because now I stayed up to dinner. At the end of dinner, there was invariably a rather curious ritual when Ball the parlour maid brought in a decanter of brandy and a glass for granny who would then make a little speech every evening to say that she had the brandy only because the doctor had ordered it. On Saturday afternoons, Granny's children and grandchildren living nearby would be invited over for tennis in her garden. After tennis, Ball would bring to a table under the big cedar tree, a trolley with tea – an Indian silver teapot with milk jug, sugar bowl and tongs to match; and scones, strawberry jam and cakes. Tennis at Wimbledon can mean different things to different people!

Cattie, Granny Ingram's retired West African kitchen maid, died during my parents' furlough in 1935–36. This happened during my term time, so I did not attend the funeral at which my father jointly officiated together with the pastor of Cattie's charismatic chapel. I am told that, at some point in the service, my father handed over to the pastor a small sum of money – Cattie's savings – which had been found in her retirement flat.

The following January, in 1936, my cousin Esther Ingram married Guy Bryan, with the reception being held in the Priory. Granny was in India, so alcoholic drinks were permitted. Mary Ingram and I were to have been bridesmaids, but due to national mourning after the death of George V, the wedding was low key, without bridesmaids. Mary and I, gingerly grasping glasses, slunk into a corner of the vast dining room and nervously sipped our first alcohol!

The international scene was becoming tenser in both Europe and the Far East and I was glad to be able to read about it unimpeded; indeed, my father encouraged me to do so. At Runton Hill, we were urged to take an interest in politics, but at the Thompsons I had been forbidden to read the newspaper[2] as *The Times* was considered to contain salacious matters unsuitable for a twelve-year-old. (*The Times* then ran fuller accounts of divorce proceedings than later.) I was not at all interested in the salacious matter, but in international affairs; however, if caught reading *The Times* surreptitiously, my pocket money was docked. My father shared my interest in the world scene and when I went to St Michaels's ensured that I had my own copy of *The Times*.

---

2 *Children's Newspaper*, a journal edited by the progressive Arthur Mee, I had been seeing since I was around six.

In 1935 I went with my parents to the Keswick Convention and in 1936 to the Church Missionary Society summer conference at Malvern. At both, there was an emphasis on "the Church" – nebulous and invisible, but still, important. (A banner in the meeting hall at Keswick had always proclaimed: "All One in Christ Jesus".) At the Malvern Conference, Bishop Stephen Neill of South India, spoke about the unity movement among Protestants there. This was a continuation of the trend dating from the Edinburgh Conference of 1910 which my father had attended as an usher. It was certainly more than I had absorbed from my previous evangelical upbringing. The significance of the Church was reinforced by the intensive study of the Epistle to the Ephesians and the Acts of the Apostles which I undertook for my School Certificate exam in 1937.

In the summer of 1935, my parents and I went for a holiday to Coverack, near the Lizard, in Cornwall, taking Janet Thompson with us. My father always had a strong attachment to Cornwall, from where our family originated. Joseph Hunkin, then Bishop of Truro, was a good friend of his and during this furlough offered him the living of the parish of Charles, King and Martyr at Falmouth. My father was, I think, minded to accept, but was dissuaded by my mother, who disliked the idea of becoming a housewife, a very low category in the feminist lexicon. The summer of 1936, as already mentioned, I went with my parents to a conference at Malvern, with its sweeping hillscapes. The conference had arranged a visit to Stratford on Avon and I took with me an African girl attending the conference and unfamiliar with England, around the town. In those days, even in a tourist centre such as Stratford, an African visitor attracted much curiosity and attention. After Malvern, my parents and I went to Gloucester and Tewkesbury and other parts of the west country. During their furlough, I can remember visiting Downing College Cambridge with my parents where, around 1925–6, my father had spent a short spell as college chaplain.

My parents' furlough coincided with a spectacular exhibition of Chinese art (often referred to as the Eumophopoulos Collection) at the National Academy in London. My father took me to see it and the perfection of the porcelain celadon-glazed bowls and vases remains printed on my mind.[3]

While with my parents during their furlough, I met some of the foremost evangelical Anglicans of the time, such as Bishop John Taylor Smith, who had been Chaplain General of the Army during the World War and Harold Earnshaw Smith (for some reason commonly known as "Annie" Smith), for long the Rector of All Souls, Langham Place, London. These were friends from my father's Cambridge days.[4] One of my mother's friends whom I met at this time was Biddy Chambers, widow of Oswald Chambers, my mother's erstwhile mentor whose Bible College she had attended and the author of the evangelical classic *My Utmost for His Highest* which, for a number of years, I read daily.

It was a consolation to my father that he was able to see his mother in the year before her death in May 1936 and then to conduct her funeral service. Granny Donnithorne was never a commanding personage in the manner of Granny Ingram but her skill in entertaining her young grandchildren and the quiet courage with which she overcame the vicissitudes of life both before the death in 1906 of her obviously difficult husband and in the thirty years afterwards, had a deep influence on the family. She was buried in the churchyard of St Mary's, Wimbledon Hill, among the graves of the Ingram family, into which four of her children had married.

In 1936, we went to Ulster to see my mother's sister, Louise Gaussen who had married a member of the Royal Ulster Constabulary. Her husband, Horace, had retired and we stayed with them in their country cottage near Belfast. Their daughter, Helen, was married to Cuthbert Peacocke, at that time Dean of Belfast, and we also spent time with them and their six-month-old baby Heather.

Cuthbert, known in the family as Cip, was the son and grandson of Church of Ireland Archbishops of Armagh and himself later became

---

3 After repeated moves for safe-keeping during the Sino-Japanese war and then the Chinese civil war, many of these artefacts are now in the National Palace Museum, Taipei, Taiwan. See *Splendors of the National Palace Museum: A New Edition,* Feng Ming-Chen (ed.), 2010, pp. 235–7.

4 See Loane, *Archbishop Mowll,* p. 55.

Bishop of Londonderry. The whole family was, of course, very Orange (Ulster Unionist Protestants, pledged to retain Northern Ireland's union with Great Britain), especially my Uncle Horace who once told me that he could tell a Catholic half a mile off by the way he nodded his head! In later years, with changing times, Cip and Helen both mellowed and were always kind to me. Louise, too, was never as Orange as her RUC husband. During his lifetime, she could not visit the Irish Free State (the Republic of Ireland). Horace insisted that "they are all savages there"; but later, she and her sister-in-law, my Aunt Lilian, much enjoyed a holiday together on the River Shannon. This trip covered 12 July, Battle of Boyne Day, which was celebrated by a hilarious and friendly cushion fight in the steamer's lounge.

The intense greenness of Ireland, the beauty of the Mountains of Mourne and the rest of the countryside we visited there made a deep impression on me. This was the only time I have been to Northern Ireland. To the Republic, I have made only five or six brief visits. It is one of the regrets of my life that I have never got to know Ireland despite having an Irish grandmother. In the 1950s, I went to Galloway and, a few years later, for a walking tour in Kerry and Co. Cork, visiting Mitchelstown where my father used to holiday in his youth. In 1983, I stayed with the Lawlers, good friends from Canberra days, when Sir Peter Lawler was Australian Ambassador to Ireland, and I took the opportunity to visit my grandmother's old home in Milford, Co. Carlow and meet my second cousin, John Alexander.

While my parents were in China I used to go and stay with my father's sister, Edith Rawlence and her husband Duncan for about three weeks every year while Hammy and Dora Thompson were on holiday. The Rawlences lived on Kingston Hill, just adjoining Richmond Park. From there it was easy to visit other uncles and aunts in Wimbledon and nearby, so I had not lost touch with them. During my parents' furlough, I saw more of my extended family than usual and some of them handed down to me the wisdom of the tribe. Two points stuck in my mind: It was essential that the Low Countries should never fall under the control of a dominant power. Also, that what the British always demand from their leaders is not brains but character.

This was illustrated by a certain politician who was clever and ambitious, but whose career had virtually ended and who would never become prime minister because he lacked character. Well, he did become prime minister – in 1940! Never after that did anyone say that Churchill lacked character; however, had he died in 1936, that might have been his epitaph. Meanwhile, the nation was still reassured by Mr Baldwin, in a famous poster leaning over a farm gate with his pipe, promising "peace in our time".

My parents returned to China in the autumn of 1936, where my father was by this time Archdeacon of the Anglican Diocese of West Sichuan and also secretary of the Church Missionary Society's mission in that province – the liaison man between the missionaries in the field there and the CMS headquarters in London. In April 1937, the secretaries of all the society's missions in China gathered for a meeting in Fuzhou, in retrospect a very timely meeting as a few months later, the Sino-Japanese War (really dating from 1931 in Manchuria) would flare up. From Fuzhou my father sent me a small card, treasured ever since, with a Chinese-style painting of the coast off Xiamen, featuring five small junks and the island of Gulangyu (formerly known as Amoy Island).

When my parents left for China, I had just begun the academic year in which I was to take School Certificate. I was somewhat young for this and my parents kept telling me that if I wished, I could postpone it for a year. I saw no need for such a postponement and the exam proved no problem. Getting it over had the great advantage of giving me two years in the sixth form before the clouds of war descended.

A few weeks after my parents left, I can remember watching from our dormitory window a distant red glow, the fire which on 30 November 1936 destroyed the Crystal Palace. The next month brought the shock of the abdication of King Edward VIII who, as Prince of Wales, had always been held up to us as the symbol of the future. When the news of the scandal became known, Mr Moule, the headmaster, when reading the usual prayer for the sovereign in the Anglican Morning Prayer, omitted the words "Thy servant" before "Edward our King". Soon it was all over, to the great benefit of the nation for whom it would have been disastrous to have had such a lukewarm supporter of the allied cause as monarch during the fateful days of 1940.

The new king, George VI, was crowned in 1937. My Uncle Duncan Rawlence's firm, Rawlence and Squarey, had offices close to the entrance of Westminster Abbey and fixtures erected for the event obstructed the view from their windows. In compensation, they were given two seats in some temporary seating put up for spectators just outside the Abbey. The Rawlences generously allotted these seats to my cousin Ilsley and myself, because our parents were abroad in the missions. So we had an excellent view point on that magnificent occasion.

St Michael's was on the whole a good school, both spiritually and educationally[5] until partially spoiled in my last year there by intervention from the Ministry of Education, when the school sought "recognized" status. It consisted in fact of three separate schools, with one name and under one Headmaster, on an extensive property at the edge of Limpsfield Common, Surrey. At the bottom of the grounds was the kindergarten, then up a steep hill stood the large red brick building where the other pupils lived and studied. One wing housed a preparatory school for boys up to thirteen years old while the other bigger sector was a school for girls up to eighteen. The headmaster's house and the chapel were between the two wings. In order to provide more parental-type care than most boarding schools, because many pupils had parents abroad in the missions, the Church Missionary Society took care to appoint a married couple who would both devote themselves to this responsibility. Every morning and evening we attended services in chapel, comprising prayer, scripture readings, hymns and psalms; every month the whole psalter was chanted. We did not resent this, and I think that many of us looked back on chapel with appreciation as a settling background for life.

5 At Runton Hill, I was about two years younger than the average in my form; at St Michael's, about one year younger. The intelligence of the pupils at St Michael's must have been affected by being children of missionaries and therefore usually with fathers who were either clergy or doctors; also, they had greater motivation, knowing that they would one day have to earn their own living, while the girls at Runton Hill had richer parents who were more able, and in those days more accustomed, to supporting adult daughters.

The headmaster of St Michael's during my time at school was a remarkable, wise and unassuming man, Ernest C. H. Moule. He came from a learned family which gave more than one bishop to the Anglican Church. The family, while bearing the patina of an old culture, was not wealthy and, as a boy, Ernest insisted that all the money available should be used to enable an elder brother to go to university while he never took a degree but got his education by deep private reading of the Scriptures and of the Latin and Greek classics. Later, Moule was sent by the Church Missionary Society as a lay missionary first to Japan and then to Ceylon (now Sri Lanka); in both of these countries he was a successful headmaster. At St Michael's he taught a Scripture class to the sixth form every week. To me, he was a Western version of the Chinese *junzi* (scholar gentleman) with a certain *gravitas*. Ernest Moule was one of the many influences which have led me towards a somewhat sceptical view of the importance of educational qualifications. Once, indeed, he did tell me that he knew I was expected to go to university but that, really, I would get a better education by going away to some quiet country place and spending two or three years in solid reading. His wife, Josephine, a cultured and kindly lady, came from a family similar to his, deeply involved in missionary work; indeed, the Moules got engaged when travelling out to the missions on the week-or-more-long journey by the trans-Siberian railway to East Asia. Josephine Moule's brother was Bishop Wood of Lichfield and he sometimes visited the school. Mrs Moule took a close interest in us, especially those with parents abroad and often invited us to their home, set in the middle of the school, and read to us while we knitted or sewed.

Sport I thought a waste of time, both while at school and later. I could never see that it matters, in the general scheme of things, whether the ball goes into one goal or the other. In later years, I tended to file sport, mentally, under the heading of crime prevention. Boys and young men have such abundant energy and it is much better that they should expend it on football than on mugging people. Girls, however, tend not to be so exuberant. That we seldom mug people is not just due to superior virtue! I could not see why sport should be inflicted on girls. I much preferred going for walks, either in the countryside looking at nature or in towns observing how people live, or perhaps gentle swimming on a hot summer day. However, I realise that for those so disposed, sport is a perfectly innocent pleasure and am happy to see them enjoying themselves at it. My own best memories of school games, at all the schools I attended, was of seeing the shadows of surrounding trees stretching across green grass in the late afternoon sun.

At school in Sheringham, I had belonged to the Brownies. At St Michael's, I joined the Girl Guide troop attached to the school. Participation in this was in a way really part of the school activities as everyone was supposed to join but we were allowed to drop out, as I did, as work became more pressing before School Certificate. I cannot remember learning much of use in it, except perhaps bandaging up a finger. Once or twice there were joint meetings with a troop from a nearby independent boarding school, of a much higher social order than our "missionary children" school, the other troop including Mary Churchill, daughter of the wartime leader. On one occasion, as part of an entertainment, she performed a solo dance.

Music I was never taught properly. I had many piano lessons at Sheringham and at St Michael's and spent hours practising. The purpose, I was told, was to be able to sight-read hymn tunes, a standard I never reached. I have always regretted not knowing more about how to listen to music and recognize different composers; this has been difficult for me because I seem to have no memory for music unless accompanied by words. I enjoy listening to the music of the great classical composers (and hate modern "pop") but cannot discuss the music later because I do not remember it except as a blur. Patricia, the wife of my cousin Ilsley Ingram, was musical like all her family and always tried to pack Ilsley and myself off to concerts, even when she herself could not go, saying, "Go – get some culture," but time seemed to be lacking. The evangelical tradition in England, unlike in Germany, neglected the place of beauty in religion as an aspect of God's self-revelation. I love good Catholic liturgy, although I have never tried or wanted to study liturgical matters in detail. My most intense liturgical memory is of Cardinal Griffin's requiem in Westminster Cathedral in August 1965.

With art, it was rather different. I think I could have got further with it if it had been better taught and later, if it had not been crowded out by other activities. As already mentioned, at Runton Hill School the art teaching was good. At St Michael's, Mrs Moule occasionally took us up to London art galleries but I cannot remember any use of the school's magnificent grounds for the teaching of landscape painting which is what I have always wanted to attempt. During the summer of 1944, on days off from the War Office, I sometimes painted in Epping Forest. Another war memory is of going to the National Gallery at lunch time to see the one "picture of the month" which was on display. In fact, I enjoyed this much more than many longer visits to art galleries which often tire me out both emotionally and physically. My favourite artists are probably El Greco, Constable and Turner.

Much later, in the 1960s, I enrolled for evening classes at the Chelsea School of Art, but all there was to paint there were green bottles. Still, I learned that there is more to green bottles than first meets the eye and also had an opportunity to dabble in oil paints. When I decided to go to Australia, I thought that now at last there would be time for painting. A kind gift from my friend Eileen Brooke was used to buy oil paints and brushes, an easel and paper. Alas, soon after my arrival in Canberra, the Culture Wars broke out there and I had, in all conscience, to use my spare time for that. The lesson to be drawn is, perhaps, that life is too short for everything, even for all good things, and that unfulfilled aspirations will find unexpected fulfilment thereafter.

I made some good friends at St Michael's with whom I continually argued about war and peace, and theological matters involved, during those pre-war years of gathering tension. Later, the war and my absence abroad cut me off from many of them, but with two at least I remained in touch for years afterwards, in one case until we were both nonagenarians. Margaret Wright, the daughter of a one-time missionary in Africa, became a Quaker and with her husband worked for some years in a Quaker mission in Madagascar. We occasionally met and corresponded fitfully until her death. Marion Phillips's father had been a colleague of my parents in

Sichuan and had died while Marion was young. She felt a strong calling to be a missionary doctor and St Michael's arranged special coaching to enable her to take the first MBBS exam (in biology, physics and chemistry) in the sixth form. She did well in her medical studies and turned down an opening which might have led to a distinguished surgical career in Britain. With a theological shift, she joined the high Anglican Universities Mission to Central Africa (which later merged with the Society for the Propagation of the Gospel to become the United Society for the Propagation of the Gospel – USPG) and went to Tanganyika (now Tanzania) where she worked valiantly for decades in often very primitive conditions.[6]

The school encouraged us to enrol in an international "pen pals" scheme. I was asked from what country I wished my pen pal to come and I replied Fiji, because that sounded exotic. I duly received a letter from a girl in Chicago with whom I corresponded for a time. Also, a letter came from Krakow, Poland from a girl named Mina Mandelbaum. After exchanging a few letters, in the spring I wrote wishing her a happy Easter. Mina replied, seemingly with a bit of indignation, to say that she was Jewish and that the Easter greeting was therefore inappropriate. I replied welcoming a Jewish friend and our correspondence continued until the tragic autumn of 1939. After the war, I wrote to the International Red Cross to find out if Mina had survived the Holocaust. In return, a request came demanding detailed information about her, which I did not have, so I let the matter drop. When I visited Krakow in 1958, I went to Mina's old address and talked to the concierge who remembered her and her sister. She had heard that one had survived but did know which it was.

In my sixth form years from 1937 to 1939, we could choose a year's course in Christian doctrine (not given by Mr Moule but by a lady whose name I have forgotten). It was mainstream Anglican of that time, with a solid and orthodox chunk of Christology. A few years later, I read Charles Gore's *Reconstruction of Belief* and found that the lessons had been taken, almost word for word, from that. I benefitted from the teacher's plagiarism!

6 See her autobiography *Surgeon or Jack of All Trades?* published 2013 under her married name, Marion Bartlett, in association with Words by Design.

On ecclesiology, of course, Gore was weaker.[7] We also had a voluntary course in Sunday School teaching while in the sixth form.

When I began my sixth form studies, in the autumn of 1937, I resolutely refused to work for the Higher School Certificate – in fact, I can remember no pressure being put on me to do so. If I went to university, it would be to Oxford or Cambridge which admitted by individual college entrance exams, more general in character. I did not want to spend two years swotting up for the rather factual Higher School Certificate. Thus I look back to my sixth form years as some of the best times in my formal education, although at the time I did dream about being able to leave school soon, get a job in a factory, avoid university and work my way up the trade union ladder into politics in the Labour interest.

My main studies in the sixth form were in history and classics with also English and French. With burgeoning political interests, I was anxious to concentrate on modern history. Fortunately, our young history and English teacher, Eleanor Reader, just graduated from Hull, insisted on my doing mediaeval history, a decision for which I have always been grateful to her. It has seemed to me to be the sort of decision that an older person with a wider view of things, especially a teacher, should make on behalf of a young pupil. In classics I read Cicero, Horace, Ovid and a little Homer, learned rudimentary Greek and read some ancient history. Also, in my second year in the sixth, I began German. In my last term at school, in the summer of 1939, I was able to arrange my time table so that I had no classes all day on Fridays until the evening, when the whole school had choir practice. It was a glorious summer – like that legendary summer when the First World War broke out – and I used to take a rug to a bluebell wood in the school grounds where I would spend the day reading Virgil's Aeneid. The first book of the Aeneid I had done for School Certificate; now I also read the other books. This has always been one of the most enjoyable and carefree memories of my life.

My father's friends, Bishop and Mrs Hunkin invited me to stay with them at their beautiful house, Lis Escop, in Truro in the summer holidays

7 Bishop Gore, at or after the Lambeth Conference of 1930 which approved contraception, which he opposed, declared that if they then accepted contraception, in a generation's time they would also be accepting sodomy – a prophet indeed.

of 1938. It was the first time I had gone away to stay on my own, except to my relatives, and I was dreadfully shy and retreated to my bedroom for long periods. However, on balance I enjoyed it, noting that they took a less strict view than the Thompsons on sabbatical activities. I kept in touch with their daughter Elspeth for decades.

In December 1938, my Ingram grandmother died and was buried in the churchyard of St Mary's, Wimbledon. The family gathering on that day was my last visit to the Priory, which was sold, first to an overseas bank which was looking for a place to which to evacuate its central London office if war broke out, and then, much later, to the next-door King's College School which, after a radical restructuring, is still using it as its junior school. The family estate in Gurgaon was sold to its tenants in 1944; they were, I heard, able to buy the land which they worked without going into debt, thanks to the high agricultural prices in India during the war. By now, they may have sold their land as Delhi expanded its suburbs and become solid members of India's middle class. Soon after Indian independence, when the Secretary General of the United Nations came to visit India, the government wanted him to see something of the new developments in the countryside and he was taken to the former Ingram-Skinner Estate. My grandmother's financial estate, less of course death duties, was divided among her children according to the terms of a trust which she had drawn up. I have always considered a large family as one of the best ways to redistribute property.

During my final years at school and in the period afterwards, I began to be aware of the theological currents that were swirling around at that time: the revolt against that modernism which I had come across briefly at Runton Hill School. God's revelation, standing out like a mountain range looming above and out of the mist of our earthly knowledge, demanded recognition. Above all, the Incarnation of Christ – the sheer incredibility at first sight of the Creator of all that is, seen and unseen, of the laws by which the universe (or universes) exist and man has come to be, the Supreme Being Who alone exists of Himself and is infinite in all perfections – that this Being should accept the limitations of becoming a human individual, at one place and at a particular time – this, if true, must be the fulcrum around which history and all human life revolves. Reading His life and words presents the age-old challenge, as expressed by one of the Fathers: either He is God or he was not a good man (*aut Deus aut homo non bonus*) for the claims He made for Himself could not rightly be made by a non-divine mortal. This belief in the overwhelming importance of the Incarnation, both for the history of the human race and for the life of each individual, has remained with me ever since.

The impact of the Incarnation, with its earthiness, carried over to the growing importance of the notion of the Church, from the "all One in Christ Jesus" of the Keswick Convention (foreshadowed in the Edinburgh Conference of 1910) to the more developed but vague notions of the Church in the Protestant ecumenical movement of the 1930s; still considered little more than a collection of Christian individuals, but with an uncomfortable feeling that it should be much more. (Around this time, an Archbishop of Canterbury – perhaps Archbishop Temple – is said to have declared that he firmly believed in One Holy Catholic Church and greatly wished that it existed.)

In July 1939, I left school and went back to the Thompsons as I had done every school holidays. Hammy had recently moved from Norfolk to a new parish, that of Southborough, near Tunbridge Wells in Kent. During that summer, I can remember attending meetings of a peace group in Tunbridge Wells that had "adopted" a refugee from Germany. A few weeks later war broke out. On that Sunday 3 September, the country was tense. In the middle of the morning service, Hammy Thompson climbed into the pulpit, announced he had just been given a message that war with Germany had been declared and, in place of a sermon, read 1 Corinthians chapter 13 – St Paul's great encomium on charity. Then an air raid alarm sounded and the service was abruptly closed. We walked home thinking the world was about to end, but the alarm was false.

For months, it was only "phoney war", without much actual fighting; it seemed that this might stretch out indefinitely. My parents' expected furlough was cancelled and, instead, it was decided that I should join them in Sichuan. Meanwhile, a few days before war was declared, children from

London and other cities, together with their teachers, were evacuated to more rural areas. The Thompsons offered to house twelve evacuees – more than the number they were obliged to take. The rectory had a large drawing room which could be divided into two rooms by pulling down a shutter; this was done and the girls bedded down on the floor in one and the boys in the other. A basement room served as a dining room; Janet and I helped with serving and supervising meals. The evacuation process in most of Britain was done in general with remarkable efficiency and the bustle it caused diverted our attention from the grim happenings in the great world.

Arrangements about my own immediate future were confused. At sixteen, I was too young for university. Also, I was very anxious to rejoin my parents in China. That depended on getting a wartime sea passage and a suitable companion/guardian for the trip. First, however, it was desirable to secure a university place for the more distant future. The state of the mail between Sichuan and Britain was poor, many letters went missing and at one time no mail arrived from my parents for three months, so the necessary plans and decisions took a long time to make. This led to a good deal of bickering between myself and my aunt Maud Crofts, who was my parent's solicitor as well as the custodian of my mother's bank account, derived from the share of the family trust fund left her by her mother. My health at the time was not good, and it was thought that, to fill in time, I should spend a term at a domestic science college at St Leonard's, on the south coast. This I did in the autumn of 1939. On health grounds, it was successful and I felt much better at the end, but as regards domestic science, less so. As at domestic science classes at school, the emphasis was always on making cakes, especially Christmas cakes, and neither at school nor at the domestic science college did I ever make an ordinary meal. In sewing, I had to make crêpe de chine underwear by hand – not a skill I have ever later needed! Fortunately, I was allowed to spend half the time at a secretarial college where I learned typing and Gregg shorthand, neither to any level of proficiency, and some elementary accounting, which I loved. Also, I had German lessons from one of the German theological students being sheltered by the Anglican Bishop of Chichester, who was known for his support of anti-Nazi forces in Germany. Here, at St Leonard's, I had more freedom than before in my spare time. On Sundays, I used to attend an early morning High Anglican Eucharist and then a mid-morning Quaker meeting. A German refugee fellow student at the college told us she was terrified when she thought of all the German tanks and aircraft she had seen, but the rest of us pooh-poohed her and felt confident in the Maginot Line.

The next entrance exam for any of the Oxford women's colleges was for St Hilda's, to be held in the spring of 1940. I took the papers, went up for interview and was told that they would keep open a place for me in the College until I returned from China, but they could not keep open a scholarship for such an uncertain time. I agreed to this arrangement. My parents' colleague, Alec Maxwell, son-in-law of Bishop Cassells who had baptised me, and who many years later himself became Bishop of Western Sichuan, was about to return to China and very kindly agreed to take me under his wing on the journey.

The war was in its initial quiescent "phoney" stage. In Britain, we were still "hanging up our washing on the Siegfried Line", as a current song went, and some thought that the impasse might last for years. We left by a channel steamer for Calais on 18 April 1940, travelling through France by rail. All I can remember of that swift journey is seeing lots of Communist graffiti on walls, at a time when the Party was banned in France. The following day (three weeks before the German invasion of Belgium) we embarked at Marseilles on a P & O ship for Hong Kong. The voyage was uneventful. Italy had not yet entered the war, nor Japan, so the Mediterranean and the Indian Ocean were relatively safe. At night, we had to observe a wartime blackout, lifted only when approaching Singapore, after our captain had signalled the British naval commander that he did not think much of the Royal Navy if it could not keep the Malacca Straits clear. From Singapore, we sailed to Hong Kong, where we disembarked. Hong Kong seemed far from the war in Europe although affected by the Sino-Japanese hostilities which had been waging in China since 1937.

Vyvyan H. Donnithorne, 1936

Gladys Donnithorne, 1936

From left: Gladys Donnithorne, Victoria Ingram and Maud Crofts, 1935

Audrey with her parents in the garden of Beeston Regis Rectory, 1935–36

Audrey with Vyvyan and his nephew Patrick Rawlence on the Helsingford River, Cornwall, 1936

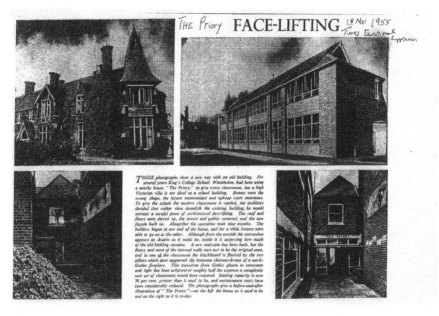

The Priory, Wimbledon – once the Ingram family home (*TES*, 18 November 1955)

CHAPTER 4

Wartime in Sichuan: 1940–43

In Hong Kong Alec Maxwell and I spent ten days, staying at Church House and buying provisions which my mother had ordered and a bicycle for myself. I had brought quite a lot of books from England as I thought I might have to face a university scholarship exam again soon after my return to Britain. So altogether we took a heavy load of luggage with us. On 14 May 1940, just as the war in Europe was hotting up, we boarded a small steamer to Haiphong, in what was then French Indo-China. At Haiphong, we had to get all our things through Customs, a tedious business for which we engaged a French *transitaire* (goods agent). Our impatience and my schoolgirl French irked him, especially since we insisted on him re-opening his office in the afternoons so that we could get the procedures completed in two to three days. "*Que femme veut, Dieu veut*" ("what woman wants, God wants") he exclaimed, throwing up his hands in exasperation. After Haiphong, we had to spend one night at Hanoi, which we reached by rail and then another day's train journey brought us to the frontier with China where we had to stop for two nights. Then we entered the Chinese province of Yunnan and travelled to Kunming, the provincial capital, on the narrow-gauge rail line which the French had built from 1904 to 1910. The railway was a remarkable feat of engineering, penetrating a region of high mountains and deep valleys; I counted, over one hundred tunnels. As the train ran only by day, we stopped twice for nights at railside inns. Disturbing news reached us from Europe of German forces sweeping into Belgium and breaking through the Maginot Line.

In Kunming, I stayed for two or three weeks in a missionary household and saw something of the city. My mother had asked me to call on friends of hers, German Lutheran Sisters who worked there. I was glad of the opportunity to make a gesture of Christian friendship across the divide of war. They received me politely though coolly, but I was shocked when a small box of biscuits I had brought them was placed on a shelf below a large picture of the Führer. From Kunming, after several weeks of delay and managing to send our heavy luggage by road, we were able to get flights to Chongqing (where the airport was on an island in the middle of the river) and thence, again by air, to Chengdu. There I was met by my parents, whom I had not seen for nearly four years. Sichuan had no railways at that time, so we went together by ramshackle bus along rutted dirt roads, to Guanghan, my parents' mission station, some thirty miles north of Chengdu.

From June 1940 until the autumn of 1941, I lived with my parents in Guanghan,[1] a county town some thirty miles north of Chengdu. The mission owned a beautiful old family house in the town with a traditional *tang* – a hall found in old Chinese homes – joined to the main house. Occasionally, services were held in the *tang,* but more usually in the church, which was along the street from our house. Between the *tang* and the street stood a series of smaller buildings in their own little courtyards. The section of the complex in which we lived consisted of three spaces, with two sets of single-storied buildings on each side of the middle space. In the centre of the space nearest to the *tang* was a courtyard where a tall *guihua* tree grew; then followed the middle space, covered but open at the two ends, where we had our dining room, then a space open on four sides, with an open-air staircase leading to a bedroom; this provided shade to the space below, which formed an open-air sitting room, furnished with a wicker sofa and chairs. The buildings on both sides of the middle space where we had our dining room, comprised on one side two bedrooms and on the other, my father's study and an indoor sitting room. Passages on

1 My parents always used the old name of the town, Hanchow.

58

each side of the courtyard led on one side to my mother's study and on the other to the well, kitchen and scullery, above which, as an extension, two bedrooms had been built, one of which was mine and the other that of Grace Liao, the senior of the band of workers whom my parents had recruited. The total effect of the house was pleasing in a traditional Chinese manner.

Water was drawn from a deep well near the kitchen. Electricity was fitful. Lights would come on in the evening "about the time the crows gather to roost" and go off around 11 p.m. The strength of the current went up and down without notice. At its lowest, we used to say we needed oil lamps to see if the electric light was on; then suddenly it would become blindingly bright and this might break the bulbs. We surmised that the power company was in cahoots with the manufacturers and sellers of bulbs. For reading, oil lamps were usually needed to supplement the electric bulbs. It was one of my jobs to fill the oil lamps (with vegetable oil because kerosene was unobtainable during the war) every day before evening, twitching the wicks with tweezers to ensure they were properly in place. These lamps were of a type which probably have been used in many parts of the world since antiquity, with wicks protruding from little pipes, one wick for small lamps and three for our larger ones.

There was only one electric bulb in each room (I am not sure why this was; there may have been some power-saving regulation to this effect) and because of the usual dullness of the light, in the evenings we dispersed to different rooms to read. My mother would also spend a long part of the evening with Grace Liao, with whom she was very friendly. After leaving Grace Liao, my mother would look in to say a brief good night to me. My father had suffered a minor stroke and, at this stage of his life, was not very talkative, although he still preached in both English and Chinese. I had the impression that my parents were yoked together primarily in a common devotion to their work, as colleagues, rather than with deep mutual understanding. I was a sort of extra addition rather than an essential constituent of the family although I always felt an instinctive bond with my father.

By the main gate of the compound which opened out on to the street, on one side was a hall, rougher than the *tang*, in which gospel talks and lantern lectures were given in the evenings. On the other side of the main gate were two rooms for a small out-patients' clinic, run by a nurse employed by the mission. This was always crowded, especially on market days, as its fees were lower than those at commercial counterparts while service was better. My mother often helped there; she had no formal medical qualifications but had acquired medical skills while living in India and then burnished them by a few months nursing training in England. In the 1930s, when Sichuan warlords fought each other vigorously, a friendly local warlord asked her to open a hospital for wounded soldiers. This she did, with some success; her most efficient assistant was a man whose "training" had consisted of six weeks as a patient in a mission hospital! My grandmother, Victoria Ingram, used to attend to injuries or sickness when camping on her estate in India if no qualified person was available. In those times and places, such skills were expected of the lady of the house. At another crisis in Guanghan in the troubled 1930s, a head had suddenly appeared above the garden wall, followed by the body of the local magistrate, climbing over to seek refuge in our compound.

We had a male cook and a cook boy – usually a young relative of the cook – and two women house-servants, who also sometimes helped with the cooking. Once, when my mother was out and my Chinese was still very inadequate, one of the women came to me with a question – was any *tang* needed? When spoken with one tone *tang* means soup, with another tone, sugar. (As mentioned above, *tang* can also mean a hall – using the same tone as for sugar.) I thought she was asking if we wanted soup with the next meal and said no; however, she had enquired if she should put any sugar in a dessert she was making, which consequently arrived unsweetened.

There was no heating in our house and the winters were quite cold and our dining room was open on two sides. My mother used a charcoal foot warmer such as was commonly used by old people in China. In winter we all dressed in padded Chinese clothes. I had a long, padded gown with a blue cotton cheongsam on top to keep it clean. In summer, like most women students, I wore cheongsams made from cotton printed fabric manufactured in Sichuan. Padded clothing was the normal method of surviving the chill north Sichuan winters as woollen garments were expensive and in short supply. As winter set in, small children would be seen to grow fatter and fatter as layer after layer of padding was added until they appeared almost as round balls, not being able to get up if they tumbled down. Then in spring they would rapidly slim. For footwear, except for special occasions, we always used the customary local black cloth shoes, handmade, with soles from rags compressed into hard slabs; these grew more comfortable as they wore out and were best when a small hole appeared in the sole. However, at that stage my mother confiscated them – I came to understand Gerard Manly Hopkins's complaint: "No longer can foot feel being shod."[2]

Our food was almost entirely very local. At Christmas or for special occasions we might open a precious tin of butter or of some other luxury from the stores which I had brought up from Hong Kong at my mother's request. Now that we were cut off from the outside world these supplies could not be replenished. My parents and I were in any case fortunate to have them at all, as most missionaries from Britain (as distinct from North America) could not afford them. It was only because my mother had independent means that she had been able to order them for me to bring up in 1940, or indeed had been able to bring me out to live with them. I do not think that any of my parents' colleagues resented my coming; none of them, as far as I can remember, had children of my age for whom the question might arise. Of course, when access to the coast was cut after 1941, routine coming and going from the Sichuan missions had in any case ceased. There had, I think, been some disapproval in the Church Missionary Society's London head office in Salisbury Square at my joining my parents. Dora Thompson's brother-in-law, Gurney Barclay, was still the Church Missionary Society's Secretary for the Far East, the executive in charge of day to day decisions about the missions in China and Japan. I saw him briefly before I left England and he did not seem happy about my going.

2 From his poem *"The world is full of the grandeur of God"*.

But to return to the topic of food, except for the delicacies mentioned from Hong Kong, all our food was local, from the vicinity of Guanghan, because no refrigeration was available. A substitute for refrigeration was the considerable trade in dried poultry and rabbits which were Guanghan specialities. Visitors leaving our town by bus would be seen with flat, opened and dried ducks and rabbits dangling on strings from their hands. I cannot, however, remember that we ever ate these dried items at home. Our meat came from fresh local poultry, goats, pigs and buffaloes; these latter were slaughtered only after a lifetime's work in the fields and so were very tough. Meat was not an everyday item of diet for ordinary people in Sichuan; its frequency in meals was a measure of a family's standard of living. Vegetables and fruit were plentiful and good. Persimmons, pomegranates, melons and citrus fruit – oranges, tangerines and pomelos – were excellent in season. Bananas did not appear in our district until the railway to Yunnan was built, years later. For drink, there was of course tea – Sichuan produces good tea – although hot water was the usual home drink of ordinary people. The famous Sichuan tea houses were the places where business was done. Milk, in local society, was regarded as medicinal, something for the sick, sold in small cupfuls measured out by the cow-owners at customers' homes. As mentioned above, our water came from a well; it was always thoroughly boiled before drinking. My mother told me not to draw it myself as my muscles were not used to this; however, sometimes when she was not looking, I did so and learned how heavy full buckets of water can be and how tiring it is drawing them from a deep well.

Most of our food was bought at local open-air markets, usually by our cook. Sometimes I visited the market, noting the sprinkling of ethnic minority people, usually referred to as Miaos, who had come to sell strange produce, often medicinal herbs, and who, in their traditional costumes, contrasted sharply with the ubiquitous Han Chinese majority.

By 1940, things were a bit quieter in the province. The central government had established its wartime headquarters in Chongqing (at that date part of Sichuan) and was trying to control the province's notorious warlords, but troubles still were frequent. On my first arrival at Guanghan, my mother suggested that I should stay at home and rest for a few days. This I readily did as I wanted to get my things, especially my books, unpacked and arranged. It was only later that I heard that the real reason for my mother's caution was that Guanghan, the county town where we lived, was locked down, with the city gates firmly closed against an angry mob of country people with complaints against the magistrate.

My parents were at this time in the first stages of detaching themselves from both the Church Missionary Society and from the Anglican Diocese of West Sichuan, of which my father was archdeacon. A number of Chinese Protestant religious workers from East China had come to Sichuan to escape the Japanese invasion. My parents recruited some to work with them at Guanghan, setting up what they called the West China Evangelistic Band. These workers lived in the small buildings between the *tang* and the street. They were of various denominations, but this meant little among most Chinese Protestants – it depended on which denomination happened to set up a mission in one's native town; when one moved elsewhere one would find another congenial place of worship regardless of label. My mother shared this attitude. My father's loyalty to the Sheng Kung Hui (as the Chinese Anglicans are called) was somewhat greater, but I felt sympathy for my father's curate, Pastor Wang, who had trained in an Anglican theological college in east China and may have had a stronger denominational attachment. The Wangs lived in premises in the compound of the church along the road some distance from our house.

The only physical links between Free China and the West in 1940 had been the French railway from Indo-China, the newly dug Burma Road to Yunnan along which trucks lurched, and also a few air services. The Japanese occupation of east China, much the most industrialised part of the country and the site of its seaports, cut off Free China's foreign trade and with it, much of the central government's revenues, of which import duties formed a major part. The outbreak of the Pacific War in December 1941, soon followed by the fall of Hong Kong and the Japanese conquest of Indo-China and Burma, closed the first two routes. Flights from India via Assam and then high over Japanese-occupied Burma (the

"Hump" route) to Kunming in Yunnan became the only link apart from radio. While government revenue fell, military expenditure swelled and inflation spiralled. China's allies, meanwhile, maintained steady the international value of its currency. The small foreign community, mainly missionaries who relied on remittances from abroad from agencies whose incomes had been diminished by the war, was hard hit. So were others on fixed incomes, such as teachers and civil servants. Some had second or third jobs in the evenings and at week-ends. Others, especially those in government employ, took bribes. Pastor Wang's family was in financial difficulty. My parents tried to help them by paying school fees for their children and getting a sewing machine for Mrs Wang on which she busily made clothing for sale.

Air raid warnings were frequent. They were of three types: the first indicated that Japanese planes had entered Sichuan's air space; the second that they had flown past Chongqing; the third that they were approaching Chengdu. Up to about an hour might elapse between the preliminary warning and bombs actually hitting Chengdu, which encouraged a lot of people, even some hospital staff, to hasten out of the city at the earlier alarms. I can not remember seeing severe damage in Chengdu. Quite often Japanese planes flew over Guanghan but, as far as I know, our town was never bombed.

Soon I settled down to the hard grind of learning Chinese – re-learning the spoken language in which I had been bilingual, though with a small vocabulary, up to the age of four but had completely forgotten in the intervening thirteen years; and also the written language, which I had never learned. Two of my parents' Chinese co-workers helped me in this task. One, from Sichuan, taught me spoken Chinese as I was anxious to regain my Sichuanese accent and the other, reading and writing Chinese characters. In return, I gave them some English tuition. One of these co-workers, Ruth Hu, and myself, together opened a small Sunday school outside the East Gate of Guanghan in the courtyard of a Christian family. This family told my parents that, before becoming Christian, they had had a number of girl babies whom they had drowned, hoping for a son.

When no son came, they eventually kept two girls. Later, they gave their daughters in marriage to pagans, for which my father chided them.

For a few weeks, we sheltered a *mutsai* girl of about eleven or twelve. A *mutsai* was a young girl who had been trafficked, usually by her own poor family, to another family, to work as a servant in return for her keep, but without any schooling, until she grew up, when she would be married off. It was better than letting the child starve, but still undesirable. The practice had long been permitted in Hong Kong, as a traditional custom, but was eventually made illegal there, after agitation in Britain; it was probably illegal in Guomindang China too, but that would not have been a consideration to which much weight was attached. Our girl had been with a wealthy family in Chengdu, located next to the Anglican mission house there. She had been beaten and otherwise badly treated and finally escaped over a wall to the mission where she was kept for a short while. Her former "owners", who had the money to be able to "influence" officialdom, demanded to be admitted to the mission compound to see if she was there. The missionaries felt compelled to let their neighbours in, but succeeded in hiding the girl from them. Everyone knew it would be useless to ask official help with the situation because of widespread corruption. It was realised that it was essential for the girl, and her rescuers, to get her out of Chengdu, so they whisked her thirty miles north to us in Guanghan. We could not provide her with a permanent home but she spent some weeks with us while a better placement was sought and I found myself, in the early days of my own studies in Chinese, having to try to teach the youngster to read the language. Eventually, the family of a pastor in another country town offered to take her as an older sister to their own small children. They would send her to school and give her board and lodging until she was old enough to earn her own living, and meanwhile she would also undertake the duties which fell to any older daughter there to help with the little ones, perhaps thus enabling their mother to earn more. Her new family was good and I hope the arrangement worked well. At that time, most people in Sichuan were living hand to mouth with the rampant inflation, and it was a problem to feed another mouth.

I often used to cycle with my father to the mission outstations in the market towns of Guanghan county where services would be held on market days when farmers came to town. We took with us small, rough locally printed copies of the gospels which I would sell *wu fen qian yi ben* (five cents each). People around were very friendly as well as curious about the strange foreigners. On some afternoons, I went for walks with my father in Guanghan and its environs; beside the Ya (Duck) River that flowed a little way outside the town walls or to the large, beautiful and tall-tree-filled park inside the town. The park contained an inscribed stone tablet which my father thought was of Nestorian origin although this was later disputed. Also in the park was a beautiful arch, one of a type which were erected in old days to honour widows who did not re-marry. At that time, a series of these arches adorned the approaches to Guanghan on the road from Chengdu. The Guanghan magistrate had intended to pull them down to facilitate a road-widening scheme but my father managed to dissuade him, pleading that future generations would value them. Unfortunately, years later, during the Cultural Revolution (1967–77) they were destroyed, leaving only the one in the Guanghan park.

I enjoyed cycling in the Sichuan countryside on the rutted mud highways or on the narrow ridges between paddy fields. The Chengdu plain was dotted with family farmsteads rather than villages, each farmstead being guarded by fierce, loud-barking dogs and surrounded with tall bamboos which provided raw material for a variety of tools and implements, mats, rain cloaks, hats and building material. The country people, though not their dogs, were always friendly. On market days, produce for sale would be carried on bicycles or in carrying baskets on poles balanced on shoulders or (especially in the case of live pigs), on wheelbarrows. Market towns had grown up, over time, at such distances apart as to enable the surrounding farmers to have one or more centres near enough to take produce for sale and return home the same evening. China counted time in ten-day periods rather than seven-day weeks, and each market town had a market day usually twice, sometimes thrice, on stipulated days (e.g. on days two and five, or three and seven), of each ten-day period. Adjoining market towns would differ in their chosen market days so that in densely populated districts, such as the Chengdu plain where Guanghan was located, there would be a market held every day somewhere not very far off.

My father maintained contact with the local officials. The county magistrate usually had an assistant with some reading knowledge of English on his staff; anyhow, my father was punctilious in taking round to the magistrate, in the course of our walks, copies of the British Embassy newsletters which were delivered to us, hoping to bolster British influence and thus the allied war effort. On one occasion, my parents and I visited the local boys' secondary school and the English master was thrust forward to demonstrate his linguistic skill. However, it soon became evident that his spoken English was almost nil and we had to save his face by pretending to carry on a conversation with him.

My father's interest in Chinese antiquities had already led to the beginnings of what was to be a very important development. In the spring of 1931 a local well-to-do farmer named Yen told him that he had found a number of stone and jade objects on his land. Vyvyan realised that a foreigner must avoid holding such things himself and approached his friend, Colonel Tao the local magistrate, for help. This led to the artefacts being lodged in the museum of the West China Union University. The museum's curator, David C. Graham, visited Guanghan, helped with excavating the site and wrote up his findings.[3] This site, Sanxingdui (Three Star Knoll) has become famous and there is now a splendid museum there. This discovery has helped re-write the early history of China. It is now realised that Chinese civilisation did not just spread out from North China but sprang from several centres, one of the centres being the kingdom of Shu, based on the Chengdu plain. Fortunately, not much more excavating around Sanxingdui was done at the time; otherwise, during the Cultural Revolution, the whole site might have suffered the same fate as the ancient arches.

---

3 "A Preliminary Report of the Hanchow Excavations", *Journal of the West China Border Research Society,* 1934 Vol. 6, pp. 114–31.

Before leaving England, I had all the usual inoculations and vaccinations, against typhoid and cholera etc. Nevertheless, within a few months of my arrival in Sichuan, I fell ill with typhoid. It was surmised that the local typhoid bug was fiercer than that against which I had been inoculated in London and future new arrivals from abroad were re-inoculated on arrival against the Sichuan type. Of course, we always drank only boiled water; it was cooled in bottles which were placed in the well bucket and sunk into the chilly well water until needed for drinking; this may have been a source of contamination. An alternative explanation for my infection was that I contracted it by eating bowls of noodles from street stalls at out-stations. Before drawing noodles out of the bubbling cauldron, the vendor would throw in some cold water to settle the contents and this water might not have been boiling for long enough to kill the microbes. The only Western-medicine doctor in Guanghan at that time was considered to have gone to seed and we never consulted him. A recently arrived missionary doctor from England, Frank Knight, was still doing language study and, as he had no medical responsibilities, he very kindly came to Guanghan where he continued learning Chinese while keeping an eye on me until the most serious stage of my illness was over. Later, my own Chinese language study was again interrupted, in turn, by scarlet fever, dysentery and pneumonitis.

Living in a country town in Sichuan, we were very isolated from the world outside China. Only powerful and expensive radios, which we did not have, were able to receive world-wide news. Postal links were very tenuous and it was hard to realise that the rest of the world really existed. China seemed self-contained like a world in itself, or rather, the world itself, largely unconscious of other lands, in the present or the past. The immensity of China in both time and space, impinged on our consciousness. Everywhere beyond China seemed shadowy and we thought of our friends there rather as one thinks of the dead. Intellectually, we knew and tried to keep up with the ebb and flow of the war in the West, but – especially before December 1941 – emotionally it was hard to believe it was real. Those around us in Guanghan were completely detached from the great world outside that we knew (and that "great world" was completely detached from life in the interior of China). In my room at Guanghan I might be reading a book on European ancient history. When I looked out of the window, I would see, in the neighbouring courtyard, a woman working a hand loom and I realised that she had probably never heard of the Roman Empire.

I had brought with me a number of books, including a few Latin classics, especially Cicero, and a Greek New Testament, which I read through, and dictionaries of both languages. My father had a small collection of English literature as well as theological works. Later, in Chengdu, these were supplemented by the university library and also the generosity of Andy Roy, an American missionary whose theology I disliked but who kindly lent me books. In the background, at his home, a number of small children ran around, including one who grew up to become a United States ambassador to Beijing.

So perhaps, in a way, I did follow the advice of my old headmaster, Ernest Moule, in getting my tertiary education by going away somewhere to do solid reading on my own. In any case, I have always thought that my most valuable higher education came about in the course of my unorganised years in wartime China.

By the autumn of 1941, my Chinese was still inadequate for academic use but I decided that at least I would like to attend lectures as an auditor and experience student life in Chengdu. So I applied to be admitted as a non-degree student at the West China Union University (WCUU) which had been established in 1914 by Protestant missionary bodies of different denominations from the United States, Canada and Britain, with North American influence predominating. Catholic institutions of higher learning existed in Beijing, Shanghai and Tianjin, but WCUU was the only Christian, and the only foreign-founded, university in the interior of China. Its most lasting institutional legacy has been its medical school which, since the Communist takeover, occupies the whole of the old campus and is called the West China University of Medical Sciences. The medical school's hospital is now the outstanding medical centre in Sichuan province. The arts and sciences departments of the former university were, under the communist government, amalgamated with the corresponding sections of Sichuan University or with other institutions and the library similarly re-distributed.

When I went from our home in Guanghan to Chengdu, some thirty miles away, I usually travelled by bicycle and often stopped for a meal halfway at Xindu where a Church Missionary Society lady lived alone. A dirt road, this was one of the main arteries of Free China, stretching from Chengdu to Xian, the capital of the neighbouring province of Shaanxi. Military lorries, going north, continually rumbled over its surface, which alternated from corrugated to muddy. For cyclists, the question on a dry day was whether to ride in a rut or on one of the ridges between ruts. In wet weather, it was a matter of squelching and slithering through the mud. Probably no road user in Sichuan had heard of a rule of the road – it was only years later, when sitting in the library of Chatham House in London, that I first learned that one had existed there. We just rode, drove or walked where there was space and the road was passable.

In 1941, WCUU was still on the outskirts of Chengdu. Indeed, some of the countryside was ensconced within the campus. When that stretch of land was being bought by the university-to-be, a farmer refused to sell his property, including his mud and straw farmhouse, which lay in the middle of the site. So the modern buildings of WCUU were built around this anomalous bit of old China where primitive agricultural practices obstinately continued alongside a university whose agricultural department was fervently promulgating the latest techniques.

It was fairly simple to secure my admission to WCUU to audit a few lectures. Enquiries were then made at the Women's College of West China Union University to see if I could live there but a regular place could not be made available for a student who, like me, had not been admitted to a regular course. It was then realised that there was, in fact, an unused room on an upper floor of the building which was intended to be for ablutions at whatever date it might be possible for water to be laid on to the building, but meanwhile had been judged unsuitable, because of its configuration and poor lighting, for use as a normal three bedded dormitory room. I was told that I could occupy it if I wished, which I gladly did. Without water in the building, we fetched it in buckets from a daily-filled giant vat at the end of the passage and emptied our potties into a large metal bucket in an adjoining room.

I was at the time the only foreign student in the university. Most of the students (including myself) were natives of Sichuan province but a good number were from families from east and north China who had taken refuge in Free China. These two groups, Sichuanese and the extra-provincials, who were often referred to in Sichuan generically as "down-river", did not mix well and at meals in the Women's College they sat at separate tables. I, of course, sat with my fellow Sichuanese. We were served different dishes as the "down-river" students disliked Sichuanese food spiced with hot chillies. In the outside society, this antagonism between locals and down-river people was widespread. I felt a certain pleasure when, bargaining with a Sichuanese accent, I was able to buy fruit in the local market cheaper than could Chinese from Shanghai! The students from Manchuria (the "northeast" in Mandarin) were a particularly close-knit bunch and could often be heard singing a mournful ditty *"jiu shiba, jiu shiba"* ("nine eighteen, nine eighteen") which commemorated the Japanese invasion of their home region on 18 September 1931. As well as individual students, whole universities had moved as institutions to Free China from the Japanese-occupied areas. Some, notably the University of Nanking and its associated women's institution, Ginling College, were accommodated in cramped quarters on the WCUU campus. This raised the intellectual level of what had been rather a backward provincial academic community.

Food in the college canteens at WCUU, whether for local students or others, was poor as at all universities in China at that time, and was supplemented by soya bean milk, supplied by some relief agency. I also made arrangements to eat frequently, in return for payment, at foreign households on the campus.

Corruption was rife, so the keys to the college rice store were held by two student representatives who doled out the appropriate amount daily to the cooks; this saved the college from accusations of cheating the students at a time when the price of rice, and of other commodities, was rising steeply from day to day. I found my fellow-students friendly. They told me of schoolmates who had gone north to join the Communist rebels but said they never heard from them because of mutual disapproval. One good friend of mine, Luo Wenyu, the niece of WCUU's Dean of Arts, Professor Luo Chongshu, was a member of the youth branch of the Guomindang. All the Chinese students had to study Guomindang ideology, although I do not think it was taken very seriously. Neither did any of my fellow students seem the least bit interested in old Chinese classics and philosophy except for one girl who was doing a graduate degree in Chinese and who had been taught the classics at an early age by her scholarly father. I was trying to struggle on my own with Confucius's *Analects* and she was a great help, but other students laughed at my interest in the Chinese classics. Another very different friend was a somewhat older student who lived in the college but was one of the numerous concubines of a Sichuan warlord who wanted an English-speaking spouse to accompany him on foreign travel. She often brought her small son to the college but I never got to learn much about her life. Years later, I heard that the warlord murdered her because she had let her affections wander.

There was, as far as I saw, no independent political activity among the students on the WCUU campus. Every week there was an assembly, with the singing of the Guomindang national anthem ("*San min zhuyi ...*" "*The Three People's Principles ...*") and the reverencing of the portrait of Sun Yat Sen. This was something generally taken for granted as an official requirement and did not seem to evoke any emotional attachment or conviction. Nor was there much enthusiasm for the war among the students or anyone else. Once, walking among some rice fields, I came across a young woman singing a sad song "*Zhongguo qingnian xiao zhi ku*" ("*China's youth know how to endure hardship*"). I got into conversation with her and learned that she was an army nurse and had just completed her training. "So now, I suppose, you will be going to the front?" I asked. "Oh no," she replied. "My family thinks that would be dangerous." She appeared oblivious of the discrepancy between her words and her song.

On another occasion when I was strolling on my own near a farm, I was attacked by four dogs. Two small ones bit my ankles while two large ones jumped up on me. Only with difficulty did I manage to extricate myself. At that time, there were no facilities for the treatment of rabies in Free China, so in the following days I gingerly visited the farm to assure myself that my canine foes were still alive and well.

At the university, I selected a few lecture courses in Chinese history, philosophy and anthropology; on the whole, because my language level was still low, these were more helpful in improving my Chinese than in imparting knowledge on the subjects being taught. However, Professor Luo Chongshu, the uncle of my friend, whose philosophy lectures I attended, had a very confused manner of speech. Sometimes, rightly realising that I was not following his Chinese exposition, he would switch into English for me. The trouble was that not only could I not understand his English but I also had difficulty in knowing which language he was speaking! This embarrassed me because when he spoke English for my benefit, I should have looked suitably appreciative. I attended some lectures, too, in physical anthropology although I soon desisted after being given the Chinese transliterations of the Latin names of various types of hominids.

During that year, to earn pocket money, I gave a few private English lessons. I also found a local journalist to give me lessons on the history of modern Chinese vernacular-style literature which, in the twentieth century, was replacing the old *wenli* (literary-style) writings and, having already delved into some Chinese classics with help from a graduate fellow-student, I read some modern authors such as Ba Jin and Lu Xun.

While at Chengdu (from the autumn of 1941 until the end of 1942) I also made a number of Western friends. Chief among these was Penelope Piercy, who had a great influence on me and with whom I remained in close contact after we both returned to England. Through her, I met others, older than myself, whom I might not otherwise have come across. Notable among these were the Molgaards, Val and his wife Margaret, an Ulsterwoman, and their small son. Val Molgaard was a Danish Lutheran pastor. He had been the representative of the British and Foreign Bible Society in Kunming,

Yunnan. After Denmark was overrun by the Nazis in 1940, Val found himself the leader of the Free Danes in Free China, all two and a half of them – himself, his young son, and a Quaker lady missionary who, while whole heartedly anti-Nazi, found the Free Danes rather too militant for her liking. In his capacity as leader of this allied contingent, Val was invited by the British Consulate in Kunming to occasional cocktail parties. This scandalised the fiercely teetotal Protestant missionary community, which it was his job to serve, and so he had to resign his position with the Bible Society. Thereupon, the British Embassy in Chongqing asked him to edit an English language news sheet as a means of providing the expatriate community, and educated Chinese circles in Free China, with more reliable information than could be gleaned from the tightly controlled Chinese press; radio reception was poor. The Chinese papers reported only the advances of the Chinese army and not its reverses, so we reckoned that if it went any further eastward it would invade California!

The Molgaards based themselves in Chengdu and had some rooms in the Canadian School building on the campus. Pen and I used to join them there. Once, Val celebrated a Lutheran liturgy – he particularly wanted to familiarise his little boy with it. On another, lighter, occasion, he had got hold of a bottle of whisky and insisted that I should taste it. Unfortunately, I disliked it so much that I have never since repeated the experience. I was looking for a Catholic missal which, like most things from abroad, was not available in Sichuan at that time. Val happened to see an old French missal and prayer book in a second-hand book shop, which I visited and bought the small volume. It has become, in an increasingly battered condition, one of my most precious possessions.

Before I left for England, in January 1943, Val asked me to take a message to the Free Danish government in London as he did not trust the post. In addition to his expressions of loyalty and good wishes, he informed them that the Free Danes were not permitted to fly the Danish flag in Free China because Denmark had recognized the Japanese puppet state of Manchukuo. On my return to London, I duly called, unannounced, on the Free Danish government at its headquarters off

Knightsbridge and without any ado was ushered in to see their Minister of Foreign Affairs to whom I delivered my message. I think he was glad of something to occupy his time.

Some Westerners with whom I struck up acquaintanceship on the WCUU campus were later numbered among the "foreign friends" hosted by the Communist government in Beijing. Ruth Weiss, a very secular refugee from Germany, fitted ill among the foreign community in war time Chengdu. Isobel Brown, the daughter of Canadian missionaries, later married David Crook and she and her husband, as well as Ruth Weiss, figured in that select Beijing group. Isobel's mother was a French Canadian and lapsed Catholic; from the Brown family, I acquired a battered old Douai version of the Bible. A Chinese biochemist, Liao Hong-ying who had studied at Somerville College, Oxford, was more inclined towards the Communists than were most of her contemporaries on the campus. Under the influence of Margery Fry, Principal of Somerville, she became a Quaker and worked in Quaker activities in China. She married Derek Bryan, a British diplomat in China, who resigned soon after the war because of his sympathies with the new government in China. They returned to Britain, where I kept in very intermittent touch with them; for years, they participated in pro-Beijing "friends of China" groups but were never extremists. Another foreign couple whom I met, during their stays in Chengdu, were Ralph and Nancy Lapwood, active in the China Industrial Co-operatives. This movement had been started by the New Zealander Rewi Alley. I was much interested in this venture, but never had close contact with it.

Although we might sometimes feel it was in a different world, we anxiously followed the scanty news available of the war in Europe, North Africa and, after December 1941, in south east Asia as well. On 8 December (the day the Pacific War broke out in East Asia, while in the USA it was still 7 December), I was returning to the campus from a dental appointment at the Canadian Hospital in central Chengdu, when I noticed a boisterous excitement on the streets. The news had arrived that after more than four years of fighting Japan on its own, China now had allies. However, this was followed by long months of devastating reports as the Japanese armies swept to the borders of Yunnan and of Bengal and two British warships were sunk in eastern waters. In 1942, some 200 bedraggled British Royal Air Force ground crewmen made their way up the Burma Road into Free China ending up in Chengdu. The small British community there did our best to help, setting up a club for them in the Canadian School on the WCUU campus.

On the entry of the United States into the war, the American-sponsored Yenching University in Beijing was shut down by the Japanese and the foreign staff interned. The students and the Chinese staff trekked on foot the immense distance to Sichuan where in October 1942 they opened Yenching-in-Chengdu. They needed more staff of all kinds, so I was hired, at the age of nineteen, as a part-time teacher of English and part-time English secretary to the Acting President of the University, Professor Mei Yi-Pao (the interned Leighton Stuart was still recognized as the official President). Mei was one of a trio of distinguished brothers, one an eminent medical man and another, Mei Yi-Chi, was president of the University of the Southwest, based in Kunming, Yunnan province (an amalgam of several refugee universities from East China), who later became Minister of Education in Taiwan.

As I did not have a university degree, I was unqualified to teach normal university courses, so I was put to instructing the "sub-freshman" English language students, English being a compulsory subject for all students at Yenching. In Beijing, Yenching demanded a high standard of English from its entrants. In Sichuan, such students did not exist, so the university had to accept many with a much lower standard and then try desperately to bring them up to an acceptable level – this was my task. Yenching's previous English textbooks were useless for this and I had to invent a very basic course, lesson by lesson. If I ran out of material before the class ended, I would ask them to count out aloud in English "one, two, three…" to ensure that there was at least some English they knew! Around forty years later, as a guest of the Sichuan Provincial Academy of Social Sciences, I visited a state bank in Chengdu where an old man introduced himself as one of my former students – his English had provided him with a rice bowl as a translator at the bank.

Half a day of my time at Yenching was spent as English Secretary to Professor Mei. He had extensive correspondence with many of the leaders of Free China (the Minister of Finance, H. H. Kung, was Chancellor of Yenching-in-Chengdu University) and, with those who had been educated abroad, he found it easier to write in English, so I typed these letters and polished his English. If he wrote these letters in Chinese, they would have to be written with brush and ink and in old-style respectful phraseology.

Our refugee institution, Yenching-in-Chengdu, was housed in a former secondary school building on a road off the southern stretch of the main north-south street in Chengdu – the present Renmin Nan Lu. Three members of the staff of the English Department, including Penelope Piercy, who already was a good friend of mine, a much older American woman Lucy Boynton, and myself, were given small cubicle rooms on an upper floor of the old wooden building which formed the women's dormitory. The windows were unglazed and instead had semi-translucent paper pasted on them and water was not laid on to the upper floor. The three of us hired a woman servant who did our washing, cleaned our rooms, carried water up to us, bought and cooked our food and boiled our drinking water. As I was the only one of us three who spoke much Chinese, dealings with her were left to me.

Our salaries were settled according to complex and constantly changing calculations. First there was the basic salary (the pre-war salary for each grade) to which was added a wartime addition plus the current cost of one *dou* of rice a month (i.e. one person's presumed monthly consumption of rice) plus a cost of living allowance which rose each month with inflation. When wealthy Yenching first re-settled in Chengdu, the other universities were afraid it would lure away their staff by offering higher salaries, so it promised to keep its salaries level with theirs. However, it found a way of semi-cheating. While staff at other universities often took side jobs to survive, Yenching gave its employees an additional "single job payment" on condition that they took no other employment. Also, it (and perhaps also other institutions) paid our salaries a few days before the end of the month, a considerable help during a runaway inflation, so that we could immediately spend it before prices rose higher.

Penelope Piercy had been a scholar of Somerville College Oxford. She graduated in Modem Greats (Philosophy, Politics and Economics – PPE) in 1938 and then began graduate work at the London School of Economics and also took a position with the Student Christian Movement (SCM) in England, which embraced a wide range of theological views. In 1941, she accepted a position with the Young Women's Christian Association (YWCA) in Free China, which brought her to Chengdu later that year, when I was at WCUU. Pen had come to China via the Burma Road, a rough and arduous highway, driving a car that was being brought to Free China (which had no car manufacturing capacity) for the Minister of Geology in the Free China government. Pen was an Anglo-Catholic who took her religion seriously and soon felt ill at ease with the Chinese YWCA'S vague and woolly theology and also with its close links with the ruling Guomindang. So she resigned from the Y and accepted a position to teach English and some philosophy in Yenching when it arrived in Chengdu. Pen was six years older than me and carried with her much of what to me was the novel and exciting atmosphere of pre-war Oxford, an intellectual stimulus which I badly needed at that time. She also brought to China some volumes of Maritain and Gilson and others, which she generously lent me and which I devoured. These works influenced me deeply, especially elements of the philosophy of Aquinas, including the concept of God as "Being". From Pen I learned quite a bit about things Catholic and she taught me the Hail Mary.

The religious life on the Chengdu Campus and at Yenching horrified Pen as much as it did me. A book then influential on the campus, written by a North American missionary there, *Jesus as Teacher,* summed up the theological flavour being propagated: that Christ should be put forward just as one of the world's great thinkers, not for Who He is. Christianity was depicted as one way of searching for the divine rather than God's revelation, His breaking out to us. Some of the few Anglicans on the campus, notably the English Reverend Bertie Lutley, differed in a quiet but persistent way from this general trend but did not make much headway against the prevailing wind. Bertie, and his American wife, Martha, who came from Boston high society, were always kind to me and I was often at their home and at their neighbours in the CMS portion of the campus, Norman and Jessie Parfit, both medical doctors who also were very helpful. I frequently visited their home and enjoyed their small children, one of whom grew up to become a notable Oxford philosopher. The Parfits were a force on the medical front in Chengdu. Jessie set up a small leprosarium on the campus. This later proved useful to us when one of our servants at Guanghan became increasingly clumsy and was diagnosed as having a neuralgic type of leprosy. A place was found for him at the leprosarium where, when I last heard, he was doing well. The Parfits also did their best to combat TB on the campus. Around five per cent of the students were said to have active TB and there was strong resistance against sufferers being quarantined; this was denounced as a foreigners' plot to deny education to the students concerned. One vacation, a girl student turned up to see me in Guanghan having cycled the thirty miles from Chengdu. Over lunch she told me that she had TB and "wasn't it silly, the doctor had told her she should go into hospital."

The Anglican Bishop of West Sichuan, C. T. Song, preached in his cathedral in Pifang Gai, a series of solid sermons on the Incarnation which I appreciated. In an early example of ecumenism, he was collaborating with Catholic scholars in translating some works by Church Fathers into Chinese. Song had been appointed bishop a decade or so earlier. As a child in England, I had been told that my father might be the next bishop but it was rightly decided that it was time for a Chinese instead. My father, in a circular letter to his home supporters, gave his strong approval to the appointment. Quite often, however, my father disagreed with Bishop Song, whom he considered modernist in theology and too close to the Guomindang and its New Life Movement.

Dissatisfied with religious observances on the campus, Pen and I found our way to the Catholic cathedral compound, at Pingan Qiao

(Bridge of Peace) where, on the evening of Christmas Day 1941 we attended Benediction in the Sisters' chapel. It was the first time I had been to a Catholic service. In the following year, I went with a group of foreigners to a Buddhist ordination ceremony held at the Wuhou Temple (also known as the Zhugeliang Temple or the Wenshu Monastery) in Chengdu and there got into conversation with some Spanish priests of the Redemptorist congregation who were also attending. (The Redemptorists had been working in the Diocese of Xichang – then called Ningyuan – as well as having a house and chapel in Chengdu, the provincial capital.) Later, one of them, Father Eusebius Arnaiz, came to see me on the campus and lent me some books. Father Arnaiz, an excellent man but dark and with a somewhat conspiratorial demeanour, seemed just the sort of Spanish cleric that had for centuries bedevilled English Protestant perceptions of things Catholic. This first reinforced and then made me face up to my own prejudices. Pen and I went to Mass at the Redemptorists' chapel in Yangshi Gai (Sheep Market Street). Quite often, we would also cycle together to an early Mass in the Catholic Cathedral compound.

Although in 1640 Jesuits had been the first Christian missionaries to reach Sichuan, the continuing presence of the Church there from the eighteenth century was due mainly to the French MEPs (Missions Etrangères de Paris – the Paris Foreign Missions). These French Fathers in Chengdu, in 1941 under the leadership of the Vicar Apostolic, Monsignor Jacques Rouchouse, were elderly with long white beards and so closely resembled my imagined idea of the Fathers of the early councils that it was with difficulty that I refrained from asking them their memories of Nicea! As regards their contemporary world outlook, it was known that a division existed among the French missionaries between those who leaned towards Pétain and those who supported de Gaulle. Pen and I often attended Mass or Benediction in the chapel of the convent of the Franciscan Missionaries of Mary. These Sisters were mostly from France and French Canada, some coming to the mission field in their late teens. They taught women and children as well as running orphanages for abandoned children. There was not much opportunity for outsiders like ourselves getting to know them well.

A Belgian lady in Chengdu, Madame Germaine Braye-Yuen (Uen), had been giving me French lessons and I think it was through her that I met Father Albéric de Crombrugghe, a Belgian Benedictine from the great monastery of Saint André in Belgium. He was much more compatible with English susceptibilities than were the Spanish Redemptorists. The Benedictines were in the process of establishing a monastery in Sichuan, outside the city of Nanchong and Dom Albéric divided his time between Chengdu and the new monastery at Xishan (West Hill) Nanchong.

The Catholic liturgy was of course in Latin which the priest said in a low voice while simultaneously the congregation chanted a rough vernacular equivalent, stopping briefly only for the words of consecration. It was similar to the chant which I heard at Mass in Polish churches many years later. Sermons were long, and in the case of an old Chinese priest in the cathedral at Chengdu, rambling, hopping from one topic to another. This reminded me of what I had heard about Presbyterians in Scotland, that no sermon was regarded as complete unless it touched on every article of the creed.

The modernism which I came across briefly at Runton Hill School and again on the WCUU campus, had in Europe brought about a revolt by theologians and philosophers such as Kierkegaard and Barth and these had come to my notice although it was not until my time in China that I read any of them, and then only such as I could get hold of there. Barth's *Credo* I especially remember with his stress on the implications of the Incarnation. Incarnational theology suggested that the notion of the Church should be more coherently defined and visible than the vague vision of the protestant ecumenical movement. My inclination was to go on believing that the Church of England was the legitimate continuation of the Catholic Church in England. I loved the Anglican liturgy, the Authorised Version of the Bible, and the old churches and cathedrals which in England are in the possession of the Establishment. I greatly feared the Catholic Church. I read anything available against the Catholic Church but it sometimes had the contrary effect, to provide evidence of the basically Protestant nature of the Church of England, as had indeed my own experience of the Anglicanism of my upbringing. Jewel's *Apology for the Church of England,* which at one time was ordered to be kept in every Anglican church, alongside the Bible, was a telling example of this. It was actually while reading Jewel that the thought first gripped and terrified me that I might, after all, have to become a Catholic. I tried as hard as I could to counter this thought. I read all the Anglican and anti-Catholic works I could get hold of, such as George Salmon's *Infallibility of the Church.* I delayed finishing Newman's *Apologia* lest the beauty of his style should sway me. I avoided the Redemptorists. But however hard I tried, the realisation grew that I would have to become a Catholic or go straight against God's will. At length, I yielded though with regret. During the months of perplexity, I had the guidance of a High Anglican RAF padre, Graham Langford, who had come to Chengdu with the RAF stragglers from Burma.

There were two other matters I had to mull over internally. If I became a Catholic, there was the possibility that I might find I had a vocation to the religious life. I did not want this, but if the good Lord called me, I would have to obey, which I agreed. Since then, no thought or sign has come that this was God's will for me. My life has continued, step by uncertain step, but every now and again something would happen that indicated I was where I should be. The second matter concerned pacifism. Interpreting the New Testament as a Protestant individual, it seemed that even defensive warfare was forbidden. I realised that the Catholic Church had a more nuanced interpretation and this I was willing to accept.

Another influence on my whole outlook on life, which probably helped me in the direction of the Catholic Church, was China's ability to bring people down to earth. Living in a world which was quite other from the Western world yet one to which I felt closely tied by my earliest childhood memories, made me hone in on the essentials which inhered in both worlds. The trends in Chinese thought and life which seemed most reasonable to me were broadly those which can be labelled as Confucian: an acceptance of the visible world as we see it and its social obligations but with a duty to use it all according to objective moral principles. Buddhism, in a way a diametrically opposite view of life to Confucianism (although sometimes blended in a Chinese manner), has always appeared to me a form of escapism, by denying the world as we experience it and with this, also denying free will. Confucianism is readily consonant with Christianity, especially with Catholic thought, but Buddhism is radically different and opposed to it. It is Christianity, too, which is consonant with the dimension of infinity – part of the image of God – which is stamped on our consciousness.

When I told my parents of my decision, they were of course horrified. I was not yet of age (the age of majority in English law was still twenty-one) and so could not be received into the Catholic Church immediately. Also, it would have been a great embarrassment to my parents if I became a Catholic in Sichuan. I was planning to return to Britain in the near future and Dom Albéric advised me to wait until I was there. Pen wrote to a High Anglican friend of hers at Oxford, Austin Farrar (who some years later tutored me in philosophy) and asked him to suggest a Catholic priest from whom I might seek instruction.

My parents had by this time resolved to break their links with the Church Missionary Society from which my father then retired and thenceforth to work independently, together with their team of Chinese fellow workers, as the West China Evangelistic Band, financed chiefly by supporters in England as well as by my mother's own resources. They would be based at Beipei, a town in the suburbs of Chongqing, the other end, at that time, of Sichuan province. (Since then, Chongqing has been made a municipality directly under the central government and is no longer part of Sichuan.) Late in 1943, my father, who had been in poor health for some time, with a gastric ulcer brought on perhaps by his fondness for eating raw chillies, flew over the Hump to Calcutta for an operation. My mother and their Chinese collaborators packed up and moved to Beipei. My parents' break with the Church Missionary Society and the Anglican Diocese of West Sichuan was not a theological rupture; my father was often still referred to as "Archdeacon" and after leaving China would officiate in Anglican churches and, for a brief spell, as the Anglican chaplain in the Canary Islands. In a way, it was more as if my parents had left for a retirement job. Their assorted fellow workers from all over China never had any official link with either the missionary society or the diocese and it might have suited all concerned that they should go elsewhere. Also, it must be remembered that my father was a Cornishman and that the Cornish are strong individualists and not noted for team spirit.

I was anxious to return to England as I felt I was missing out on the experience and responsibilities of my generation. On the way, I would visit my father, who was now in hospital alone in Calcutta. So early in January 1943, I left Chengdu for India to be with him until he was well enough to go to the hills to recuperate, and then I would return to England.

Above

Outdoor sitting room in the mission house at Guanghan, 1930s or early 1940s. On the left can be seen part of the ladder leading to a sleeping loft used in hot weather

Left

The courtyard of the Donnithornes' house at Guanghan, Sichuan. The guihua tree was destroyed during the Cultural Revolution when the Red Guards stacked Bibles and other books round it and set them alight

The arches destroyed during the Cultural Revolution (1967–76) on the road between Guanghan and Chengdu. Photo taken by Vyvyan H. Donnithorne, 1936 or early 1940s

CHAPTER 5

A Wartime Journey and Life in Britain: 1943–45

The first part of my journey to Britain in January 1943, the approximately 200 miles from Chengdu to Chongqing, I did by crowded open lorry, putting my suitcase beside me and sitting on my haversack. The road and the vehicle both left much to be desired and we had to stop for a night before reaching our destination. I had to stay for a few days in Chongqing before I could get a flight over the Hump to India. This gave me an opportunity to call at the Catholic mission there and attend a talk by Archbishop Yu Bin of Nanjing who had come to Chongqing with the Guomindang government to which he was close. The Archbishop also gave me a lengthy interview of which, by some extraordinary chance, I still have the notes. He outlined the framework of the Catholic Church in China at that date, with 130 mission units – apostolic vicariates (headed by a bishop), apostolic prefectures (headed by a monsignor) and independent missions (headed by a priest) serving around four and a half million Catholics; there were over seventy bishops of whom twenty-five were Chinese and five Chinese monsignori. The Church ran numerous primary schools, more than 200 middle schools and three tertiary institutions – Fujen University in Beijing (then called Peiping), Aurora University in Shanghai and the Tianjin College of Commerce and Industry, all three of which were continuing to function under the Japanese occupation. He also spoke about the current low ebb of philosophy in China. Maritain's *Introduction to Philosophy* had been translated but not yet published. Christian classics were being translated by a combined team of Catholics, Protestants and non-Christians.

Chongqing was at that period subject to frequent bombing. This limited the times when civilian aircraft could take off from the airport which was on an island in the river. As the Hump flight was Free China's only lifeline with the outer world, every ounce of cargo space on inward flights was precious; on outward flights, the reverse held true, as apart from a little mail, there were almost no exports to take. Therefore, I was allowed to stagger on to the weighing scales before departure carrying as much hand luggage crammed with books as I could manage, a heavy rucksack on my back and many bags in my hands. We stopped briefly at Kunming and then went on the longest and most dangerous stretch of the journey, flying high over Japanese-occupied Burma. Those who made the flight frequently, such as King's Messengers, were given oxygen; the rest of us merely had to sign a document to say that we did not suffer from any heart complaint and then felt so rotten during the flight that it would have seemed quite a relief to be shot down. Having passed safely over Burma, where some of the toughest battles of the war were being fought, we stopped at Dinjan in Assam and spent the night in a government rest house. We were a strange assortment of people as we sat around the dining table that night – I can remember two exhausted Irish priests who had been escaping from a Japanese advance, and other bedraggled survivors.

The next morning brought us to Calcutta where I stayed for a few weeks in an Australian missionary household, visiting my father every day in hospital until he was well enough to go to the hills to convalesce. I also had time to explore Calcutta, its slums and its prosperous parts, a few months before the severe famine which hit Bengal later in 1943. In Calcutta, I made a number of friends, Indian, Chinese and Western. On first meeting them, the Chinese and Indians would separately say how much they had in common, having both suffered from Western imperialism. Then, when I got to know them better, they would change tune and complain bitterly about the other, Indian or Chinese, saying how incomprehensible they found them. My impression was that the gulf between Chinese and Indian outlooks on life was wider than that between either of them and the West.

In Calcutta, I met a missionary who had translated some of the works of Rabindranath Tagore, the Bengali poet and great literary figure, into English and I read some of them. I visited Santiniketan, the cultural centre and university which Tagore had founded with his Nobel Prize money and met a relative of his, I think his brother. The great man himself had recently died but his spirit lived on in the Bengali atmosphere, much softer, gentler and more intellectual than that of the "martial races" of central and northern India with which the Ingram and Skinner families had been associated. Also, I went to the small French colony of Chandanagore, near Calcutta. Except for old buildings, including the church that I visited, there were few signs of French influence but rummaging around in a second-hand bookshop, I found a battered French dictionary which I still possess.

I bought a third-class rail ticket from Calcutta to Bombay via Benares, Agra and Delhi and hired from the railway a bedding roll, returnable in Bombay. I travelled in a "ladies only" carriage and, in the evening, I persuaded my fellow travellers that if the luggage was taken down from the luggage rack to the floor, I could sleep on my bedroll on the luggage rack which would make room for them to lie down on the sitting space; like that we all had a good night. Next day, I alighted at Benares, where I spent a day watching the bathing rituals in the Ganges and passed the night, on my bedding roll, in the ladies' waiting room. Some more hours in the train brought me to Agra. About five miles from Agra, in a village called Etmadpur, lived a missionary uncle, George Ingram and his wife May. They knew I was coming but not the exact day or time as my travel was somewhat erratic and they had no telephone to alert them of my arrival. So I hired an obliging chap to carry my luggage and set out walking on dusty roads through the heat of an Indian summer to Etmadpur, arriving somewhat bedraggled. They took me to see the Taj Mahal in Agra but, unfortunately, it was encased in scaffolding for repairs. After a few days at Etmadpur, I fell ill with hepatitis (then known as jaundice) and had to spend a month at a government hospital in Agra. I shared a room with a local Anglo-Indian girl and spent the time reading a life of Nehru and watching a stately long-legged bird which seemed to own the hospital yard. The illness left me weak, so I had to cancel my proposed visit to Delhi and to the Ingram Estate, which was at the time in the process of being sold to the tenants. In my convalescent state, it was thought best to travel straight on to Bombay with a missionary friend of my uncle who was going there, though this entailed upgrading my ticket to second class.

In Bombay, I spent six weeks in a hostel for students, trying to get a berth on one of the few part-passenger part-cargo vessels bound for Britain at that stage of the war. The long delay led to my enquiring about the possibility of enlisting in the WAC (I) – the Women's Army Corps (India) – but refrained when told that to allay anxieties of Indian families, members were not deployed outside India. From a Catholic source, I had an introduction to a dockers' trade union which I visited and had an interesting conversation about their work. I fear that their members may have suffered severely in an appalling explosion that occurred in the docks a few months later, which wartime censorship prevented being widely known for years. While in Bombay I was asked to write an article for the Sunday edition of the *Times of India* on the journey over the Hump from China to Calcutta. This was my first ever publication.

Bombay, a long established port which had become India's chief manufacturing centre, attracted over the centuries a great medley of different peoples including the Parsees – Zoroastrians who had fled from Persia before Moslem advances and who, by astuteness, became one of India's richest communities – and the Portuguese, descended from the sixteenth century adventurers who had intermarried locally and in Bombay formed distinct groups, one known as East Indians and the other as Goans, having come to Bombay from the ancient settlement at Goa. The majority of Bombay residents are, of course from the various strands and castes of Hindus as well as Moslems, Sikhs and Christians of non-Portuguese background. The presence of the Portuguese has made Bombay the chief centre of Catholic Christianity in India. While there, I savoured something of the strong Indian devotion to the Sacred Heart of Jesus which can sometimes seem foreign to Anglo-Saxons but which accords deeply with Indian spirituality.

Our ship, the City of Hong Kong, left Bombay for Britain early in May 1943. It carried far fewer passengers than its cabin space allowed and I had a four-berth cabin to myself. This may have been due to low demand for berths during the war or because of limits imposed by lifeboat capacities. We expected to sail via the Cape of Good Hope, as allied ships had been doing since the summer of 1940. As this would entail a long voyage, I was asked to give lessons to three children on board, one of whom was the eleven-year-old Parvine Helen Razavi.[1] Parvine's mother, a British woman married to a Persian who held a high position in the British Petroleum Co., was travelling to England with her daughter and a younger son, Lawrence, whom she taught herself. It was the beginning of a long and valued friendship, still continuing with Parvine and her children and grandchildren. Our first stop was the southern Indian port of Cochin, where we took on a cargo of tea and pepper, with some carpets to fill up spare space, and had several days to see that ancient town with its old Catholic church and separate synagogues of white Jews and black Jews (I think both have now left for Israel). Our next stop was at Colombo after which we sailed south west towards the Cape. One morning we woke up to find the sun in the wrong direction. We were given no explanation but soon found ourselves back in Colombo where we learned that we were to sail via Suez. The allies had just taken the Pantellarian Islands between Sicily and North Africa and this meant that by hugging the coast of North Africa, it was reasonably safe for allied merchant ships to transit the Mediterranean. On our way, we viewed, sailing in the opposite direction, the huge naval armada making for the allied invasion of Sicily. Our little convoy sustained one loss when we saw a small vessel torpedoed. We were told that it was able to hobble to the nearby coast of North Africa and that there had been no casualties.

---

1 I am grateful to Mrs Parvine Helen Merrillees (née Razavi) for giving me access to her own account of this voyage. See Parvine Helen (Razavi) Merrillees, *Memoirs 1932–1963 & Happy Ever After,* privately published, 2015.

A strict blackout was of course observed after dark, throughout the voyage. Our cabin portholes were permanently closed and blacked-out so the heat in the cabins was intense. Fortunately, we were allowed to sleep on deck under the stars and every day the sailors carried our mattresses up and down from our cabins. Before going on deck at night I used to read Compline from my Latin-French missal prayer book; the Psalmist's phrase *"a negotio perambulante in tenebris"* ("from trouble afoot in the dark") has always since then for me referred to torpedoes. Frequent lifeboat drills were held. On board there were, as passengers, a number of merchant navy officers going to Britain for redeployment and they were naturally made captains of lifeboats, being given large, heavy-duty torches for the purpose. As the voyage dragged on, food became progressively worse as supplies diminished. Shipboard morale lowered. The merchant navy officer-passengers complained that our captain, who had come out of retirement because of the war, was not up to his job. To mark their dissatisfaction, they went on strike from their lifeboat duties and handed back their torches. They assured us, that in case of emergency, they would act, but we disliked the fact that they would then be without their torches. We had several warnings of attacks by submarines or from the air, but never came to any harm.

We spent two weeks in Spanish waters off Algeciras, near Gibraltar (Gibraltar waters being reserved for allied naval vessels), waiting to join a convoy that was coming from the Cape. Our stay coincided with the tragic air crash which, on 4 July 1943, killed General Władysław Sikorski, President of Poland and Commander in Chief of the Polish forces. On one of our two permitted shore visits, I went to his lying-in-state in the cathedral at Gibraltar. For the rest of the fortnight, we stayed aboard, reassured by the constant swishing around us of British naval launches which the cooperative Spanish authorities allowed to prevent hostile action against allied merchant ships. Finally, we left Algeciras to join a larger convoy which had come around the Cape and then we sailed far out into the Atlantic to avoid the enemy-occupied continent, encircling Ireland before disembarking at Liverpool on 20 July 1943.

On disembarking, we were interrogated by Immigration to find out where we had come from, to determine if any of us might have information of interest to the British war effort. This resulted in my being summoned shortly afterwards to the War Office in London where the first officer I saw caused me some dismay by his obvious ignorance of the situation in Free China. He was rather shocked to hear my accounts of low morale and corruption there. However, I was then sent on to see Major Jack Storrs who headed MI 2b, the sub-unit of Military Intelligence which included China in its remit. Then I realised that the first man was in MI 5 and his job was to vet me to see if I was suitable to be sent on further. Jack Storrs, who had been in Chinese Maritime Customs, was obviously au fait with the situation in Free China and asked me sensible questions such as the state of roads on which I had recently travelled.

I was of conscription age and so had to register for war work. The ATS (later the Women's Royal Army Corps) was not at that time recruiting anyone over eighteen, so it was not for me. Before long, however, I received a notice directing me to be a Junior Civil Assistant in MI 2b in the War Office (supposed to be the equivalent of a second lieutenant, but paid less),[2] in the sub-unit headed by Major Storrs.

Military Intelligence in the War Office was divided into various departments, each headed by a Lieutenant Colonel, a regular (professional) officer on relatively short-term assignment to the War Office. Lieutenant Colonel Wren, who at that time headed MI 2, which covered intelligence relating to the war against Japan, was a few months later posted to Burma where he was killed. He was succeeded at MI 2 by Lieutenant Colonel Brian Montgomery, younger brother of Field Marshall Montgomery. MI 2a dealt with the Japanese armed forces and MI 2b, where I worked, with everything else – reports from various sources, matters concerning allies such as China, and maps of East Asia.

My initial salary, including wartime supplement, was £177 a year; on attaining the age of twenty-one it rose to £250. Major Storrs tried to get

2 This ranking was to permit us to see top secret documents which were supposed to be restricted to those of commissioned rank or equivalent.

me a further rise because of my knowledge of Chinese. This was refused as it was not a requirement of the post and could not be made a requirement because, if I left, it would have been almost impossible to recruit anyone else with this qualification. As I did not have a home but had to rent a room, I had to depend in part on my mother's generosity.

When I arrived, MI 2b occupied a room in the basement of the War Office in Whitehall; ventilation was poor so we were given two-hour lunch breaks. Some months later, as the Pacific War was accorded more importance, we moved up to the ground floor, to a room fronting Whitehall but the windows were brick-blocked to avoid the possibility of top-secret papers floating around Whitehall if windows were broken by bomb blasts; air quality continued to be bad.

One of my minor duties in the War Office, on which I was told not to spend too much time, was to draw up an Order of Battle for the various Chinese armies and armed units criss-crossing China, about which the Western allies were ill-informed. The Guomindang government at Chongqing, with which we were of course allied, had sent us some rather doubtful information about their forces but we had nothing about those of our other allies, the Communists in north west China (with whom the Guomindang was, in fact, at war, despite the so-called united front), nor about our enemies, the troops of the Japanese puppet government of Wang Jingwei, nor about the straggling units of changeable loyalties which meandered around between different sides. So I collected such scraps of information as were available and was given cards, on each of which I wrote particulars of one of the known units. The top right corner of each card I coloured according to the unit's allegiance (sometimes having to re-colour the cards of the stragglers). Then I found an old cardboard shoe box at home which I brought to the office. The cards fitted well into it – and the War Office had an Order of Battle of the various armies of China.

The military in the War Office worked a six-day week and took it in turns to do night duty. Civilians worked an eleven-and-a-half-day fortnight. The night duty officer had to write an "I (intelligence) report" on intelligence relating to enemies on the Pacific War front or to happenings behind enemy lines. This report had to cover not more than one page to be readable at top levels. One night the MI 2b night duty officer's telephone rang and a gruff but instantly recognisable voice asked, "On what grounds do you refer to Myitkyina as a city?" (Years later, I discovered that in fact the Burmese town, Myitkyina, had a Vicar Apostolic – who is usually a bishop – and therefore, presumably, its church could be considered a cathedral, which raises the town to the status of a city according to the traditional English definition – but by that time Winston no longer needed earthly information.) Of course, the knowledge that our reports were read carefully at the very top was a boost for morale.

Once, some bombs destroyed most of the vehicles in Horse Guards Parade, where the Admiralty parked its cars and the next day, to our delight, sundry admirals came, caps in hand, to the War House begging for cars! On a much grimmer occasion, on a Sunday morning when we were working at our desks, a flying bomb landed nearby. After a decent interval, Storrs rang the relevant operations department to ask where it had fallen. "The Guards Chapel" was the reply. We all looked at our watches – it was 11:30 a.m. "That will have promoted a lot of guardsmen," Storrs drily remarked.

One day the door of our room opened and a large man entered, loudly announcing, "I am Cantlie of China." He was Lieut. Col. Kenneth Cantlie, son of Sir James Cantlie, a notable medical man in nineteenth century Hong Kong who co-founded the Hong Kong College of Medicine, which eventually grew into the University of Hong Kong. On retirement to London, Sir James was instrumental in securing the release of Sun Yat Sen from the Chinese Legation where he had been imprisoned. His son seems to have been active in China, but I have never known in what role.

The officers in MI 2b all had some East Asian experience or knowledge. Ivor Trevor had been manager of the Hong Kong-Canton Railway, Capt. Mitchell had worked in Malaya; Cecily Cox had lived in Japan for some years and knew the language. An American liaison officer, Capt. Lynn, who joined us for a time, spoke Chinese and was the only one in our sub-unit, apart from myself, who could read the language. Major Storrs remembered some spoken Chinese but I do not think he could read it. My small book atlas of the provinces of China, which had travelled with me over the Hump, contained the only Chinese language maps of that country I ever saw in the War Office. Lynn and I spent a long time pouring over it trying to discover a place in Manchuria whose name some report had garbled. When we thought we had found it, and the news was cabled across to the States, apparently some kudos accrued to the old War Office. This reminds me, one thing I heard there was that until the early twentieth century, the War Office had in its files a contingency plan for war with the United States. Perhaps it was the half-American young Churchill who had it torn up when he was First Lord of the Admiralty.

We saw Lord Halifax's dispatches from Washington (where he was British Ambassador) in so far as they related to China matters and were amused at the infatuation of that dignified and devout old man with Madame Chiang Kai-shek, for whom he considered no praise too high. We also received the reports of the British Army Aid Group which operated in Japanese occupied Guangdong in areas near Hong Kong. Captain H. Brown, the officer covering activities in Japanese-occupied Burma, had a map of that country hanging by his desk on which he stuck pins indicating the latest known positions of General Orde Wingate's Chindits. A curtain hung to cover the map, which was of course Top Secret, to shield it from the sight of those who might enter the room, such as document-carrying clerks, who were not cleared to see material of that classification.

My parents returned to England in November 1943 just in time for my twenty-first birthday. They stayed with my aunt Tina Ingram in the flat in Wimbledon village which she occupied after the Priory had been sold. Tina was a keen amateur photographer and as a war job had joined the staff of the Daily Mirror, as a toucher up of press photos – one picture had originally depicted the Lord Mayor of London with his tongue out – Tina rectified this and felt that she had done something to keep up morale! During the fly bomb time, all civilians not engaged in war work were told by the government to leave the London area if they could and my parents went to Weston-super-Mare for some months.

While in China, I had written to give up my place at St Hilda's, Oxford and had contacted Somerville College to say I would like to try for a place or scholarship there in history. On returning to England, I did so again, asking for suggestions for preparing for the entrance exam in London in my spare time from the War Office, and was put in touch with a Somerville alumna, Lady (Mary) Ogilvie, much later Principal of St Anne's College Oxford. She very kindly agreed to coach me in the evenings after work and did everything possible to help me. I joined the London Library; my extended lunch hours, given because of poor ventilation, meant that after a quick slice of bread and margarine bought nearby, I could get to the London Library in St James's Square and do some reading. The Somerville entrance exam was broad-based. I took it in history, specifically mediaeval history. There was, if I remember rightly, one paper on this, one general history paper, an essay and a general knowledge paper; also, a translation paper provided the opportunity of attempting translations from Latin, Greek, French and German, of which Latin and one modern language were obligatory.

I took the exam early in 1944 and was summoned to Oxford for an interview. I was offered a scholarship to read either history or Greats (classics) or Modem Greats (PPE – Philosophy, Politics and Economics). I chose History, but after one term changed to PPE. I may have impressed the Somerville scholarship committee by demanding that my final interview be as early as possible in the morning as I was required to be back at the War Office by the afternoon. I celebrated the scholarship by buying a small second-hand three-volume edition of Dante's *Divine Comedy* in Italian, realising that I might not have time to read it, or to learn Italian, before I retired, decades later. Now I have been retired for more than thirty years and still have not achieved either of these goals.

On my return to England, I had also contacted Penelope Piercy's friend, Austin Farrer of Oxford and he suggested that I should ask Father Daniel Woolgar OP, formerly at Blackfriars Oxford but then at St Dominic's Church, Haverstock Hill, North London, for Catholic instruction. So, one evening a week for six months, I had the benefit of Father Daniel Woolgar's quiet and thorough teaching. He received me into the Church on 7 March 1944 (at that time the feast of St Thomas Aquinas) at Haverstock Hill. My sponsors were Dorothy Razavi, whom I had met on the voyage from Bombay and (in absentia) Germaine Braye-Yuen (Uen), my friend in Chengdu. I knew hardly any Catholics in England. A few weeks later, I was confirmed in Westminster Cathedral by one of the Westminster auxiliary bishops, Archbishop Myers. My sponsor was a half-Japanese friend, Mrs Betty Russell, whom I had recently met. Before long, she and her daughter returned to Japan where I once tried to meet her, at her home in Yokohama, but she was ill so I saw only her daughter. Some years later, Father Woolgar went to the Dominican missions in the West Indies where I once met him when I visited Jamaica in 1983. In his later life, he devoted much time to church music and would suddenly break off a conversation and hum a little tune. I remember him with gratitude.

On D-Day, 6 June 1944, the War Office was a mixture of exhilaration and apprehension. We had seen cryptic references to "Operation Overlord" but knew no more than the general public about when it would eventuate. We did little work on that day but rang up Operations, as often as we dared, to find how things were going in Normandy. We relieved our tension by seeing who could write the worst poem on rhododendrons. For a few hours, the Pacific War was forgotten. Some weeks later I attended the Thanksgiving Mass for the liberation of Paris. De Gaulle had already returned to France but much of the French Government was still in London, so this was a major occasion, concluding with the odd experience of hearing the Marseillaise sung in Westminster Cathedral.

That summer, south-eastern England suffered an intensive bombardment by flying bombs – explosive missiles sent off from land-based launchers on the continental coast nearest to us. After flying their maximum range of several hundred miles their hum would become fainter, their engines would turn off and they came hurtling down. The RAF managed to shoot down many of the bombs as they crossed the channel and the countryside of Kent and Surrey. It was agreed that once the missiles reached the London area, they should not be shot down but left to fall where they would. To shoot them down over the poorer east London and thus protect the wealthier western part of the capital, would have been invidious. So, after the air raid warning, we would hear the flying bombs grow ever louder until the dread moment when the engine suddenly turned off and we would duck under furniture. I was once blown down, but in the gentlest possible manner, by the blast from one, which fell on Exhibition Road near my digs. I had been running down to the basement when the window broke opposite the flight of stairs where I was and suddenly I found myself sitting down. I picked myself up and then heard another bomb coming so I continued my descent to the basement. I was a fire warden in my block and took turns to be on duty for a couple of hours on many nights and was given training in crawling through a smoke-filled corridor; this I found had a good effect on my hay fever. I was fortunate to have a basement where I could spend the nights on the floor in the room of a kind friend, Ellen Avery, also in the War Office. Many Londoners at that time took refuge in underground train stations, passing the nights lying on the platforms, covered with the grey blankets which I think London Transport doled out. In fine weather, I would often, as my only opportunity of exercise or fresh air, cycle to the War Office from South Kensington where I lodged and it frequently seemed that a fly bomb was chasing me as I dashed round Hyde Park Corner.

On days off, after March 1944 when I was no longer working for the Somerville exam, I would sometimes go by bus to Epping Forest which was just outside the range of the flying bombs and settle down in some sunny spot to make crude paintings of the woodland. On other days at lunch time, I might go to the National Gallery and look at the "picture of the month". Most of its treasures had been stored for the duration in some Welsh fastness, but every month the Gallery risked bringing one to London to refresh us and raise the morale of the home front. Sometimes, I might spend lunch time in St James's Park delighting in the ducks, thinking of a line in a poem I had once learned: "From the troubles of the world, I turn to ducks." Often, in a primitive eatery near Charing Cross underground station, I lunched off a slice of bread and margarine, sometimes sprinkled with sugar. Civilian staff were not eligible to use the military canteen where my uniformed colleagues ate, emerging with a verdict on the "plat du jour" which made my mouth water. The War Office civilian canteen was not as good and the queue impossibly long.

On rare spells away from the War Office, I sometimes went for refreshing visits to Pen Piercy's parents at their beautiful old house and garden in the Cotswolds at Burford. My first visit was soon after my return from China when I spoke to them of the time that Pen, their eldest daughter, and I were together at Yenching-in-Chengdu. Pen was still abroad, now in uniformed war service. Her father, William Piercy was a leading figure in the City of London, in the Baltic timber trade and in the early unit trust (mutual funds) movement. At a low point in the war, when Britain, standing alone, was running out of oil, Piercy was summoned before a cabinet committee and asked what he knew about oil. "Nothing at all," he replied. "I have never had anything to do with the oil industry. On that, you must ask someone else." "Splendid," was the answer. "You are just the man we want." He was forthwith dispatched to Washington to head a British oil mission, which had to be led by someone completely neutral between rival oil companies, to squeeze the last drop from every possible source. Mary Piercy, Pen's mother, showed me great kindness and over the next few years was a major support, having far more understanding of the academic and religious worlds in which I lived than any of the older generation in my own family. In 1945, the new Labour government found itself handicapped by its shortage of supporters in the House of Lords, so to remedy this, it created ten new peers. Among these was William Piercy, one of the few Labour supporters in the City; another new peer was the Master of Balliol College Oxford, Sandie Lindsay, whose son Michael had been on the staff of Yenching in 1941 when the Pacific War broke out and who, with his Chinese wife, managed to leave Beijing and reach the Chinese Communist hold out in Yenan, Shaanxi province. The Piercy family was disappointed that their newly ennobled father did not attend to his parliamentary duties assiduously enough to qualify for the parliamentary petrol ration.

My solicitor uncle, Robert Ingram, who in the First World War had been a pilot in the Royal Flying Corps, was recalled to the RAF as a Squadron Leader at Fighter Command. His family rented a house in a nearby north London suburb and I occasionally spent a few days there with them. Churchill many times visited Fighter Command which of course was the nub for the defence of the country. Robert's admiration for the great man was strengthened by their common loyalty to Harrow School. Some years later, I accompanied Robert to Harrow's annual commemorative evening of "Harrow Songs" which Churchill, as usual, attended. One of the songs, *Forty Years On*, had now added some lines: "and Churchill's name shall win acclaim from each new generation". Years later, Churchill's lying in state in Westminster Hall was a profoundly moving occasion. I joined the all-night queue, stretching in front of Lambeth Palace and winding across the Thames as we said farewell to part of Britain's history.

During my early time at the War Office, I lodged in the flat of a French lady in Roland Gardens, off the Fulham Road, in the parish of the Servite Fathers. Later, I moved to a private hostel in Queensberry Place not far from Brompton Oratory. During the War, a bunch of governments-in-exile clustered around Knightsbridge and the Oratory was their parish church, with very international congregations. I came to connect different altars in the Oratory with particular flying bombs which had fallen while I was hearing Mass at that altar. For years, I associated one altar with a bomb which had demolished a nearby MacFisheries.

One occasion late in 1944, which has been etched in my memory, was a crowded and emotion charged meeting held in Westminster Cathedral Hall during the siege of Warsaw. As the Nazis clung on to Poland and the Red Army approached from the east, the Polish underground forces were determined to seize the moment and secure the liberty of their country from both tyrannies. The Polish Uprising, also known as the Siege of Warsaw, continued for weeks. The Soviet armies ceased their advance. They were very content to see the cream of the Polish underground resistance being demolished by the Germans as they knew that the same stalwart fighters would also resist them once they had taken Warsaw. The RAF (which included Polish airmen) and the Americans dropped military and humanitarian supplies to the Polish resistance in Warsaw but they could only take light loads because of the long two-way flights. If they had been allowed to land behind the Soviet lines and refuel there, the help given to the Poles in their desperate situation would have been much greater. The Westminster meeting, mixed Polish and British, demanded that the allies put heavier pressure on the Russians to co-operate. After the meeting, I wrote to my local MP on the matter and got back a sniffy letter saying that civilians should not try to interfere in the strategy of the war.

The war had brought sad losses to my immediate circle of family and friends. While I was in China, David, the youngest of the Thompson boys, who was a fighter pilot in the RAF, died in a flying accident. My cousin, Anthony Crofts, son of my Aunt Maud, was killed by a flying bomb which came down in Surrey when his regiment were having a sports day while waiting for the Normandy invasion. This changed my attitude to these bombs which at that time were a part of daily life. I had a rather casual, perhaps fatalistic, attitude to them at first, taking reasonable precautions but not worrying much. Then, when I saw what consternation Anthony's death had caused in the family, the bombs began causing me more alarm. A few months later another cousin, Roger Rawlence, was killed when a shell landed on his tank in France. He was poised to go into the family firm of Rawlence and Squarey, estate agents for country properties in west England, to replace his father who was wanting to retire. Roger had taken a degree at Cambridge relevant to this career. Despite an effort to get some other member of the family to fill the gap, it was in effect Roger's death which eventually led to the demise of that long-established firm.

My double first cousin, Tom Ingram, a professional soldier, was dismayed when he broke his ankle during his unit's sporting activities and was disabled for D-Day, but the family was heartily relieved. Tom was an unselfish chap and would always have risked himself to help a comrade; both his father and his wife's father had been killed in the First World War and his wife was pregnant with their first child. Later that year, Tom, still hobbling, his sister-in-law, Georgette Lubbock (née Ashmead-Bartlett) and myself, had dinner together at a Chinese restaurant in Soho on the day of his daughter Philippa's birth. Through Tom and his wife Tesa, I got to know Tesa's aunt, the historian Gladys Scott Thomson. Gladys was a Somervillian who, after some university appointments, worked on the Duke of Bedford's archives and authored several books. Gladys soon came to regard me as a protégée and gave me very useful help and advice from that time, throughout my years at Oxford and while I worked at University College London.

My cousin Ilsley Ingram, after taking a medical degree at Cambridge, entered St Thomas's Medical School, London. His studies were interrupted by a recurrence of tuberculous, but eventually, with tremendous efforts, he completed his course and qualified. Another medical cousin, Patrick Rawlence, joined the Friends' Ambulance Unit and went out with this to China. I never met him there but it formed a link between us in the future, although I seldom saw him again. The Thompsons' eldest son John also qualified as a doctor. He married another doctor and had a rural practice. Their second son, Tom, with a degree in English from Cambridge, after a spell with British Petroleum in the Gulf, became a teacher and with a growing family, emigrated to New Zealand. Janet Thompson also became a doctor, married another doctor and with him went out to Morocco where they worked for many years and brought up a large family.

As far as I could tell, the attitude of everyone I came across in England after my return in 1943 was one of determination; I never consciously encountered any defeatism. Hostility, of course and some hatred, was evident but not, I think, to the degree that is reported in the First World War. I was sometimes surprised that I found it so easy to fulfil the injunction to love our enemies. The very effort we were making to defeat them seemed to deflect emotions of hatred. It was easy to realise that among the enemy airmen flying overhead in bombers, there were some with whom I had much more in common than I did with many of my fellow countrymen. I hoped they would be shot down but also that the aircrews would survive and that in any case eventually "we would all come merrily together in heaven". With allies, it was different. They had to be lived with and tolerated. I was amused how thankful I was that not even the gospels bid us love our allies! One remembers Churchill's comment that his heaviest cross was the Cross of Lorraine.[3] Of course, I was a hundred per cent in favour of the American alliance – it would have been idiotic not to have been – but it was really intolerable when a young woman could not walk through central London without being accosted by GIs.

By the end of 1944, poor ventilation at the War Office, plus having to sleep in the basement of my lodgings because of air raids, and probably also the earlier months when I was working for the Somerville exam every evening and week end, had worn me down so that I was like a limp rag. My own doctor said I must leave the War Office immediately and get into the open air. However, as I was of conscription age, I had also to see a Ministry of Labour doctor to confirm this advice. She was very helpful and said that people reacted differently to poor ventilation and lack of air and that I obviously could not take it. So she agreed that I must leave the War Office for a country job and advised that in future I should avoid working or living in a basement or where there was poor ventilation. So now, more than seventy years later, I live on the eighteenth floor – but breathing the polluted air of Hong Kong and suffering from asthma.

Despite leaving abruptly, I parted on good terms with my colleagues at the War Office and with an encouraging "Certificate of Service", presumably drawn up by Major Jack Storrs, the head of MI 2b and a veteran of the Chinese Customs Service, saying, inter alia, "Displayed an intelligent interest in her work and is of a type on whom reliance can always be placed. (Has a good knowledge of China and experience of the Far East.)" Storrs later became manager of a factory in Queensland and, through a chain of circumstances, we once had a telephone conversation when I was working in Canberra, although we never met in Australia.

My run-down health would have precluded me from being accepted by the Women's Land Army in which my cousin, Jenefer Rawlence was serving. Through the Women's Farm and Garden Association I was put in

---

3 The symbol of General Charles de Gaulle, the leader of the Free French, who did not react easily to France's lowered status during the War.

touch with an elderly lady, Mrs Bray, who wanted help on her small-holding at Knockholt, near Orpington, Kent, where she grew vegetables and kept chickens, ducks, geese and bees. So for six months I had an agreeable and healthy life, growing vegetables and looking after poultry – for which she gave me board and lodging (including the extra cheese ration to which I was entitled as an agricultural labourer) and five shillings a week, which she soon raised to seven and sixpence. Sometimes I was dispatched on my bicycle to take some produce to the market at Sevenoaks. The smallholding had a number of soft fruit bushes – raspberries, currants and gooseberries – and soon I learned how gooseberries got their name; geese, if given half a chance, will strip a gooseberry bush of all its fruit in a jiffy. Mrs Bray was one of the wonderful women who bind rural communities together with their activities. Among other things, she was Chairman of the local Pratts Bottom Women's Institute, so I had an opportunity to participate in that admirable English countryside organisation. Also, I took the opportunity to try to improve my defective knowledge of English literature. I had studied some Chaucer for School Certificate years before and wanted to continue from there to modern times. I read *Piers Plowman* and then went on to the Elizabethan era, postponing Shakespeare as needing a large chunk of time which I would find later to read the plays I had not covered at school (never accomplished!), and beginning Spencer's *Fairy Queen*. Alas, I have never got further. From the time I went up to Oxford, until late in my retirement, I never had time for reading just for pleasure.

The nearest Catholic church to the smallholding was Holy Innocents at Orpington to which I used to cycle. The parish priest, Canon Slocombe, once called a parish meeting on the question of building a parish school after the war. In the absence of a church hall, we gathered at the back of the church and he told us of discussions that had been going on about it but said that it was the parishioners who should decide on the school because they would have to pay for the building. The recently passed Butler Education Act, the framework for Britain's post-war educational re-structuring, laid down that the running costs of all voluntary aided (i.e. church) schools would be met by the state, as would half the cost of building improvements in existing voluntary aided schools but for new schools, the sponsoring body would have to bear the full cost of building. So the good Canon said he would leave it for us to decide whether the parish should build a school or not. He then went off to the sanctuary to pray while we talked it over. All of us favoured building a school and called him back. He said, "Thank God for that," and the matter was decided. As a result, we felt an added obligation to play our part; for some years, I continued to send my mites back to Orpington for the school.

I was in Kent at the time of the election that took place that summer after VE Day (victory in Europe) but before VJ Day (victory over Japan). My vote was still in London so I had to go up there to cast it. Soon after this, I was able to quit my job on the smallholding in order to have time to do some reading before the Oxford term began and also to be with my parents who were planning to return to China in the near future. They had gone back to my aunt Tina Ingram's flat in Wimbledon village and I joined them there. Thus, I was able to be in the huge crowd which gathered in front of Buckingham Palace to celebrate on the evening of VJ Day. That night I returned to Wimbledon tired but thankful and spent the next few weeks preparing for Oxford.

PART TWO

University Life
in Britain: 1945–68

CHAPTER 6

Studying in Post-War Oxford: 1945–48

I did not enjoy Oxford. It was definitely the least happy time of my life. My overwhelming memory of those years is one of physical exhaustion. At the end of the war, my health was run down despite its improvement during the months on the smallholding in Kent. Without those months, I doubt if I would have survived Oxford.

The war years, especially those in China, I have always felt, were the most valuable part of my higher education. However, I still had no qualification and by now I realised that one was necessary. I was nearly twenty-three when I went up to Oxford and was at a stage of my life when I wanted to do something more practical and active than studying. I found academic work tedious and burdensome and wrote essays slowly. Throughout my course, I had to write two essays a week. I was anxious to be thorough in my reading for each topic, not just skimming for what the essay subject narrowly required. I was therefore continuously in a crisis to get an essay done in time for it to be handed in before the tutorial, and this usually meant working late into the night. Apart from a good amount of drinking coffee, socialising with friends, and some Catholic chaplaincy events, I had little in the way of relaxing leisure activities. There were, at least in the first year, attendances at some lectures that I went to just out of interest, in subjects outside the ambit of my official courses;

meetings of the societies I joined and which I was determined to attend – the Conservatives, the Chung Hwa (China) and the Indian Majlis; and, occasionally, the Celtic Club, because of my Cornish ancestry – but these scarcely provided relaxation. I think that I went twice on the river during my three years at Oxford.

When I was awarded a scholarship to Somerville, in the spring of 1944, I had taken the papers in history but I was told that I could also hold the scholarship to read Modern Greats (Philosophy, Politics and Economics – also known as PPE) or for Greats (Latin, Greek, Ancient History and Philosophy). I would have enjoyed Classics the most, specialising in the history of the later Roman Empire (a fluid period that has always interested me) in the fourth year. However, I was afraid that Classics might immure me in an academic career while I wanted to take part in the contemporary world. So I decided on History and, for my first term, Michaelmas 1945, I read that subject. However, I did not get on well with May MacKisack, the history don, who was a dyed-in-the-wool academic and could not understand that anything outside the academic world was significant. She saw no reason why allowances or exceptions should be made for those of us who had spent the war years on non-academic pursuits. To her, entry to Oxford, and especially to Somerville, was a privilege beyond compare.

To me, however, the need to go to university was a burden imposed by society. It was as if the great world said that unless you undergo this particular form of processing, we will do our best not to give you the opportunity to exercise whatever intellectual talents you may have. In the past, women had always been the bearers and carriers-down of culture within families and had been helped in this role by not having to undergo the processing imparted to their brothers by universities, professional training and apprenticeships.[1]

Now, though, in the name of liberation, this advantage was removed. Without a university qualification, one would always be considered inferior. For specific technical tasks, of course, prior training or apprenticeship is necessary. People should not be let loose on the public to perform surgery

1 Would Jane Austen really have benefitted from a PhD?

or to build bridges without proof of knowledge and ability to do these tasks. For occupations where a general capacity for getting on with people and getting things done are the most important qualifications, such as the civil service, administrative jobs or the non-specialised forms of teaching or nursing and for non-technical business affairs, the usefulness of a university degree rests not on the formal education (an internship type of training would be more useful) but on the simplification of recruitment procedures it yields. It is also easier for a miscellaneous set of people to work together if they have been through the same type of processing. The most important part of tertiary education is that provided by the university as a club. These opinions, and my resentment at the practical necessity of going to a university may have been due in part to the fact that my least favourite aunts were those who were university graduates.

At the end of my first term, after a fight and thanks to sympathy from the Principal, Janet Vaughan, who was also trying to adapt to university life after a war spent in other pursuits, I transferred to Modern Greats. This was, perhaps, an improvement on three years to be spent largely within the confines of British history. However, PPE was a mishmash of ill-assorted chunks of information, often at cross purposes. Thus, in one and the same week one might be writing an essay on the causes of the trade cycle and another on Hume's denial of the principle of causality. I always wondered what would happen if, in confusion or perhaps on purpose, the trade cycle essay was composed around the doubtfulness of the principle of causality. (The reaction to one's essay would inevitably be, "Your essay is irrelevant: answer the question asked.") I considered theory of knowledge an illogical component of any course of study because unless we are capable of objective knowledge, study is useless. In PPE, there seemed to be a prohibition on looking at life as a whole and making coherent sense of it. A secular university has to opt out of this and leave it to the chaplaincies. Perhaps, PPE is based on the dogma that there is no coherent sense in life.

Economics at Oxford at that time was looked at primarily from the viewpoint of the state, of politicians and civil servants. I left without any idea of how a firm actually works or even how to run the financial affairs of a middle-class family. Margaret Roberts, with her grocer's shop background, must have known much more about this than did most PPE students. It is fortunate that she read chemistry.

Part of the problem presented by economics as an academic discipline is a natural tension between this abstract view of the world of livelihood and that of the business people who make the real-life decisions in it. Perhaps the better the business instinct, the worse the economic theorising; a discontent with academic life and a desire for more active pursuits may help towards an understanding of more practical people.

Connected with this was another constant source of friction: the manner in which anything outside the syllabus, narrowly defined, was considered irrelevant. Sometimes I tried to brighten up a dull essay on some topic in the theory of knowledge by a reference to Chinese philosophy – this was definitely criticised as irrelevant. I realised that any Thomist references would be even more damning. What was "relevant" was what was currently under discussion at Oxford or had been in the last few years. I realised this in my first term of philosophy, when I was tutored by Philippa Foot. Later, with the help of my old friend of China days, Pen Piercy, I was fortunate enough to be able to transfer to Donald Mackinnon, a profound and stimulating thinker. With him I had four tutorials on Kant's Metaphysics as well as a term on moral philosophy. Later, when Mackinnon left Oxford, I was able to get another friend of Pen's, Austin Farrer, as philosophy tutor.

In history, the same problem of "relevance" also cropped up. Mary Macdonald (later Mrs Proudfoot) once gave me an essay on the reasons for the critical opinions of the English towards Ireland. She knew I was a Catholic and, no doubt, she thought she would thereby force me to delve into the reasons for British scorn of Irish religion. She did not know that I was of partly Irish Protestant Ascendancy background and had been brought up an old-fashioned evangelical. I was able, therefore, to write the essay from the back of my head and she commended it. However, I found it so boring that I tried to brighten it up by comparing the British failure to understand the Irish with their equally glaring failure to get on with Bengalis. In both cases, I surmised, the British were unable to sympathise with a more imaginative people. This final part of my essay was criticised as irrelevant.

Modern Greats was, apparently, confined entirely to Western civilization. If anything else was desired, it was necessary to go into a ghetto such as (then was) a degree in Chinese. Chinese would have been much the easiest degree for me to have done as I already had a moderately good knowledge of the language, but this was something I did not want to do as I wished to be in the thick of things that were currently happening, wherever they were, and not exclusively things happening at Oxford. I felt that I was being blinkered and urged to forget my previous life.

For the two special subjects which the PPE degree required, I chose 19th century British economic history and economic theory. For the first, I had an excellent tutor, Lucy Sutherland, at that time Principal of Lady Margaret Hall, and I enjoyed the subject. I was advised to take economic theory, against my better judgment, because it was said to be advantageous in applying for jobs in the economics field. I have never seen the point of it. Economic theory, at least on a large scale, operates when all other conditions are equal, and in social sciences they never are. It is the differences in human conditions and reactions that interest me. Graphs and equations in economic theory seem to be attempts to explain things which are more easily explained verbally. There are some very specific circumstances where economic theory can be useful, such as in certain types of markets.[2]

When I was at Oxford, the sub-speciality of game theory was about to explode on to the world but while this may be useful in understanding or manipulating commodity markets or the stock exchange, it has not been relevant to matters with which I have had to deal. Never while working on the Chinese economy, did I derive benefit from the time I spent studying economic theory. (I bracket it with learning the Chinese transliterations of the Latin names of various hominids and the making of crêpe de chine underwear by hand, as the most wasteful parts of my formal education.)

---

2 Also in economic forecasting using digital material and perhaps more so in future in dealing with robotic policy. Here economics will merge with information technology, but old-style economics – human economics – will still be important.

I shared, with Phyllis Wightman, tutorials on economic theory with John Hicks, a future Nobel laureate. Hicks was an agreeable person and later, when they visited Australia, I got to know him and his wife Ursula (whose work in applied economics I found more palatable) much better. At the time he taught me, Hicks' interest was centred on the relationship between long and short-term rates of interest, and he had charts of the two rates above his mantelpiece which he would spend long hours contemplating. Part of the trouble about economics may be due to the oxymoronic words "social sciences" into which the subject is slotted: science – in order to make it respectable in modern life – but with an inbuilt tendency to fit it all, or as much as possible, into categories susceptible to mathematical treatment; "social", however, involves human behaviour, which cannot, and should not, be reduced to mathematics.[3]

Another great trial in my Oxford course was the fact that two subjects had to be studied simultaneously every term, with an essay and a tutorial every week in each. I found the continual switching from one subject to the other extremely stressful and inhibiting to deep study of either. It was like being on a constantly switching conveyor belt – to get through all essential topics it was necessary to go on to the next one before having thoroughly thought through the first. I was always exhausted by lack of sleep aggravated by the poor food – e.g. whale meat – which the College provided, through no fault of its own but because of the shortages of the immediate post-war period, when rations were often below wartime levels. Also, because of post-war energy shortages, the College was always cold in winter, especially in our rooms where we could have our electric heaters on for only two hours a day; there were some bitter winters at the time.

---

3 "In my view, every economic fact whether or not it is of such a nature as to be expressed in numbers, stands in relation as cause and effect to many other facts, and since it NEVER happens that all of them can be expressed in numbers, the application of exact mathematical methods to those which can is nearly always waste of time, while in the large majority of cases it is positively misleading; and the world would have been further on its way forward if the work had never been done at all." Alfred Marshall, letter to A. L. Bowley, 3 March 1901, *Memorials,* p. 422. (This quotation was once circulated – by Marian Bowley – at a staff meeting of the Department of Political Economy at University College, London.)

One thing I definitely appreciated about the Oxford educational system is that it purposely discourages students from going to lectures – the important work consists of tutorials (although I thought there were too many of these) with one or two undergraduates alone with the tutor, and the essays and reading done for each tutorial. As lectures were scattered around the city and the streets congested, it was impossible to attend many. It was usual to savour a few lectures from particularly notable figures in one's field of study, especially if the lecturer was about to publish what might be an important book and an examination was imminent. Also, in the year before finals, it was worthwhile to attend some lectures given by examiners to see what was on their minds. Otherwise, lectures were often attended because they were on some subject in which one was interested but did not have time to study closely. Thus, in our first year, Mary Low and I regularly attended a course on Jewish history given by Cecil Roth. The weekly lecture, given late in the afternoon, was sometimes followed by a social. I think the lecturer rather assumed that the attendees would be Jewish, and regarded these gatherings partly as a pastoral occasion to bring them together. One week, the lecture was given by a visiting Jewish scholar who spoke with extreme warmth and admiration of what Pope Pius XII and other Catholics had done to save Jews from Nazis. This was before the Soviet disinformation campaign about Pius began.

The pleasanter parts of Oxford life centred round the friendships I made at Somerville and elsewhere and also attendance at the Catholic Chaplaincy Mass every Sunday morning and at other gatherings there. Monsignor Vernon Johnson (V. J.) and Monsignor Valentine Elwes (V. E.) were invaluable supports. However, I was disadvantaged, at the Saturday evening Chaplaincy socials, by the fact that my upbringing had left me without any knowledge of ballroom dancing for which, in any case, I have never had any ability. This, and my general tiredness during these years inhibited me from getting to know many of the men students around.

The preachers at the Sunday Masses included some of the outstanding clergy of the time; Monsignor Ronnie Knox, who had been Oxford Chaplain before the war (when the chaplaincy served only male members of the University), used to preach once every term. After the Mass we would adjourn, with the visiting preacher, to the chaplain's large sitting room where we had an informal discussion with him. Gabriel Marcel, the French philosopher, visited the Chaplaincy one Sunday when the sermon was given by the philosopher Father Victor White from Oxford Blackfriars. After Mass, they were both at the informal sitting-room gathering where they had a light-hearted discussion on the question whether immortality might ever be predicated for animals, tentatively suggesting that it might be possible in the case of animals which had developed some human characteristics by close contact with human beings! St Aloysius church, at that time still staffed by Jesuits (the poet Gerard Manley Hopkins SJ had been resident there and I felt the proximity of his spirit),[4] and Blackfriars were conveniently near Somerville and I frequently attended them on weekdays. During vacations, when I was in Oxford, I would go to Sunday Mass at St Aloysius and afterwards observe the Pakenhams and Michael Fogarty and others chatting together outside the church. I joined a discussion group at the Catholic Workers' College which, like Ruskin College, prepared students who had been manual workers, and often active in trade unions, for the Oxford Diploma in Economics. It also gave them a grounding in Catholic social teaching. The only other undergraduate who took part was Dermot de Trafford who later became a prominent businessman.

My first day on coming up to Oxford, in October 1945, was memorable for several events. I went to the Chaplaincy and met Monsignor Vernon Johnson. Then the Somerville Bursar, knowing that I had lived in China, told me that there was a Chinese girl among the other first years and she had given us rooms near each other. Thus, she said, "You can speak Chinese to her so that she will not feel lonely." That evening, I knocked at Mary Low's door, went in, and began speaking Chinese to her so that

---

4 An intriguing reference, which I have not been able to follow up, occurs in the note on Gerard Manley Hopkins's poem *St Winefred's Well*: "When I was writing my Demeter for the lady-students of Somerville College ...". *Poems of Gerard Manley Hopkins*, Robert Bridges (ed.), 2nd edn., 1930, p. 119. Re-issued in the Oxford Bookshelf in 1937.

she would not feel lonely – only to find that she knew no Chinese and had never been further east than the French Riviera. However, it was the beginning of a firm friendship which is still going strong after seventy years.

That same evening, I sought out the college secretary of the political party of my choice. As I handed over my subscription, I remember thinking, "What can this girl, who has come straight from school, know about politics compared to me who has been knocking around the world for the last six years?" However, I realised later that, even then, Margaret Roberts (later Thatcher) already probably knew much more about politics than I will ever know. In the following year, I took over from Margaret as College Secretary for the Conservatives. Once, I remember, Margaret, who was reading chemistry, mentioned that she hoped, after Oxford, to go into industry, so I asked if she would be applying to ICI. She said that ICI was bad at employing women in professional-level jobs; so it was in some other firm that she got the experience that later enabled her to boast of being the first British Prime Minister to have worked in industry. Margaret was very competent rather than brilliant and she never wasted energy on introspection or on subjective internal conflicts. At that time, she was rather dumpy and not nearly as good looking as later. Perhaps the Conservative Central Office did a good job on her when she was first accepted as a candidate.

I attended quite a number of meetings of OUCA (Oxford University Conservative Association) but did not have either the time nor, perhaps more importantly, the social abilities to get anywhere in it. I joined a study group on colonial matters, which met in Christ Church, and can remember having to run across the Great Quad as the clock struck ten o'clock, when all women had to be out. On another occasion, when Lord Templewood (the former Sir Samuel Hoare of the Hoare–Laval pact fame when Foreign Secretary) had addressed us, we all then retired for coffee to the Randolph Hotel. I was the only woman in a group of about a dozen gathered round the great man, talking to him. After a bit he turned to me, smiled sweetly and said, "Are you beginning to take a bit of interest in politics now?" I ignored his query and countered with a rather obscure question about the Government of India Bill on which he was the opposition spokesman in the Lords.[5]

My Somerville friends, with most of whom, if now alive, I am still in touch, included Rosalind Chamberlain, who was reading medicine and later became a consultant psychiatrist. She married Peter Bearcroft of Balliol and I am now godmother to one of their daughters and one of their granddaughters. Other friends included Teresa Dyer from Bombay, of the East Indian community of that city (not to be confused with the Goans, although both are of partly Portuguese origin) and her future husband Bernard Kay who was reading Chinese. In subsequent years our lives crossed several times, in Hong Kong and later in Laos where the Kays invited me for a memorable Christmas in 1968 when Bernard was in the British Embassy in Vientiane. Lalage Bown was an exhilaratingly lively friend who later played an important role in the development of tertiary education in different parts of Africa. Esther Unger (Ehrmann), a faithfully practising Orthodox Jewish refugee, was the daughter of a learned rabbi; I enjoyed the occasions when I was able to step in as a *shabbat goye*. Esther later taught in universities in the West Indies, London and Israel. She married a rabbi and lives in Jerusalem, helping to bring up her nine grandchildren and, at last count, five great-grandchildren; she has also run an on-line course on the Torah. Cecile Offen (Kessler) who read PPE and later worked in UN agencies, was also one of my circle. In one way or another, I kept up with them all, if only by Christmas cards and inter-continental telephone calls. With Phyllis Wightman (Ticciati) I not only shared some tutorials but later delighted in her small sons. Elspeth Kennedy, who was embarking on a distinguished career in mediaeval French literature had, like me, worked at the War Office, and Ann Whitaker was another older post-war undergraduate with whom I kept up occasionally.

---

5 On the clause about protection for the Dalits (formerly known as the scheduled castes or untouchables). My uncle George Ingram was a friend of Dr Ambedkar, the leader of the Dalits and accompanied him to Chartwell to meet Winston Churchill, then Leader of the Opposition.

Valerie Corcos, after achieving a first class in French and Russian, became librarian of the Russian section of the St Antony's College library, married a retired Danish seaman and settled down very happily in a beautiful village near Oxford to bring up a family. I often visited her during the rest of her life when I came to Oxford. She would pick me up, usually at the entrance to Somerville, and drive me to her home. Carmen Blacker had taken a degree in Japanese at the School of Oriental Studies, London before coming up to Somerville to do PPE two terms before I left. Our common East Asian interests drew us together and I once stayed at her home, meeting her father, Carlos Blacker, the demographer whose views I would later spend much energy controverting. It was remarkable that Jeanette Dawe, the oldest of our year, was the only one I am certain came from a working-class family, but her father had by then become a full-time union leader. She had obtained a diploma at a teacher training college and then, I think, taught for some years after which she managed to get to Oxford on an inadequate scholarship which the college tried to supplement by giving her part-time evening work at the college gatehouse. Anne Martin, who came up to Somerville in 1946 to read PPE will always have an affectionate corner in my heart. Brilliant, eccentric and rather wild, she later held a number of academic jobs in different parts of the world before her mental problems led to an early tragic death. To us of the post-war crowd, Anne – who came up at age seventeen – seemed to embody some of the youthful wildness we had foregone because of the war, and I have always felt a bit guilty that we may have egged her on a little. A friend, with whom I lost contact, was Patricia Avis, a South African. She read medicine and early on married Colin Strang, who later became a professor of philosophy. I attended her wedding and grand reception. The marriage collapsed; subsequently, Pat married the Irish poet Richard Murphy. I tried to keep up with her but lost touch.

Patrick S. S. Yu, reading law at Merton College, and a future star of the Hong Kong Bar, was one of the Chinese students whom I got to know. In his rooms at Merton he threw crowded, cheerful and noisy parties. Years later, he told me that at his parties I must have met his friend C. P. Hsu but really it was almost impossible to remember whom one had seen in those boisterous gatherings! Francis C. P. Hsu later became the first Chinese Bishop of the Catholic Diocese of Hong Kong, but at that time he was an agnostic with whom Patrick often argued, trying to convince him of the Catholic faith. Some years later, he was converted through the agency of a devout and simple Jesuit, Father Gurrin (no, a simple Jesuit is not an oxymoron, although rare) and then gave up his promising career in the Hong Kong Civil Service to enter a seminary.

I also got to know two Dutch girls who had come to England under a scheme which brought young people from the continent to learn English while supporting themselves in jobs. They were working in the Somerville kitchen and had not been given the promised opportunity to attend English classes. In addition, their only companions were the other maids, local girls whose heavily accented English the Dutch girls found difficult to understand and did not want to emulate. Eventually, more suitable jobs were found for them; one, Hanny Bijvoet, going to look after the children of a prominent Oxford figure whose wife wrote children's books but, according to Hanny, neglected their children.

Two extra-curricular but firm friendships with members of the Somerville Senior Common Room were with Elizabeth Anscombe[6] and Lucy Brown. Elizabeth at that time had some research fellowship at the college. Occasionally, she left her eldest daughter Barbara, then a toddler, in my room for me to babysit while Elizabeth attended a meeting. In later years, when I visited Oxford, I would sometimes come across Elizabeth at an early Mass at Blackfriars and she would take me back to their home in St John Street for breakfast. Barbara, the oldest child and the most practical of the family, would be getting breakfast while the rest were engaged in fierce exchanges, perhaps on arguments about the existence of God; I am strongly of the opinion that the existence of God should be taken on faith until after breakfast! Lucy Brown was a

---

6 One of the most distinguished English philosophers of the twentieth century and later Professor of Philosophy at Cambridge. Her husband, Peter Geach, was also an eminent philosopher.

historian, specialising in nineteenth century British history. She taught at the London School of Economics for many years and I have kept up with her and several times have stayed in her house in Ealing.

As earlier noted, when I went up to Oxford, I was nearly twenty-three and it may be that if I had gone up at around eighteen, I would not have been so irked by it. The undergraduate system is (or was) geared to dealing with those in the eighteen to twenty-one age group and it is not fair to judge it by its impact on a student who was five years older. Others of the post-war crowd often felt the same and there was a psychological division between the post-war intake and those straight up from school. The habit of "gap years" had not then become common. If I had attended a university where regular attendance at lectures was expected, I do not think I could have endured three years. The enveloping atmosphere of academia ground me down increasingly and towards the end of my time at Oxford I tried to find ways of escaping it. I went to some meetings of the Women's Farm and Garden Association in South Oxford (the organization through which I had found Mrs Bray, on whose allotment in Kent I worked in 1945) and also the City of Oxford Young Conservatives (for which I was eligible because I was on the Oxford electoral roll, having no other address in Britain); indeed, I once went as one of their representatives to a Conservative Party Conference. In any case, I made many good friends for life at Oxford while acquiring a qualification which has been my rice bowl. For both I am grateful.

China had, as with many people, brought me down to earth, politically as well as in other ways. In British universities in 1945, especially in the social sciences, the left-wing trends which had swept the Labour government into power that summer, tended to hold sway in the senior common rooms, perhaps more than among undergraduates. Some of us doing PPE felt disadvantaged by this and at least once, I thought I was subjected to a biased assessment. The Principal, Janet Vaughan, while generally popular and whom I always found kind and supportive, was regarded by many of us as a perpetual adolescent as far as politics was concerned. Once, she gave an informal talk after returning from visiting some place where

Soviet troops had just arrived. She was thrilled to find that they seemed like normal human beings and implied that this nullified any ill effects of their presence. "Do you know – they were drinking coffee from paper cups!" Reacting to this atmosphere may have hardened Margaret Roberts' outlook.

During my first term at Oxford my parents sailed to Hong Kong and from there went back to Sichuan, to Beipei near Chongqing where the band of Chinese workers, formerly at Guanghan, had settled as the West China Evangelistic Band. This meant that I did not have a home in Britain where I could go in vacations and relax, recover from the exhaustion of term time and get sympathy and encouragement. Of course, this problem was also shared by students from abroad who were unable to return to their home countries in vacations, although in their case the problem was more generally acknowledged and help given, while I was just another UK student. The vacations were always a problem and a worry for me during my time at Oxford as I had to find somewhere economical to stay where I could get work done; and of course, like everyone, I wanted to see something of the continent from which we had been cut off during the war.[7]

In a way, the lack of a home in England was worse now than during childhood. My tuition fees and term time keep were covered by the Further Training and Education Scheme for young people who had been in the services or on other war work – it was much more generous than the way UK students in the early twenty first century are treated[8] – but it gave a very exiguous sum for vacations, assuming that recipients would be living at home or would find a job. Oxford, however, really expected us to do the reading in vacations which we did not have time for in term and this I needed to do. My parents gave me an allowance (paid through my aunt

---

7 Restrictions on money for holiday travel abroad were severe for years after the Second World War. At first, only fifty pounds sterling a year was permitted. However, for most of us, our own impecunity was at least as restrictive.

8 But, at the same time, the war generation was disadvantaged by beginning their working lives, and therefore their progress up the incremental ladder, at a later age; and finally retiring with fewer annual superannuation payments having been made.

Maud Crofts[9]) to compensate financially for the lack of a home, but there was still the question of finding a place where I could get the necessary academic work done. Sometimes Pen Piercy invited me to spend some days in her flat in London, which I always enjoyed, but her invitations were unpredictable. I stayed in College for as much of the vacation as was permitted; as a scholar, I could do so free of charge which was, of course, a great incentive. Once I spent time in digs in south Oxford, but that was discouraged as it was thought better to go out of Oxford as indeed was my own preference. Without a home, I had to store all my possessions in my room at Somerville. Fortunately, the room I was given in my first term had large cupboards so I kept it for all my three years, although otherwise it was not very attractive, on the ground floor of Penrose building, looking out on some sheds at the back. If I had not needed so much storage space, I could, in a subsequent year, have moved to a much nicer room.

For the Christmas vacation of 1945, after my parents left Britain, I went to relatives in the London area. While there, at some occasion when my extended family gathered, an aunt made disparaging remarks about inter-racial marriage which stirred me to mention that our own family was of mixed race, Victoria Ingram being Anglo-Indian. Uproar immediately irrupted at my mentioning the unmentionable. Many of the older generation had deliberately decided to forget it and assumed that their descendants would either never hear of it or, if they did, would likewise decide to forget. Their disapproval of any relative, such as myself, who might suddenly blurt this out, was clear. Aunt Lilian took me aside a day or two afterwards and explained that her daughter Esther, some eleven years older than me, had got engaged in the 1930s but when her fiancé's family discovered that the Ingrams had Indian blood, they insisted on the engagement being broken; (a different reason for the breaking off of the engagement was given by Lilian to another cousin). After that incident, I felt that I could not invite myself to the homes of my senior relatives for vacations, and avoided them

---

9 Whenever she sent me a cheque from my mother's account, Maud always said that it was a present "from your mother." This was, of course, legally correct and I knew it, but in my reply, I always thanked her for the gift "from my parents". I resented the unequal financial status of my parents.

at a time when my need for a home environment was greatest. My double first cousin, Esther, and her husband, Guy Bryan, were living at that time in Oxford where he was the local manager of Barclays Bank, but I never saw them during my years at Somerville.

Naturally, I was eager to explore the continent as soon as possible. In 1946, I wrote to the International Federation of Catholic Students (I may have forgotten its correct name after the years) asking to be put in touch with a Catholic family near Paris where I could go as a paying guest. In the summer of 1946, I spent an agreeable and interesting couple of weeks with the Beriots at Breuillet, seeing something of Paris as well as getting to know one of those great solid Christian families which will ensure the survival and flourishing of the Faith in Europe. I have remained in intermittent but warm touch with several generations of them in the nearly seventy subsequent years.

One of my Somerville friends, Ann Petre, the daughter of an old recusant Catholic family, invited me to her home for the Christmas of 1946. I had to cut short this pleasant stay to attend a conference in Germany. Thanks to the initiative of an official of the British Control Commission in Germany, a joint Catholic and Protestant Anglo-German conference was held at Münster in December 1946 and January 1947. The conference was hastily organised and the religious mix was unusual in those pre-ecumenical times. The participants were university people, recruited – as far as the British side was concerned – from the Union of Catholic Students and the Student Christian Movement, and from the appropriate graduate bodies – on the Catholic side, this was the Newman Association; I do not know how the Protestant graduates were selected. The German participants were drawn from both Catholic and Lutheran organisations. Many of the Catholics, especially the local Münster ones, had been those who had gathered round the courageous old Bishop of Münster, Clemens von Galen, the "Lion of Münster", who had died shortly before and was buried in his partly-ruined cathedral. Known as a valiant opponent of the Nazis, he was much venerated in the Catholic community and has now been beatified. Margret Maué, a young medical doctor with whom I made friends, had (with, I think, her future first husband) been part of the von Galen group. She was now one of the organisers of the conference; her husband had gone missing on the Eastern Front.

When, late in the Michaelmas Term, the Union of Catholic Students had asked for volunteers to attend the conference, I applied from Oxford, where I was then in my second year. The British Control Commission in Germany arranged our transport to Münster by train – travel was still very difficult on the continent. I travelled with one of the Newman Association (the UK Catholic graduate organisation) contingent and we were the first international participants to arrive at Münster. It has always been a quiet source of pleasure to me that I was the first foreign student to arrive at what I think was the first international civilian conference held in Germany after the War.

Much of Münster had been destroyed by allied bombing. The conference organisers had a problem finding facilities for it. The conference meetings were held in the Catholic seminary, Borromeohaus, where all the male non-local participants were lodged; this was unheated. The women were put into Martin Lutherhaus, a large building a considerable distance away. We were privileged to be in one of the few heated buildings in Münster that very cold winter, because half of Martin Lutherhaus was used as a hospital. Going back at night after the meetings, we walked between eerie snow-covered ruins. We were told it was estimated that the rubble would not all be cleared until around the end of the century.

The atmosphere at the conference was friendly though sometimes tense. Some named persons had been invited to attend from the Soviet-occupied zone in East Germany. Participants arrived from that zone, but not the ones that had been invited, and they could give no reasonable account of how they had been selected. The German participants tended to register their approval of anything by stamping their feet rather than clapping their hands, perhaps a habit learned under totalitarianism. Senior Catholic members of the British delegation included Father Paul Crane SJ of the Catholic Social Guild and Professor Hilary Armstrong, later of the

University of Liverpool; they took a firm line when discussing topics such as responsibility for the war and their views appeared to meet with wide acceptance from many of the Germans. The British Protestant participants included a number of Quakers who tended to attribute the war to almost everyone equally.

The local rations in Germany at that time were very meagre but Catholic farmers had given supplies so that the food at the conference was better than normal. We were also able to go to the NAAFI (British army canteen stores) and bring away food to give to local friends. Margret Maué took me to a particularly needy family living in a dank basement to give them some of these supplies. Margret's husband, on his last leave, had told her "First we must defeat the Soviets; then we will come home and deal with them" – and he gesticulated in the direction of the local Nazi headquarters.

The Christmas of 1947 I spent very happily at the home of my cousin Marcelle and her husband Jack Reay-Smith and their two small sons (their youngest child, Hilary, had not yet been born). They lived in Durham near Bishop Auckland, Co. Durham and so were far removed from any swirling currents of family disapproval; in any case, they were too sensible and kindly to care. Jack had stood in the General Election of 1945 as Conservative candidate for Bishop Auckland, one of the strongest Labour seats in the country, held at that time by Hugh Dalton, who became Chancellor of the Exchequer in the new government. Jack must have put up a good fight because it led the Conservative Central Office to enquire if he would be interested in standing for a winnable seat at some future date. He had to turn down the suggestion because, with a young family, he could not afford to close his one-man solicitor's firm in the north of England and live in rented accommodation in London on a parliamentary salary, especially when he might lose his seat in the next election.

I was always fond of Marcelle and her elder sister Joy, daughters of my Aunt Ruby (née Ingram) and her husband Philip Pitt. As children, they had a difficult time. Their father was a barrister whose lack of success in his profession soured him as well as impoverishing his family. Possibly Granny Ingram gave them some help, but they lived in a much poorer part of Wimbledon than others of the family. The girls both went to Wimbledon High School, from which Marcelle won an Exhibition to Oxford Home Students (which later became St Anne's College) and read English. She was for a time on the editorial staff of the weekly journal *Time and Tide* and then married an Oxford friend, Jack Reay-Smith. Joy became a nurse and went to India in the army nursing corps. It was during my parents' furlough that news came that Joy had suddenly married an army other rank, Ronald Ross, and was pregnant. The bossier of the aunts were scornful of her, but I think my mother and Aunt May, also a missionary, were kinder. Ronald, whom neither I nor most others of the family ever met, soon abandoned his wife and their son, Philip Keith. Joy later became matron at King's School, Canterbury where Philip was educated before joining the army himself. I tried to keep up with Joy and Philip, but seldom had opportunities to meet. Both have now died. Philip served in the East Anglian Regiment in Aden and Germany; after retiring, he worked for a time in the War Office. Once I had the pleasure of staying with him and his wife Rosalind.

One vacation I spent in Manchester, living in a hostel and reading in the famous Rylands Library. I was anxious to see something of the Catholic community in the north of England which had, from the early nineteenth century and perhaps earlier, formed the bulk of the Catholics in England. From the Catholic Social Guild and the Catholic Workers' College at Oxford I had received useful introductions.

The summer of 1947 I signed on for a German course at the Zurich College of Technology and lodged comfortably with an electrician and his wife, Herr and Frau Hans Vokinger. The prosperity of Switzerland was an enjoyable novelty after the impoverished state of Germany and France, or even of post-war Britain, but it was rather expensive. I found a chain of cheap restaurants set up by a women's temperance society and by eating in them, I was able to save money to go elsewhere to have a glass of wine which otherwise I could not have afforded. After the course ended, I went on for a few days of youth hostelling in other parts of Switzerland. I remember an excellent hostel in Ticino but regretted I would not be able to visit it again as I would soon be twenty-five, the upper age for visitors to Swiss youth hostels – presumably to protect tourism. The good lady in charge, however, would have none of this, declaring that I could continue to come as "*hier bin ich die regierung*" ("here I am the government").

Fortunately, I had solved the post-Oxford job problem early in 1948 when I accepted a Research Assistantship at University College London, although I hoped that this would only be a temporary solution. This was a great relief but, despite it, early in the summer term of 1948, some weeks before Schools (the final exams), I was not at all well, fainting suddenly on a hard floor and breaking some front teeth, necessitating taking time for dental appointments. Janet Vaughan, our ever-watchful principal, exercised her medical judgment by arranging for me to go away for a week to stay with a kind friend of hers, Molly Hoyle, the headmistress of a school in Stroud, Somerset. This pulled me up and I managed to struggle through the term, although hay fever, especially in the summer, and migraine as usual gave trouble. Mary Ogilvie, as throughout my years at Oxford, was very kind and invited me to come to rest between papers in the Principal's lodge at Jesus College where her husband was Principal (much closer than Somerville to Schools). A few weeks later, her eldest son, James, was tragically killed in a mountaineering accident in Switzerland.

The day I left Oxford, after Schools, I did not know where I was going to spend the next night. I had arranged to stay with Pen Piercy, but the evening before I received a telegram to say she could not have me after all. As I had already bought a ticket, I went up to London with all my worldly possessions which, in default of anywhere else, I had stored in my cupboards at Oxford. With most of my things stowed in the left-luggage office at Paddington Station, I called at a convent hostel in Bloomsbury. I explained my predicament and showed them my letter of appointment at University College which they accepted in lieu of a reference. I stayed there for two or three days while I looked for something more permanent.

That summer, as a complete and economical change, I signed on for a fortnight's agricultural camp on the border of Lincolnshire and Nottinghamshire, picking potatoes. These agricultural camps, for which anyone with free time was urged to volunteer, were a feature of wartime and post-war Britain when labour was in very short supply. Work was tiring but we had the satisfaction of being paid every evening, usually with three solid half-crowns; or when we had worked extra hard and long, with a crisp ten-shilling note! It provided me an opportunity to visit Lincoln Cathedral and Sherwood Forest and also of mixing with a completely different set of people. A group of lads from the East End of London (then a notoriously poor area – now increasingly gentrified) talked about their tiffs with "the Jew boys" there. It was almost the only time I have ever heard anti-Semitic remarks in Britain and I asked them what they had against the Jews. All they could say seemed to be that they were "other", a role soon taken over by coloured immigrants who after the war began crowding into London from the West Indies, Pakistan and elsewhere.

Shortly after that, I joined Pen Piercy, her sister Priscilla and Pen's friends Michael Maurice and Christopher Maude on a motor trip, in Michael's ancient Rolls, to the south of France. We spent some time at Les Beaux, an extraordinary prehistoric town on a craggy rock. From there we explored other places in Provence and then went on for a day to Lourdes. My companions were High Anglicans and were happy to join the evening procession. After Lourdes, I left my friends and took a train to Geneva where my most compatible economics tutor, Helen Makower, was working in a UN agency and had invited her old pupils to visit her. Continental train journeys in those early post-war years were ordeals and I spent much of that night's journey standing on one foot in a jam-packed corridor. Still, we were in the post-war euphoria at being able to get to the continent at all. In Geneva, Helen roped me in to help collect figures about the Hungarian leather industry.

Another journey to Switzerland came rather unexpectedly. My cousin Dr Ilsley Ingram, during the latter part of his convalescence from TB, found what was supposed to be a light job at a sanatorium at Montana where he met and got engaged to a former ward sister, Patricia Forbes Irving, from his old hospital, St Thomas', London. The wedding took place in the Anglican chapel at Montana on 25 September 1948. The problems of travel and of life in general at that time meant that I was the only member of either the bridegroom's or the bride's families who could get there. They asked me to be a bridesmaid, together with a friend of theirs who was a patient in the sanatorium. I arrived with one day to spare before the wedding and someone swiftly made me a bridesmaid's dress. The wedding went well, and the refreshments after it. Then there was a great rush for the bridal pair to change and go by a hired car to catch a bus to take them to the Alpine village where they had booked their honeymoon. Owing to shortage of transport facilities, I was pushed into the hired car with them and deposited at the station in the valley to return to England. The speed and the terrifying manner in which that car hurtled down the mountain were such that I told the bridal couple that, if we survived, I would remind them of it on every anniversary of their wedding, which I did whenever I was with them for the anniversary, until their Golden Wedding and beyond.

CHAPTER 7

University College London, and South-East Asia Research: 1948–52

While at Oxford, I was unsure of what to do afterwards. I certainly did not want to work for a post-graduate degree because I was thoroughly tired of academia, and I had also been brought up with the traditional British scorn of higher university qualifications. Sir Frederick Ogilvie was at that time chairman of a committee which dispensed postgraduate scholarships to Harvard and he asked me if I would like to apply, even after he knew that I had achieved only a second in Schools. This, however, was the last thing I wanted. My experience in Chengdu had put me off North American higher education. In any case, I had had more than enough of being a student and I wanted a job, although preferably not an academic one. My upbringing had instilled in me an instinct that a university was where one went to qualify for a profession or to get a general introduction to society but whose doors one did not darken in later life; like adolescence, it had to be passed through but without dallying. A professor was, in my childhood, rather a figure of fun, unpractical and usually qualified by the adjective "absent-minded". The senior doctorates of Oxford and Cambridge, DLitt and DSc, were part of British tradition – they were not qualifications but were usually awarded towards the end of a career as marks of achievement – but PhDs were for Americans or verbose Germans and were considered un-British. Indeed, I can remember being carefully instructed as a child at Beeston Rectory that, if ever any of our British visitors had, perhaps for convenience, acquired a PhD while working in the States, it would be impolite to address him as such; his indiscretion should be over-looked. One uncle of mine, whenever mention was made of PhDs, would murmur "Phoney Doctor." Vestiges of this deeply-ingrained attitude towards academia have, effectively, remained with me ever since.

Neither did I want to be in government service as it would curb my independence. During the war, it had been different. At that time, we had all lost much of our freedom, willingly, because of the constraints of war. As a career, however, I did not want to have to support and implement policies with which I might not agree.

Of course, I prayed for guidance in this important decision about my future, but as throughout my life, no sudden inspiration came into my head; but by following rational steps, things turned out all right and later I could see evidence of guidance. In this case, it came in the form of the very suitable but unexpected position that turned up at University College London, which fitted me for the future paths in my life.

In my second year at Oxford, I went to the university careers bureau and said I would like something in business or finance. They immediately asked, "Can you type?", this then being a necessary skill for a woman wishing for a job in these spheres. I had done a typing course and could type quite quickly but very inaccurately and did not improve with practice, so I gave up that idea. A tutor suggested that I apply for a job on the *Economist*. I did so, giving a number of distinguished Oxford figures as referees, but my application was not even acknowledged. In order to be able to concentrate on the fast-approaching Finals, I had to get something settled about my future. I had no home in England, so on leaving Oxford I would need immediately to find somewhere to live and that would mean paying rent. At that time, I was somewhat alienated from the older members of my extended family, who might otherwise have put me up.

An academic job would be the easiest to find and would not be a long-term commitment. I answered an advertisement for a research assistantship in the Department of Political Economy at University College London and was summoned for an interview. The head of the department, Professor George C. Allen, had lived and worked for some years in Japan and had written extensively on the Japanese economy. He noted my China background and thought I would be suitable for a project he had in mind – to study the influence on the economies of various Asian countries of Western firms which had operated in them in modern times. At the interview, I was asked if I wanted an academic career and replied firmly, "No," but on being further asked if I would be willing to do an academic job for two or three years, I said that would be all right. I thought, "Perhaps two, but not, I hope, three." I stayed at University College London for over twenty years, from October 1948 until December 1968 as research assistant, then lecturer, then reader. I liked the department, which concerned itself with the economic behaviour of human beings in all their variability and I found most of my colleagues there congenial, but was never really reconciled to being an academic. What made it tolerable was that from around 1957 on, I was working on contemporary China. I would much rather have been in China doing something active, but that was unthinkable in Maoist times. The nearest I could get was to follow what was happening, as far as I could, day by day, and this is what I did. For the first few years, however, I worked on other topics, including historical issues in China.

The Department of Political Economy at University College was, as its name suggests, the oldest or one of the oldest economics departments in the country. The last head of the department before the war had been Hugh Gaitskell, but only as a reader, not a professor. By the summer of 1945, he had been elected to Parliament and soon came to hold a leading position in the new Labour government. In 1947, the department began to be reconstructed after the war when George Allen resigned his chair at Liverpool to take the Jevons Chair at UCL; and three others, who like him had been wartime civil servants, were appointed to senior positions in the department: Herbert Tout, Marian Bowley and Alfred Stonier. One young economist, Douglas Hague, had been appointed to an assistant lectureship in 1947. In 1948 three more new recruits augmented the staff: Wilfred

Corlett, a statistician, Ann Nicholson and, as a research assistant, myself. A few years later, Ann Nicholson became Mrs Corlett and I am the proud godmother of their elder daughter. Douglas Hague and Alfred Stonier co-authored what became a standard economic textbook. Douglas soon went on to a chair in a provincial university and later to the position of economic adviser to Margaret Thatcher and a knighthood. In the course of time, others joined the department, including Leslie Pressnell (a banking specialist), Stanley Sturmey, Margaret Paul (née Ramsey – a sister of Archbishop Ramsey of Canterbury),[1] John Spraos and Dipak Mazumdar. It continued to be a reasonably harmonious department with a very pleasant annual gathering in the Allens' house and garden in Surrey, as well as attendances at the students' Jevons Society annual dinner and a summer river party. In 1951 Hugh Gaitskell, then Chancellor of the Exchequer, was guest of honour at the Jevons Society dinner. The student president of the Society congratulated him on getting a more remunerative job than he had had before the war as head of the department. Gaitskell replied, "More remunerative, but less secure."

In 1948, UCL was still run down and dishevelled as a result of the war, with several units housed in temporary structures. The main buildings had not been hit and, as college tradition demanded, Jeremy Bentham's embalmed body, ensconced in a glass case, kept watch outside the council room; but whether it continued to be brought in to attend council meetings, I never heard. Nearby, bomb sites were very evident. One lay gaping for years on the corner of Gower St. and Gower Place, next to Euston Square underground station, brightened, like many other bomb sites, with tall, wild red flowering St John's wort.

Throughout my twenty years at University College London there were three Senior Common Rooms – Mixed, Men's, and Women's. The WSCR had better coffee, less tobacco fumes, more comfortable chairs, more papers and journals and was quieter. Individual conversation was easier there. When with male colleagues, we all went into the Mixed Common Room; if

1 Years later, on the day when her brother was visiting the Pope, I took Margaret out to lunch. She, like most of her family was irreligious, but was proud of her brother, rather in the way an unmusical sister might be proud of a brother who excelled in music.

alone, I usually chose the WSCR. I remember once when a retired WSCR member, a centenarian, came back; she had lived in India in her youth and told us in her low voice how she came to Britain across the Suez isthmus by land, before the canal was cut. The Mixed Common Room was noisier, especially the group around John Haldane, the biologist, which every now and then broke out into raucous laughter. Men guests were allowed into the Women's, but no women were allowed into the Men's. Sometimes votes were taken on whether all SCRs should be mixed and voting was very close. I always voted to retain a separate WSCR as I never attached such importance to equality or discrimination as to want to lower the status of women to that of men. My departure for Australia at the end of 1968 may have been decisive in ending segregation and, perhaps, the good coffee.

The Department of Political Economy was housed, within the University College campus, in what had been an ordinary residential building, part of a row fronting on to Gordon Street and Gordon Square. The building, if I remember rightly, consisted of three floors and a basement which provided, through the building's back door, the usual way to the rest of the College. There used to be a tree at the back of the building, but years later this was cut down despite a letter of protest which I had written to the College Secretary. I worked in this building for the first sixteen years of my time at UCL, from 1948 to 1964, sharing a largish office at first with one or two other junior members of the academic staff and then, when I began to work on China, with just my own research assistant. As I acquired more and more journals and stacks of copies of *The People's Daily*, bound together month by month, the room became cramped. The whole department badly needed more space. My sub-unit was the obvious choice when part of the department had to be hived off, and this happened from the autumn term of 1964, when the College rented premises in Tottenham Court Road, a few minutes' walk from the campus. There, my research assistant Tsu-tung Emslie and myself each had a room, with space for the publications we brought with us, and there was also, I think, a small room for John Chiu-Hon Wong, an economics graduate of the University of Hong Kong who, in the early 1960s, came from Hong Kong to write a thesis on Land Reform in China under my supervision. Originally, he was from Guangdong and, as a secondary school pupil, had taken part in the land-reform programme. On the ground floor of this building was a pub, the Mortimer Arms, and this proved useful as a place to which the China Seminar, which I had started, could adjourn for refreshments, supper and continuing informal discussion.

In 1948, Professor Allen was envisaging a book on the impact of Western firms in China and Japan on the local economies. He had close links to the Royal Institute of International Affairs, also known as Chatham House, and it arranged a dinner to which were invited the heads or other senior members of major firms which had been engaged in trade with East Asia and whose help we would need. They proved co-operative and, for the next year or so, I went around interviewing members of these and other firms and anyone else who might throw light on our subject. I also read up anything available in publications or elsewhere.[2] Then I made a first draft, topic by topic, for what was published in 1954 as *Western Enterprise in Far Eastern Economic Development,* jointly authored by G. C. Allen and myself.

A great gap in our endeavour was the absence of Chinese sources. The civil war in China, followed by the Communist victory, meant it was impossible to search for information there. Little, if any, Chinese written material was available. Looking back on it, we might have tried to tap some of the Shanghai businessmen who had fled to Hong Kong, but at that time they would have been submerged in their own problems and indeed little was known about who had come. The Japanese section of the book was entirely Allen's work. He gave it to me to read for comments but I cannot remember that I changed even a comma. I asked him to include a note in the book to say that he alone had written the part on Japan, as I did not want to appear to claim an expertise on the Japanese economy which I totally lack. He, however, declined. I handed over to Allen my draft of the China chapters and he re-wrote my preliminary version with great improvements.

---

2 The Jardine papers (with material on the early days of that firm) had not yet been released.

Meanwhile, I began work on our second volume, *Western Enterprise in Indonesia and Malaya* (it was not until after Singapore had split from Malaya that the latter became known as Malaysia). As before, I began by reading the literature available and interviewing staff in Britain of the UK firms with business in these countries. Then I wanted to visit these countries to investigate matters on the spot. This was the time of the Malayan Emergency when groups of Chinese insurgents, inspired by Mao's success in China, had organised themselves in the jungles of Malaya to struggle against British colonial rule. I was warned against the problems this situation would present, as well as about the unsettled condition of newly independent Indonesia. However, the Bank of England's Houblon-Norman Fund gave me a grant to cover the costs of several months' field work in South East Asia.

Leaving by sea from Southampton in December 1951, I touched at Algiers where I visited the *souk* and then spent Christmas, without any Mass on board, in the Red Sea. Passengers were invited down to a lower deck to see the fine nativity decorations put up by the devout Goan sailors who manned the P & O liners. On St Stephen's Day, we docked at Aden where I visited the local Catholic church and met the valiant Sister Gesuina, who ran a school of constantly shifting multiracial pupils, and also the cheerful Vicar Apostolic who laughingly described himself as "Bishop of Mecca". Bombay was our next stop and there I had an enjoyable visit to the home of my old Somerville friend, Teresa Dyer. On 8 January 1952, we arrived at Singapore.

I already knew Professor Tom Silcock of the newly established University of Malaya (which was situated in Singapore) whose father, Arnold Silcock, I had met when he was a Quaker missionary in Chengdu. Tom had arranged for me to stay with Tan Ek Khoo, a well-connected businessman, and his wife and small children in a convenient location in Singapore. Then I began a round of several hundred interviews that was to continue for the next seven months.[3] Those I talked to in Singapore included university

3 My notes of these interviews are deposited in the Menzies Library, Australian National University, Canberra and I have not had the opportunity to read them again before writing these memoirs. I have, however my five-page report to the Houblon-

staff and research students, expatriate and local government, consular and UN officials, people of different nationalities and races in the rubber and other produce trades, in banking, insurance, shipping, real estate and other lines of business. I visited a wide range of factories and the Straits Trading Company's tin smelter on Pulau Brani. Also, I accompanied members of ICI's staff on visits to smallholders (chiefly vegetable-growers). At the Office of the Registrar of Companies I went through both the pre-war and most recent share registers of some local companies to examine the extent of the sale of shares by Europeans to Malayans (chiefly Chinese) and I read some relevant works at the Raffles Library, but lack of time prevented me from making as much use of it as I would have wished.

In March, I motored through southwest Johore with Ungku Aris, President of the Johore Rubber Smallholders' Association, visiting rubber smallholdings and government offices. Aris was a very knowledgeable and useful contact; regrettably, he was killed in an air crash not long afterwards. From Johore, I went to the ancient city of Malacca, a complete contrast to Singapore. While Singapore was a tribute to the achievements of modern Overseas Chinese, Malacca quietly carried the memory of the early Chinese pioneers. I was privileged to meet Dato Sir Cheng-Lock Tan, the doyen of the Malacca Chinese community, and to see his magnificent old house. I also met the Estates Director of Dunlop Malayan Estates Ltd.

After the peace of Malacca, I was reminded of the current realities of the Malayan emergency when I travelled from there, in a convoy of armoured cars (with the male members of our party carrying rifles), to one of the Dunlop rubber estates in Negri Sembilan. There I spent a night before returning, in like manner, to Malacca, from where I took a bus to Singapore.

A week later, on 22 March 1952, I sailed on a KPM (Koninklijke Paketvaart Mij.) ship to Jakarta, which had only a few years previously been metamorphosed from being Batavia, the capital of the former Dutch East Indies, to becoming the capital of a large but disorganized sovereign nation. Thanks to introductions which I had to Catholic missionaries in Singapore,

Norman Foundation in which I listed many of my activities.

I had met there a papal emissary, Bishop Carl van Melckebeke, who had been expelled by the Communists from his diocese in Ningxia, China, and was subsequently appointed Apostolic Vicar for Overseas Chinese. He asked Archbishop de Jonghe, the Apostolic Delegate to Indonesia (i.e. the papal representative), to help me.

Archbishop de Jonghe kindly contacted convents throughout the country, requesting them to give me hospitality. This was a huge advantage. Indonesia was still unsettled after the Japanese occupation, followed by the struggle for independence. Hotels would have been very variable and anyhow expensive; staying in local convents in a way provided assurance to the businessmen and others whom I needed to meet and who were quite unused to visiting researchers, especially young women, that I was not an irresponsible adventurer nor a wild radical come to denounce them and their doings. It also made my visits much more interesting as the Sisters were close to, and in some cases included members of, the local people. The only problem was that, when I was about to leave and wanted to pay for my stay, the Sisters would almost invariably refuse to take payment. This placed me in a quandary because I could not in conscience live off the kindness of those who themselves were leading very simple lives. So I had to press something into their hands which would cover the costs of my stay and say, "Well, please take this for your school/orphanage/clinic," which they could not refuse. This was possible only because the Houblon-Norman Fund, in its wisdom, demanded just a general report of the use made of its grants, not a detailed accounting with receipts. As a result, by not staying in hotels, I was able to stretch their grant to cover several months more in South East Asia than originally envisaged. Much of my internal travel in Indonesia had to be done by Air Garuda, partly to save time but also because many roads were unsafe due to local civil unrest. The coastal road from Jakarta to Semarang was considered particularly dangerous. It was Air Garuda and the KPM which kept the country together.

In Jakarta, where I stayed in the Ursuline Convent, I had interviews with Indonesian government officials and with the staff of the British and American embassies and of the Netherlands High Commission, of the university, the British Chamber of Commerce and similar bodies, and of the POB (a federation of trade unions). I also interviewed lawyers and businessmen of various nationalities and races, including some engaged in the export of produce and others in the import trade, in plantation estates, in shipping, railways, civil aviation, banking, insurance and other lines. I visited the Bata Shoe Factory, the General Motors Assembly Plant, Unilever's soap factory and (with ICI), some batik factories. I also went to the Bogor Botanical Gardens.

In April, I spent a couple of days visiting the Anglo-Dutch Plantations of Java Ltd.'s estates (the Pamenoek and Tjassem Landen – usually known as the P & T Lands), a huge enterprise where I saw rubber, tea and other crops and visited rubber and tea factories. Later that month, I flew from Jakarta to Bandung where I went to a technical rubber goods factory, a quinine factory, a weaving mill and a tea estate, and had interviews with members of ICI's staff, with the Bandung Textile Institute and with the President of the Badah Pusat Serikat Seberoja (a federation of trade unions). From Bandung, I flew on to Semarang where I visited three factories and workshops and met some businessmen, including a particularly helpful ICI manager. From there, I went by air to Surabaya and then on to Makassar in Sulawesi (Celebes).

Makassar was a different world from Java. With its beautiful long, curved beach, it looked a paradise, but the far end of the bay was rebel-held territory and driving outside the city was unwise. Even within Makassar, as I soon found, things were not too safe. I was staying in a staff bungalow in the compound of the Catholic hospital. The flight from Surabaya had been rough and I felt very tired. Directly I got to my room I locked the door and threw myself on the bed and fell asleep. When I woke, I saw that a second door into my room from outside, which I had not noticed, was open and my handbag, which I had placed close to me, was missing; it contained my passport, my cash and travellers' cheques and much else besides, but fortunately not the name and telephone number of the local honorary British consul, which I had been given. I rang him and was amazed at the style and efficiency with which the crisis was resolved. The honorary consul turned up quickly in a black Rolls flying a Union Jack, every bit the emissary of the Great White Queen come to rescue a damsel in distress. He told me not to worry, that the passport could be replaced, the travellers' cheques cancelled and reissued and, until then, funds could be supplied to keep me going. As it turned out, the thief had thrown away my big handbag within the hospital compound and it was soon found, with my passport but without my purse or travellers' cheques. It took a few weeks to replace the travellers' cheques but meanwhile I was kept financially afloat by loans.

At Makassar, I had interviews with members of the staff of the local university, with the head of the Coprafonds (the official body with the monopoly of copra exports from East Indonesia) and with businessmen engaged in the produce trade, in importing, shipping and banking. I also had a memorable visit to an exporter's godown where spices, notably nutmeg and mace, were being sorted on the floor in the manner that they had probably been sorted for centuries, although in the past twenty years press-packing had been substituted for trampling in the packaging.

After a week in Makassar, it was with regrets, despite my troubles there, that I left that ancient trading post and my helpful friends in that city, and flew on to Bandjermasin in south Kalimantan (Borneo). This was, again, a new world, much more primitive with its tropical jungles and wide unbridged rivers. Here I visited a variety of ventures, including a Western-owned rubber factory and rubber estate, a Chinese tannery and Hadji Samad's diamond-cutting factory at nearby Martapura which I reached by canoe. In addition, I interviewed businessmen, chiefly Dutch, engaged in rubber and other exporting trades, in importing, banking, insurance, shipping and civil aviation. After Kalimantan, I returned to Java, flying from Bandjermasin to Surabaya, but sad that I did not have time to visit other islands of east Indonesia.

East Java, of which Surabaya was the chief port, had been the centre of the sugar industry, the first large-scale Western economic interest in Java. From Surabaya, I twice went to Pasuruan, where I visited the long-established Sugar Research Station and several factories. In Surabaya, apart from talking with a variety of businessmen, I also visited four big factories and the Dry Dock Company (Droogdock Mij.). From Surabaya, I went to Semarang by train and from there I visited a sugar factory and its sugar gardens and talked to people in the industry. I went on, by road, to two ancient centres of Javanese civilisation which still played a significant part in national life, Jogjakarta and Surakarta, where I visited batikeries and talked to Indonesian businessmen in the batik trade. I gathered information on the effects on local economic life of the destruction of sugar factories during the recent struggle for independence and visited a village where this had occurred. In central Java at that time, Islam did not seem deep-rooted and the influence of earlier faiths such as Buddhism and Hinduism seeped through. However, during the war of independence, a few years earlier, some Moslems attempted to identify Islam with Indonesian nationalism and Moslem extremists had killed ten Dutch Jesuits in that district.

Of course, I went to see Borobudur, the famous partly-ruined Buddhist temple outside Jogjakarta. In those days, there were no tourists swarming around. On the whole vast site, I think I saw only one other person. I sat there for some time, absorbing a scene of calm and serenity, the only sounds being occasional cockcrows.

From Jogjakarta, I flew to Jakarta for a few final interviews there before leaving Java. I saw the manager of the BPM (Bataafsche Petroleum Mij.), a subsidiary of Royal Dutch Shell, whose oilfield in Sumatra I planned to visit. I also made a last, fruitless effort to get an interview at the headquarters of SOBSI, the then-powerful Communist trade union organisation which was reported to have strong backing from Beijing. The leaders of the non-Communist unions with whom I spoke complained of the scanty support they had received from the international free trade union movement.

At the end of May, I left Jakarta, where the Ursuline Convent had been the base from which I travelled round Java, Sulawesi and Kalimantan, and flew to Bangka where I saw some open-cast tin mines worked with dredges and interviewed businessmen in the pepper trade and other branches of commerce. I also visited a pepper garden worked by a Dutch religious brother. From Bangka, I flew to Palembang in Sumatra where I visited

BPM's oilfield at Prabumuli and their refinery at Pladju and had interviews with some of their staff and with the manager of a Dutch trading house.

Then I flew to Padang on the west coast of Sumatra and experienced another of those tremendous switches in scenery and atmosphere from one part of this vast and variegated land to another. Padang was much quieter than the east coast of the island and I enjoyed my stay there. I talked with Dutch and Indonesian importers and exporters and visited a couple of factories. Another flight across Sumatra brought me to Medan – again a major shift in landscape and lifestyle. On the way across, we could see below us the large Lake Toba, with an island in the middle. Medan was much more in touch with the outside world, with Singapore and Malaya and elsewhere. Here I once more talked with staff of British, Dutch and Chinese merchant houses and visited the AVROS Research Station (for rubber and certain other crops) and also a British-owned rubber estate. On 12 June, I embarked on a small steamer for Singapore after an unforgettable but rushed eighty days in Indonesia. I have only once been back to the country – on a brief visit from Canberra to Jakarta many years later – but will always cherish warm memories of it.

After my return to Singapore in mid-June 1952, I had a few more interviews and then went by train to Penang. Here I lodged at the Convent of the Dames of St Maur, whose order I knew in England, and I enjoyed seeing more of this old trading centre which previously I had viewed only on short port stops. At Penang, I had interviews with officials, merchants, plantation estate staff and shippers, and visited a large tin smelter. Then I flew across the peninsula to Kota Bahru in Kelantan, in the relatively undeveloped north east of Malaya. Here I lodged in a "dak bungalow", a government-built rest house for visiting officials and others. In addition to the usual round of talks with businessmen, I also went to a Malay weaving mill, Chinese rubber, rice and timber mills and an Indian match factory. Western businesses had a much lower impact here and it is notable that Kelantan kept the Moslem weekend (Thursday afternoon and Friday) rather than the global Christian one. (Here, the Catholic church held its principal Mass of the week on Friday, which I attended.) From Kota Bahru,

I flew south-west to Ipoh, at that time a rather small and quiet town but an important tin-mining centre with a largely Chinese population where I had interviews with staff of big Western mining companies and smaller Chinese ones. I visited the Perak River Hydroelectric Company's dam and power plant at Chenderoh and also talked to a bank manager.

After Ipoh, I flew on to Kuala Lumpur, the capital of the Federation of Malaya, where I spent a fortnight seeing government officials and many different businessmen. I visited rubber processing factories, a tin dredge, the new Lever Brothers' soap and edible oil factory and, at the nearby town of Klang, the Bata Rubber Shoe Factory and a Chinese factory in the same industry. At Kuala Lumpur, I also had interviews with the Federation of Malaya's Trade Union Adviser and with the General Secretary of the Plantation Workers' Union of Malaya.

Then I flew back to Singapore for a few final interviews and also made another visit to Johore to see the Guthrie Group's oil palm estate at Layang Layang and the United Malayan Pineapple Growers and Canners Ltd.'s factory at Sendai. After seven months strenuous work in South-East Asia, I sailed from Singapore on 7 August 1952, arriving in England on 2 September to sort out everything and to find new accommodation before the academic year began in October.

CHAPTER 8

University College London – Turning to Contemporary China Research: 1953–60

While I had been away in Southeast Asia in 1951–52, Professor Allen had finished going through and re-writing my rough draft of *Western Enterprise in the Development of China and Japan,* and soon it was taken to the publisher. It came out in 1954 and was well reviewed. Meanwhile I settled down to use my interview notes from South East Asia to draft *Western Enterprise in Indonesia and Malaya.*

At this time George Allen was a member of the British government's Monopolies Commission. The American Marshall Plan had included a provision that some of the counterpart funds should be used on research on British industry in the twentieth century, particularly on the relationship, if any, between innovation and the structure and organization of industry. Someone in the Board of Trade suddenly noticed that this item had apparently been overlooked and turned rather desperately to Allen. He called a departmental meeting and put the situation before us, asking if anyone would be willing to take a British industry and study it from this angle. Several of us agreed and were told that funds would be provided for research assistants, and also that we would each get an extra £100 a year on our salaries to compensate for diverting our research plans to make these studies. I was happy to have an opportunity to see something of a British industry, choosing rubber manufacturing because I had been looking into rubber growing. I travelled around the country visiting various factories and other associated institutions and interviewing their staff.[1]

After gathering material and writing it up, I sent copies of what I had written about different companies to them, as I had promised, before sending my manuscript to the publishers. (This is usual when university researchers ask for co-operation from firms and individuals; George Allen and I followed this procedure with the two *Western Enterprise* books.) I had heard considerable criticism of the Dunlop Rubber Company, at that time by far the largest rubber manufacturing company in Britain, as I went around other companies and bodies connected with that sector. My chief judgements on the British rubber industry, however, were those which reflected on the British economy as a whole – first and perhaps foremost, the much larger size of the American market, especially in automobiles, which of course restricts the market for tyres, and therefore also the resources available for innovation in the British industry; secondly, the greater secrecy and lesser willingness in Britain than in America to produce new products, which I suggested might be due to the lesser use in Britain of market research, a practice which reduces the risk of deciding to produce things which turn out to be unwanted. I mentioned several inventions relevant to the rubber industry which had been made in Britain but were not generally accepted here until taken up abroad; but I also noted Dunlop's role in the two main British rubber manufacturing innovations in the twentieth century – latex foam and the combined invention by the firm of both the well-base rim and the tyres to fit it; also, the company's invention of anti-static rubber in 1933. I noted that no private firm could be blamed for the chief reason for the slowness to use synthetic rubber in Britain, which was primarily attributable to an allied strategic decision taken in the Second World War to concentrate the manufacture of that product in the United States. Subsidiaries of foreign companies in Britain had a major part in the initiation of new developments and their introduction into the country and

1 My interview notes for the project are deposited in the library of the London School of Economics and I have not had an opportunity to consult them while writing these memoirs.

these foreign subsidiaries kept the British market more competitive than it would have been without them. I concluded that "little evidence has emerged, in the course of our study, to link innovation with the degree of monopoly or of competition" in the British rubber industry.

Dunlop was not satisfied with what I had written and asked me to come to see them. The company secretary and another person grilled me for some hours. I agreed to make some inconsequential changes of a few words but refused to alter my main conclusions. Dunlop's then wrote to University College to complain. Professor Allen, as head of my department, was informed and he mentioned it rather casually to me, asking me to look over what I had written again, but not to change anything if I did not want to. I made no changes and that was the last I heard of it. University College benefitted considerably from corporate donations but did not rely on them, and was fully able and willing to prevent this consideration from interfering with academic work.

Two subsequent points may be noted. After my *British Rubber Manufacturing* was published in 1958, a review copy was sent to the *Rubber Journal,* the chief British journal on the industry, but no review was to my knowledge ever published, an indication that Dunlop's was willing and able to use its influence to suppress criticism. The second point is from Wikipedia: "Dunlop failed to adapt to evolving market conditions in the 1970s and after taking on excessive debts was acquired by the industrial conglomerate BTR in 1985. Since then ownership of the Dunlop trade names has been fragmented."

Western Enterprise in Indonesia and Malaya was published in 1957 and had good reviews. *British Rubber Manufacturing* appeared in 1958; I was happy with such reviews as it had. When the completion of these two tasks was in sight, I had a tenured appointment as a lecturer at University College and was wondering about my future research. Sometimes, I considered trying to leave academia and enquired about administrative and advisory UN positions in the newly independent African countries, but I heard that there were already too many British appointees and that preference was being given to under-represented nationalities.

On a visit to Oxford, I saw Colin Clark, Director of the Oxford Institute of Agricultural Economics, a famous and controversial economist whom I greatly admired. Colin had liked my Catholic Social Guild booklet on population and resources (see Chapter 10) and asked if I would be willing to come to work with him on these matters. We walked round and round the large grassy space which constitutes Oxford University Parks, discussing this. I was flattered but turned down his suggestion. First, I did not have the mathematics for at least parts of demography. Then, the alternative field of work which I was considering, the contemporary Chinese economy, was badly in need of cultivation. A few economists in the United States and Japan were showing an interest, but no one in Britain. I wanted to know what was happening in Sichuan and in the rest of the country. Journalists had no free access to China and news was scanty. I discussed the matter with Professor Allen and with others in Chatham House and elsewhere, and they were encouraging. I was the only young British economist – perhaps the only young Western economist – with first-hand knowledge of China, so I set my hand to the plough.

I gathered whatever information I could find from people in Britain – Chatham House, the Foreign Office, journalists, business houses, the pro-Beijing "friendship" groups and others. I used to attend the regular monthly China lunches at Chatham House, beginning, I think, in the middle of 1959, which brought together (under "Chatham House rules") those with special interest and knowledge of China from government offices, the press, universities and business. My most knowledgeable contact at the Foreign Office was Martin Buxton, a young diplomat who had been temporarily in charge at the British Embassy, which was then located at Nanjing, at the time when the Communist Army took the city.

In 1957, academic work on the Soviet Union was better developed in Britain than was research on contemporary China, and I soon came to know two excellent and helpful Soviet specialists who were working at the London School of Economics: Alec Nove, an economist, and Leonard Schapiro, a political scientist. I attended their seminars, where a number of prominent international Soviet specialists gave papers. Later, when Alec

Nove left for a chair at Glasgow, Peter Wiles took over from him at LSE to work on Soviet economics and he and I often swapped information and ideas. LSE had no Mainland China specialists but their Sovietologists were interested to know how far Soviet patterns were being transplanted in China and were willing to help me understand those patterns. Victor Funnell, an old friend, who had been working in the Chinese section of the British Broadcasting Corporation, enrolled at LSE to do a PhD thesis in political science on the Chinese People's Liberation Army, with Leonard Schapiro as his supervisor. I was asked to be a joint supervisor to provide support on the Chinese side. Victor's parents had been missionaries with the China Inland Mission in Sichuan and he had been born in the province. Later, Victor and I often met in Australia when he was working at Adelaide and I kept up with him until his death in retirement in Italy. I was a frequent visitor to LSE and had an open invitation to its Senior Common Room which, of course, was an international meeting point for economists, and there I met Friedrich Hayek and other leaders in the field.

The nearest that LSE had to a Mainland China specialist was the anthropologist Maurice Freedman, who had done important work on the multiracial divisions in Malaya and on the Chinese community there and in Hong Kong. He also wrote an interesting book on the Jewish community in Britain. Maurice and his wife Judith became good friends of mine and I kept up with them after I moved to Australia. During the student unrest in the late 1960s, Maurice was on the governing council of LSE and much of the radicals' ire was directed at him because of his critical attitude towards their movement. At the School's Annual Oration towards the end of 1969 (when I was in London on study leave from Canberra), Maurice, among others, was on the platform when rowdy students (or perhaps outsiders masquerading as students) jumped up and took over the meeting. They pinioned Maurice against a wall and it looked as if they might do him violence. I was in one of the front rows and saw and admired his calmness. A few years later, Freedman was given a Chair at Oxford and a Fellowship at All Souls which provided him with a quieter life to carry on his anthropological research, and once I had a very pleasant dinner with him there. When I was visiting England a few months after Maurice's death in 1975, Judith invited me to attend the dedication of his tombstone and also, beforehand, to lunch at their flat together with just herself and the officiating rabbi.

In that era the huge, disjointed, loosely connected Communist bloc in the world threatened and challenged the West to counter its power and influence, while for those researching communist societies the challenge was to understand their methods of operating and ways of life. We were always looking for holes and cracks through which we might observe their workings.

The "Polish Autumn" of 1956, following the "Hungarian Spring" a few months earlier, showed a weakening of Soviet authority in Eastern Europe. The "Hungarian Spring" had enabled a number to escape from behind the folds of the Iron Curtain to the west, but while some of us had tried to help these refugees,[2] there had been no two-way access. However, after 1956, Poles were able to make visits abroad for professional purposes and similar openings were available for Westerners to go to Poland. Responding to this, the Soviet specialists at LSE arranged, under UNESCO auspices, an Anglo-Polish Economics Seminar at the School in September 1957 which I attended. There, I met, among others, Krysztof Rey, an economist from Warsaw. I heard him ask the way to Portman Square and I guessed immediately that he wanted to go to the Newman Association, in the setting up of which the London Poles had played a large part. Recently, at the Newman Association, I had got to know a Polish historian, Marzena Pollak, who it turned out was a good friend of his whom he was anxious to meet (they had once been fellow detainees when a group of Warsaw students was arrested). This was the beginning of my contacts with Poland, to which I made eight visits in the 1950s and 1960s. Others whom I got to know at this conference included Antonina Kloskowska, a sociologist from

---

2 I co-operated with other members of the Catholic Women's League in looking after a young Hungarian architect and his wife and daughter who had escaped to England. Specifically, I helped him draw up his curriculum vitae. Those used to a Soviet-type working environment had no experience of these documents as they just had jobs allotted to them with no choice for either employee or employer.

the University of Łodz and Jozef Nowicki of the Polish Central School of Planning. In later years, I also met again two of the senior economists in the Polish delegation to the conference, Jan Drewnowski (and his wife Jadwiga) and Włodzimiers Brus.

This was the first real tear in the Iron Curtain which had been dividing the world for ten years. Now the way existed for visiting, though guardedly, a Communist-ruled land and talking there freely, in private, with friends. To those of us engaged professionally in trying to penetrate the Iron or Bamboo Curtains (which were long conjoined) this presented both intellectual and emotional opportunities. The Chinese government was adopting institutional economic structures from the USSR and other socialist countries, and so I jumped at any chance to learn how these were functioning anywhere. Also, of course, I wanted to find out how the Church was surviving in these lands. Therefore, as soon as possible after those initial contacts at the LSE conference and at the Newman Association, I resolved to visit Poland.

Next summer, in July 1958, I temporarily abandoned my immersion in the reports spewing out from China that summer, Mao's Year of the Great Leap Forward, of agricultural records being broken by impossibly large margins, and went for nearly a month to Poland. I travelled by train from the Hook of Holland, with a special visa to permit my transiting East Germany to Warsaw, where for the first two nights I stayed in the rather expensive hotel which was all I could book from London; then I was able to move to a cheaper one. The more senior economists I had met at the LSE conference were mostly out of Warsaw during the vacation, but I was able to contact some of those with whom I had made friends and really wanted to see, such as Krzysztof Rey, Jozef Nowicki and Antonina Kloskowska. Also, I had interviews at the Institute of Internal Trade, the Ministries of Internal Trade and of Foreign Trade, and at the Polish Committee for International Scientific and Technical Co-operation.

I had brought with me for gifts as much as I could in the way of tinned and packaged provisions and of Nescafé (a great luxury at that time in Poland), so I felt able to accept the kind invitations to homes of friends, many of whom were scraping to make ends meet. The Rey[3] family, especially, were very hospitable and insisted on my spending most evenings in their cramped flat in Pługa St. Three members of the family worked in government offices and Krysztof, the economist, had a university position. All day they had to bottle themselves up and be careful not to say the wrong thing, especially because they were of a "bad class background" and were also practising Catholics. When they got home, all the frustrations of the day would burst out, often with everyone speaking at the same time. They tended to take a hard line in religious matters, complaining that the Catholic periodicals, the weekly *Tygodnik Powszechny* and the monthly *Znak,* by refraining from trenchant enough criticism of the government, were paying too high a price in order to be published. Their most severe criticism, however, was reserved for the Pax movement which was established by the communists in 1947 to provide a religious veneer to essentially communist policies. Mr Rey, the father, had been in the wartime underground and had a part in transmitting to Britain information about the German experiments that led to the V1 and V2 flying bombs.

When war broke out in 1939, Krysztof Rey had been a sickly child and his mother, fearing for his survival in war-torn Warsaw, had managed to get him to a convent in the Tatra Mountains, where he spent some years in bed and in a wheelchair and was educated by his mother and the Sisters. Later, he gradually improved in health and after the War, as the universities slowly re-opened, he began to study economics.

Poland had some good economists who, under the veneer of Marxism required by the regime, tried to teach Western-style economics. This may have accounted in part for the mathematical bent of Polish economics – few senior Party members could follow such work. Krysztof explained the greater importance of economic theory in eastern Europe than in the west by the fact that a market economy is an organism which does not need a theory while a planned economy is a mechanism which does. Economic planning concentrates on the allocation of scarce resources and this lends

---

3 Later, sometime after the fall of Communism, Krysztof Rey reverted to the old-style family nomenclature of "de Werszowoc Rey".

itself to a mathematical approach; a market economy, depending more on human variables, does not. He said that within the economy the real problem that defied Party discipline was technical restraints. In Poland the technicians, the "know-hows", were the economic group which wielded most power. They had undergone less brainwashing than other groups. The intellectuals were too disorganized; the peasants, too backward and static, were losing their ablest members through upward social mobility. In the past twenty years, he thought that the "esprit de corps" had gone from Polish society except for the Church; and that Polish Catholicism was individualistic.

Krysztof's elder sister, Helena, had her junior secondary schooling in Łwow (then in Poland, now Łviv in the Ukraine), where the family had lived before the war, followed by underground secondary schooling near where her mother and brother were staying in the Tatras. (The German occupying forces had closed all but primary education in Poland.) When the Warsaw Uprising began in 1944, Helena became a nurse in a medical unit and moved casualties through sewers beneath the city. Most of her unit were killed. She was taken prisoner but managed to jump off the train that was moving them to a camp. After the war Helena enrolled in the faculty of law at the University of Poznan, but because members of the resistance were being hunted down by the Russians, it was thought advisable for her to leave the university and lie low. She therefore went home and first worked in a bank and then in the Polish Chamber of Foreign Trade; and later enrolled in part-time external courses. It seemed impossible for Helena to pursue further studies in Poland and she was not qualified to be admitted to a British university. However, it did prove possible to arrange for a private scholarship for her to study for a non-degree Oxford diploma in economics at Plater College (formerly known as the Catholic Workers' College), where she was admitted in 1959 for a two-year course, after which she returned to Poland. She found much stronger left-wing sentiments among her British Catholic fellow students in the College than she had ever come across among her Polish contemporaries and colleagues in a Communist Polish government office at home.

Antonina (Tola) Kloskowska, whom I had met at the LSE conference in 1957, was Director of the Department of Sociology at the University of Łodz, a large industrial town two or three hours from Warsaw by train. She invited me to stay with her and her mother at Łodz. Unlike many of my other Polish friends, Tola was an agnostic, but appreciative of her cultural-religious background; her mother was a practising Catholic. Tola had studied the socio-economic history of Łodz industry where, she said, the factories had often been Jewish-owned, a fact which had given rise to bad feeling towards Jews, but these were the strains of a plural economy such as Maurice Freedman and I had observed in South East Asia (Chinese and locals), not the Nazi type of racism which arose, extraordinarily, in Germany, where Jews were seemingly well-assimilated. Poland, like other Slav lands, for long had almost a caste society – aristocrat and peasant castes (both composed of indigenous Poles) and a Jewish merchant caste. Anti-Jewish feeling was commoner among peasants than among aristocrats; if Jews converted to Christianity, they were assimilated to the aristocracy, which therefore acquired Jewish blood – this probably also contributed to the strong intellectual streak in the Polish aristocracy. In my experience in Poland, there was no anti-Semitism among the aristocratic Reys, in contrast to Jozef Nowicki, who was of peasant stock and had historic gripes about Jewish money-lenders and employers, although totally opposed to Nazi-type racist anti-Semitism.

My next trip from Warsaw was with Helena Rey to Czestochowa, to Jasna Gora, the shrine of the "Black Madonna", the ancient icon reputed by legend to have been painted by St Luke. We travelled by bus through the sunny countryside to reach our destination for the Feast of the Assumption, 15 August 1958. Small roadside shrines, decked with flowers, abounded. The first Mass of the Assumption was to be celebrated at midnight when the famous picture, above the altar, was unveiled. The painting is extraordinarily moving, reflecting all the sorrow of Poland's history, with slight shifting of expression as the light changes. The Cold War was at its height and I was a bit startled, but not shocked, to find that at the altar rails to receive Holy Communion, I was kneeling next to a uniformed officer of a Warsaw Pact army.

In August, harvests were in, so farming people from across the country streamed to the national shrine for the Assumption. The Communist government refused to put on extra trains and buses to facilitate this movement, so groups could be seen walking along the roads towards the shrine. Next day, crowds covered the adjoining mountainside where a youthful priest was preaching. Helena told me that he had a great following among the young and was soon to be ordained a bishop. I did not catch his name, and neither, of course, did I understand his Polish sermon, but he may well have been Father Karol Woytyła.

From Czestochowa I went, on my own, to Krakow where, when I was walking down a side street, a woman ran up to me. She had seen my foreign-looking clothes from a distance and had mistakenly thought I was a friend of hers who had recently returned from abroad. When she found that I was a foreigner and did not speak Polish she switched to English. She gave her name as Teresa Plater and said she was a singer in the local opera company. After a bit, she asked me where I was going and by then I judged it was safe to tell her that I was looking for the office of *Tygodnik Powszechny*, the Catholic weekly. She said the people who ran it were her friends and immediately took me there and introduced me to the editor, Jerzy Turowicz. He very kindly spent some time showing me around the city and talked to me about their problems. At Krakow, I also met and had a long conversation with Professor Stefan Swiezawski, who had a chair in philosophy in the Catholic University of Lublin, to which he commuted from his home in Krakow. Post-war, no philosophy apart from Marxism had been taught in Polish universities, except at Lublin, where philosophy had blossomed. Now the Lublin philosophers had teamed with Professor Adam Scharf, President of the Philosophical Institute of the Academy of Sciences, who was a leading Marxist philosopher but, like many Polish experts in Marxism, with wider sympathies. A joint programme of the two groups had been entered into the official government-approved plan of the Institute of Philosophy. These Krakovians, Turowicz and Swiezawski, whom I was privileged to meet in 1958, have since become known as key members of the *Srodowisko* (milieu) surrounding Karol Woytyła, the future Pope John Paul II. Swiezawski and his wife were very close to Woytyła, who often visited their home and had a major role in the religious education of their children.[4]

Teresa Plater's family had links with Cardinal Sapieha, who was the de facto leader – the inter rex – of the Polish people during the German occupation and the Communist period until his death in 1951. Stories, some of which Teresa recounted to me, abounded about his attitude towards the occupiers. Once, the Nazi commander in Poland, Hans Frank, intimated he would like the Cardinal to invite him to dinner. Sapieha agreed and served each of them one small potato and some ersatz coffee made from acorns – a typical meal for Krakow residents during the war. Another time, a secret messenger from Rome reached the cardinal, with a handwritten letter from Pope Pius XII, deploring and denouncing the treatment of the Poles by the Germans. Sapieha read it once and immediately threw it in the fire, saying that if it fell into the hands of the Nazis they would make it the excuse for another pogrom. His pleas to the Pope about the futility of denouncing atrocities and, indeed, the counter productivity of doing so, are said to have led Pius to desist, for which the Pope was later bitterly criticized. Teresa Plater, who lived with her old mother, had helped some Jews to hide in a hut deep in the forest and brought food to them at night but did not tell her mother for fear that the old lady might inadvertently blurt it out. She was distraught when she found that her mother had written to a friend, "Teresa goes out alone at night; I do not know where or why."

Polish friends had insisted that I should visit the former Nazi concentration camp at Auschwitz, not far from Cracow. When I got there, I was abashed by the banality of it. Perhaps I had expected something wild and terrible. Instead, the camp consisted of dull, low, brick buildings, seemingly designed by unimaginative bureaucrats. Guides took visitors round in different language groups. At that date, most tourists in Poland came from the Soviet Bloc so the languages were usually Slavic and

4 George Weigel, *Witness to Hope,* pp. 95, 130–4.

German. I tagged on to a German group and we slowly walked through the grim place, including a sight of the starvation bunker where St Maximilian Kolbe and his companions died. At the end, we were told to hurry to the station as the last train back to Cracow was about to leave. So there was no time, for which I must admit some relief, to visit the other site, the gas ovens where the actual killings took place. Auschwitz warns of cold, well-organised wickedness, under the banner of *"arbeit macht frei"* ("work brings freedom").

After my 1958 summer visit to Poland, I returned to London and to following the Great Leap Forward in China. Before I could get down to serious work on the Chinese economy, other matters needed attention. My Chinese language skills had grown rusty since I left Sichuan in 1943 and had to be honed. Then I had to link myself to the international network of China-watchers who were trying to penetrate the smokescreen that had been put up to prevent the outside world from seeing what was happening within one fifth of the human race. The best place to accomplish both of these tasks was Hong Kong. I put in for grants to cover the cost of a long visit there. The Ford Foundation was a bit suspicious – young would-be China specialists were often motivated by a political agenda and I was asked how I became interested in China. The interviewer was rather nonplussed when I replied that I had been born there.

A Junior Sinologues Conference was held at Cambridge in September 1959 and there I met a number of Soviet specialists on modern China including M. I. Sladkovski who had written a history of Sino-Soviet trade and was about to publish a work on Chinese commerce with other socialist countries; Julia Berezina, the author of three books on Chinese natural resources and Mr Sucharchuk, a specialist on Chinese agriculture.

In October 1959, I set off for Hong Kong, stopping on the way at Delhi and Bangkok. At Delhi, I saw a few of the Indian China specialists, both officials such as V. V. Paranjpe of the Ministry of Foreign Affairs and also members of the staff of the Indian School of International Studies at Sapru House and others. I went to see St James' Church, a magnificent domed edifice, built by my great-great-great grandfather,

Colonel James Skinner, to fulfil a battlefield vow. One Saturday, I visited the former estate of my grandmother in Gurgaon District, then some miles from Delhi but now, perhaps, part of the city's suburbs, where I met Parshadi Lal, formerly assistant manager of the estate, who took me around. He had summoned a number of old retainers and introduced them, having coached me on the size of tip which should be given to each. It came to be quite expensive! Parshadi showed me the *tappa*, the administrative headquarters of the estate, with the manager's bungalow and other buildings.

In Delhi, at first, I booked in at the Marina Hotel, in Connaught Circus (later, Connaught Place), an old-style hostelry where guests negotiated separately with different providers for each service such as laundry and shoe cleaning. The atmosphere differed greatly from a modern hotel and I found it relaxing. Then I accepted the kind invitation of the parents of my young colleague, Dipak Mazumdar, whom I had met when they came to London for Dipak's wedding, and stayed a few days with them in the official bungalow which they occupied, Dipak's father being a retired senior civil servant. It was the Hindu festival of Diwali and they took me around some of the temples they were visiting. The coincidence, that year, of Diwali, with myriad small lights shining everywhere, and the Feast of All Saints, was strikingly symbolic. From Delhi, I flew to Bangkok, where I visited the headquarters of the Economic Commission for Asia and the Far East (ECAFE) and also met Sir Alexander and Lady MacFarquhar, the parents of Roderick MacFarquhar, who at that time was at the beginning of a brilliant career in modern Chinese politics.

The University of Hong Kong gave me an Honorary Visiting Fellowship in the Department of Economics and I soon also enrolled in one of the University's Chinese language classes where one of my fellow students was David Wilson who many years later became Governor of Hong Kong. Stuart Kirby was Head of the Economics Department and others there included Ronald Hsia and Edward Szczepanik. Edward, his wife Ann and their four children became good friends of mine. He had been in the Free Polish Army, fighting in Italy. At one stage, the Allies were faced with a need to bomb targets in Bologna and it was feared that much damage might be done to cultural treasures, but I heard that Edward devised a complicated scheme by which this was avoided while the Allied objectives were achieved. The Poles, when they reached Rome were greeted by the Polish Chargé to the Holy See, whose diplomatic immunity had enabled him and his family to remain there throughout the war. In Rome, Edward met, and became engaged to, one of the chargé's daughters, Ann. He was discharged in England, studied at LSE and then embarked on an academic career. From Hong Kong, Szczepanik moved to a position in Pakistan with the Ford Foundation and later to the FAO in Rome. I kept in touch with the family over the years, and helped in finding schools for the children. Edward and Ann retired to Lewes in Sussex and then, as a post-retirement job, Edward became prime minister of the Free Polish Government in London that continued for many decades after the war. Once he took me to its handsome headquarters in Eaton Square which he was planning to sell with the intention of providing scholarships for students from Poland to study in Britain. Ann had died a few years before and the children were pursuing careers in England. Edward later told me that when Lech Wałensa came to power in Poland, he was anxious to be seen as the successor to the Polish Government-in-exile in London, not to the puppet Communist government in Warsaw. So Wałensa came to London, where Szczepanik handed over to him the seals of office, and then both went to lunch with John Major in Downing Street. On his death in 2005, Szczepanik was given a state funeral in Poland.

A pleasant surprise was to find that Edmund Blunden, one of my favourite modern poets, was at Hong Kong University as poet in residence at the time and I remember a very enjoyable lunch at his house on the campus. Another notable contact at the University was Henri Vetch, the head of the University Press, who had lived for many years in Beijing as a publisher. He had been jailed for a considerable time by the Communists, making match boxes for long hours on end. It may have been this experience which propelled him into extreme eccentricity. He was a philological freak although an agreeable one, interrupting every few words of a conversation to delve into the derivation of a word he had just used. Another friend I made at Hong Kong University was Margaret Yu, then a lecturer in the Department of English and the sister of Patrick Yu, whom I had known at Oxford and whom I now met again.

The Vice-Chancellor of the University of Hong Kong at that time was Lindsay Ride, an Australian medical man who had been Professor of Physiology there before the war. Escaping from a Japanese prisoner of war camp, he became commander of a small guerrilla unit, the British Army Aid Group, which operated in Japanese-occupied areas in south-east China, near Hong Kong. While in the War Office in 1943–44, I had read the reports put out by this unit, so I was glad to meet Ride and to hear about his exploits first hand.

The Universities Service Centre (USC) in Argyle Street, Kowloon had been established with funding from American sources, primarily, but not exclusively, for academic students of contemporary China. Hong Kong was the chief centre for those wanting information about what was happening on the Mainland of China, which was closed to all but a very limited number of foreigners – only diplomats, severely restricted, a few journalists, similarly circumscribed, and a handful of businessmen; also "friends of China" helped so long as they paid their dues in loyalty and usefulness. Trying to penetrate China's "Bamboo Curtain" was frustrating and the Centre provided invaluable practical as well as intellectual morale boosting – desks for visiting scholars, cheap daily lunches at which visiting academics, locals or resident graduate students would often give informal talks followed by vigorous discussion, frequent lectures and other events, opportunities of meeting others, perhaps more experienced than oneself, working in the same field, with the same problems and the same disheartening circumstances. Snippets of news and gossip could be picked up and mutually evaluated, as well as information on the availability of publications and on the arrival of newcomers from across the border. Hong Kong had sprouted several booksellers specialising in smuggled Mainland publications and I went around them, assiduously buying anything useful I could afford. The Universities Service Centre was headed by a succession of able directors, including a former British diplomat, Joe Ford, and John Dolfin.

A sister organisation, the Union Research Institute (URI), collected probably the best library available anywhere outside China at that date of contemporary Chinese books, journals, newspapers and documents of all sorts, and also set up a cuttings library which could be consulted. Later, it was learned that some of both centres' funds came from the Central Intelligence Agency, but this in no way crimped their style. Many of the younger set of participants in USC's activities were radical, sometimes boisterously so, especially during the Vietnam War, and it was a lively and invigorating place. On at least one occasion, a senior member of the US Government had to be deflected from visiting the Centre for fear of disturbance.

The large US Consulate General in Hong Kong (often referred to, in the long years before the US recognised the People's Republic, as "the embassy that is not in Beijing") was always a valuable source of information and ideas. China experts from the State Department, the CIA and other official agencies were rotated to Hong Kong. With outside academic and other China specialists, there would be genuine if discreet discussion, not just putting out the official line, which would be left to the press department of the consulate. I also visited a number of the other consulates in Hong Kong, many of which at that time had staff members charged with China-watching. The British Foreign Office and other British agencies had staff in Hong Kong among whom was Bernard Kay whom I had known when he was reading Chinese at Oxford and whose wife Teresa was with me at Somerville. They now had three young girls, the eldest of whom, ten-year-old Fanny, was the most observant (or at least the most outspoken) critic of my admitted deficiencies in dress that I have ever had. Before going to see her, I took more care of what I wore than with anyone else I have known. However, she made up for it later by permitting me to continue to use her childhood name of Fanny, while insisting on others addressing her as Francesca. She is now a successful novelist.

A particularly valuable contact in the field of China studies was Father Laszlo Ladany SJ, a Hungarian Jesuit who, after having been expelled from his North China mission, worked for many years in Hong Kong. He brought out, virtually single-handed, a weekly newsletter – *China News Analysis* – which was deeply admired by the more sober China-watchers, while being ignored or attacked by those supportive of Beijing. He also maintained clandestine contact with many Catholics inside China and was sought out eagerly by those, not only Catholics, who escaped to Hong Kong. Then, and at later dates when in Hong Kong, I used to go, after attending the Sunday Morning English Mass at Ricci Hall, to visit him in his room in the Hall's basement. He spent hours listening to Chinese radio news reports and was the most skilled operator anywhere for picking out changing nuances in them. He was foretelling the Cultural Revolution long before other observers of the Chinese scene. His files of information on the Mainland were legendary. Father Ladany was one of the strong individualists whom the Society of Jesus, sometimes with difficulty, is able to accommodate (perhaps Father Jorge Bergoglio, later Pope Francis, is another). Like Father Bergoglio, he was not always at ease with his confrères and tended to live and work apart from them. Most of the Hong Kong Jesuits had thrown themselves into caring for the colony and had a notable part in its revival after the Second World War. Father Ladany's heart was ever with the Catholics on the Mainland, tyrannised by the Communists, whom he had been forced to abandon; and especially with those of the underground. I shared his sympathy for the underground, but because of my personal experience, realised that whether Catholics were above or below ground depended largely on geography, not on the intensity of faith; so on this we often differed. In his youth, he excelled in the violin and might have become a professional concert player; now he said his skill had declined and he would no longer play for others, but "only for the angels".

J. R. Jones, at this time Political Adviser to the Hong Kong Bank, had before the war been the Secretary of the International Settlement in Shanghai and was a depository of all the scandal of the Western community on the China Coast over the last several decades. After 1945, J. R. (as he was widely known – I never learned his Christian names) had performed a very useful service to the Hong Kong Bank by sorting out and finding a solution to the trouble caused by the Japanese wartime administration in Hong Kong issuing notes in the name of the Bank. He was also a recognised arch-druid at Welsh Eisteddfods, and had obviously colourful experiences as some kind of British agent in East Europe at the time of the Bolshevik Revolution, including being present at the famous "Miracle on the Vistula" when the Poles defeated the Russians in 1920. J. R. was planning to write a history of the Hong Kong Bank and at one time asked me to write it jointly with him. However, I wanted to concentrate on present-day China. He had a small but comfortable boat, flying the Welsh Dragon in the South China Sea, on which at weekends he would entertain his friends, including myself, taking them to islands then seldom visited though now in some cases completely built over.

Other Western friends whom I first met in Hong Kong at this time included Michal and Rosie Giedroyc. Mike, who came from a Lithuanian-Polish princely family, had escaped from Poland through the Soviet Union, with his mother and sisters, in an epic journey which he later chronicled.[5] When I met them, he was working for HAEC at Hong Kong Airport. Later, they settled at Oxford where I often enjoyed their hospitality.

To get more opportunity to speak Mandarin, I lodged with a Mainland family not far from the University; their amah's little boy, Zhishan, was a constant source of joy and amusement – I think that I also amused him. In addition, to improve my Mandarin and to get even a sanitised view of the Mainland, I watched as many mainland films as possible; in fact, I went to the cinema more than at any other time of my life. My parents were in Hong Kong for much of my visit and I frequently visited their flat in Kowloon Tong and saw something of their work, including roof-top schools on the resettlement blocks, and the old people's home that my mother opened near Shatin. She took me into the Walled City, which she used to visit regularly. On Sunday afternoons, I used to go to the Maryknoll Sisters at Homantin,

5 *Crater's Edge*, Bene Factum Publishing Ltd., London, 2010.

then a resettlement area, where I helped Sister Maria Regis and others with an "English club" which gave children an opportunity to practise speaking English.

At the time of this and my other early visits to Hong Kong, air conditioning was not widespread and was lacking where I stayed. In the humid heat of a Hong Kong summer, I was too exhausted to do much work after supper. While the city had already become a major financial centre in the 1940s, the introduction of air-conditioning facilitated its growth into a financial and intellectual hub. Without this facility, it would have been difficult to recruit and retain the talent necessary for Hong Kong's development.

Japanese scholars were known to have done a lot of work on contemporary China and I was anxious to learn from them. So from Hong Kong I went to Japan for a month, arriving by sea at Yokohama, having stopped on the way at Hiroshima, where I mourned the unspeakable effects of the first atom bomb. I lodged in Tokyo at the luxurious International House of Japan, a cultural centre which accommodated visitors from abroad, set in a magnificent traditional Japanese garden in the middle of the city.

George Allen had given me useful introductions including to his old friend, Saburo Okita, of the Japanese government's Economic Planning Agency and I saw him and Ayakoto Okozaki, Director of the Bureau's East Asia Economic Research Institute who had made a number of visits to China, including conversations with Mao and Zhou Enlai. At Hitotsubashi University, I met Shigeru Ishikawa and Hideo Yamada with both of whom I continued in contact for many years. Shinkichi Eto of the University of Tokyo I had met at Cambridge earlier at a Junior Sinologues Conference. He had been brought up in Shenyang (then Mukden) and spoke Chinese. He was working on the history of the Chinese Communist Party and its inner conflicts, and on the effect on the Party of the Japanese invasion. Shinkichi was a Presbyterian (Scottish missionaries had long worked in Manchuria) and his interests included the history of Christian missions in China. He was a survivor of the Nagasaki bomb.

Another friend I was able to see again was Yoshio Kawashima, whom I had met in 1952 when we were fellow passengers on a ship from Singapore to England. Now I also met his wife, Toyono, who entertained me at their home. Later they moved for some years to Vienna where Yoshio was the Japanese representative on the board of the International Agency for Atomic Energy; on his return to Japan, he held several senior government positions connected with the atomic energy industry. I did the round of a number of research bodies and libraries, visited the Jesuits' Sophia University in Tokyo and met the recently ordained Father Peter Milward SJ from England. He gave me a beautiful Japanese-style ordination card which he said he gave to Westerners, while reserving a Western type one for Japanese friends – cultural sensitivity has sometimes to be exercised in a complex manner. My interest in the sociology of religion drove me to visit the headquarters of Tenri-kyo, one of the great number of new cults which had recently blossomed in Japan; a curious phenomenon. In addition, I spent a few days in Kobe where I visited Kobe University and met Tadao Miyashita and some of his colleagues and then enjoyed a weekend in Kobe and a day in Kyoto before returning to Tokyo and thence by air to Hong Kong.

In 1959–60, rumours were spreading in Hong Kong about severe hardship on the Mainland and messages reached those with relatives there begging for money or food. Official reports still spoke only of success and progress. Other rumours told of growing dissension between the Chinese and Soviet governments, until then strong allies.

I planned to return to the UK via Moscow, so that I could attend the 1960 Orientalists' Congress to be held there in August. I had hoped to travel by train on the Trans-Siberian Railway which would have been much cheaper. I had long wanted to go by this legendary route, but the necessary visa to travel through China was not given in time. So I had to re-schedule my journey to fly from Hong Kong to Delhi, and then via Tashkent to Moscow. This gave me the magnificent sight of the morning sun rising over the Himalayas and also an interesting two-day stopover in Tashkent before the old city was destroyed by earthquake. The old and new cities of Tashkent belonged to different ages and cultures, the old being Uzbek and the new, Russian. In the old city, outside the mosque before Friday prayers, stood an ancient goatherd, with his flock, selling milk by the cupful. In the Orthodox church, just outside the new city, I met an elderly lady from an aristocratic Russian family with English connections, who spoke English. She told me that a new clampdown on the Church was in progress.

Apart from its formal programme, the 1960 International Orientalists' Congress in Moscow provided a fascinating observation post on both the Cold War and on the burgeoning split between the Soviet Union and China. To confirm the Hong Kong rumours, I asked my Moscow "minder", a Russian post-graduate, if all the expected participants had come. She replied that quite a lot had not arrived and on my asking if all the no-shows were from one country, she just smiled! The non-attendance of the Chinese irked the Soviets but it did not deflect them from their main goal for the event, which was to try to ensure that all future meetings of the International Orientalists' Congress (which, in their view of things, was considered an important tool of soft power) should be held in one part or other of the then Soviet Empire and thus effectively captured. The international participants, through quite a lot of hard work and determination, managed to thwart our hosts' subterfuges and the next congress was scheduled for New Delhi. Twice during this gathering, I experienced a sensation which I have never had before or since, of being drugged. Once, after I had drunk a cup of coffee in a lounge in my hotel, I suddenly began feeling very sleepy and it was only with difficulty that I got back to my room and threw myself on my bed before falling into a deep sleep from which I awoke only a few hours later. The second instance was similar, but not so intense.

In the course of the Congress, I was able to talk to members of the China Section of the Soviet Institute of the Peoples of Asia including G. A. Ganshin, head of the Economics Division of the China Section, while members of its staff took me to the Lenin Library and helped me to buy books. I also met Glunin of the Politics Division of the China Section.

In the two memos which I wrote on my return to England to the Hayter Commission, which had been set up by the Universities Grants Commission to review developments in Oriental, Slavonic, East European and African Studies in Britain, I urged "collaboration as far as possible with Soviet research on modern China. The difficulties are obvious – the strong political bent of the Soviet work and the unwillingness on their side, as yet, to talk freely about China. However, the Soviet research workers may gradually open up if cultivated assiduously and are more likely to respond to British than to American approaches." I pointed out the "lack of persons in Britain who have a knowledge of the Chinese language and a background of Chinese experience and who at the same time are conversant with a branch of the social sciences", that "demand may be expected to rise for such persons as the influence of China impinges more and more on the world at large" and that use should be made of the Chinese Language School at the University of Hong Kong to teach British students. "No amount of study in the West can be a substitute for living in a Chinese environment. At present the most accessible places where this can be done are Hong Kong, Singapore and Taiwan." I recommended that information should be sought of courses in this field in the United States especially Harvard and also of the five-year course at the University of Moscow in Chinese language, history, geography and economics. In a separate memo, I mentioned the urgent need to recruit well-qualified Chinese to supplement British home-grown resources in the field of modern Chinese studies, with assurance about career prospects: "It is believed in the East that Asians are debarred from holding chairs in Oriental Studies in at least one British institution."

The journey from Moscow to London I made by rail and sea, stopping on the way in Poland and in Berlin. In Warsaw, I saw my old friends the Reys, Jozef Nowicki and Tola Kloskowska. Tola had now moved to Warsaw and at her flat there I met Professor Janusz Chmielewski, a philologist who held the chairs of Chinese at both Łodz and Warsaw Universities. I later visited Chmielewski in his department in Warsaw. No one in that university was working on contemporary Chinese society but, as part of the Soviet bloc, they had for years received some periodicals which the Chinese government banned for export to the West. They had some duplicate copies which they did not want and were glad to barter them for subscriptions to Western journals which they had not been able to afford because of stringent limitations on foreign exchange. Also, they were willing to supply photocopies. In this way, I was able to obtain, and then make available to others in the West, a quantity of useful material. The librarian of the Sinology Department was the splendidly named Alexander Macedonski who, I understand, claimed descent from his namesake. I visited, too, the Oriental Institute of the Polish Academy of Sciences where Professor Chmielewski also headed the Chinese Department. While in Warsaw I had an interesting interview with a Mr Lobman who had spent ten years in China as a PAP correspondent, and I met Edward Zakrzewski of the Polish Institute of World Affairs, who was later Polish Military Attaché in Beijing.

From Warsaw, I continued by train to West Berlin which was, in 1960, tightly held by the allied occupation forces, despite Soviet attempts to strangle its economy. I spent a couple of days in Berlin, visiting the Frei Universität which was one of the manifestations of the liberty which distinguished the Western part of the city from its surroundings. I arrived back in London in mid-September 1960, in time to sort things out before the beginning of the new academic year.

CHAPTER 9

China Studies in London and Elsewhere: 1961–68

Now, having returned to London, I got down to the hard work of writing on the Chinese economy. I was very fortunate to find an excellent research assistant, Mrs Tsu-tung Emslie, née Mei, the niece of Professor Mei Yi-Pao for whom I had worked in Chengdu in 1942 when he was Acting Principal of Yenching. Among other duties, Tsu-tung helped shore up my crumbling Chinese and checked extracts from English language sources, such as the radio monitoring reports, with reports in Chinese sources (when we had them), to ascertain correctness in translations. Every bit of information relevant to the economy that penetrated the bamboo curtain between China and the world outside had to be collected and carefully filed. Present-day researchers, with access to digital data storing technology, may not appreciate the effort involved in all of this.

Some of the chief sources of information were these transcripts of monitoring of Chinese radio stations, both national and provincial, put out by the British and American governments. These were published daily and I always read them carefully, if quickly, marking out items to be extracted and filed. At first, I had no photocopying facilities and all extracts had to be copied by hand or in typescript. By filing items on similar topics or places together, sometimes new information could be gleaned and connections made. Then there were such Chinese publications as were available abroad. At one time, these amounted to little more than the *People's Daily* (*Renmin Ribao*) – which Mrs Emslie bound, month by month, into large, cumbersome, brown paper covered volumes, and the *Red Flag* (*Hong Qi*) periodical. Later, the number permitted for export was increased while the ingenuity of smugglers added to our source material. As mentioned elsewhere, from the 1960s, as a result of the Sino-Soviet split at that time, I was able to get hold of more Chinese publications, especially local newspapers, from academic sources in Moscow and Warsaw and by placing subscriptions to Chinese journals in East Berlin. Useful books from the Mainland were almost non-existent and, when I began working on the contemporary Chinese economy in 1957, few books of use had been published in English. Also, I sought out as many business people, journalists, diplomats and others as possible who had visited or had dealings with China, as well as such Chinese who were able to retain links with relatives and friends on the Mainland.

Western academics working on contemporary China had no chance of getting a visa for Mainland China except for a few selected "friends of China" such as Joan Robinson of Cambridge, whose qualifications for the favour were their political stance combined with prior ignorance of the country. When the rest of us applied, we were met by complete silence. In the 1960s, I wrote to the Chinese authorities asking for a "return home permit" (*hui xiang zheng*) such as is given to Overseas Chinese wishing to visit China, saying that I had been born in China and that I am a "national (i.e. ethnic) minority Overseas Chinese" (*xiaoshu minzu huaqiao*). China claims to be a multi-ethnic country so why, I asked, should Overseas Chinese all have to be of the Han race? In the more than half a century since my application, I have never received a reply to my question.

There seemed to be little purpose in researching a minor item in the economy if it was uncertain how it fitted into the larger picture, so I decided that the first thing to do was to get a general overview of the whole. This, I naively imagined, could be done quite quickly, in a matter of months, and I began in 1958. The resulting work, *China's Economic System*, was not completed until November 1966 and published the subsequent year.

I covered the economy sector by sector. Two chapters were devoted to collective agriculture, followed by one on state farms, agricultural machinery "stations" and forestry. Then came a chapter on the conjoined topics of water conservancy and electric power, then chapters on the organization of industry and on industrial labour and management, with another on handicrafts, small-scale industry and urban communes. The next chapters were on mining, on transport and on internal and foreign trade respectively. Then came chapters on state procurement of agricultural produce, on the fiscal system, on banking, currency and credit, on price policy and on economic planning, followed by a concluding chapter to try to pull together various strands. In the last sentences I surmise that "in future years ... new patterns will emerge, but in the long run they will be moulded by economic requirements and not primarily by political desire. For the superstructure of even a Marxist state is not above being shaped by the play of productive forces."[1] Appendices follow, on remittances from Overseas Chinese, on insurance and on State Council offices, ministries and bureaux. The bibliography covered forty-four pages and the index twenty-one pages.

Each time I worked on a new sector, it would throw up fresh information which might compel major, or at least minor, corrections to be made in the earlier sectors, which then had to be re-written. Thus, before the task was ended, I had in fact written most of the book several times over. These were tedious, tiring and rather lonely years, but the compensation was that I felt increasingly close to what was happening in China. This was also of course very distressing, although we did not yet know the full horror of the Mao famine and other tragedies.

The best time for writing, I found, was in the late evening; colleagues had left, the telephones were off and I did not then have to hurry back from the Tottenham Court Road premises to the College to teach a class or attend a departmental meeting. I was able to get down to writing, uninterrupted except for going off to an evening Mass at St Charles Borromeo's in Ogle

1 Audrey Donnithorne, *China's Economic System,* New York: Frederick A. Praeger, 1967, p. 511.

Street or, in later years, at the Chaplaincy in Gower St., followed by a quick supper there or at some other local eatery. Shortly before midnight, I would run off to catch the last inner circle train from Euston Square to Kensington High Street. Crawling cars, slowing when a woman was sighted, infested central London at night; I would stick out my tongue and then hear the glad sound of acceleration. Sometimes I missed the last train and walked home, about five miles. This was especially invigorating during one bitter winter when my snow boots crushed the icy slush. At one time, I used to make a practice of working through the night on Fridays (on Friday nights the cleaners did not come in the night to do our rooms in Tottenham Court Road) and then catch an early morning train home. On these occasions, I heard the horses of the Household Cavalry being exercised along Tottenham Court Road at crack of dawn.

I would come to College rather late in the morning, missing rush hour and getting in around 10 a.m. Like that, I could do household chores before leaving home and find a seat on the underground to read the morning paper. Tsu-tung Emslie, who came in at around 9 a.m., would have dealt with the notes I had left for her the previous night, about checking references and uncertain translations. I would go through the new material that had just come in – the BBC's daily monitoring reports from many Chinese radio stations, national and local, as well as the American daily *Survey of the China Mainland Press,* and also any Chinese journals or other material which had arrived.

Around 1960–61, the School of Oriental and African Studies (SOAS) woke up to the fact that it was doing nothing on the economy of contemporary China and appointed two young economists to be trained in Chinese studies. Cyril Phillips, the Director of SOAS, assured George Allen that he wanted to co-operate with what was being done at University College, so I invited the two new trainee China specialists along for lunch at UCL to find out their plans, expecting to hear that they were going to Hong Kong and/or Taiwan to learn Chinese and to imbibe something of Chinese life. However, they said they were set to learn Chinese in London and then to embark straight away on work on the Chinese economy. I was aghast and may have said so too plainly. I thought of the British tradition of Sinology and studies of Chinese life and culture which had been built up by generations of consular officers, Chinese Maritime Customs officials and missionaries who had lived years in the country before writing about it. SOAS, if short of cash itself, might surely have obtained grants from some foundation to start the new project on a firmer footing.

However, the young men and their seniors at SOAS pushed forward with a rush job on the understanding, so they implied, that rapid promotions would come their way; and so it happened. No doubt I approached the matter undiplomatically and also, I think, George Allen may have been rather naive in his dealings with Phillips – George himself being straightforward even in academic politics, while the SOAS Director was a consummate practitioner of the art. The unofficial motto of a certain famous public school is said to be "make a gent quick", which can be beneficial, but to "make a China specialist quick" is a betrayal of academic integrity.

The first book by one of SOAS's new experts was on the peasants' private plots in Chinese collective agriculture, rightly pointing out that their productivity per unit of land was far higher than in the collective fields. However, it also contained around fifty pages devoted to fertilisers in Chinese agriculture in the 1950s, when chemical fertilisers had hardly begun to be used. (The first chemical fertiliser plant in China opened in 1956.) These pages concentrated on pig manure and did not even mention night soil, an omission which elicited derision from readers who had lived in China. However, on the strength mainly of this book, the author was before long given a chair. A little earlier, both the SOAS China specialists (the above author and his colleague) and then, a bit later, myself (after *China's Economic System* had been completed), had been promoted to readerships in the University.

In 1961, I was invited to give a paper at a conference held by the University of Hong Kong that September as part of the celebrations of its 50th anniversary. I left London on 24 July, stopping on the way for three nights in West Berlin. From there it was possible to get to communist-controlled East Berlin where I succeeded in placing subscriptions to some important Chinese journals to which I could not subscribe directly from London but which the East Berlin agent was willing to forward to me.

From Berlin, I flew to Warsaw and went on to Wrocław to see Maria Łatyk, whom I had met in London when she was taking an English course. She had very much hoped to be able to stay longer in England, and had indeed been accepted as a student by a teacher training college but could not obtain the necessary visa. She overstayed her original visa and was arrested. I visited her in detention but could do nothing to prevent her deportation. Maria had a sad lot. As a girl, she and her mother were forcibly moved from Łwow (Łviv) when it was incorporated into Ukraine (then part of the USSR) and sent to Wrocław, which had been the German city of Breslau before the Soviets shifted Poland westwards after the war. The Łatyks had no relatives in Poland and, when her mother died, Maria was alone in the world with few close friends. She had a dreary room, without its own facilities, in a run-down tenement block and eked out an existence from an ill-paid office job. I stayed at a nearby hotel and spent the intervening day with her. She embarrassed me by plying me with lavish food and drink. I tried to keep in touch with her afterwards, but she fell ill and died a few years later.

While in Poland in 1961, I saw some of my old friends and contacts, including the Reys. I also had a long interview with Pajecka, Director of the Research Board of the Planning Commission of the Council of Ministers. From Warsaw, I flew to Moscow where I spent a day visiting the Institute of the Peoples of Asia, with which I had already formed a link the previous year at the International Orientalists' Congress. I spoke with Glunin and his colleague A. G. Yakovev of the Political Division of the China Section. The Institute of the Peoples of Asia was being reorganized with the establishment of a new Institute of the Economics of Socialist Countries, but some economists, including Ganshin, were to remain in the old institute.

The Sino-Soviet political rift had led to the Moscow researchers receiving fewer Chinese journals and newspapers; the provincial newspapers, for example, were no longer arriving. In 1961, no one from the institute had gone to China and neither were they expecting anyone to go the following year. "So," I remarked to them, "the division is now not between the Socialist camp and the West but between China and the barbarians." "Not quite, but something like that," Glunin replied. I asked them how far they thought China's then current agricultural difficulties were due to bad weather and how far to mismanagement. Glunin hedged his reply by saying the picture was very complicated but that the root of the problem was the general backwardness of Chinese agriculture, especially the lack of mechanization. I asked why China was currently buying grain from Canada and not from the Soviet Union. He replied, "China may think Canadian wheat is more tasteful," and was emphatic that it was not a question of price. I asked their opinion of Chinese statistics and Glunin said China had in the past studied Soviet statistics, "but it is not just a problem of method and organization but of personnel – and some other problems." In reply to my further questioning, he said that they had not had any Chinese statistician come to Moscow to consult with them, and he smiled. A member of the institute accompanied me to the Lenin Library and I checked the catalogue to see the most recent Chinese economic and political journals and newspapers entered in it.

In Delhi, I broke my journey again to accept a kind invitation from our old family friend, Parshadi Lal, to stay at his home in Sihi, a village in Gurgaon District. Parshadi was the chairman of the village *panchayat* (council) and he showed me what the villagers were doing to improve the roads and drainage in the village. He asked me to send him a note, which I gladly did, for him to forward to the government authorities, urging the construction of an approach road to Sihi from the main Delhi-Muttra trunk road. Parshadi was a Brahmin and had to observe certain rules of separation from non-Brahmins, including foreigners. At meals with them, he would eat from a tray on his knees, not from the same table as his guests. Similarly, he had built a comfortable guest room, where I stayed, separate from his house. His elder brother, Jiwan, whom I met, had also been employed by the Ingram Estate, but for years had retired from active work and lived alone in a hut in the fields, absorbed in meditation.

From Delhi, I flew to Hong Kong, arriving so as to have a month before the beginning of the University of Hong Kong Jubilee Conference of 1961. This gave me time to do the lengthening round of China-watchers and institutions, as well as to see my parents and friends. The conference went well, although there was some embarrassment for those of us attending social activities hosted by the Department of Economics, owing to the obvious rift between Professor Stuart Kirby and Edward Szczepanik, the next most senior member of the department, with the professor in the room where the event was being held while Edward was sitting on the steps of the building outside. Harald Munthe-Kaas, of the Norwegian Broadcasting Corporation, was an interesting younger participant. He had rather better access to Mainland China than most other Western Europeans or, of course, North Americans. It was at this conference that I first met Michael Lindsay (Lord Lindsay of Birker) whose name I knew well from my days at Yenching-in-Chengdu after he and his wife Xiaoli had escaped from the original Yenching in Beijing to join the Communist guerrillas in Yenan. Others whom I may have met on this occasion in Hong Kong, or perhaps on later visits to Hong Kong, included a savvy and gallant American couple, Dan and Lois Tretiak for whom I had great esteem – Dan suffered from severe physical deformity, but this did not deter him from being a percipient observer of the Chinese political scene, as was his wife Lois, an African-American who later set up her own consultancy in Beijing. Geoffrey and Colina Lupton also became good friends around this time. Geoffrey was in the Colonial Service and rose to be Commissioner of the New Territories. I visited them once in their splendid mansion in Taipo where Colina, who at one time worked on the *Far Eastern Economic Review*, dispensed hospitality as the First Lady of the New Territories.

In the summer of 1962 there was an economics conference in Vienna at which George Allen had some leading role. I went, and remember a pleasant boat trip with George and Nell Allen and others on the Danube. This visit gave me the only opportunity I have had to see that beautiful city. After the conference, I went by rail to Warsaw where I again met my friends in the University Chinese Department and the Oriental Institute about microfilming Chinese journals, and then went with Krysztof Rey to Zakopane for a couple of days hiking in the Tatras, staying overnight at one of the communal mountain huts, perhaps one of those in which Karol Woytyła lodged on skiing trips with young friends. After that I returned to Vienna, where I met Hubert and Norma Breitenfeld and their two little boys, with whose family I had lived ten years earlier at Northfields, London. Thence I returned by rail and sea to London, after which I buried myself again in the writing of a tediously long book.

In 1963, I was not able to spare time from writing to get to Poland. I went for a SELIPO (see Chapter 11) colloquium in Louvain but do not think that otherwise I went abroad that summer. In the following year, 1964, I again visited Poland, stopping for two nights at Poznan, where my friend Marzena Pollak was now living at home, ill with a tumour on the brain. Then I went on to Warsaw and saw my friends there, and also called at the Chinese Department of the University and at the Oriental Institute. The institute's librarian had been to North Vietnam since I last saw him, and reported that the food situation was very bad. The number of Russian experts in North Vietnam had fallen, but there were still a couple of thousand as well as a number of Poles. However, only one Polish student was still there and none in China as far as he knew.

From Warsaw, during the 1964 summer vacation I went to West Berlin where Martin Buxton, whom I first knew from the Chatham House China lunches, was now attached to the Allied Control Commission. He and his wife Jacqueline had invited me to stay with them. It was always interesting to visit that small enclave, sustained by airlifted supplies while the Soviet authorities, then controlling East Germany, enforced an embargo on goods by surface. I was anxious to talk to Alan Winnington, who from 1948 to 1960 had been the *Daily Worker* correspondent in China and was thought to be the only Westerner who had heard a famous speech of Mao Zedong in which Mao was reported to have said that China need not fear atomic bombs because even if half the population was killed, there would still be many people left. Now Winnington was based in East Germany. He had been threatened in Britain with charges for treason, for allegedly trying to subvert allied POWs during the Korean War, and the Foreign Office had refused to renew his British passport. My host, Martin Buxton, said he had no objection to me contacting Winnington; in fact, I think he was interested in news about him. When I telephoned, Winnington invited me to lunch in his apartment in East Berlin and I went over on the underground as I had done previously to place subscriptions to the Chinese journals which had since been arriving regularly. He confirmed that Mao's speech was as reported, that Mao had said it did not matter if half the population of China perished by nuclear weapons because there would be plenty of people left. Winnington spoke critically of things in China. As for East Germany, he remarked he knew the people detested their rulers, adding "but they deserve it". He seemed intensely lonely and stressed that his loyalty was to the *British* Communist Party. At the end of lunch, he asked what I sensed was a loaded question: "Would you like tea or coffee?" When he left England in 1948, there was still a class differentiation between the two and he may not have realized that this had all but disappeared. I played safe, and said, "Tea".

The accuracy of the report of Mao's speech, with his nonchalance at the prospect of half the population of China being killed by nuclear bombs, is consonant with his apparent indifference to the millions of famine deaths in 1959–61 which could have been averted. It may be debated whether it is worse to be killed out of hatred, as the Nazis murdered the Jews or to be allowed to die because "one does not matter".

The fortnightly China lunches at Chatham House provided a useful venue for discussion and exchanges of information for a relatively select few (the SOAS China economists rarely attended) but I thought there was room for a wider forum. In the autumn term of 1963 I began a Contemporary China Seminar, held on alternate Wednesdays at 5 p.m. in term time. It continued, except when I was out of the country, until the summer term of 1968. At first, it was held in our departmental seminar room. From the autumn term of 1964, it moved to the rooms which Tsu-tung Emslie and myself then occupied, in Tottenham Court Road. This meant that, in the course of the evening, the seminar could be adjourned to the Mortimer Arms on the ground floor, where those who wished could continue the discussion over liquid refreshments and also, if desired, a good pub counter meal. The seminar proved popular, drawing chiefly graduate students and academics from several colleges but also a number of outsiders with China interests.

Seminar paper-givers were drawn from across Britain and also included visitors from abroad as available. In October 1963, the series was started off with a paper by Victor Funnell, then a graduate student at LSE with myself as a joint supervisor (graduate students are useful because they can easily be pressured into giving papers). This was followed by papers by W. A. C. (Ian) Adie of St Antony's College, Oxford, by John Gittings of Chatham House, Ronald Hsia of the University of Hong Kong and Jerome Chen of the University of Leeds. In the next year our paper-givers included Jack Gray and James McIver, political scientists of SOAS, Maurice Freedman of LSE, Conrad Brandt of Berkeley, Hsieh Chiao-Min of Leeds, Stuart Schram, at that time at the Centre d'Etudes des Relations Internationales, Fondation Nationale des Sciences Politiques, Paris, my student John Wong Chiu-Hon, George Moseley of Harvard, and Barbara E. Ward of Birkbeck College. Isaac Deutscher, the biographer of Stalin and Trotsky, opened a discussion on the Sino-Soviet controversy. While basically we concentrated on China, we had a paper on Mongolia from Owen Lattimore of Leeds and one on North Vietnam from P. J. Honey. In 1965, we had papers from, among others, Colonel Wheeler of the Central Asian Research Centre, J. Chinnery of SOAS, Harald Munthe-Kaas of the Norwegian Broadcasting Corporation, Dick Wilson, formerly editor of the *Far Eastern Economic Review* of Hong Kong, Sybille van der Sprenkel of Leeds, Peter Wiles of LSE, Hugh Baker also (at that time) of LSE; Mark Elvin of the Institute of Oriental Studies, Cambridge, opened a discussion. Paper-givers in the following three years (with gaps when I was away for considerable periods) included David Lai of LSE, Derek Waller of SOAS, W. Drew of the Foreign Office Research

Department, Eric Chou, the former editor of the *Ta Kung Pao*, Hong Kong, Rhoads Murphey of the University of Michigan, W. L. Blythe, formerly Colonial Secretary, Singapore (on the topic of secret societies), Mah Feng-Hwa of the University of Washington, Seattle, Coral Bell of LSE, Colina MacDougall of the *Far Eastern Economic Review*, Geoffrey Lupton of the Hong Kong government, Michael Yahuda of the University of Southampton, Kevin Bucknall of SOAS, Aubrey Raymond of Pembroke College, Oxford, Dennis Duncanson of LSE, and Arthur Huck of Melbourne and the Institute of Strategic Studies, London. During the autumn term of 1968, no seminars were held as I was fully occupied with my impending departure for Australia.

Attendance, if my memory is correct, was usually between ten and twenty-five and the discussions were lively, both during the actual seminar and in the convivial gatherings afterwards in the pub. As seen by the list of seminar givers, a wide range of opinion was covered. I think the seminars served a useful function in disseminating information and views on contemporary China and in bringing together a nucleus of people knowledgeable about the situation there. It was certainly one of the most enjoyable episodes in my academic life.

During my years at UCL, in addition to books and my extra-curriculum writings such as the booklet on population and resources for the Catholic Social Guild (not something that could be included in an academic CV), I also published some fifteen articles – two on South East Asia, one on the pan-Communist Council for Mutual Economic Aid, using material derived from interviews in Poland, and the rest mostly on various aspects of the Chinese economy. My focus was on internal trade, economic planning and finance. Professor Allen was trying to help his friend Bill Holland revive the journal *Pacific Affairs* after its problems under Owen Lattimore's editorship during the McCarthy times, and encouraged me to write for it, which I did in 1954 and 1959. In the 1960s the new journal at SOAS, *China Quarterly*, provided an obvious home for articles by British China specialists and I had two pieces there before hostility from the SOAS China economists blocked that opening; but a Sovietologist friend,

Alec Nove, helped and published my two-part article on state agricultural procurement, which had been refused by *China Quarterly,* in his journal *Soviet Studies.*

In 1963 a Centre for Chinese Studies was set up at the University of Leeds, under Owen Lattimore, an American with extensive experience of China and Mongolia followed by a controversial political interlude in the United States. While I never worked closely with him, he built up a lively and important centre at Leeds where I had a number of friends. In 1965 the Leeds Centre hosted its first conference, where I read a paper. This occasion also gave me a last opportunity to see Gladys Scott Thomson, who was dying in a Leeds nursing home, an old friend to whom I am greatly indebted.

Joseph Needham's *History of Science in China* which he edited in many volumes, was another major development in the field of Chinese studies in Britain at this time. I reviewed the volume on agriculture in this series, favourably, if my memory holds. I am aware that Needham has been criticised for the uneven quality of his huge work and also for bias. The concept, however, was praiseworthy, although much more research must be done both in the West, and more especially in China, on the whole subject. The most acute question is why the advances in scientific knowledge did not lead to practical results as in Europe and North America. My own conjecture would be that in China the major immediate reaction to food shortages may have been a rise in infanticide. In eighteenth and nineteenth century Europe, the stronger taboo on infanticide (and abortion) meant that hygienic improvements, and the consequent rise in survival rates, caused more pressure to be put on the adoption of new means of production, as well as on migration and the development of new sources of food in America and Australia. In China, population pressure in the early nineteenth century did of course lead to a migration of people from the North China plain to Manchuria, which soon became a grain surplus region. I would surmise that the large cohorts born in the years after the Mao famine of 1959–61 were a major factor in the breakdown of collective agriculture, and the resumption of private farming, in the late 1970s and early 1980s. This was not initiated by government policy, but like so many of the better trends in China's economic policy, resulted from government recognizing and yielding to the inevitable, accepting (at least de facto) that its role was to ease, not stunt, such transitions. To return to Needham, because his historical work did not directly impinge on mine, while in London I did not meet him. However, in November 1977, on study leave from Canberra, I had a pleasant lunch and talk with him in Cambridge.

In 1965, I paid a brief visit, my first, to the United States, at the invitation of the Association of Atomic Scientists (an organisation with much wider ranging interests than its name suggests), which was holding a Conference on China at the University of Chicago. For the first day or two, the schedule was tight and I did not have time to leave the campus. On the third day, I went outside and found I was in a black ghetto and, on asking my way of a young boy, I could hardly understand his reply. The university campus was a mainly white enclave. Another surprise came when I attended Mass on the Campus. At the "Kiss of Peace", I turned to the nearest person to me and gave the usual greeting "Peace be with you", to which he replied, "Nice to meet you." I did not expect the vernacular in the liturgy to be taken to such extremes.

In addition to the usual closed conference with papers given and discussed, there was a public meeting in the large ballroom of the Hilton Hotel. The topic was, I think, the People's Communes or something similar, and I was one of the speakers. Another speaker was Professor Joan Robinson[2] of Cambridge whose *Economics of Imperfect Competition* was one of the most tiresome books I had to read at Oxford. She had "discovered" China, and its Maoist government appealed to her political sympathies as, a generation earlier, the infant Soviet Union had entranced the Webbs, the founders of the London School of Economics. Joan Robinson was a prominent "Friend of China" whom Beijing welcomed to tour Potomkin units of collective agriculture and other well-prepared sites attesting to the glittering success of an economy which had recently led to the worst famine

---

2 A sister of Michael Maurice, whom I knew well and liked and often met with Pen Piercy, but Joan and Michael were very different.

in human history. Professor Robinson gave a rousing laudatory speech on "communes I have seen", while I read a paper putting together the many fragments of information I had gleaned and scrutinised, drawing tentative conclusions from them. Naturally, it elicited a lukewarm response; an academic discourse is unlikely to arouse enthusiasm from a non-specialist audience. Joan Robinson, however, gave her hearers just what they wanted about a subject of which neither she nor they really knew anything.

Meanwhile, I plodded on with drafting and redrafting *China's Economic System*, with the emphasis on the post-Great Leap relaxations of the economy under the influence of Liu Shaoqi. Colleagues and friends very kindly read chapters in which they might have a special interest and George Allen read every chapter with care and discernment. Some topics required especially careful treatment, notably that of the efficiency or otherwise of food distribution during the years 1959–61, about which we now know much more of the disastrous story, thanks to the works of two Chinese authors, Yu Xiguang: *Dayuejin Ku Rizi: Shangshuji* (2005) and Yang Jisheng: *Mubei: Zhongguo Liushi Niandai Dajihuang Jishi* (2008) and, in English, Jasper Becker's *Hungry Ghosts: Mao's Secret Famine* (1996) and Frank Dikötter's *Mao's Great Famine* (2010). When I took my manuscript to the publishers, in November 1966, many were still denying that anything bad had happened. I knew that that was untrue, but the full extent of the tragedy was still hidden and, despite my suspicions, I was determined not to exceed the facts that I knew, so I wrote:

"Some have claimed that, over the years of scarcity, from 1959 to 1961, the available supplies were fairly spread out over the country so that none actually starved. This has, however, been disproved by the publication of issues of secret military papers of 1961, which tell of numerous deaths among soldiers' families in the disaster areas [reference given]. Also reports coming to Hong Kong from Guangdong province in those years spoke of extreme malnutrition and high death rates from deficiency diseases. 'Non-producers' in cities in various parts of China are also known to have suffered severely. An interim conclusion is that the food situation during the hard years, and even in more prosperous times, has been extremely patchy, that conditions have varied greatly between one part of the country and another, and even from one district to another; that variations from year to year and from season to season have been extensive and, of course, that different categories of consumers have fared very differently. Priority groups – workers in major industries, intellectuals, those in receipt of remittances or food parcels from abroad – had, on the whole, a diet adequate to maintain health throughout the time of shortage. The great coastal cities and the conurbations of Liaoning benefitted from the purchases of foreign grain. Some areas of lesser political and economic importance and untraversed by foreign visitors, experienced much rougher conditions in the hard years."[3]

There were times during those years of writing when I thought the book would never be finished, and that I had set myself an impossible task. Professor Allen also admitted, after it was published, that sometimes he had wondered whether it could be completed. However, finally, in November 1966, I took the manuscript to the Bloomsbury office of the publishers, Allen and Unwin. As well as the English frontispiece, I put in one in Chinese, with the book's title and my Chinese name written by a good calligrapher.

The next week, I left for Eastern Europe, first for a few days in Poland, spending two nights at Poznan, where Marzena Pollak was ill at home, with a tumour on her brain. Her father was the curator of a museum of Polish history in Poznan. Until her illness, Marzena had been teaching Polish history and doing research at the Lublin Catholic University. Her research was centred on the Teutonic Knights, a topic which the Communists used to twist Poland against the West. Marzena set herself to study it as impartially as possible and to write what she discovered. One of her teachers, and later a colleague, had been Karol Woytyła.

After Poznan, I spent a couple of days in Warsaw where, as well as seeing old friends, I met, in the Chinese Department of Warsaw University, Roman Slawinski, whose wife was from Changsha, Hubei province, and some others who told me that few Polish students now wanted to study Chinese. It was felt that there was little future in Poland for Chinese studies

3 Donnithorne, *China's Economic System*, p. 312.

because relations with China were in limbo and they could not publish much about it, either in praise or in criticism. I also called at the Polish Institute of World Affairs whose oriental specialists seemed to alternate between working there and in the Polish embassies in China and Vietnam. We also discussed the supply of Chinese journals.

From Poland, I went on to Moscow, arriving on 16 November 1966 in the middle of a Russian winter, experiencing some of the coldest weather I have ever known. Walking the streets of Moscow, I used to wriggle my nose to prevent it getting frostbitten! I had come on a visit to the Institute of Oriental Studies under the Anglo-Soviet Cultural Agreement. A previous request for such an invitation, made a year or two earlier, had met with a refusal from Moscow; now, with the worsening of Sino-Soviet relations, my visit was acceptable. I gave a paper (I forget the exact topic) at the institute and it was received well on the whole. They took exception, however, to two points. One was when I mentioned that, in some units (and I gave examples from Chinese written sources), the director and the Party Secretary were one and the same person; this, they said, was impossible (it is akin, of course, to having one person as both financial officer of a company and its auditor) and second, strong objection was expressed to my remark that the controlling elite might be weakened by the fact that membership of the Party was often sought from career motives rather than from political conviction. I was able to go through and note down the institute's holdings of Chinese publications, especially journals and local newspapers – these latter were unavailable to us. They indicated that they would be willing to provide copies for scholars in the West. My Soviet hosts also secured me a ticket to the Bolshoi for a notable performance of *Giselle*.

From Moscow, I flew to Almaty (then known as Alma Ata), in Kazakhstan, where I spent a few days. The Soviets, determining to make it an oasis – "the greenest city in Central Asia" as it was known – had filled it with trees, a form of city planning which I strongly approve. There, I was told that, during the "bad years" in China in the early 1960s, some thousands of Uighurs from Xinjiang had crossed the border to the Soviet Union and that they had been re-settled on state farms. I asked to visit some such farms, but was refused. In Almaty, I met some Russians who had lived in North East China until relations deteriorated when they came over the frontier. These were extremely anti-Maoist: "Mao was worse than Hitler," one remarked. During the War, Germans from the Upper Volga region had been resettled in Kazakhstan and these comprised a high proportion of the residents of Almaty and were more sophisticated than the locals. I got into conversation with an ethnically mixed group of women students from the German Department of a local university and the ethnic German girls were horrified when Kazakh students asked me if London was as big as Almaty. In the park, I noticed that local and Western-looking children were playing together; race relations in Almaty seemed quite good. On Sunday, I attended divine liturgy at the Orthodox cathedral (made of wood, if I remember correctly). One of the congregation gave me a holy card of a Russian-style Madonna, while I gave him a rosary. In Almaty, I hired a car and was driven out towards the Altai Mountains (called Tianshan in Chinese), a range that straddles Xinjiang and Kazakhstan, but I was not allowed near the border. It is a fine stretch of country, with huge sloping mountainsides.

The return journey to London I broke for a long weekend in Warsaw, where I saw the Reys and also Professor Chmielewski of the Department of Chinese at Warsaw University. He spoke about the Cultural Revolution in China which he thought had two main objectives: first, it was a war of succession; and second, it was a struggle for ideological continuity in which the Party was hoping to win over the young through the Red Guards and to ensure continuity for at least another forty years or so. In the event, this proved successful for organisational, but not for ideological, continuity.

Having completed the writing of *China's Economic System*, I was also free to accept an invitation to the United States for a visiting professorship at the American University in Washington DC for the first semester of 1967, to take over teaching on contemporary China from Michael Lindsay, who was going on study leave. I had met Michael several times and found him congenial. The Lindsays were still in Washington when I arrived in February 1967 and kindly invited me to stay with them in their home in suburban Chevy Chase until I found a flat, which I did, in New Hampshire Avenue, near Dupont Circle. I was taken aback at the de facto segregation that existed in Washington. In the large block of flatlets where I lived, I do not think I ever saw a black person; but a few streets away, I found myself in a completely black neighbourhood, though otherwise not much different from the nearby middle-class white areas.

At American University, I had more teaching on China than at any other time in my career and there was much more general interest in contemporary Chinese matters than in Britain at that time. Some of my classes were in the evenings; when the students signed up, I invited them to put down their day employment, although I did not insist on this. Most came from a gamut of government departments and agencies, which made for interesting discussions. As well as my students, while in Washington I was of course continuously in touch with more senior China specialists in government offices and at universities in Washington: George Washington, Georgetown (Father Joseph Sebes SJ) and the School of Advanced International Studies at Johns Hopkins; and those, too, at the World Bank.

Two of the most knowledgeable US official China experts whom I met at the time were the Jones brothers, whom I thought of (Welsh style) as "Jones the State" and "Jones the Agency" respectively. I was somewhat baffled to discover the existence of several competing official intelligence agencies, each not keen on divulging their findings to the others. One particularly valuable contact was the economist Wu Yuan-Li (Y. L. Wu, or "Y. L." as he was usually known). I do not think he was already at the Pentagon in 1967, but later he rose to be the Deputy Assistant Secretary there at a time when this was the highest public office ever held by an ethnic Chinese in the States. His work on Chinese energy resources was particularly noteworthy; and then and later I found him a valuable professional discussant. While in Washington I wrote a memo on the Chinese economy to the Joint Economic Committee of Congress and gave evidence before it.

Through mutual friends I met Wong Lin-Ken, the recently arrived ambassador to the United Nations of the Republic of Singapore, newly independent after having been thrown out of Malaysia by the Malay-dominated government. He asked me to introduce him to some of the academic China specialists around and so I arranged a tea party one afternoon at American University (an evening party there, with drinks, was impossible owing to its Methodist affiliation). Wong made a short speech to the assembled group about his new republic, beginning, "When, through no fault of our own, we achieved independence ..."

I also made the rounds of many other centres of China studies in the States, and usually gave seminar papers. These included Chicago, where I attended the Association of Asian Studies Conference; Cornell, where I had the pleasure of seeing my old boss from wartime Yenching-in-Chengdu, Y. P. Mei, and met his son, a professor at Cornell and also John Lewis; the East Asian Centre at Harvard where I met again John Fairbank, John Lindbeck, Ezra Vogel and Dwight Perkins. Wherever possible I made a point of getting to know the China librarians at the major centres of research on China. This proved mutually beneficial when I was able to get hold of microfilms of Chinese journals and newspapers, usually banned from export, through contacts first in East Berlin and then in Moscow.

One difference I came across in academic life in the States compared with Britain was that discussions at seminars were much more aggressive. Participants had to jump in with their comments while others were still speaking, not wait for a pause, as was more usual in the UK. Otherwise, one would end up having said nothing.

In June 1967, after term ended, I flew to Los Angeles and stayed at Santa Monica where I visited the Rand Corporation and also met Barry Richman of the University of Los Angeles. While there, I went inland to Valyermo where the Benedictines whom I had known in Sichuan had, in 1956, made a new foundation. Dom Albéric de Crombrugghe who had been very helpful to me in Chengdu, was one of the founders. He had taken American nationality and with it, a new name, being discontented with his aristocratic Belgian patronymic. The monastery, St Andrew's Priory, occupied a beautiful site deep in the countryside. It was a great joy to see Dom Albéric once more. In addition to him, there were two other refugee monks from Sichuan whom I met there, one Belgian and one Chinese. Both have since died, and also Dom Albéric, but after their deaths, Brother Peter Zhou, having spent decades in prison, was able to leave China, rejoin his community and make his solemn profession, thirty-four years after his simple profession. The monastery has since given rise to an annual arts and crafts festival but still retains an interest in its Sichuan roots. The memories of the monks are treasured in the Diocese of Nanchong.[4]

My next stop was San Francisco and then Stanford University from where I went on to Seattle, giving papers and seeing China-oriented academics, many of whom I had already met either at conferences or in Hong Kong. At Seattle, I stayed with Frederick Brandauer and his wife Marie, with whom I shared an interest in Christianity in China. After that, I went on to Vancouver, my first foray into Canada, where I was welcomed by Bill Holland, the doyen of East Asian studies at the University of British Columbia and an old friend of George Allen. That weekend I was able to spend a day with my cousin Geoffrey Ingram, son of my uncle Robert who, with his wife Elspeth, now lived in Vancouver where he practised as an obstetrician. It was pleasant to see how well he had settled and to meet his young children. They took me to a rousing performance given by the Royal Canadian Mounted Police.

I had taken *China's Economic System* to the publishers before I left England, but as every author knows, that is not the end of the job of getting out a book. Proofs followed me to Washington, which I had to read and correct (it was a work of nearly 600 pages). The index was compiled in London and sent to me; I was not happy with it and re-made it myself – largely, if I remember correctly, late at nights during my rushed tour of California and adjacent parts. I forget where I received the proofs of the final version of the index but it was an immense relief when they were at last dispatched back to the publisher, together with the proofs of the book cover. At the same time, I did my best to keep up with the new material that was pouring in from China about the Cultural Revolution. The daily

---

4 Brother Zhou has published poems he composed and committed to memory in prison (having no writing materials there) as: *The Faithful Dove Flies Against the Wind (A Chinese-English Bilingual Text)*, St Andrew's Abbey, Valyermo, California, 2013.

radio monitoring reports and the *Survey of China Mainland Publications* were mailed to me from London, wherever I was. I read them, marked them up for extracting and filing and returned them to Tsu-tung Emslie. All this brought home the turbulence that was sweeping through China. The grimness of the situation for friends and for the Church there was well understood by all of us who had our ears to the ground but we had no hard facts. In the West, student discontent and political froth was beginning to blow up, although at American University in Washington this had been little evident.

After Vancouver, I flew to Honolulu where I briefly visited and gave a paper at the East-West Center at the University of Hawaii, before going on to Hong Kong which I reached late in July 1967. I spent eight weeks there, going the rounds of the ever-growing community of resident and visiting China-watchers and getting up-to-date with the latest news, rumours and publications. Li Choh-ming, the Vice-Chancellor of the Chinese University of Hong Kong, invited me to lunch at his university as he did whenever I visited Hong Kong during his tenure there. He was the author of a small but excellent book on the Chinese statistical system and was always a valued professional contact. While in Hong Kong, I was also able to see my parents again in their flat in Kowloon Tong. My father, especially, was feeling the weight of his years.

My former student, John Wong, had successfully completed his PhD and had returned home to Hong Kong. Before leaving London, he had firmly told Tsu-tung Emslie and myself that in Hong Kong he intended to look for a traditional Chinese bride. However, it was not long after he returned home that he announced his engagement to Aline, a Hong Kong girl with a PhD from Berkeley! They were married in Kowloon in August 1967 and I was glad to be present. They have lived happily ever after, mainly in Singapore where they have both had successful careers, John as a professor in the University of Singapore and Research Director of the East Asia Institute, and Aline having been at one time in the Singapore Cabinet and, later, the first Chancellor of the Singapore University of Social Sciences.

During this visit to Hong Kong, I went for a day to Macau which had been hard hit by its own offshoot of the Cultural Revolution. I saw the ruins of the British Consulate, which had been sacked. Everywhere there were slogans: "Down with Imperialism", "Down with America" and (near the canidrome!) "Down with Running Dogs". On a church wall, I even observed a daubing, "Down with the Blessed Mother of God", which I thought was one of the strangest fulfilments of her prophesy that "all generations shall call me blessed".

In that summer of 1967, Hong Kong also was disturbed by riots, spilling over from the Mainland's Cultural Revolution. Jack Cater, an able official of the Hong Kong Government who later became Colonial Secretary, was in charge of response to the troubles. Barbara E. Ward, the anthropologist, was in Hong Kong that summer and she was close to Jack and Peggy Cater, whom I also knew, so I was constantly updated on the inside story of the tangled events, by them or by Bernard Kay who was now in Hong Kong. At one time, it was surmised that a leading figure from the Mainland (perhaps even Zhou Enlai) might appear at the Hong Kong border, seeking asylum, and it was debated who would be the best person to interrogate him in depth.

Parvine Razavi, whom I had first known when she was eleven and whom I had taught on that far-off wartime voyage to England, had married an Australian diplomat, Robert Merrillees, now stationed in Cambodia and they invited me to stay with them in Phnom Penh. So from Hong Kong I flew there, first spending a day on my own at Angkor Wat, going around those astonishing remains at a time when very few visitors were present. I hired a tuk-tuk and, with little common language, succeeded in getting the driver to take me round from one site to another, all swathed in forest growth. At each site, on my arrival, an attendant would emerge from nowhere to show me around, again with few words. From Angkor Wat, I flew to Parvine and Robert at Phnom Penh. That weekend they took me for a long drive and a magnificent picnic; drinking chianti in the jungles of Cambodia is one of life's rarer pleasures. However, in the years ahead, I looked back on this occasion with a certain gloom. Memories of that idyllic day were blighted by the horrors that befell Cambodia soon afterwards.

Singapore was my next stop on my journey back to Britain. I had been asked to speak at the Pyramid Club. I also visited the Economics Department at the University of Singapore as well as seeing Anne Wee, the anthropologist I had met some years previously in Hong Kong, and others who were working on aspects of Chinese society. I was able to catch up with two students I had known at Campbell Hall, UCL. Ellen Wong Hee Aik had embarked on an academic career that was to lead to a chair in Biochemistry at Singapore University and Teh Huey-beng was practising as an architect.

Early in September 1967 I went on from Singapore for a fortnight in India, mostly in New Delhi, where I met scholars and officials working on Chinese matters and gave a talk at Sapru House (the headquarters of the Indian Council of World Affairs), where I spoke with S. L. Poplai. I also met R. K. Nehru, a former Indian ambassador to China and a cousin of Jawaharal Nehru, and called at the Ministry of Finance and the Agricultural Price Commission to discuss the differences between India and China in the division of revenues and expenditures between various layers of government and also in farm price policies.

My Aunt Tina (Evangeline) Ingram, my mother's youngest sister, had returned to India after the War and was living in the hill station of Mussoorie, where she had set up and worked in the sanatorium of the Tibetan school which the Dalai Lama established there; my Uncle Robert Ingram having provided most of the funds for the sanatorium. Now, because of age and ill health, she had retired and lived quietly in her bungalow in that mountain town. None of our family had seen her for some time so I was determined to go, although unfortunately I did not have much time. I took a night train, with a sleeper, from Delhi to Dehra Dun where I hired a car up the steep road to Mussoorie. Tina's small house was crowded with some pieces of furniture which I recognised from the Priory, her mother's home in Wimbledon; a large signed photo of the Dalai Lama hung on the living room wall. She was well looked after, with a couple of live-in women servants and a cook and houseboy who lived nearby, but she seemed lonely, not now being able to go out and having few local acquaintances. That afternoon she sent me to pay a quick call on two of her few good friends there, the Terings – the headmaster of the Tibetan school and his wife.

On the street, I saw some nice-looking apples, costing not much more than they would in England, so I bought a bag for Tina who was pathetically grateful and said that normally she could not afford them. I was surprised, considering her household arrangements and reported it back to my Uncle Robert, who managed the family finances; he thought it was just imagined financial anxiety brought on by old age. Our distant cousins, Brigadier Michael Skinner and his wife, lived some miles away, on the road between Mussoorie and Dehra Dun, but they never visited Tina and neither had she contacted them – I think a hangover from the old days, when the darker members of a multi-racial family and the fairer members would keep apart. However, the Skinners had put Tina on the list of people to whom they sold the high-quality eggs produced on their chicken farm, for which there was excess demand, probably because government price regulation may have prevented the raising of prices to permit the functioning of the laws of supply and demand. Next day, I had to leave Tina, regretful that I had not allowed more time to be with her; she died two years later and I was the last of the family to see her. Tina was one of the few in her generation willing to respect our family's links with India.

On my way back to Dehra Dun station, I had arranged to call on Michael Skinner, who was most welcoming. He gave me lunch in his magnificent mansion, Sikander Hall (our common ancestor, Colonel James Skinner, had been known colloquially as "Sikander Sahib"), and then showed me the bungalow a little distance away, near their chicken farm, where he and his wife (who, unfortunately, was away) now lived. The partition of India, at independence, had bitterly impacted the Skinner family. Michael's father went to Delhi railway station to farewell Moslem relatives who had decided to leave for Pakistan. An inter-communal riot broke out at the station, in which some of the departing Moslems were dragged from the train and killed. Michael's father, in despair at what was happening, went home, took a gun, and shot himself. However, Michael's career in the army flourished, he was made colonel of the family regiment, commonly known as Skinner's Horse, and retired a brigadier. A saying at the time on the effect of independence on the Indian Army went "Gurkha officers for Gurkha regiments, and a Skinner commanding Skinner's Horse."

On my return to Delhi, I was able to see another distant cousin, Rosie Skinner, who lived in an old people's home sponsored by the British High Commission. My Aunt May, George Ingram's wife, had known her when George and May were missionaries in India. I also met other Skinners, including a confident young electrician who, I sensed, represented the new Asia with a modern trade at his fingertips.

My last stop on my return to London was at Geneva, where I spent a few days with an old friend from the Newman Association, Eileen Brooke. Eileen, considerably senior to me, was a statistician who had long worked in the UK Department of Statistics and was an expert on the statistics of mental health. She had then moved to the World Health Organisation in Geneva. Father Roger Fox, whom I had known when he was Chaplain to Seamen at Singapore, had returned to his monastery at St Maurice, not far from Geneva, and I was able to fit in a short visit to that beautiful and inspiring centre of monastic life.

Late in September 1967, I returned to London, in time for the beginning of a new term in what was a changed Department of Political Economy at University College. George Allen had retired and no successor had yet been appointed. I was sorry to have missed his retirement dinner but sent a telegram which was read out on that occasion. Also, as my *China's Economic System* was published in October, I had the opportunity to pay tribute to him in my preface. I owe him a great debt. Apart from myself, George Allen was the only person in the department – or indeed I think, in the College – who worked on East Asia. He brought to economics the common-sense approach of his native English Midland business community together with a sympathetic and imaginative understanding of human beings in their variety, whether in Britain, Japan or elsewhere; also an intolerance of ideological waffle. George and his wife Nell, a devoted couple, grievously disappointed at having no children of their own, had opened their home to refugees from Nazi Germany. He was often called on to help with government affairs, during the War in the Ministry of Economic Warfare and, in later years, as a member of the Monopolies Commission.

In March 1968, I attended and read a paper at the International Orientalists Congress in Dublin. At the Congress dinner, I was placed between the British Ambassador to Dublin and the Irish Chef de Protocol. The ambassador's previous posting had been in Jakarta where he won plaudits for calmly walking round the blazing building, playing his bagpipes, as a radical mob burnt down the British Embassy. As a reward, he was moved to Dublin, considered a quiet and pleasant pre-retirement job. He told me that he had little to do and had spent the whole day fishing. He then went on to make a somewhat disparaging remark about the land of his current post. At that, I turned to the charming Irish official on my other side and conversed with him for the rest of the dinner. The following autumn, the "Troubles" broke out in Ulster and I have always wondered if they might have been prevented by greater British watchfulness in the Republic. After Dublin, I visited the Columban Fathers in Navan and then spent a weekend with Ann Power in Bray, Co. Wicklow. I had first met Ann at a retreat, probably at the Cenacle Convent at Grayshott, Surrey. Later, she married Richard Power, an Irish civil servant and spare time poet, some of whose work had been published. He died early, leaving Ann with a family of young children to bring up – and probably before his poetic talent had matured.

The contemporary China economics specialists, and the administration at SOAS, continued their hostility. They were much better placed than myself to bargain with foundations for grants. At around this time, negotiations for China studies with some foundation were under way. Maurice Freedman, now at All Souls, was on the committee dealing with this and he told me that the SOAS representatives were against anything being given for my work; Maurice was able, with difficulty, to secure me a small allocation. I saw that my future did not lie in London. While I had enjoyed my months in America and found it stimulating, I realised that I was temperamentally unfitted for American academic life. Having just completed a major work which was receiving mainly good reviews, I was well placed to look for a new job. At that time, early in 1968, Tom Silcock, who had resigned from the Vice Chancellorship of the University of Singapore, was visiting the Australian National University (ANU) at Canberra, so I wrote to him asking if he had heard of any vacancy there. He handed my letter to Professor Heinz Arndt, head of the Department of Economics in the Research School of Pacific Studies at ANU who was immediately interested and wrote to me suggesting that I should apply for a professorial fellowship in his department as they wanted to begin work on the Chinese economy. I was planning to go to Hong Kong again during the 1968 summer vacation and ANU said it would pay the extra cost of adding on the Hong Kong-Canberra return flights so that I could visit them for an interview. I went, I liked what I saw of ANU and Australia, and, after due procedures, was given the job.

After my Australia visit, I spent a couple of months in Hong Kong, China-watching – getting the latest news of the unrolling of the Cultural Revolution, meeting scholars at the University Service Centre and elsewhere, going the rounds of the consulates and business firms, where now I often had long-established contacts, seeing Hong Kong officials such as Jack Cater, Kenneth Topley (and Margery, his anthropologist wife), and David Wilson whom I had first met when he was a language student at Hong Kong, and later in London when he was at the Foreign Office China desk. He was now Political Adviser to the Governor of Hong Kong. Han Su-yin, the author, whom I had met in the States in 1965, was visiting Hong Kong and I had a chat with her. She said that the Chinese authorities had written to her about the two houses she owned in Beijing and that the proper thing would be to write back giving them to the state; however, she said she would not do that so that when the present troubles subsided, she would still have them. She admired Madame Mao as a feminist icon.

Another new contact made on this visit to Hong Kong was Leo Goodstadt, who had joined the staff of the *Far Eastern Economic Review*;

his Hong Kong born wife, Rose, whom he had met at Oxford, eventually became the Hong Kong government's most senior social work professional. In subsequent years, they both made tremendous contributions to Hong Kong society. They both became and remain my close friends. I do not remember on which visit to Hong Kong I first met Lynn White of Princeton and his wife, Barbara Sue, but it was probably in the 1960s. They often visited the city on his lengthy preparation for a distinguished career as a political scientist writing on contemporary China, notably on Shanghai. Lynn is now a retired professor but, in my mind, he is still "that bright young graduate student"!

I gave a seminar paper in the Department of Economics at Hong Kong University and attending it was a young woman named Olga Kramer from the Far Eastern State University at Vladivostok where she was in the final year of a six-year course in the Department of Oriental Languages. She had a knowledge of Mandarin and, for the third time, had come to Hong Kong as an interpreter on board a Soviet ship, the m/v Grodekovo, which was being repaired in a Hong Kong shipyard. In previous years, Soviet vessels based on Pacific ports had been sent to Dalian or some other Communist Chinese shipyard for major repairs. Now, with the worsening of Sino-Soviet relations, Hong Kong ship-repairing facilities were used instead. This gave the Vladivostok scholars of things Chinese a rare opportunity to explore the academic resources of Hong Kong (as a general rule, Hong Kong at that time did not give visas to Soviet citizens) and in this I was glad to help Olga. I took her to see the Union Research Institute, which impressed her greatly. She was the first student in Vladivostok to study the Chinese economy; her supervisor was a specialist on the economy of Chile and had written on trade between that country and China, which apparently made him the nearest to a specialist in China's economy available. There was no ethnic Chinese teaching the language in her university. In return for my help, Olga invited me to dinner on her ship, followed – I could not understand why, because I had already eaten heartily – by another meal in the dockyard quarters of the two superintendents of Soviet ships at the Kowloon docks.

All this involved lavish and lengthy meals with a wide variety of liquid refreshments, both wines and vodka. I tried to keep contact with Olga, but failed to do so, hearing that she had moved to Moscow.

During the first part of my visit to Hong Kong, my parents were there and I saw them often. My father, though obviously ageing, was well. They had been invited to Korea and decided to go by sea rather than by the more stressful air flight. I saw them off; then on the short voyage, my father had a stroke, so they immediately returned to Hong Kong where he was taken to the Matilda Hospital on the Peak, which at that time had a special arrangement for the care of missionaries. I visited him there and he seemed peaceful and in good spirits. I told him I would be back soon on my way to Australia.

In 1968, once again, I broke my journey between Hong Kong and London at Warsaw, to savour what was happening in the western part of the Communist world. I saw Krisztof and Helena Rey and their family and called on Professor Chmliewski at the Chinese Department of Warsaw University. Helena's time in England at Plater Hall, her improved English and her Oxford diploma in economics had strengthened her position in the foreign trade bureau where she worked and where her bad political background had previously told against her. I made a one-day trip to Poznan to see Marzena Pollak, who was now terminally ill. Marzena died in 1971 and I sometimes invoke her prayers.

I returned to London in September 1968, just in time for the new term, having already sent in my resignation from my readership at the University of London to take effect at the end of the year. That final term is rather a blur in my memory. I gave one of the College's public lunch-hour lectures and various other papers, including one to a graduate seminar at Oxford. I also spent a few days in Paris and in Brussels, giving lectures and seeing China specialists including my old friends the Ruhlmanns, and meeting General J. Guillermaz, an authority on the Chinese army. In those weeks, I also had to say goodbye to many friends, colleagues, family and godchildren, clear out my UCL office and my flat and dispatch most of my possessions, including my books and China files, to Canberra by sea, keeping with me only what I could take by air. I wanted to send change of address notices to my friends around the world, which I planned to do with my Christmas cards.

Then I heard from my mother that my father was sinking. Marian Bowley, at that time acting head of our department, said I could take compassionate leave and go the week before term ended. Pat Ingram, in her usual wonderful and competent way, came to my rescue to get all my packing done and change of address notices sent out, and on 4 December I left London. My mother met me at Hong Kong Airport and said that we should go at once to see my father in hospital which we did. He gently smiled in recognition when he saw me but could not speak. He then lapsed into semi-consciousness until, a week later on 12 December 1968, he died very peacefully with me at his side. The next day, I registered his death and on 17 December his funeral service was held at St John's Anglican Cathedral, before burial in the Happy Valley Colonial Cemetery.

I stayed on for a week in Hong Kong. I had always been much closer to my father than to my mother. She had a tight circle of evangelical missionary friends into which I did not fit and she realised this and it irked her. So I think she was thankful when I arranged to spend Christmas with my old Oxford friends the Kays in Laos, where Bernard was now in the British Embassy. By flying the risky and unpopular Royal Air Lao, a visa was given immediately, while for those who insisted on other airlines, the wait could be long. I spent ten interesting days and a good Christmas in Vientiane with the Kays and their three young girls. The Vietnam War was still being bitterly fought. I was allowed to fly in the embassy plane on a trip covering the Ho Chi Minh Trail stretching through Laos. Then I made a visit on my own to Luang Prabang, the ancient capital, for a short stay over the New Year, and after that returned for another three weeks in Hong Kong and from there flew to Canberra. In Australia, a new lifestyle awaited me.

CHAPTER 10

Extra-Mural Interests – Civic, Religious and Social: 1948–54

My early years at University College were lived against the backdrop of the Chinese civil war and the Communist victory in 1949. My mother was still at Beipei, near Chongqing with her Chinese co-workers. In 1949, some urgent health matters had brought my father to England so he was not there when the Red Army overran Sichuan (of which Chongqing was then a part). My mother was confined to her house for over a year and was frequently interrogated. When asked what she thought of the Communists, she replied that she admired their energy. I was thankful that my father was not there then, because he might not have been so diplomatic! They had already heard how badly some of their friends and others had been treated at the Communists' hands. My mother was not able to get out of China until the summer of 1951, when she was deported to Hong Kong and eventually arrived in England in September of that year. Meanwhile, my father took a short-term position as Anglican chaplain in the Canary Islands.

Before I began working at University College London, I moved to a small attic room in Beaufort Gardens, off Knightsbridge, a part of London I had got to know during the war. Soon I joined the South Kensington Young Conservatives and we were asked to volunteer for some minor local government tasks. I was appointed to the managing committee of a group of North Kensington primary schools, one of which was in what was then a poor area. These appointments were made on recommendation of the local political parties in proportion to their seats on the borough council. The principal duty of the committees was the appointment of teachers, especially head teachers, and there was always a member of the London County Council Education Department staff present at the meetings to guide us and take minutes. The only time when we divided on political lines was once on whether to give the contract to maintain some school gas equipment to the state-owned gas board or to a private company! However, it provided an opportunity to visit the schools quite often and to get to know their problems. Being a school manager also led on to school care committee work. This normally meant being present at the medical examination times of the children and liaising with parents who had not been present. I was not free to come in the daytime, so I was asked to help with a few special cases which could be visited or otherwise handled in the evenings and at weekends. These cases, which were interesting and included both ends of the social scale, I would discuss with the LCC social worker who could be seen out of office hours; and then I might visit the families, if necessary, at weekends.

Apart from these activities, and a bit of canvassing in North Kensington, I did not do much with the South Kensington Young Conservatives. However, Margaret Roberts (later, Mrs Thatcher), then Conservative candidate for Dartford, was once invited to speak. It was thought that she should be given something to eat before the meeting, but the branch had no funds for this (we were all poor in those post-war years). As I knew Margaret, I offered to see she was fed, although I, too, could not afford to take her out for a proper dinner. Instead, on my little plug-in electric cooker on the floor of my attic room, I cooked up an awful meal of stew, which nevertheless seemed to sustain her for her talk, though I have always felt ashamed of entertaining her so badly!

In London at that time there were others of my old Oxford friends. Mary Low was doing a DipEd; I often saw her and through her met Gregory Chan, whose family in Malaya were friends of Mary's parents. Many years later, in Australia and then in Hong Kong, I came to know Gregory and his wife Margaret and family much better. I also visited Mary's family in Hove – I had already met her brother Peter when he cycled up to Oxford from Beaumont School to discuss with the Oxford Jesuits his possible vocation. I was surprised when one day, out of term, I returned to my room in Somerville during the morning and found him there having breakfast. He needed to be fed and Mary's room was (as often) in a state of chaos so she very sensibly put him with his breakfast in my nearby room (perhaps slightly more orderly, but not much) – quite all right by me because we often shared things, but rather a surprise. He became a Jesuit, was ordained and did good work with them, including with their foreign mission promotions in Britain and with rover (senior) scouting. Some years later, while taking some rovers camping in Wales, Peter was tragically drowned in a canoeing accident.

Another old Oxford friend was my former tutor, Helen Makower, who had left Somerville for a readership at the London School of Economics. Pen Piercy now had a senior position in the Ministry of Technology and she remained a constant support whose flat I frequented, as during my years at Oxford. Another old friend from China who turned up was Father Graham Langford, formerly the high Anglican RAF chaplain who had come to Chengdu with the RAF ground crewmen escaping from Burma in 1943. He had since become a Catholic and after a short time in a seminary, had been ordained in the Catholic Church.

Hanny Bijvoet, the Dutch girl who was working in Oxford to learn English, had returned to the Netherlands where the Bijvoets had a substantial bulb-growing business at Haarlem. In the summer of 1949 I went to stay with her large, flourishing, old-style Dutch Catholic family, safe now after wartime troubles; some of the boys had hidden on shelves of bulbs to avoid being conscripted for war work by German occupying forces. The Bijvoets' bulb fields spread over the flat countryside, sprouting a post-war revival of prosperity. Like other Dutch Catholics, they now felt secure, indeed complacent, after centuries of discrimination by their Calvinist fellow-countrymen. "The majority is born," said one of their family friends to me, meaning that now more than half of Dutch infants were being baptised in the Catholic Church. It was a short-lived triumphantilism before a precipitous decline of all Christian practice in the Netherlands, showing that each generation must be evangelised afresh. Moslem immigrants began replacing Christians of all confessions who, largely because of the decline in faith, were not being born. The Bijvoets took me to see the dikes which protect their country and to the Edam cheese market. After leaving Haarlem, I went by myself to other parts of the country, taking in Amsterdam, especially the fine van Gogh Museum, the Arnhem war cemetery, the cathedral at s'Hertogenbosch and a brief visit to Rotterdam.

A year or two later, Hanny visited me in London; then I heard nothing until a letter arrived in 1953 saying that she had married a couple of years earlier, and that since then she had two miscarriages and now was again pregnant; she begged for prayers that this time everything would be all right. Her husband was a thirty-five-year-old widower, with six young children. "So I got six little children at once. We are a very happy family and the children are fond of me." I prayed, as requested, and occasionally wrote but, as no letter came, I eventually gave up writing, realising that Hanny must be very busy. Years later, after I had moved to Australia and was planning a visit to the Netherlands for professional reasons, I tried again. A letter came back to say that Hanny had died two years earlier. "I am Astrid. I am seventeen and I am her eldest daughter." Astrid's father did not know English and had asked her to write. Later, on a visit to the Netherlands, I met Astrid, who was in her third year at university and had an attractive one-room flat not far from Amsterdam University. Then I went to her home, at Bloomendaal near Haarlem, and met her father, who owned a shop which was doing well; and four others of her mother's six children, all of whom seemed to be flourishing, as were her six half-siblings, several of whom were married, one having emigrated to Australia.

Londoners, in the late 1940s, were becoming conscious of West Indian immigrants streaming in from their home islands to take advantage of the many job openings in Britain. Some, indeed, were recruited directly by

London Transport and British Rail. At that time, all the peoples of the British Commonwealth had a right of free movement to and residence in the United Kingdom and I was glad to see them make use of this right to come to what many had been taught to regard as the "Mother Country". This, of course, brought problems; I can remember seeing groups of new arrivals sitting on the pavements outside Waterloo Station and wondered what plans they had in mind. It seemed fitting, however, that, as the old empire wound down, its far-flung peoples should mingle at its capital, as the peoples of the later Roman Empire often sought to come to Rome. At first, at least, the West Indians, in contrast to others, seemed happy, rather than resentful, to claim a relationship to Britain; just as I felt happy that Britain had once been a province of the Roman Empire.

Those immigrants who came as students rather than to seek work posed specific problems. Monsignor Frederick McClement, a retired naval chaplain, had been appointed Catholic Chaplain to the University of London soon after the war. Before long, he realised that his ministry was to be different from what he'd expected. During these years, students from all parts of the world, especially from British colonies, began pouring into Britain and primarily to London, to fulfil a pent-up demand for a higher education that was only beginning to be supplied in their home countries. Many were quite unprepared for life in a strange land and felt desperately lonely on arrival; they needed more and different care, socially as well as spiritually, from that traditionally given by university chaplaincies. Mgr McClement found his time and attention were increasingly distracted from his responsibilities to the mainstream British students in London, and the Cardinal therefore appointed him as full-time Chaplain to Overseas Students in London while Monsignor Gordon Wheeler (later Bishop of Leeds) succeeded him as Catholic Chaplain to London University.

Mgr McClement continued very busily trying to contact the swelling numbers of overseas students. He wrote to the bishops in the main countries of origin, asking them to send him the names of Catholics they knew had come to study in Britain, together, if possible, with addresses and institutions to which they were going, but this took time to produce results and these were only partial. Hostel accommodation was totally inadequate, the newcomers had difficulty finding digs and often met with prejudice, especially the Africans, who were the most numerous. To help him, I joined the committee which Mgr McClement formed. We had to find out where the students were, contact them and put their particulars, especially their ever-changing addresses, on a card index, so that they could be invited to functions, whether spiritual or social, at the Overseas Students Chaplaincy, which now had its own premises. They wanted to meet their fellow countrymen, so some functions had to be held for students from each of the main countries of origin. Most of the students, especially the Africans, were not ready to be assimilated en masse with British students. We appealed to local Catholics to befriend individual students and invite them to their homes and help them find somewhere to live.

The Cold War was breaking out. Official circles became alarmed because the Communists were alert in contacting the overseas students and were notably successful with the first wave to arrive, which included Kwame Nkrumah from Ghana as well as others who later rose to prominence. Sometimes, the Communists were overzealous, as in the case of one student who was permanently alienated from them by being awoken by an eager Party member at six on his first morning, after an exhausting journey to England! A large government-funded hostel (I think run by the British Council) was opened in Hans Crescent, off Knightsbridge, while an official Adviser to Overseas Students (Mary Trevelyan, whom I often found useful) was appointed with an office in Bloomsbury.

Some overseas students were older and more mature. Among these, one whom I got to know was a law student at University College, Benedicto Kiwanuka, who came with his wife, leaving their young children at home in Uganda with extended family. At that time, he was a supporter of the Kabaka of Uganda, who was in exile in London and whose cause aroused vigorous enthusiasm among the Ugandan students there. In later years, when Kiwanuka became prominent in Ugandan politics, they clashed. After being, briefly, the first Prime Minister of independent Uganda, Benito retired from politics and resumed his legal career, rising to be Chief

Justice. Idi Amin, then in power, tried to make him bend the law to suit Amin's tyrannical purposes. Kiwanuka remained firm and Amin had him seized and murdered; according to one account, Amin killed him with his own hands. One day, Benito may be remembered as the Thomas More of Uganda.

Another African law student whom I met was Dilmot Dillsworth, the town clerk of Freetown, Sierra Leone, who had been sent to burnish his legal knowledge at the Inns of Court in London. His wife Jeanne, who came with him, was pregnant and in October 1950 I was asked to be godmother to their son, Dennis.

The year 1950 was a Holy Year and my old Oxford friend, Mary Low and I resolved to go to Rome together for Easter and, because we were short of cash, to hitch-hike there. After crossing to Boulogne, we were standing beside the road, hoping for a lift, when a friendly local came up and insisted on taking us where we could get a free meal – a canteen set up to feed striking Communist dockworkers. That night, we got as far as Paris on a furniture van and, without resting, went on to Switzerland. Then, fearing we would not get to Rome before the Sacred Tridium (the three days of Good Friday, Holy Saturday and Easter Sunday), we took a train. After concluding our pilgrimage and exploring Rome, we went home, by train, via Monaco, where Mary's parents were then living. While staying with them, they packed us off to the Monte Carlo casino, giving us some money to spend there. We duly went, and found a lot of elderly people sitting round a gaming table looking bored, so we left and instead visited the cathedral where we put the money in an offertory box.

Around 1950 my cousin Ilsley Ingram took a research position in Edinburgh and their two elder children, Sarah Jane and Nicola, were born in that city. The first time I met Jane she was in a carrycot on a luggage trolley at London's King's Cross station, early in 1951 when her parents came to show off their beautiful baby to the extended family. Later that year I saw them again when I went up to Edinburgh to give a paper to the British Association for the Advancement of Science, which included a section on Economics (rather unsuitably, according to my views!). One of the gathering's excursions provided me with the only visit down a coal mine I have ever made; this left me with the conviction that mining, at least in the small tunnels along which I crawled, was an unfit occupation for human beings and should be ended, or fully mechanized, as soon as possible.

On another visit to Scotland a little later, I went to see my cousin Tom Ingram, who was in a military sanatorium near Aberdeen. After the war, he had been deployed to the Greek frontier, Conditions there were miserable, with a high incidence of tuberculosis, which he contracted very severely and had to be invalided out of the army. After I had seen Tom, I set off hiking towards the nearest highland youth hostel. On my way, I came across a number of parked vehicles and learned from the attendants that this was an excursion from nearby Balmoral. They said that the royals would soon be back. Sure enough, before long I found myself in the presence of the King (KGVI), followed by the Queen. In his usual kindly manner, the King asked me where I was going and my route. With a rucksack on my shoulder, I managed a somewhat inelegant curtsey!

From time to time I saw something of the Thompson family, with whom I had spent most of my childhood. The infrequency of these contacts did not spring from any unwillingness but from the fact that we were scattered and, for the young, at a particularly busy stage of our lives. Hammy Thompson had left the parish at Southborough, Kent, for a quieter benefice in, I think, Hertfordshire and I visited them a couple of times, once for the baptism of one of his grandchildren. The eldest son, John, qualified as a doctor, married another doctor, Eleanor, and had a country practice in Lincolnshire until his sudden death from a heart attack in middle age. At once time he was in partnership with a son of John Lechler, our old doctor in my childhood days in Sichuan. Tom, the second son, married Marjorie, whom he had first met in Norfolk, and worked for a short spell with an oil company in the Gulf before recycling himself as a teacher. After some experience in England, he emigrated with his wife and young children to New Zealand. I stayed with him and Marjorie a couple of times before they left. The Cold War had begun and he told me that, wherever he was, he feared that if it intensified, he would probably be called up again and he wanted to leave his family in a safer place than England was then deemed to be. The youngest Thompson brother, David had, sadly, been killed in a flying accident in the RAF. Janet qualified as a doctor and married a doctor, Farnham St John; they went to Morocco where they set up a hospital and worked for many years, while bringing up a family of five boys and a girl. I saw her occasionally over the years, but not often. Her mother, Dora Thompson, after Hammy died, went to live with them in Morocco until her death.

When I arrived in Singapore in January 1952 on my research visit to Malaya and Indonesia, I had not only introductions to academics and businessmen, but also to missionaries. The main men's congregation working in Singapore and Malaya was the Paris Foreign Missions (MEPs), and they had laid solid foundations for the Church. Bishop Olçomendy of Malacca (but resident in Singapore which had long supplanted in size and importance the older trading and mission centre in Malay lands) reminded me of his confrères whom I had known in Chengdu ten years previously, with his long white beard and timeless demeanour. Modernity, however, was abruptly intruding on the whole of society after the war, especially on the Chinese, who were more open to the outside world than the Malays: and the returning British colonial officials were anxious to adapt the administration to it. In 1948 the University of Malaya was founded, based in Singapore. The first generation of Chinese immigrants had no time for intellectual pursuits but their descendants had wider interests. These years also saw a Communist insurgency in the jungles of Malaya. To withdraw the rural Chinese population from the control of the guerrillas, the government resettled the scattered Chinese country dwellers in 400 new villages, fenced around and closed at night.

These changes brought fresh challenges and opportunities to religious bodies in Malaya. A few Jesuits, led by Father Patrick Joy SJ, an Irishman and former Provincial of the Jesuits in Hong Kong, had come to Malaya on a temporary basis; the Diocese of Malacca (which at that date comprised the whole of Malaya and Singapore) invited thither some Catholic missionaries who had been expelled from China, but seemed chary of encouraging more to come. Father Joy was in despair at the lethargy of the local diocese to respond to the government's urgent requests to send church workers to live and help in the new villages. The French missionaries seemed incapable of making informal contacts with British officials or to communicate with them in any effective way.[1]

Father Joy felt that the Jesuits, whose own position in the country was not assured, must not be seen to criticise the local diocese but told me that lay people were better placed to do so and that the way would be through the Apostolic Delegate, the papal representative in Britain. As a new Catholic, I knew nothing of all this. Father Joy also deplored the lack of interest about British colonies of the British Catholic laity. He took trouble to help me meet people who could give background information to suggest what the Church should be doing. Notably, he gave me an introduction to Michael Hogan, Attorney General of Malaya, in Kuala Lumpur who, when I was in that city, very kindly invited me to lunch one Sunday, together with the senior British military chaplain. Attorney General Hogan told me that General Templer, the British commander in Malaya during the Emergency, had complained that Catholics were doing little to help in the new villages.

Another policy of the British colonial rule soon drew my attention. The end of the war, as almost always at such times, saw a quick rise in the local birth-rate in Singapore. This set off a Malthusian hysteria and the government took fright, launching a vigorous campaign, with posters all over the city, to promote contraception. One British official whom I interviewed said the he could not cope with the rapidly rising population growth. I also interviewed a Chinese nurse who ran a branch of the Family Planning Association. She had few clients and was not a happy person but, after chatting a bit, it turned out that the chief cause of her unhappiness

---

1 It is difficult now (2018) to realise how different the mindsets of the British were from the French just after the war: now the gap between educated people in Britain and the continent is so much less. It is not only the Chunnel that has invalidated the old British headline, "Fog in Channel: Continent Isolated", and whatever was the equivalent French expression of disparagement of the offshore islands.

was that she had only one son and no other children. The FPA's Singapore literature was holding up a three-child family as the ideal to which it aimed to reduce family size in the city: a couple of generations later, the present Government of Singapore desperately wishes to promote three-child families to prevent depopulation or the replacement of the present inhabitants by immigrants. In Indonesia, a woman Socialist Party Member of Parliament told me that the question of contraception had come up in a discussion group and she feared that its adoption in Indonesia would cause the country to "become top-heavy with old people, like Britain" (like Britain, already in the 1950s).

In Indonesia, missionaries were finding the government of the newly independent country friendlier to the Catholic Church than had been the former Dutch colonial authorities, who were strongly biased in favour of the Calvinists. Local Catholics had been well-represented in the struggle for independence and this also had the support of the mainly Dutch Catholic missionaries, some of whom subsequently took Indonesian citizenship. The Internuncio, Archbishop G. de Jonghe, whom I met, said that "relations between Church and state in Indonesia are the best in Asia." The outstanding figure in the Indonesian Church was Bishop Albertus Soegijapranota SJ, the Vicar Apostolic of Semarang. He was the first Javanese bishop and had been consecrated in the 1930s at a time when there were few Indonesians in public life, and was a personal friend of President Sukarno. The bishop told me that he was eager for Indonesian Catholics to have more international contacts.

The strong connection between the Church and Javanese culture was especially evident in Jogjakarta, the traditional centre of Javanese civilisation. Java did not appear deeply imbued with Islam, which was a relative newcomer to the island, being introduced only a century or two before the first arrival of the Europeans. I did not feel I was in a country of Muslim civilization. The position of women was different, while art showed strong evidence of Buddhist and Hindu influences. From the early twentieth century, the Church in central Java had been embedding itself in Javanese life and culture, in its liturgy and other ways.

This was very evident in a little village called Gandjoeran, about ten miles from Jogjakarta, which I visited. There the mission was originally founded with the assistance of a Catholic Dutch family who had owned a local sugar factory in the village and had run it on lines in accord with Leo XIII's encyclical *Rerum Novarum*, with a workers' union, in the days when such things were very rare in the Indies. Now the Dutch family was gone and the sugar factory was gone, but the church, convent, hospital, orphanage and schools remained and flourished as parts of a completely Javanese Catholic parish and diocese.

There had always been a segment of the independence movement which wanted to equate Indonesian nationalism with Islam. Moslem extremism existed and sometimes became violently manifest, even in central Java as in the killing of ten Dutch Jesuits during the independence struggle. The predominant view of the independence leaders, who included a Catholic, was, however, inclusiveness as embodied in the "Pancasila", which forms part of the Indonesian Constitution,[2] and which listed Christianity among the religions of the country.

Inclusiveness was less apparent in attitudes towards the Chinese minority who had previously been rather close to the colonial rulers. After the Communist victory in China, the new government in Beijing attempted to influence Overseas Chinese communities, especially in South East Asia, although later there seems to have been some back-tracking when Zhou Enlai signed a treaty with Indonesia in 1955, abolishing the jus sanguinis and ending joint nationality for ethnic Chinese there. An extensive system of Chinese schools had grown up in these lands and Chinese diplomacy was directed to staffing them with Mainland Chinese teachers. In Indonesia, a considerable proportion of the Chinese had become Catholic and at this time the Church was struggling to set up Chinese Catholic schools.

Half the Catholics of Indonesia were on the island of Flores, in the eastern part of the country which I did not visit because Western enterprise, the focus of my research, was of lesser importance in that region. Another

---

2 The Pancasila are: belief in God, democracy, humanitarianism, nationalism and social justice.

part of Indonesia which I did not see, except from the air, was the Lake Toba region in central northern Sumatra, where the Church was growing among the Bataks, who had never been Moslem. In contrast, Aceh, in north and north-western Sumatra, where Dutch colonial rule was not strong, has become a centre of militant Islam.

On my return to Britain I contacted Archbishop Godfrey, the Apostolic Delegate and, at his request, sent him a memorandum setting out points about the Church in Singapore and Malaya which Father Joy had made to me. In November 1952, I saw him at the Apostolic Delegation in Wimbledon; he had obviously read my memo carefully and asked sensible questions. I had thought it too delicate to mention, in the memo, that the Attorney General had been my source for the remark of General Templer complaining of Catholic inaction in the "new villages", so Archbishop Godfrey questioned me on this and I was then able to tell him. A few months later, the *Tablet* asked me to write a piece, which I did, emphasising the importance of making the best use of the missionaries who had been expelled from China, as well as the needs of the Church in Malaya and Singapore and the obligation of British Catholics to take more interest in what was happening in British colonies. In the following year or two I gave talks to the Newman Association and others on South East Asia and on economic development and population matters, which were becoming a live topic in Britain, too, in the early 1950s. Father Joy had also indicated that a letter to the Jesuit General, giving my impressions of Church life and work in South East Asia, would not be amiss. So I wrote, stressing the importance of the work of the Jesuits among the growing number of tertiary students in Singapore and in the developing intellectual life there. In reply, I received a kind letter from the General, Father Jansens.

My old friend, Father Paul Crane SJ of the Catholic Social Guild asked me to write the Guild's 1953 Yearbook, on the topic of population and resources, I agreed and produced, in my spare time, a booklet which he entitled, *Is the World Heading towards Starvation?* (I would have chosen a more sober title – but his choice was no doubt better for publicity purposes.) Colin Clark, then Director of the Oxford Institute of Agricultural

Economics and one of the few academic economists writing sensibly, and ethically, on population, gave it a good review in the *Tablet* and, many years later, the American demographer Julian Simon warmly approved of it;[3] but it is not the sort of publication that can be wisely included in an academic curriculum vitae. However, it has given me satisfaction to see how right I have been proved in relation to resources but sad that the population controllers propelled humanity towards the demographic gloom which is likely to overshadow the twenty-first century.

In 1954, I attended the UN Population Conference in Rome, which I remember as being dominated by Gunnar and Alva Myrdal, a Swedish couple of population experts. While in Rome, I lunched with Dr Luigi Gedda, the noted Catholic Action leader, geneticist and expert on twins. At the weekend, I was invited, blissfully contrasting with the conference tensions, to a sunny beach near Rome and a delicious fishy picnic lunch, by Gerda Blau, an old friend of George and Nell Allen whom they had housed when she was a young refugee.

I have retained a great interest in demography and, as already mentioned, once was offered an opportunity to switch my professional work to that field but I have never spent much time on it since the 1960s because of other demands. In 2008 Matthew Connelly of Columbia University's *Fatal Misconceptions*[4] vindicated my criticism of the population controllers of the previous century, both for their coercive ways and for being unnecessary. However, he still approved of the contraceptive methods which made it possible. These methods are now proving to be counter-evolutionary, leading to net reproduction rates below the level needed to sustain population, bringing about a rapid ageing and demographic decline in the societies affected. This is seen in the countries where such methods

---

3 In 1985, I sent Julian Simon a copy of my Catholic Social Guild booklet and in response he wrote: "Your booklet, *Is the World Heading towards Starvation?* is absolutely wonderful. When I think that you wrote this thirty years ago, I am awed. And it still reads very well indeed, requiring no updating, though data which have become available since then certainly would be helpful." Letter, Julian L. Simon to the author, 9 December 1985.

4 *Fatal Misconceptions: The Struggle to Control World Population*, The Belknap Press of Harvard University Press, 2008.

are widely practised – e.g. net reproduction rates of about 1.2 in Japan, Hong Kong, Taiwan and Korea, and of around 1.6 in many Western lands (sometimes higher where there are large immigrant communities who maintain old ways of life, masking an unsustainably low level in the original host population): a rate of 2.1 is necessary for population stability, or perhaps 2.3 in China because of the skewed sex ratio.

If there ever were human or hominid lineages in which natural family planning was easier to practise and did not need strong motivation or self-discipline, these would very likely have had a fertility rate below the reproduction level and therefore they would not have survived. Natural selection would have weeded out such lineages. Natural family planning, just because it is often practiced half-heartedly, without determination or strong motivation (so long as it is combined with a taboo on abortion and infanticide), would therefore seem to be the only method of birth limitation consonant with the survival of the human race. The problems which surround the practice of natural family planning and give rise to scornful criticism of it as being inefficient, are the cause and proof of its evolutionary soundness; it is the failures of natural family planning which enable the human race to survive.[5] In any case, children unwanted at time of conception are usually wanted at time of birth by their natural or adoptive parents and probably even more so in later life.

A few months after I returned to Britain in September 1952, Mgr McClement, Catholic Chaplain to Overseas Students in London, was diagnosed with lung cancer and died in August 1953. A younger priest, Mgr John Coonan, was appointed in his place and did well. He moved his chaplaincy further from University College and was able to employ some staff. So, after helping him take over, and while keeping up with those overseas students whom I already knew or happened to meet, I gradually shifted my spare time activities in other directions.

5 This is supported by the findings of my friends the late Drs John and Lyn Billings on their work with natural family planning in China which are very relevant to this topic. In China, the motivation was strong (failure would be met with forced abortion) and the success rate of natural family planning very high, as high as with the pill. The results of their visits to China have been published only in Chinese specialist journals and should be made available to a wider readership.

CHAPTER 11

More Extra-Mural Interests – Personal, Newman Demographic Survey, Culture Wars and Malta Interlude: 1954–68

The 1950s began as years of hope in Britain. The war had been won; Nazism and Fascism had been overthrown, although the gloom of Communism engulfed eastern Europe. Materially, things were at last improving. In the immediate post-war period, rations had actually become worse and even potatoes were at one time put on the ration; the reason given was that now food had to be found, not only for Britain but also for the continental countries whose agriculture had become run down during the war. Then there came an upturn. I can remember, in Kensington, seeing a queue at a greengrocer's which I quickly joined, as one did at that time, without knowing what desirable item happened that day to be on sale. This time it was oranges and, when my turn came, I asked how many could be bought. To my astonishment, and bewilderment, the answer was, "How many do you want?" It was long since I had considered oranges in this light. Immediately I had to decide how many I could carry home; how many I could eat before they went bad (I had no fridge) and how many I wanted to buy at that price – the consumer economy was being revived.

On my return from South East Asia in 1952, I found digs in Hampstead but as this did not prove very satisfactory, I was glad when a new friend of mine, Mrs Johanne Breitenfeld, asked if I would like to lodge with her family in their house in Northfields, Ealing, in west London. I had come to know Johanne and her husband, Walter, at the meetings of Logos, a discussion group which Walter had founded and which met fortnightly at the Newman Association. I think it was Roland Hill, then at the *Tablet*, who introduced me to Logos and the Breitenfelds. Roland, like the Breitenfelds, was a refugee, he from Germany and they from Austria. Johanne, née Schönborn, was related to Marie Woodruff (née Acton) wife of Douglas Woodruff, then editor of the *Tablet*; Johanne's mother was also first cousin to the morganatic wife of the Austrian Archduke whose murder with her husband's, at Sarajevo in 1914, triggered off the First World War. Walter, much older than his wife and a widower when he married her, had been a civil servant in the old Austro-Hungarian Empire and was devoted to the Hapsburgs. In Vienna, he had founded and chaired a discussion group of Catholics and Jews and it was known that his name was on a list of people the Nazis wanted to arrest. So, on the day of the Anschluss in 1938, Walter managed to slip across the frontier to Yugoslavia. His wife could not go with him because some of their children were away from home but, at the first opportunity, she told the children they were going for a day's river trip and, without taking any luggage to avoid suspicion, turned the key in her front door, left their house full of beautiful furniture and all their possessions, sailed down the river to Yugoslavia and did not return.

Later, the Breitenfelds came to England. Walter, who of course had lost his pension, was too old to get a job but Johanne worked as welfare officer in the Austrian Embassy in London, a position which was often stressful and entailed long hours. Walter stayed at home and did the cooking – delicious Austrian dishes, even if I was often so late back from work that they had to be heated up for me. He also founded Logos as a successor discussion group to that which he had chaired in Vienna. The London Logos met at the Newman Association in Portman Square and consisted partly of refugees, mostly with a Jewish background such as Roland Hill (originally Hess) and Dr F. Elkisch, a psychiatrist and disciple of Jung; but also of English Catholics such as John Dingle, a journalist, and his wife Monica, and myself. This environment gave me a link with the old intellectual traditions of Central Europe.

I enjoyed the couple of years when I lived with the Breitenfelds and their children, Hubert, Elisabeth and Walburga, and especially my friendship with Johanne. Then in 1955, University College circulated the women academic staff with a recruitment notice for the position of Deputy Warden of Campbell Hall, the College's hall of residence for women students (accommodating around a hundred, if I remember rightly), close to the College in Bloomsbury. As my research on Asia now constituted most of my academic work, I did not have much contact with students so this would be a way to fill that gap. The duties at the Hall would not take up much time and would be compensated by the fact that I would no longer have to commute. Also, it would provide me with free board and lodging and no transport costs so I would be able to save quite a bit. I applied for the position and was duly appointed from the beginning of the academic year 1955–6.

The Warden of Campbell Hall was Kathleen Law, an Australian biochemist considerably older than myself. Either she or I would preside at dinner every evening and once a week the meal would be of a more formal nature. Every morning for half an hour, we would take turns to be on duty in the college office to issue "late keys" to anyone wishing to be out after 9 p.m., when the front door would be locked. They were supposed to give a reason for wanting a key but it could be vague – "dinner with friends" or "going to the theatre". If anyone with a late key had not returned and signed the "late book" by 11 p.m., the one on duty had to stay up until the errant girl came in. Once I had to ring the emergency number of the Ethiopian Embassy at midnight when a high-born Ethiopian girl whom I knew had friends there, failed to come back. It turned out she had decided to stay the night with her embassy friends. Postgraduates, of course, were given permanent late keys.

On some evenings, I used to have students to coffee, three or four at a time, to try to get to know them better, giving special attention to those from abroad. At Chinese New Year, I would provide a little money for the Chinese girls to buy the ingredients for a special dinner which they would cook. Some of those whom I came to know at Campbell Hall I have kept up with. Wong Hee Aik went on to a successful career at the University of Singapore, being appointed a professor in the Department of Chemistry at quite an early age. I visited Patricia Carstens (Mrs Koster), another former postgraduate at the Hall, when I went to Vancouver Island where she had married and was bringing up a family. Claudia Carasco (Mrs Johnson), from St Lucia in the West Indies, I later stayed with in Jamaica. She held a senior position as an economist with the Caribbean Commission and I have remained in touch with her and her children. Kay Hunter (Mrs Vadon), some years later when she needed lodgings, stayed in my flat in Kensington for a few months and I have kept up with her. I left Campbell Hall when I went for an academic year to Hong Kong in the autumn of 1959.

By the early fifties contacts with the senior members of my extended family had grown warmer and the aunts whom I had found most difficult were becoming old. At Christmas and sometimes at other weekends, I often went to my Uncle Robert Ingram and his wife Dorothy at their beautiful old house and garden at Claygate, Surrey. Robert and Dorothy were very kind and welcoming and they and Connie, their competent cook and general factotum, fed me well, made me feel relaxed and found me a quiet place to work when they were watching television in the drawing room in the evenings. Their three sons all married Surrey girls. One of their sons, Christopher, like his father a solicitor but not in the family firm, was active in the Liberal Party and became a local councillor. He lived close to his parents and I often saw him and his wife Felicity and their three children, but Robert's other children were widely scattered – Peter and his wife Sheila lived in Lisbon where he was the local manager of a British insurance company, Margaret had gone to Canada as a nurse and then married an Ontario farmer while the youngest, Geoffrey, an obstetrician, practised in Vancouver.

My cousin, Ilsley Ingram, with his wife Patricia and their children, moved from Edinburgh to Claygate, Surrey, not far from Uncle Robert's house, in the 1950s when he took up an appointment in St Thomas' Hospital, London, where both he and Patricia had trained and she had been a ward sister. Their Claygate house was next door to another cousin, Maurice Ingram and his wife Jill, who was also a "Nightingale" nurse from St Thomas' Hospital, and their four children. This brought many of my extended family closer together socially as well as physically and made it easy and pleasant for me to see them frequently. Both families had young children and it was a joy to get to know them as they grew older. Ilsley became a noted specialist in haematology and was eventually given a chair in the subject at St Thomas' Medical School. His wife, Patricia, was a wonderful support, not only for him and their children, but also for the wider family, especially for me. Jane, their elder daughter and Nicola her sister, both in turn became head girls of St Mary's School, Calne but, while being intelligent, were not academically inclined. Jane, after a secretarial training and a Blue-Ribbon cookery course, went on to become a professional social worker and Nicola, a nurse, whose adventurous instincts led her to participate as medical officer in Royal Geographical Society expeditions to tough places, such as Borneo jungles. John Stephen, Ilsley and Pat's son, after Westminster School and King's College London and degrees in biochemistry, joined the VSOs (Volunteers for Service Overseas, a UK official agency) and worked with them as a soil scientist in Nepal and different parts of Africa. Jane, Nicola and John (commonly known as Poss, Hokey and Wid) have been the members of the next generation in the family with whom I have been closest in touch and their later careers will be mentioned below.

My double first cousin Maurice Ingram became a submariner in the navy, retiring as a Lieut. Commander. He later tried to establish a prawn and eel growing business in Somerset, using waste hot water from a local nuclear power plant. In this, he made a name for himself, becoming

Chairman of the Fish Farming Sub-committee of the National Union of Farmers, writing on the topic and once being referred to by the *Guardian* as a "prawnographer". However, Maurice ran into many difficulties and had eventually to sell out to a Norwegian fish farming tycoon who kept him on as manager. When he retired from that he became a Somerset County Councillor in the Conservative interest and Chairman of the County Environment Committee. His children, Caroline, Tom, Liz and Jamie I saw less often after they moved to Somerset where they, and several others of my extended family, lived in the village of Kingston St Mary, near Taunton.

Rosemary, the only surviving child of my Aunt Maud and her husband, John Crofts, who had followed her mother to read law at Girton and then become a solicitor, married another young solicitor, William Vaughan. This solved the problem of the future of the family law firm as Bill entered the firm and, when Robert began to retire, in instalments, took over from him the chairmanship both of it and of the Lambeth Building Society with which the firm had long been involved. Rosemary dropped out for a time while their children were young but kept her hand in by doing voluntary legal work at home for the National Trust; later she resumed work in the firm where eventually a third generation, their daughter Mary Vaughan, also joined them. Indeed, when he grew old, Bill described the firm as being "run like a French restaurant," with the work being parcelled out to different members of the family, including a son who sometimes helped with the accounts. Mary Vaughan (Mrs Hugo Wynn Williams) was the third generation of women lawyers in the family, a fact which was given some publicity. After Bill's death, the firm was wound up; small family firms of solicitors were losing out to huge, often international, competitors. Rosemary's marriage to Bill Vaughan had caused some raised eyebrows in the family because the Vaughans were Catholic and the wedding was according to Catholic rites. Still, Bill had been a fighter pilot in the war, which made him more acceptable and, as Rosemary's mother, my Aunt Maud, remarked, "It might have been worse – he might have been a socialist." Fortunately, Bill was a staunch Tory.

During the 1950s and 1960s I kept in touch with my Dillsworth godson and his family, at least when we were all in England. The parents and little Dennis returned to Sierra Leone when he was still an infant. His father had been born in Liberia but had moved across the border to Sierra Leone where he rose to be Clerk to the City Council of Freetown, an important man in the city, and he returned there to resume his position. After a couple of years, his wife Jeanne came back to London with most of the children. She was a sensible woman with firm principles and was not willing to put up with her husband's irregular ways and behaviour; besides, she wanted to be nearby when the older children were ready for tertiary education in Britain. She bought a large house in London and financed herself by taking in children of fellow countrymen who wanted a good home for their young who were being educated in England.

The three UCL Senior Common Rooms jointly held a children's Christmas party to which members brought their children (and in my case godchildren). It was amazing to observe that various academic figures whom one never would never have suspected of it, suddenly became quite human when accompanied by small progeny. Once or twice, I brought Dennis and his brother Simeon, two years older. Perhaps on the first occasion Dennis was really too young because he began bawling and I had to remove him bodily to the sanctuary of the Women's Senior Common Room. There he continued to yell and threw a heavy metal ashtray across the room. "Poor Dennis, he is tired," I remarked. To this, four-year-old Simeon replied with elder-brotherly hauteur, "Dennis is not tired. It is just that he wants to be naughty."

The eldest Dillsworth child, Florence, was already a teacher in Sierra Leone and went on to become a headmistress and then both Mayor of Freetown during the civil war and a member of the peace committee charged with trying to quell it. I became confirmation sponsor to the youngest daughter, Jeanne, a few years older than Dennis, my godson. In his late teens Dennis went to Sierra Leone to "find his roots". There he was troubled by the social and economic gap between his relatives' servants in Freetown, who were locals from the bush, and his own class, the "colonists" who had returned to Africa from the States; he was even more troubled to find that the servants did not resent this. He returned to England where his academic deficiencies were compensated by his excelling in football. He played in the junior team of a well-known London amateur football club and, for the only time in my life, I checked the football results in the paper! One of his elder brothers, Edward, was the first black footballer to have played in a cup final (also amateur) at Wembley. Their splendid mother, Jeanne Dillsworth, died when Dennis was sixteen. I was abroad at the time but was relieved to learn that an elder brother was keeping a close eye on Dennis and giving him an allowance from the rent of rooms in the property their mother had bought in London.

During the fifties and sixties, I also acquired several new godchildren. Wilfred Corlett, a statistician, and Ann Nicholson had joined our department at University College at the same time as me. A few years later, they announced their engagement. Ann was a Catholic convert and I was asked to be godmother to one of their three children, Clare. Four years later, I was happy to acquire another goddaughter, Charlotte, the eldest child of my old Oxford friends, Peter and Rosalind Bearcroft. A few years later they moved to a large house and garden at Barming, outside Maidstone, where I often visited them. Rosalind was by now a consultant psychiatrist while Peter was an executive of British Rail and at one time the right-hand man of Lord Beeching in his revamping of the British railway system. The newly revived Carmelite foundation at Aylesford was nearby and several times I went there with them, and occasionally made retreats, as an alternative to the Cenacle Convent at Grayshott, Surrey. My earliest visit to Aylesford was soon after its re-opening, when I was accompanied by an American academic visitor to UCL, Mary Dolciani and her mother; Mary was in the early stage of a distinguished mathematical career. I wanted to show them that England was not as pagan as at first sight. Soon, another goddaughter was added, Antoinette, the child of my old friend Parvine, now Helen (née Razavi), the wife of Robert Merrillees, an Australian she met when they were both studying in London, where he was doing a PhD in archaeology. It has been one of life's joys to watch these youngsters grow up, although, unfortunately, for most of the time at a distance.

Optimism in the fifties was especially strong in the Catholic community in Britain. The role of the Christian democracy parties in reconstructing west Europe came as a surprise to the growing number of secularists in England; in fact, the British Control Commission in Germany at first sidelined Konrad Adenauer and did not consider his party, the Christian Democrats, seriously. The re-making of west Europe was led by Robert Schumann of France, Alcide de Gasperi of Italy and Adenauer, all practising Catholics with strong Catholic followings, while a major role in the first beginnings of what was to grow into the European Union was being undertaken by the Belgian Paul-Henri Spaak who, while not religious himself, was sympathetic to the religious movements of the time. Spaak's Catholic daughter married an English diplomat, Michael Palliser, whose sister Brigid was an old Somerville friend of mine. Palliser played a key part in the United Kingdom's accession to what was to become the European Union. These developments gave confidence to British Catholics who now felt themselves no longer an ignored minority but the component of British society which had the readiest understanding and links with the world's wider currents. One of the best contemporary books on the European movement, *Christian Democracy in Western Europe 1820–1953*, was written by my friend Michael Fogarty. However, even in the hopeful 1950s, foreshadowings of the future violent "culture wars" (as they later became known) that marked the rest of the century and beyond, were growing, as I had seen on the population front in Singapore in 1952; also in 1954, when I attended the UN Conference in Rome on Population and Development.

In Britain, a new Catholic professional class was maturing and one manifestation of this was the founding of the Newman Association for Catholic graduates, with a club and office house in Portman Square London. Much of the early initiative for this came from Polish exiles in London, while financial backing was provided by a Dutch Catholic charity. Its club house soon became a centre to which Catholic visitors from all parts of the world gravitated. Phan Quan, a Vietnamese exile, turned up there after the 1954 Geneva Conference on Indo-China, where he said he had been a "people's representative"; he gave me his name card and a picture of Our Lady of Vietnam. His wife had been killed by the Japanese during the war. Now he was opposed both to the French and the communists. He told me that there was no hope for his country, "No hope, no hope." After a short while, he stopped coming to Portman Square and disappeared.

The Newman Association ran regular courses of lectures on theology, scripture, philosophy and other cognate subjects; there were also more general lectures by a wide range of speakers once or twice a week, beside a variety of social occasions and a cheap canteen open every evening. I spent a good deal of my spare time there, or at the Overseas Students Chaplaincy. Particularly, I recall lectures given by Richard O'Sullivan QC on the Common Law, which he depicted as emerging, from Anglo-Saxon England onwards, as people thought out how members of a Christian society should interact; in contrast to Roman Law, based on *"quod principi placuit, legis habet vigorem"* (whatever the head of government wishes, has the force of law), with law coming down from the top. As well as the general activities, the Association gave rise to specialist groups, notably the Newman Demographic Survey, in which I was deeply involved (see below) and the Philosophy of Science Group, led by the physicist Peter Hodgson. The Newman Association usually had a good chaplain who was a great support to all. I remember especially Father Herbert Keldany who held this position for many years and was an early promoter of ecumenism.

Other great changes were taking place within the Catholic body in Britain, even greater than those in British society as a whole. Previously, the centre of gravity for English Catholics had been the north west of the country, especially Lancashire. It was to this area that, in the nineteenth century, the often-famished Irish Catholics had poured in, and also Catholics from the Scottish Highlands and Islands, to man the factories of the industrial revolution and to form the most solid Catholic communities in England of the nineteenth and early twentieth century, sometimes alluded to in London sermons as "the pious Lancastrians". After the

Second World War, the economy of England tipped towards the south east, and from manufacturing to services. It was an era of social mobility. The children of the north English manual working class were better educated, with the coming of mass access to secondary and tertiary education, and many of them were entering professional and other white-collar jobs, so they tended to move south to where these jobs were proliferating. The proportion of Catholics among this demographic sector brought about a considerable change in the composition as well as the size of the Catholic community of southern England.

In addition, after the war, immigration from Ireland grew but it now included a larger number of educated professionals. Ireland had long produced a surplus of doctors and many Irish medical men were already to be found in Britain. Now they were joined by a flood of Irish nurses, teachers and other white-collar workers who could quickly be assimilated into English Catholic parishes. The traditional type of Irish immigration of the previous two centuries also continued, with Irish labour being responsible for much of the rehabilitation of English roads and railways after wartime neglect as well as for rebuilding bombed cities. Without them, post-war recovery would have been difficult. The low birth rates of the inter-war years in England and the disinclination of the better educated young people for these jobs, provided ample openings for the immigrants – as the same factors did in the next half century for immigrants from the West Indies, Pakistan and elsewhere.

The assimilation of the less skilled Irish manual workers into the mainstream of the British Catholic community was slower and more difficult than that of immigrants in the professions. An Irish priest at the time told me that it was thought better to encourage the less educated to keep together in mainly Irish parishes – as for example in Kilburn, north London – so that social pressure would help them maintain the stricter habits of their homeland rather than being infected with what was even then the much laxer sexual mores of the English. The new British National Health Service gave added incentive for unmarried pregnant Irish girls to escape the stigma they felt from neighbours by coming to Britain to have their babies. Once I spoke to an Irish priest in London about this problem and he was furious with me – he implied I had added yet one more to England's wrongs against his land by suggesting that any unmarried Irish girl might ever get pregnant. Yet this was at a time when, in some London parishes, there were weekly appeals from the pulpit for Catholic families to adopt or foster these infants.

Another small, but significant, addition to the Catholic population came from the Poles who settled in Britain, notably in London and in Scotland (where many Polish army units had been stationed). The Polish Government-in-Exile was based in London until Edward Szczepanik handed over the seals of office to Lech Wałensa in 1990. The presence of the Poles, despite their relatively small number, raised the intellectual and social profile of British Catholics and played a significant part in getting the Newman Association, a society for Catholic university graduates, established and securing suitable premises for it in central London.

The celebrations in 1951, to mark the centenary of the re-establishment of the English Catholic Hierarchy, was a demonstration of this new Catholic confidence. The publicity given to it, the large meetings, such as that at Wembley Stadium, the fact that many were emboldened to go around wearing the distinctive Centenary badge, all this seemed to indicate that the Second Spring was warming into early summer. A garden party was held in connection with the celebrations at St Mary's Teachers' Training College (as it then was) at Twickenham, where I had the pleasure of meeting Bishop Joseph Kiwanuka of Uganda, the first indigenous Catholic bishop in black Africa since the days of the early Church.

The pastoral requirements to deal with the increase and changes in the Catholic community, especially in south England, were immense. One of the most urgent needs was for more Catholic schools. The Butler Education Act of 1944, one of the first foundation stones for post-war Britain, passed in 1944 while war still waged, had laid down plans for secondary education for all children. It also stipulated partial state help for the building, as well as the whole recurring costs, of "aided" schools, run by religious bodies, notably the Church of England (which provided many of the village schools throughout rural England), the Catholic Church and the Jewish community. During the discussion on post-war education, concern spread throughout the Catholic community about the future of their schools. I can remember a huge and noisy meeting that filled the Albert Hall, with rows of buses disgorging northern coalminers coming to demand a better deal from the government for Catholic schools. The historic Protestant Non-conformists were never very keen on setting up their own schools and had relied on Sunday schools, the closing of many of which was one of the signs (or causes?) of the steep decline in their parent bodies in the twentieth century.

The Catholic Hierarchy had little idea of the number of Catholic children for whom they should be providing nor where they were, although estimates of these figures were essential for negotiations with the government on the provision and siting of new Catholic schools or the extension of existing ones. Some of us in the Newman Association felt that information on this should be collected and analysed. The leader of this group was Anthony Spencer, a statistician and economist who at that time was employed in the Internal Revenue. Others, included Ronald Barley, an actuary and at one time President of the Society of Actuaries; Eileen Brooke, a statistician working in the government's Statistical Office; an accountant, Niall Roberts; and myself. In October 1953, we decided to set up the Newman Demographic Survey (NDS) of the Catholic community of England and Wales and organised a committee and sub-committees. Anthony himself, who became the director, was by far the most active and undertook the bulk of the work. The first objective of the NDS was to estimate the size and structure of the Catholic population of England and Wales.

The *Directory of the Catholic Church in England and Wales* printed figures each year for the Catholic populations of each diocese. We noted that in some years the figures for a diocese might register an unexpected jump, either up or down, in the size of its Catholic population. These statistical discrepancies in any particular diocesan figures seemed to coincide with changes in the bishop's secretary, one of whose duties was to circulate the parish priests annually to ask for the estimated numbers of Catholics in their parishes, which, of course, could often be little better than an informed guess. The parish clergy knew that these numbers (together with other factors) would be used to calculate the contribution each parish should make to general diocesan expenses. Therefore, the clergy had an incentive to minimise, as far as their consciences would allow, the number of their parishioners. The bishops' secretaries would realise this bias and, to rectify things, would add a figure to make up the total diocesan population. A new secretary would follow this procedure, but might have a different notion of the figure to be added, and this would account for sudden discrepancies.

The education sub-committee of the NDS, consisting of Ronald Barley and myself, was charged with the task of making a census of all Catholic schools in England and Wales in January 1955 with particulars of their enrolments in terms of age, sex and whether or not pupils were Catholic. No list existed of the Catholic schools of the country and no one seemed to know even the definition of a Catholic school. Once, someone informed me that they had come across one in a Welsh seaside town so I wrote to the parish priest about it. He replied saying that the school was indeed owned and run by a parishioner of his, but of the thirty children attending, only three were Catholics and as there was no special provision for their religious education, it could not really be called a Catholic school. From the returns received from the schools, we were able to publish the first census of Catholic schools in England and Wales. From 1959, this census was repeated annually (but by that time my academic work and absences from the country precluded me from participating), until the NDS was wound up in 1964 and the task was taken over by the Catholic Education Board.

On the basis of projections from infant baptism statistics, figures for immigration and emigration and from mortality tables, we made rough estimates of the number of Catholic children of different ages for the next couple of decades and with tentative guesses of the internal movement of the Catholic population, we tried to estimate the number of school-aged children for individual dioceses.

We also tried to work out the effects of different types of education on Catholic children with respect to their later adult practice of their religion. On this, we came to the unexpected, though tentative, conclusion that a grammar school education, even one at a non-Catholic grammar school, was more likely to lead to continuing adult practice than would education at a Catholic non-selective secondary school or just a Catholic primary school; although adult practice was, indeed, higher if the person's grammar school was Catholic. However, our findings tended to show that a higher education, of whatever kind, had a healthier effect on future practice than a scantier schooling. We speculated that this might be because of the habits of discipline and perseverance instilled by more education; leading to the conclusion that much lapsing of young adult Catholics was due to indifference fuelled by laziness and indiscipline rather than deliberate abandonment of the Faith.

However, studying religious statistics and sociology leads to a realisation of the uncertainty and haziness in this field and a need to take into consideration the cultural backgrounds of increasingly mixed populations. For example, the growing immigrant communities in a land such as Australia, with large numbers of a Chinese or Vietnamese heritage, must greatly increase the percentage who describe themselves as of "no religion", but are really rather "with no religious affiliation". They are not indicating they are atheists, and are often with a spirituality, such as a traditional Chinese belief in "heaven", a strong moral force suffusing the universe: they must not be confused with those of a lapsed Christian background.

Because everyone working on the survey was very busy with their own daytime jobs, the whole enterprise was somewhat haphazard. For example, Ronald Barley and I planned to hold brief weekly lunchtime meetings of our sub-committee, but more often than not were unable to do so. I think, however, that the information we were able to gather helped the Catholic Education Board and the hierarchy in their plans and negotiations with government bodies, and laid a basis for more methodical collection and study of church figures in the future. However, the survey became even more chaotic than before as a result of the Suez Crisis in 1956. Anthony Spencer was an officer in the Territorial Army and was immediately called up and sent to Egypt, where he was one of the relatively few casualties. His wounds took a considerable time to heal and he languished in military hospitals. During Anthony's absence, I tried to keep the survey going, but only on a "care and maintenance" basis, as I had no time for more. On his return, differences became apparent, within the committee, on the management and future direction of the survey and several of us, including myself, withdrew. In 1959–60, my visit to East Asia kept me away for ten months and, as far as I can remember, on my return I took little further part in the NDS. Any papers I had about the survey, I deposited in the Catholic Records Office and I have none now that I can consult. Anthony Spencer continued to work in the field of religious sociology and in fact left the Inland Revenue to make a career in the subject at Queen's University, Belfast, and later as a freelancer.

I am not able to assess the difference the Newman Demographic Survey made in the battle for Catholic schools, although I have heard the information gathered was useful in negotiations. However, the great contribution of these schools to civic harmony should be recognised. It may well be that it was largely because of them that, when the "troubles" broke out in North Ireland, there was hardly any IRA activity in England among the second generation of Irish immigrants. Catholic schools provided an atmosphere more conducive to assimilation than would have the more alien, to them, environment of secular institutions. They were shown that those from a Catholic Irish background could blend acceptably and securely with the English people.

A priest from Malta, Father R. Cirillo, enrolled for a MA course in our department at UCL with a view eventually to teaching economics in the University of Malta. As I was the only Catholic on the staff of the department at that time, it fell to me to take him around and introduce him to people. In return, he introduced me to his fellow countryman, Father Dennis Mintoff OFM, who came to London a little later to improve his English. Father Mintoff was a younger brother of Dom Mintoff, at that time the Prime Minister of Malta, who was in constant strife with both the British colonial authorities and the Church. It was a turbulent time in Maltese politics. I was able to find accommodation for the young Franciscan and took him and Father Cirillo to the Newman Association and elsewhere.

Father Mintoff urged me to visit Malta, saying that his sister would gladly put me up. I demurred, thinking that he ought not to promise this on behalf of his sister, who did not know me. Then he returned to Malta and from there wrote to me repeating the invitation and saying that his sister was expecting me soon. I thought that I would very much like to see Malta, especially if I could stay with a Maltese family; however, knowing that the Mintoffs, except for Dom, were not well off, I replied saying I would gladly come on condition that I should be a paying guest.

On my arrival in July 1957, I was met at the airport and told that the Mintoffs had held a family conference and decided that the sister, with whom I thought I was to stay, did not speak enough English, and that it would be better for me to stay with their brother Dom, the Prime Minister, and his wife, an Englishwoman. I was a bit bewildered by this turn of events, but felt happier that evening when I found myself playing games on the floor with the Mintoffs' two daughters, Anne aged eight and Joan, aged six. Dom was always kind to me but I felt somewhat overawed by him – he was rather a force of nature. However, I got on all right with him and, before I left, he asked me to find him an economic adviser. (I later suggested someone recommended by Professor Allen, but nothing came of it.)

Moyra Mintoff, née Bentinck, soon became a firm friend. Moyra and Dom were an unlikely match. Her father, after retiring from the Indian Army, settled in Cheltenham. Patriotic and kind-hearted, the Bentincks had responded to appeals to offer hospitality to students from the empire. Dom Mintoff, studying architecture in England, fell ill and the Bentincks offered to host his convalescence. Moyra helped look after him – and, to the consternation of her family, the two became engaged. The Bentincks were Anglicans but the marriage was by Catholic rites and Moyra was always faithful to her promise to bring up the children as Catholics, even though her husband soon abandoned the practice of his religion.

Duty was the guiding star of Moyra's life. At that date Malta was still a British colony. Dom entered politics and clashed with the British. Around then, the Duke of Edinburgh was posted to a naval position in Malta, accompanied by the young Princess Elizabeth. The royal couple sent an invitation to the Mintoffs. Moyra, following her husband's instructions, dutifully wrote declining what to her must have seemed a royal command.

I went around Malta with the Mintoffs and others and took Anne and Joan for a weekend to a little country hotel. Another day, I visited Gozo, the small neighbouring island, which was famed for the isolationism of its people. An outsider, trying to educate them away from this, once led a group to the top of its highest hill, so that they could see that their island was just a speck in the ocean. They looked down at the island beneath them and the sea beyond, and exclaimed: "Isn't Gozo big!" I was kindly given a tour of Gozo by a member of a British family, the Stricklands, who were long established there.

Father Cirillo told me that, while in Malta, I ought to call on Archbishop Gonzi, which I willingly did. At that time, Dom Mintoff was in conflict with the Church. The Archbishop realised it was thanks to Moyra that the children were being brought up as Catholics, and he appreciated this. When I came to his residence, I found crowds and crowds of obviously poor people, mainly women and children, rather casually pouring in and out. It was apparently where everyone went with their troubles, whether material or spiritual. I noticed that when a priest was walking along a street, children would run up to him asking a blessing. The Church was clearly and naturally bound up with everyday life.

Before long, the Mintoff girls were sent to school in England and were based at their grandmother's home in Cheltenham. Sometimes, when going to Malta, they would stay with me for a night, being fetched from Paddington station and brought to my flat by that useful firm, Universal Aunts, which took them to the airport the next morning. After I moved to Australia, it was more difficult to keep up with the Mintoffs but I once or twice saw Moyra in England before her death in 1997. Since then, I have intermittently been in touch with Anne and Joan but have never been back to Malta. Still, the beautiful island, and the Mintoff family, hold a warm place in my heart.

When I returned to Britain from East Asia in September 1960, I stayed with my uncle and aunt, Robert and Dorothy Ingram, in Claygate until the end of the year, commuting to University College. This was a pleasant and relaxing place to live after my hectic period of travelling, while I looked for something more long-term. The college advertised a vacant flat in a block it owned for staff accommodation in Hornton Street off Kensington High Street, and I successfully applied to rent it from the beginning of 1961. This was the first time I had a place of my own and it involved buying furniture and household equipment.

If the fifties, in my recollection, was an era of hope, the decade of the sixties was dismal, signalling Western Europe's swift slide towards the irreligious and promiscuous society which it was soon to be. The coming of the contraceptive pill at this time boosted sexual laxity. The year 1963 stands out in my memory as perhaps the worst, the *annus horribilis*. Harold Macmillan, the Prime Minister at the beginning of the year, who represented much of the best in British public life, fell ill; and at roughly the same time his government was mired in an unsavoury episode brought about by a junior minister's affair with a woman linked to the Soviet Embassy. Macmillan had to resign because of his health, ending a great career on a sour note. Lord Home, the Foreign Secretary, was appointed Prime Minister, renounced his peerage and fought a by-election in Perthshire. For a few weeks, we had a refreshing interlude with reports from the Scottish countryside replacing sleazy news bulletins but, for most of the year, the papers seemed full of scandal and dirt. Then, on a different but also doleful note, President Kennedy's assassination, in November, brought the final horror.

The Second Vatican Council was, of course the outstanding Catholic event of the 1960s. I was so engrossed with the writing of *China's Economic System* that I did not have time to follow it closely or to read the council documents as they were published. However, I very much wanted to visit Rome while the council was going on, as presumably such an event would not happen again in my lifetime. Margaret Feeney, the energetic organiser of the Catholic Institute of International Relations,[1] urged me to go to Rome and contact the representatives of orders and congregations which had previously worked in China, to see if they were doing anything to track what was happening in China and to prepare for the day when it would be possible to return there. I readily agreed, and arranged to go in September 1965.

Of course, I was already well acquainted with the Jesuit Father Ladany's outstanding work in Hong Kong in listening to and piecing together fragments of news and bringing out, with very little help, his weekly *China News Analysis*, which I, like all other serious China-watchers, always read. However, apart from him, none of the other orders and congregations seemed, as far as I could find out, to be doing any of the careful following of China news which we secular China-watchers in universities and government agencies around the world were attempting. Nor were they preparing literature in the simplified Chinese characters in which the younger generation in China were being educated. Before going to Rome, I wrote to Father Michael O'Neill, then editor of the Columban journal, whom I already knew, saying, "There seems to be a great lack of informed interest and study in Catholic circles about what is happening on the Chinese Mainland. By now we ought to be looking more to the future rather than just bemoaning what has been lost there. I have no clear-cut policy which I want to push – only a few suggestions about lines that might be followed up e.g. that linguistic developments on the Mainland should be followed and a beginning made ... in producing Catholic literature that would be understandable to those educated in present day China". In Rome, I met Father James Kielt, Superior General of the Columban Fathers, who told me that they had two young priests who were learning Chinese; one (perhaps both) was studying at Columbia University in New

---

1 The body into which the war-time Sword of the Spirit had morphed and which later, I think, may have merged into Hinsley House.

York. Later, he wrote to me in London to ask for suggestions for what work these two should do after learning Chinese. I suggested that they should get qualifications and experience in teaching English as a foreign language because I had heard that the Chinese authorities had just begun allowing in some native English teachers. Years later, I learned that one of these two young Columbans was Father Edward Kelly, with whom I was to work in Hong Kong, including jointly founding AITECE, an organisation for sending English teachers to China.

Father Patrick Joy SJ, whom I knew in Singapore in 1952, was now back in Ireland. He gave me an introduction to Father Herbert Dargan, the Jesuit Assistant General for the Far East, but he was out of Rome; so instead I saw Father Andrew Varga, the recently appointed Assistant to the General for the mission to atheists, which the Pope had given to the Jesuits. Father Varga, a Hungarian, was a friend of Father Ladany, whose work he said it was intended to expand and to develop from it a centre for the study of China. I also spoke with Bishop Juan Velasco, the expelled Bishop of Amoy, now the Vicar General for the Chinese in the Philippines. Another former China missionary whom I met was Father Schneider of the Divine Word Society.

The Chinese government did not allow the Catholic bishops in Mainland China to attend the council; indeed, many were in prison, but to show future generations that these had not been forgotten, invitations from the Holy See were written to each legitimate bishop on the Mainland and filed in the Vatican archives. The bishops from Taiwan of course attended. One evening, standing outside St Peter's at dusk, I saw them gathered, waiting for their bus to take them back to where they were staying. One of them, Archbishop Yu Bin of Nanjing, who had gone into exile with the Guomindang government, I had once met in Chongqing, but I did not think he would remember me and I was too shy to go and greet them.

In London, I continued to frequent the Newman Association in Portman Square in the evenings and at weekends. CAFOD, the Catholic Fund for Overseas Development, was founded in 1964, under the chairmanship of a retired diplomat, Sir Hugh Ellis-Rees, and I became the Newman Association's representative on its first Board.

The Catholic Chaplaincy to London University moved, at some stage, to St Patrick's Church, Soho Square, with Monsignor Coonan remaining chaplain. In Gower Street, opposite University College, some Sisters ran a hostel for business girls. It grieved me that church-owned premises in such a strategic position should not be used for a more appropriate purpose and I sometimes prayed about it. In the summer of 1966, it was announced that Monsignor Bruce Kent, then secretary to Cardinal Heenan but whom I had known when he had been a curate in my parish in Kensington, was to become the University Catholic Chaplain. I mentioned this to my colleague, Mary Douglas, the anthropologist, and she immediately told me to arrange to bring him to dinner with herself and her husband at their home on Holly Lodge Estate, Highgate. Contacts with the Douglas family, and their invitations to me, were a constant pleasure and refreshment during my time at University College and later, on my visits to England from Australia and Hong Kong. In earlier days, I had been invited to the First Communions of their children, then later for dinners where sometimes I met their friends, such as Archbishop David Matthew, whom Mary had known when he was Apostolic Delegate to British East Africa; and Jim's relative, Mgr Dôle of Rouen, who helped me visit that city. So, at Mary's behest, I arranged for Mgr Kent to go to dinner at the Douglases'. After dinner, he kindly gave me a lift home, driving via Gower Street. As we passed the convent hostel, I pointed it out to him and remarked that it should be the university chaplaincy. He agreed and the next morning rang up the Sister Superior there to discover that her order was in the final stages of negotiating its sale to the University College Hospital Medical School. He asked her to delay signing any contract and persuaded Cardinal Heenan (who rose from a bed of sickness to look at the premises) to find the necessary funds to enable the diocese to buy it as a university chaplaincy.[2]

---

2 Bruce Kent, in his autobiographical *Undiscovered Ends*, written after he had left the priesthood, gave a slightly different account. He said there that I had drawn his attention to the hostel building on another occasion, at University College. There was such an occasion the previous week (both are in my 1966 diary) and I might have

At a later date, I clashed with Mgr Kent. It was in the middle of the Cold War, and the British government had raised the defence budget. He plastered the chaplaincy's Gower Street windows with posters denouncing this. I was on his chaplaincy advisory committee and objected to his action, one reason being that some students were up on army scholarships and they might be discouraged from coming to the chaplaincy by the posters. Mgr Kent took the posters down, and generously does not seem to have held the incident against me. In his *Undiscovered Ends,* he described me as being "a very traditional Catholic", a description I hope to continue to deserve.

In the 1960s, pundits from the right and the left continued to bombard the public with horror stories of a coming crisis of over-population. Perhaps the general hopefulness of the 1950s made it easier to publicise gloomy prognostications, or encouraged the media to do so. Drastic policies of population control were demanded, especially for third-world countries. The Catholic Church was a favourite target as a barrier to this, especially after the publication of the encyclical *Humanae Vitae* in July 1968. Many Catholics were swept along with this tide, as regards both their private lives and their public attitudes. The *Tablet* capitulated to public opinion, as it has continued to do on many occasions since then – giving rise to the soubriquet "*Tablet* Catholic". (I had been too busy, after the end of Douglas Woodruff's editorship, to follow closely what had happened to the paper. At one time, I stopped getting the journal, in disgust, but later resumed because I needed it for news.) Pressure was put on the Holy See, on Pope Paul VI, to modify church teaching on contraception. In the autumn of 1968, I attended a public lecture given at LSE by Lord Robbins (Lionel Robbins), one of the most distinguished economists of his day, in which he denounced *Humanae Vitae* in the most intemperate language I have ever heard in an academic discourse.

I had attended the UN Conference on Population and Development held in Rome in 1954 and had been writing and speaking, in Catholic milieus, on the general topic of population and resources and, with others

---

mentioned the hostel to him then, but I can remember pointing it out to him as we drove down Gower St. after the Douglases' dinner.

working on the Newman Demographic Survey, I had gone to gatherings on the sociology of religion held at Louvain. For these reasons, I was invited to meetings of an amorphous group know by the acronym of SELIPO (Secretariat de Liaison pour les Etudes de Population). I do not have a very clear recollection of the SELIPO meetings which I attended at Louvain. Probably I missed many of them because in 1965–68 I was travelling a lot on my academic work, was in the final stages of writing a large book and, later, was arranging to move to Australia. I think that I gave all my SELIPO papers to the Catholic Records Office in London before leaving for Canberra. The only significant ones which I have at present are a list of members, dated March 1969, and a copy of a letter from myself to the Secretary of SELIPO on 21 April 1969 (copied to Father S. de Lestapis SJ, the Holy See's representative on SELIPO), a letter in reply from Father de Lestapis dated 5 May 1969, and a copy of his letter of the same date to the President of SELIPO.

The significance of SELIPO is that a number of its members were appointed to the Pontifical Commission on Population, Family and Birth set up by Pope John XXIII in 1963 and which concluded its work in 1966. SELIPO members, as listed in March 1969, numbered thirty-four, including one spouse (Mme Rendu); of these, twenty-seven were lay, six were clergy and one a Sister (Rev Mother M. E. Lippits of the Medical Mission Sisters); eleven were Belgian, five British, four each from France, Italy and the Netherlands, and two each from Germany, Spain and Norway. My memories of the discussions are vague but I remember that opinions among members were very divided, both before and after the publication of *Humanae Vitae* on 25 July 1968. Opposition to the encyclical was strong among those from the Low Countries; the British members were split – Colin Clark and myself supporting *Humanae Vitae* and Anthony Spencer against it; I am uncertain of the stances of Dr John Marshall, a British psychiatrist who was a member of the Pontifical Commission, and of Father A. McCormack MHM.

Early in 1969, Canon de Locht of Brussels, who opposed the encyclical, drew up a questionnaire which was circulated to members, seemingly aimed to distance SELIPO, which had always been a Catholic organisation, from supporting *Humanae Vitae* (I do not now have a copy of the questionnaire). In reply, on 21 April 1969, I wrote: "I should like to put forward the suggestion that all officers of SELIPO should be required to affirm their support for the principles enshrined in *Humanae Vitae*. For membership of SELIPO, I would not exclude those who are in the process of coming round to support the Christian position as set out in the encyclical but who as yet are not ready to give this position their full support. But any person who openly opposes the encyclical should have no place in SELIPO." I sent a copy of my letter to Father de Lestapis, who replied on 5 May 1969, giving it his strong approval and saying that he was considering resigning from the organisation; he enclosed a copy of a letter, of the same date, which he had written to the President asking if SELIPO was a Catholic organisation, as had been assumed since its foundation; because, if not, it was merely duplicating other organisations; if this was not decided in the affirmative he would resign at the next general meeting. After this, I cannot remember hearing again from SELIPO. By this time, I was in Australia where, I had in vain hoped, the culture wars would be less acute.

Some vocal dissenters claim the invalidity of the teaching of the encyclical *Humanae Vitae*, by reason of its non-reception by a large swathe of Catholics, clerical and lay, at least in the Western world. The same phenomenon has, however, occurred before, without anyone, as far as I know, ever saying that this threw doubt on the validity of the teaching of the Church's Magisterium. From 1435 until 1890 a succession of popes had issued encyclicals and other documents denouncing slavery. These condemnations were ignored by those, lay Catholics and even clerics, to whom they were directed, who continued to use and trade in slaves,[3] exhibiting the same non-acceptance, indeed defiance, of Church teaching, as have their twentieth and twenty-first century counterparts in regard to contraception.

Meanwhile, in Britain, the new fight was on abortion. The Society for the Protection of Unborn Children (SPUC) was founded, probably in

3 Joel S. Panzer, *The Popes and Slavery*, Alba House, 1997.

1966. Its first public meeting, in January 1967, a tumultuous affair which I attended just before leaving for the US, was held (in, I think, Caxton Hall), possibly while the Abortion Bill was before parliament. I remember the early stalwarts who ran SPUC – Elspeth Rhys Williams (whose brother was, at one time, MP for Kensington South) and Phyllis Bowman, who mortgaged her home to keep SPUC going.

It was not until the next century that the demographically disastrous effect of twentieth century population practices became apparent. It is no mere co-incidence that the same practices which are proving non-compliant with the survival of societies should also be those which were condemned in *Humanae Vitae*. The laws of evolution and the teachings of *Humanae Vitae* derive from the same Source. Soon I would find myself in the antipodean theatre of the Culture Wars.

Above
The British Catholic delegation to the conference held at Munster, Germany, standing outside the largely ruined cathedral, January 1947

Left
Audrey, 1958

Audrey in the New South Wales countryside, on the Lawler family's country holding, 1970s

Public audience with Pope John Paul II in St Peter's Square, April 1983

Left
Gladys and Vyvyan Donnithorne outside their flat in Kowloon Tong, 1961

Below
Visiting Father Vincent Chu SJ in a basement room down a lane in Shanghai which he shared with his brother and sister-in-law and their adult son, May 1980

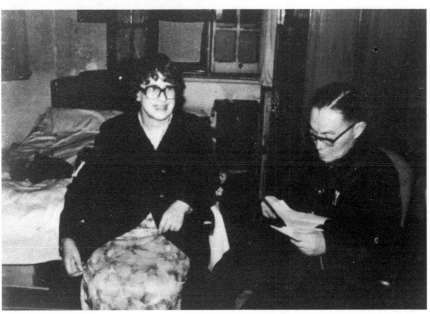

The Vietnamese seminarians Joseph Tran Dinh Trong (L), John Tran Ahn Tu (R)
with Audrey, outside her house in Canberra, 1981

PART THREE

Life in Australia

CHAPTER 12

Australia, and the Australian National University: 1969

The Australian National University (ANU) had been established in 1946 as an integral part of the country's post-war development, a national centre for research in the natural and social sciences.

ANU and University College London (UCL) were very different institutions, their differences tracing back to the purposes for which each was founded. ANU celebrated the coming of age of a vibrant nation, still rather unsure of its identity or its place in the world but vigorously debating these topics. The new university was to create a spirit of self-assurance and to explore Australia's international milieu. UCL, in contrast, was founded to provide a better chance of intellectual development and upward mobility to a large, diverse and disadvantaged segment of English society. It was drab but solid while ANU was glittering but trendy.

Both were secular institutions but in rather different ways. Some of UCL's ideologically secular founding fathers trumpeted its irreligion while it was denounced by the Anglican establishment as "the Infidel College". Nevertheless, its official history highlights, among other snippets, the story of the poor Irish widow who donated her life savings to help build a college which would be open to the young of her community who were excluded from the Anglican King's College on the Strand. The official view of UCL, as I understood it, was not to lay down that the students should be without religious instruction but, since the original students were for the most part living at home, to leave that to them and their families to decide and, if given, of what kind. In my day, and I hope now, UCL's Law Faculty, which usually had a number of Jewish students, was punctilious in finishing lectures and classes early on Friday afternoons so that all could get home before the Sabbath began. This signals that the College recognises that there is, or may be, a gap in a complete education which it is unable or unauthorised to fill.[1] This does not, of course, stop some academics trying to fill the gap in an imperialist manner, by trying to push the boundaries of their own discipline, probably in the social or biological sciences, to embrace the outer bounds of reality.

ANU's secularity, like that of Australia's as a whole, was somewhat different in tone. Because Australia has no established religion, there was not that note of defiance which tinged UCL's foundation. Around the time when I came to Canberra, Australian official policy on education was in fact becoming less secular. Gough Whitlam's achievement while leader of the opposition was to oversee a change in the ALP's attitude towards faith schools, accepting the need to subsidise those, predominantly Catholic, which had long struggled without government support. This won over many voters of ethnic Irish background from the Democratic Labor Party (DLP) which had emerged as a result of the previous savage in-fighting between Labor Party factions. One side effect of this lowered temperature over secularisation may have been that it was in the late 1960s that three residential halls with religious affiliations were established on ANU's campus – the Anglican Burgmann College, and the Catholic John XXIII College (with a chapel) and Ursula College. I heard that objections were raised by some of the founding fathers of the university, notably Sir John Crawford, but their existence seemed soon to have been accepted.

UCL, as an older institution, had more "body" to it than ANU, which sometimes seemed to attach more importance to the surface, to appearance and to the present day and current trends and fashions. UCL felt neither a

---

1 Cynics would say it was because the college benefitted from Jewish philanthropy, notably that of Marks & Spencer.

compelling allegiance to its own time zone in history nor a need to attach itself to the latest trends. ANU's bias towards superficiality and novelty was aggravated by its being located in a new and artificial capital city untempered by historical gravitas. ANU proclaimed "we are the future" while UCL was content to recognise that it lived somewhere in the midst of time.

UCL benefitted from having a large faculty of engineering. Engineers tend to be, literally, down-to-earth men, not ideologues (I hope the environmental movement has not changed this). ANU had a School of Forestry which supplies a similar, literal, grounding role, but it was small and not very influential in the university's life. Perhaps ANU would have been improved by incorporating the Commonwealth Scientific and Industrial Research Organisation (CSIRO) which includes, inter alia, an important agricultural research segment. Discussion of universities often decries their tendency to become vocational schools. This tendency can easily be overdone but recognition is due to the help given by intellectually demanding vocational courses, in anchoring down to reality the more waffly types of social or literary studies.[2]

ANU was all newness and excitement; UCL was, seemingly, dull and boring. Yet I found it easier to work while I was in London. I could get on with my writing or whatever without distraction. At ANU people were always bustling around the corridors, with more interruptions, if only for the need to be sociable and appear at the morning and afternoon coffee breaks. In later years when government indulgence to the new university weakened, the demand for reports on work done was a serious impediment to getting any solid work done at all. I do not think that I could have written *China's Economic System* at ANU, although it was that book which got me the job there. Attempts to ensure that work is done tend to lead scholars to concentrate on writing many inconsequential articles quickly,

2 George Allen claimed credit for the much smaller degree of student unrest at UCL in the late 1960s compared with LSE because it was his opposition that had stopped the College from opening a Department of Sociology. My own opinion is that sociology is a respectable field of study at the graduate (or older student) level, but is not suitable for undergraduates who have not had much experience of society and who first should learn some history.

recycling one piece of research in different formats instead of working on difficult topics that really matter.

Another great difference between UCL and ANU was the much greater closeness to government, both physically and socially, that existed in Canberra where, spatially, little more than an artificial lake separates the university from the Federal Parliament and government departments. The smallness of the Canberra community, at least in my time, meant that academics and politicians met and interacted much more than in London. Australian academics, especially in the social sciences, often knew many politicians and senior civil servants from college, or even school; the smaller population of Australia making this more likely than in the United Kingdom.

At first it was intended that ANU should take only graduate students but just before I arrived an undergraduate section was added when the existing Canberra University College was absorbed into the new university. The original research part of the University consisted of separate research schools, numbering five, I think, by 1969. The Research School of Pacific Studies (RSPacS), to which I belonged, was charged with work on the political, economic and social matters of the other countries of Australia's region – East and South-East Asia and the islands of the Pacific Ocean – but apparently excluding New Zealand. Other research schools included those for Social Sciences, Physical Sciences, Biological Sciences, Earth Sciences and eventually also the Curtin School of Medicine. Both the Research School of Pacific Studies and the Research School of Social Studies (RSSS) were housed in the Coombs Building, an extraordinary amalgam of three conjoined hexagrams built on three levels; designed, it was said, to force colleagues to intermingle because they frequently got lost and had to ask the way.

The national capital, Canberra, dated only from 1910 and its development had been stunted by the two world wars and the intervening depression. After the Second World War, its growth accelerated rapidly, on a suburb-by-suburb basis – successively five, ten, twenty, then more "suburbs searching for a city", as the saying went. In 1969, however,

Canberra was still a small town with a population of around 150,000, although it was one with exceptional facilities – cultural, medical and in respect of communications; and with an international element contributed by numerous embassies – a convenient and pleasant place for living except for its restrictive economic and social basis. It was a one-industry, one-company town, the company being the federal government.

ANU's campus comprised a stretch of well-treed country, near Black Mountain, a notable feature of Canberra's landscape. In 1969, it was still a series of building sites, with new structures continually appearing; the Menzies Library was still being built when I arrived. Large stretches of grass and trees continued to cover much of the campus. I enjoyed seeing so much greenery – a complete opposite to the grey, crowded collection of old buildings in a compound in the middle of a great metropolis which I had known at University College London. ANU was neither gated nor enclosed by a wall or fence. The university as a whole, and each department, were much more sociable than UCL. Everyone lived in Canberra and commuted by car. Parking was no problem. UCL colleagues, in contrast, often lived in distant and widely separated suburbs of the capital and many came to the college only on days when they had lectures or classes or if there was a departmental meeting. At ANU almost everyone turned up every day, and at mid-morning and mid-afternoon gathered round the departmental coffee urn and chatted.

The founding fathers of the Australian National University were still very much in evidence – indeed in control – on the campus when I arrived in 1969. Sir John Crawford, the Vice Chancellor of ANU, I had first met when I was interviewed at Canberra in 1968; previously he had served as a top civil servant and played a major role in the post-war economic changes in the country. H. C. (Nugget) Coombs had been the permanent head of the Department of Post War Reconstruction and then the first governor of the Reserve Bank of Australia, before helping to found ANU and becoming its Chancellor from 1960 to 1968. After that he devoted much of his time to his abiding interest in the Australian Aboriginal people but was still often on the ANU campus.

The research schools were divided into departments, according to academic disciplines. The work of the Research School of Pacific Studies' Department of Economics had been chiefly on South-East Asia, especially Indonesia, which was the focus of work of the head of the department, Professor Heinz Arndt. As a young man, Heinz Arndt escaped from Germany to England as a refugee, studied at LSE and after the war had taken an academic job in Australia where he had and was still progressing through a whole spectrum of political views from the extreme leftist outlook with which he arrived in Australia to the more moderate membership of the Australian Labor Party from even which, in the 1970s, he resigned. He was, for many years, on the editorial board of Quadrant, a journal of literary and political comment sponsored by the Australian Association of Cultural Freedom.

David Bensusan-Butt, like me a professorial fellow in the department, had been closely associated with Maynard Keynes at Cambridge, his help being acknowledged in the preface to Keynes's *General Theory*. David claimed that his ancestor had attended the same London synagogue as the economist Ricardo. The artist, Camille Pissarro, was his uncle and David himself was artistic. He was no longer publishing much but played a major role as an economic adviser to the Australian government, notably on tax matters. Sundrum, also a professorial fellow, a Tamil with no other name (on getting to know him, instead of switching to first name terms, one dropped the "Mr"), was born in Burma, of Tamil descent. He researched southeast Asian economies and was a member of Aung San Suu Kyi's group of economic advisers. Colin Barlow was a younger member of the department, working on southeast Asian agricultural economic matters; his father, whom I knew slightly, had a chair in engineering at UCL – I think he was an ally of George Allen in UCL internal politics. I often visited Colin, his wife Ruth and their five children at their home in the suburb of Cook where they had a splendidly productive vegetable garden. Ruth has since died and Colin later married Ria, the daughter of a former Indonesian ambassador to the Holy See and they both are now very active in an NGO for agricultural development in Indonesia which Colin founded after his retirement. Ruth Daroesman, an American who had long lived in Indonesia, was another colleague who became a good friend and very helpful on many occasions. She had been brought up a Christian Scientist, but later became a Catholic. Wang Gungwu, then head of the Department of History in RSPacS, a renowned historian of the Chinese diaspora, was a great support in promoting studies of contemporary China, especially when he became the RSPacS Director. Still later, after I moved to Hong Kong, it was good having him as Vice Chancellor of the University of Hong Kong. Gungwu's background and career gave him an ability to look at China, both its past and present, as a mainlander, an Overseas Chinese and an outsider – feeling, as well as studying, the unfolding troubles of the country.

Pierre Ryckmans and his wife Han-fang became close friends of mine and I was quite often at their home and knew their four children. He was soon to become celebrated as the author, under the pen name of Simon Leys, of a number of devastating criticisms of Mao and his China. Pierre taught in the Department of Chinese History in the School of General Studies, the undergraduate section of ANU (although it had begun also to take graduate students). Pierre's professional interests centred on Chinese art and literature; as he grew older, he also wrote on maritime matters and other topics, apparently veering away from China as being too painful a subject. He was certainly one of the most distinguished scholars on the campus. Another colleague with whom I soon made friends was Harry Rigby, a political scientist working on the USSR, and his wife Norma, the parents and grandparents of a talented family. Their son, Richard, undertook graduate studies in modern Chinese history and later entered the Australian diplomatic service. He married Tai-fang, a sister of Han-fang Ryckmans; the sisters came from an Anhui family which had taken refuge in Taiwan.

Canberra was an interesting place for the student of religious sociology. Its rapid post-Second World War growth from around 10,000 in 1945 to around 150,000 by the time of my arrival in 1969, came about first by the movement of public servants from the federal departments which had been in Melbourne; these departments swelled, as in many other lands, when governmental functions expanded in the mid twentieth century. The recruitment of academic and non-academic staff for the new university added more residents. The increased numbers, of course, needed services of all kinds – bringing in medical, educational, banking and legal professionals, technicians, artisans and shopkeepers. Canberra did not, though, attract large businesses or the top echelons in banking and financial services, which remained in Melbourne and Sydney.

At the beginning of the twentieth century, most Australian Catholics were the working-class descendants of poor Irish immigrants. In the first half of the century, through the Catholic school system, many rose in the world by entering professions in which it was possible to do well through intelligence and hard work without money or family connections, notably in public service, medicine and law. In the new capital with its large public service sector and little private business, they were disproportionately represented, Catholics forming a rather higher percentage of the population than in other parts of Australia. They had, however, moved without their extended families; in its early days Canberra was a city without grandparents. This is detrimental to the passing down of religious and other traditions, but the general public, as distinct from the academic community at ANU, was more Catholic than I had known in Britain.

Australia involved for me a new and more affluent lifestyle with a higher income and a rise in living standards. For my first nine years there I lived in the very comfortable University House, one of the early buildings of the new university, designed as a residence for university visitors, graduate students and such academics, usually single and always without children, who opted to live there. It also provided congenial faculty club facilities for all colleagues who wished to join – a kind of grandiose senior common room. I had a two-room suite but without cooking facilities (indeed, cooking was forbidden) looking out on to the grassed central court with trees and a lily and goldfish pond. University House provided three high-quality, substantial meals a day for residents and it was not possible to rent accommodation without paying for these meals. I put on a lot of weight while living there.

University House was only a few minutes' walk from the Coombs Building, so there was no daily commuting, though to get across the campus on foot took some time, let alone going to the shops and other facilities or to visit friends in their widely scattered homes in the suburbs. Public transport was poor so, for the first time in my life, I had to get a car. (I had a motor scooter for a few years in London, but did not use it much.) I had passed my driving test (at the fourth attempt) in London in 1958 but had almost no subsequent experience of driving. The morning after my arrival I went to get an Australian licence. I produced my UK licence and asked how to get a local one. Instead of answering my question, the woman at the counter asked, "What is the maximum speed in a built-up area?" I replied that I had arrived only the day before and did not know but said that in the UK it was 30 mph. She smiled and said, "Here you can go faster," and forthwith gave me a licence. I bought a second-hand car and had some more driving lessons but was still a very nervous driver as I set off, at much less than even 30 mph, along the rather empty streets of Canberra.

My first long drive, during the August holiday in 1969, was to attend a conference at which I had been asked to give a paper, in Adelaide, over 600 miles away. When I set forth on this trip, I had never overtaken a moving vehicle. An hour or two later, I found myself, in the countryside, behind a farm tractor and I pulled up all my courage and accelerated past it! I took three days on the trip, stopping at motels on the way, before reaching Adelaide and giving my paper. While there, I also saw John Bonython, a member of a prominent Adelaide family who had looked me up in the telephone book and contacted me when he came to England. In both the Donnithorne and the Bonython families there was a belief that, long ago in Cornwall, the two families had been one and my grandfather and the then head of the Bonython family had corresponded on this at the turn of the 19th and 20th centuries. During my week at the conference, John Bonython and his family were very hospitable, showing me around the city and, on the Sunday, took me to lunch at their mansion in the Adelaide hills. Before long John left again for England and I did not have further contact with his family while I was in Australia. My old friend and former student from London, Victor Funnell, was now a lecturer at Flinders University in Adelaide, and it was pleasant meeting him and his family there. From Adelaide, I drove along the coast road to Melbourne, discovering, on the way, the Southern Ocean, of which I am ashamed to say I had never previously heard.

At Melbourne I saw three friends, the Sinologue Harry Simon, whose father I had met at SOAS, and two whom I had known in Hong Kong – Arthur Huck, a scholar who had written on the Chinese in Australia, and Bob Beveridge, a China political scientist who had worked in the University of Hong Kong library as an assistant to Henri Vetch and who was now teaching the politics of contemporary China at Monash University. Monash students were notoriously left-wing, strongly Maoist, and Bob was encountering fierce hostility because of his moderate approach to the Chinese scene. I always consider him one of the heroes of the Cold War.

By the time I returned to Canberra I had begun to experience a little of the vastness and variety of Australia and also some of its beauty. No one had told me how beautiful Australia was, but I came mentally to absorb its colourings – the red or yellow shades of the earth, the dull olive green of the gum trees and the greyish green of the wattles, the wide blue of the sky. It seemed to breathe out an ancientness that contrasted and clashed with the trivialising newness of a city such as Canberra with suburbs popping up one after the other. Canberra is a very convenient city in which to live but after some years there, I became irked by its tidiness. The wide green verges that line its suburban streets I wanted to change into vegetable plots or cover with untidy market stalls and artisans' benches. The attempt, really rather bogus, at rigid separation of residence and livelihood always troubled me. For me, economics is centred on how people make their living and the evident scorn of livelihood matters by the Canberra planners displeased me. When I bought a house, I was constantly writing articles and letters there in the course of my academic duties, but no one seemed to worry. However, a man across the road opened a business consultancy, working at home, and all his neighbours were circulated by the authorities to enquire if they objected.

My next long drive, in May 1970, was to Broken Hill, a run-down mining town remote from most other human settlements, in the interior of New South Wales. It had become a favourite dwelling place of artists – the distinctive colourings of the Australian landscape were in strong evidence and also no doubt rents and other living costs were low – so the town had sprouted many galleries. The long day's drive from Canberra was not without problems. I got stuck trying to cross a creek and had to be pulled out by other motorists, ever helpful to their fellows in the outback. The rescue and assistance services provided by the National Road and Motoring Association (NRMA), too, I often found useful on various occasions.

My third long drive, in August 1970, was to Bourke, a small town in the New South Wales outback where there was a sizable Aboriginal community. By that time, I had got to know Nuggett Coombs, who kindly gave me introductions there. Since my arrival in Australia I had been fascinated by these first people of the country – "the fierce, gentle, mysterious, fugitive, ever-present people of the Australian Bush"[3] – and had attended lectures on Australian Aboriginal prehistory. (This prehistory had continued into the 1960s when an Aboriginal group was found which had had no previous contact with the outside world.) I was not able to stay long enough in Bourke to learn much, but had a glimpse of the complexities facing these first Australians in finding a fitting place in the national society.

I met the Missionaries of Charity (the Mother Teresa Sisters), who had established a good rapport with the Aboriginal community in the district, helped by their brown Indian skins. Out of Bourke's total population of some 3,000, Aboriginals numbered around 520, mostly of mixed blood and from many different tribes, so their traditional social structures had been lost, often along with their tribal languages. I talked with one full-blood old man, George Macdermott, a patient in the local hospital, who had been born into a Queensland tribe when its traditional society was still functioning. He had taken part in corroborees and spoke his tribal language.

3 J. J. Eddy in *Britain and the Australian Colonies 1818–1831: The Technique of Government*.

George had no formal schooling but learned to speak and read English later, when he worked on a cattle station. Now there was little opportunity to speak his own tongue because his daughter and grandchildren, who lived on the Bourke Reserve, did not speak it.

A major problem was that, having forgotten their tribal languages, because of the tribal diversity of the urban migrants, many Bourke Aboriginals were not fluent in English either; so many parents did not speak much to their children except for commands. Therefore, the youngsters might never have heard a complete sentence spoken before they came to pre-school where they had to be taught to speak properly. I visited the government pre-school which had been opened the previous year and was racially mixed. Experiments in intensive speech practice were under way and high-protein snacks provided to counter malnutrition. The Aboriginal children in the pre-school were said to be more stable emotionally than the white children because they were showered with affection in their extended families.

Most of the Aboriginals still lived on the reserve but the Department of Welfare was building houses for them in the town, some close together near the reserve but others deliberately scattered; six were about to be occupied. Aboriginal men, when they had jobs, might be drovers, sitting on horses all day while the more competent were in the meat works, but employment was scarce. Spare money tended to be spent on drink, gambling and taxis – sometimes jumping into a taxi to visit relatives living hours away, rather than waiting for an infrequent bus. I went to the reserve three times, twice with staff of the Department of Welfare and once with the Indian Sisters. I also met Father Murray, the Catholic parish priest who had worked in the outback for sixteen years. He said that around 20 per cent of the children in his parish school were Aboriginals. The previous Sunday, some fifteen Aboriginal children had made their First Communion and, in their special attire for the occasion, they walked together from the reserve to the church, to give them a sense of their own dignity. I went to a special Sunday Mass where most of the congregation consisted of Aboriginal children. Major modifications were made in the first part of the service where the epistle and gospel were paraphrased. The epistle – a difficult passage from the Epistle to the Romans – was perhaps necessarily morphed into asking if the children knew what a letter was and if they had ever received one; and then telling them about St Paul writing a letter to Christians in Rome.

The Indian Sisters aimed at building self-esteem among the Aboriginal women by, for example, teaching them to sew, as a result of which they were beginning to dress better. The Sisters also encouraged the Aboriginals to paint their shacks and keep them nicely and to grow vegetables in the reserve. I met Billy Reid, an Aboriginal community leader who worked for the local council and was also pastor of his own church. He thought that the future for New South Wales Aboriginals lay in assimilation and not in separate identity, although this might be possible for those in the Northern Territory. He was against too much in the way of handouts to Aboriginals but stressed the need for adult literacy classes to cater for school dropouts.

Staff of the Department of Welfare with whom I spoke were critical of the police attitude to Aboriginals. There were no Aboriginal policemen anywhere in Australia. Some 90 per cent of Aboriginal men had police records and this limited their job opportunities – railway jobs were barred to those with such records as well as demanding minimum educational standards which Aboriginals could seldom reach. Locally, at Bourke, discrimination against Aboriginals was found in Rotary and the Bowling Club. My informant had tried to get some admitted but was rebuffed. He thought the Aboriginal reserve in Bourke would remain for another twenty years as members of the community were gradually moved into the town. He had wanted the Indian Sisters to be allowed to have a place on the reserve, but the Welfare Department turned this down.

At weekends, I often drove into the countryside, sometimes taking visitors from abroad who were staying at University House. The Tidbinbilla Nature Reserve was one favourite destination where it was always possible to see kangaroos and emus. Emus could sometimes be fierce, especially when food was in sight – once I had to make a quick get-away in the middle of a picnic because of aggressive emus. A drive to Tidbinbilla often included a visit to the huge space telescope nearby. Another short trip from

Canberra was to Captain's Flat, an old mine settlement with the original grey weatherboard housing, abandoned by the miners years ago and now providing cheap accommodation, often taken up by those on long-term welfare such as the disabled. A disheartening place in some ways, but also somewhere with a relaxed and undemanding atmosphere for those who had to drop out of more competitive lifestyles. The old gold-mining town of Braidwood and its surrounding district was another easily accessible centre to visit. In my first years in Australia, I often visited country areas at weekends and delighted in the "wide land"; although as time went on, I had less time for such relaxation.

CHAPTER 13

Contemporary China Studies in Canberra: 1969–72

Before long, I became somewhat more knowledgeable about the Australian political scene. Like many local academics, I was an associate member of the National Press Club and often attended its lunches, at which prime ministers and other senior politicians frequently spoke. Some years later, I joined the Australian Liberal Party (roughly the equivalent of the British Conservatives) but was never active. Several times at their functions, I met John Howard, at one time Prime Minister, and other leading figures. After Gough Whitlam, formerly leader of the Australian Labor Party and Prime Minister, ended his stormy parliamentary career, he moved for a time to an honorary research position at ANU and had an office quite near mine. Sometimes he came and borrowed books on China from me – I always managed to get them back, but sometimes with difficulty! He was genial and if I met him elsewhere, at some reception – or once in a restaurant in Chengdu – he would, in his customary manner, bend down from his great height and place a kiss on my cheek; I wondered, because of my opposition to some of his policies, if I should turn the other cheek. When necessary for work purposes, of course, my usual contacts would be with public servants (who, in the UK, are known as civil servants). Soon after arrival, I paid a call on the Secretary of the Department of External Affairs, Sir James Plimsoll; otherwise, I contacted public servants according to the topic and level required.

The recognition of the Communist government of China in Beijing constituted a major party-political controversy at the time of my arrival in Australia. In the immediate past, during the early Cultural Revolution, China had not seemed anxious for recognition; indeed, was not very conscious of the outside world. Nor did it appear that substantial benefit would accrue to Australia from such a step. Now, the situation had somewhat changed. The Australian Liberal government, like the USA, still continued to recognise the Guomindang administration in Taiwan. Recognition of Beijing was not something I had ever opposed; before or around the time of British recognition, I had written an article in the Jesuit journal *Christian Order* in favour of this, which I regarded as merely an acceptance of reality and not as a mark of approval, as it was often regarded in the USA. The Liberal government in Australia already had the matter under consideration and would probably have granted recognition as soon as it had seen the USA was moving in that direction; meanwhile there was sense in keeping in step with its most powerful ally. Therefore, all the hullabaloo which the Australian Labor Party (ALP) was making about recognition was no great matter.

A little time before the Federal Election of 1972, when relations with China were a hot political topic, I sent the Ministry of Foreign Affairs a draft of a suggested statement of policy on the subject. My draft statement concluded with a consideration of China's UN seat – bearing in mind that at the time the USSR had effectively two seats in the UN General assembly because of the separate status assigned to the Ukraine, which was (at that time) de facto but not de jure a part of the USSR: "Relations between different Chinese administrations are the concern of the Chinese people. In order to smooth out the exigencies of the present situation brought about as a result of historical circumstances, two seats in the UN should be allocated to China for the period of the next ten years. It is to be understood that one of these seats should be occupied by a representative of the administration of the Taiwan province of China."

The political conflict surrounding China at that time in Australian politics may have delayed ANU's embarking on contemporary Chinese studies. In 1967, the university had taken a step towards introducing work on the Chinese economy when they appointed Professor A. W. H. (Bill) Phillips to a chair, with the promise that he could devote half his time to the study of China's economy. Phillips had made his name at LSE as the proponent of what became known as the "Phillips curve" – linking the rate of unemployment to changes in wage rates. His earlier diverse and variegated life had included visiting China and also learning some Chinese as a prisoner of war in Indonesia. He was anxious to study the Chinese economy and, being by origin a New Zealander, welcomed the opportunity to do so nearer home. However, as soon as he arrived in Canberra, he was in such demand from universities and government departments all over Australia to expound on his former field, that his desire to work on China was thwarted. Bill strongly supported my appointment and gave me great help on my arrival at ANU. Unfortunately, soon afterwards, he suffered a severe stroke and had to take early retirement; and, with his wife Valda and daughters, left for New Zealand where he died in 1975. I think I would have enjoyed ANU more if Phillips had been around longer.

ANU was generous in its provision of field work resources and in study leave, so individual academics did not have to approach foundations for these purposes. This both helped to overcome the "tyranny of distance" which had stunted a remote colony's intellectual life and also attracted scholars from abroad, such as myself, to work there. Thus, I would be able to visit Hong Kong every year for a few weeks, keep in touch with the world of China-watchers (and with my mother) and, when it became possible, also to get to the Mainland. From Hong Kong, by a frugal division of the five-yearly allocation of study-leave time and of funds, I could most years travel to the UK where I could get short honorary university visiting positions in London or Oxford and remain in contact with former professional contacts and distant library resources (more important in pre-Internet days) while staying with extended family and friends nearby.

Even before I arrived in Canberra, I was of course well aware of the significance of Australian exports of grain to China and so I decided to work on China's internal grain policy which helped determine its imports. I gave the original draft of this as a paper to the Adelaide conference in August 1969 and, after adding new material in Hong Kong while there in October, arranged for it to be published as a monograph by the Economic Research Centre of the Chinese University of Hong Kong.

In Hong Kong, I heard that visas were being readily granted to go to Guangzhou to pick up the Pakistan Airways flight from there to Karachi and thence to Europe. The visa permitted me to spend one night in China – this was a tremendous thrill after having been unable to get to the Mainland for twenty-six years. An attempt to get a visa for a longer stay was unsuccessful. However, in the few hours I had there, I was able to go around, by car and on foot, and get some idea of Guangzhou, where I had never been before. I also visited the Guangzhou Export Fair, which was being held at that time. On entering the fair, still rather nervous and dazed at finding that I was actually in the People's Republic, I suddenly found myself violently assaulted, with arms thrown around me – I thought I was being arrested. When I came to, I saw that it was an old friend from London, Peter Marshall, Secretary of the Sino-British Trade Council, who was beside himself with surprise at seeing a Western woman in those surroundings.

From Guangzhou, I flew to London in mid-November 1969 and spent six weeks on study leave with an office and a visiting position at LSE, where I gave a paper to Peter Wiles's Soviet Economics Seminar and went to other seminars and occasions, including the Annual Oration which, as mentioned in an earlier chapter, was broken up by hooligans. I also took the opportunity to attend a Chatham House China lunch and visit St Antony's, Oxford, and the University of Kent. I gave a paper at a Working Session on Twenty Years of Communist China held at the University of Ghent, chaired by Daniel Ellegiers, where I met a number of continental European scholars of contemporary China, including Jürgen Domes, then of the Free University of Berlin. Before going to Australia, I was beginning to have contact with some of the university centres of contemporary China studies that were springing up in France, Belgium and the Netherlands, and now, thanks to ANU's study-leave provisions, I was able to continue and expand my contacts with them.

Scholars interested in contemporary China were scattered throughout the ANU, in various departments of our own Research School of Pacific Studies and also in the undergraduate School of General Studies. One of the first things I did at ANU was to begin holding China lunches, in one or other of Canberra's Chinese restaurants, where anyone concerned with contemporary China – academics, graduate students, government officials, the press and others – could gather, with someone giving a paper or starting a discussion. However, something more formal was also needed, and it was decided to set up a Contemporary China Centre, based in the Research School of Pacific Studies, to which all academic staff and graduate students in the university with modern China interests would automatically belong, alongside, of course, their existing substantive positions in other schools and departments of ANU. I was appointed head of the Centre with Stephen FitzGerald, a young man in the Department of International Relations, RSPacS, as my deputy. It was also decided to inaugurate the Centre by holding an international conference on contemporary China in August 1970. Finance was provided for this from a Ford grant to invite five international participants from abroad – Shinkichi Eto and Shigeru Ishikawa from Japan, Michel Oksenberg and Dwight Perkins from the States and David Wilson, at that time editor of *China Quarterly*, from Britain. A prominent French scholar of Chinese society, Jean Chesneaux, who worked on labour relations in China, was already visiting ANU, so he also attended. A bevy of academics came from inter-state and from New Zealand as well as a number of officials from the Australian Departments of External Affairs and of Defence and some Canberra-based diplomats.

The conference went off well. The only incident that sticks in my memory is that during some discussion session about I cannot remember what (perhaps the Cultural Revolution) a wild young Australian scholar, in the course of a diatribe, boastfully threw in a description of how he had broken into some politically unacceptable academic's office in the United States and caused havoc with his papers and books. I was chairing the session, and while there was no suitable gap for me to intervene during the discussion, at the end I said that I could not let the session end without an expression of disapproval of the violent disruption of scholarly work which had been boasted about during the session. My words were greeted with complete silence and no one remarked about them to me until around ten years later, when I happened to meet one of the Japanese who had been present and he mentioned that he had been impressed by my intervention. It illustrates the atmosphere of acceptance of unruly behaviour in some university circles during the stormy 1960s and 1970s.

Other ANU academics, not directly working on China matters but peripherally concerned, included a number of international relations specialists who could be drawn on for discussions and advice and were useful to have around. This especially applied to members of the strong Department of International Relations at RSPacS in the 1970s and 1980s and included Hedley Bull and, in my last years at ANU, Coral Bell, whom I had known earlier in London. Another well-informed China-connected friend was Jocelyn Chey, who in those years alternated between academia and the Australian diplomatic service, and later became Australian Consul General in Hong Kong. Stephen FitzGerald, my deputy head in the new Contemporary China Centre, was a bright junior academic in his early thirties from Tasmania with a previous spell in the Australian diplomatic service. He was also adviser on Chinese matters to Gough Whitlam, the Leader of the Opposition. In June 1971 Steve accompanied Whitlam on a visit to China, which received much publicity in Australia. The immediate recognition of the Beijing government became a plank of the ALP's programme in the Australian general election the following December.[1]

The building up of a good collection of modern Chinese material in the new Menzies Library was a prerequisite to developing contemporary China studies at ANU. We advertised widely for a suitable librarian to take charge of this task and in November 1971, when I was in Hong Kong, I interviewed and was impressed by Y. S. Chan, a librarian at a major

---

1 For Stephen FitzGerald's account of these years see his *Comrade Ambassador: Whitlam's Beijing Envoy*, Melbourne University Press, 2015.

public library in the city. He was duly appointed and made a name for himself by the ways he hunted down usually unobtainable publications from booksellers and other sources throughout China on his trips there. Soon the Menzies Library, together with the National Library of Australia, possessed collections able to support research, even more essential in that pre-digital age.

ANU was also willing for me to recruit research assistants from abroad; at that time Australia had a dearth of suitable candidates. I was fortunate in finding Flora Chan, a young Hong Kong graduate who proved very efficient. Later, it was possible to recruit locally, and my final research assistant was Philippa Kelly who, among many other merits, patiently gave me my first initiation into the mysteries of computing. I was not an apt student! Anton Ikonnikov, an Australian of White Russian origin, brought up in north east China, with a command of both Chinese and Russian and an extensive knowledge of Chinese minerals, was appointed as a Research Officer in our department. He assembled and published useful material on China's mineral resources and development. The Contemporary China Centre began publishing papers, in booklet form. In 1972, I contributed one, *The Budget and the Plan*. In the same year, the *China Quarterly*, under a new editor, published an article of mine, "China's Cellular Economy", which attracted considerable attention, including in China where (without consulting me) it was translated and published some years later.

In 1972, my colleague, Pierre Ryckmans, spent six months in China as Cultural Attaché in the newly-opened Belgian Embassy. Based in Beijing, he was able to make seven trips to other parts of China including Shanghai, Suzhou, Wuhan, and Guangzhou. He came away with the impression of a heavily bureaucratic, elitist society where people were wary, shaken and exhausted by the Cultural Revolution. On several occasions, Pierre saw fistfights on the streets. At two universities, he asked to visit the Chinese literature department and, in both cases, excuses were given why it was impossible. He sat in on literature classes at middle schools and found standards low, with the texts mostly political. I asked Pierre to speak at one of our informal China lunches. He replied: "I feel quite reluctant to talk in public about my experiences in China. I have little to tell, and what I have to tell is not nice. Here there are very few people now ready to understand these unpleasant truths (in fact in Canberra I think you are the only person who really feels the same way as I do on these matters) – especially in the time of universal Maoist euphoria. So what is the point of talking? I shall not be able to convince our friends who are still in this euphoric mood – I shall just lose their friendship and get myself a label of anti-Maoism which could bar me from further contacts and eventual return to a country I love more than my own."[2]

Pierre's words well describe the atmosphere surrounding those of us working on contemporary China affairs in Australia during these years. When Stephen FitzGerald, the deputy head of the CCC, drew headlines, first as Whitlam's China adviser and then as Ambassador-designate, my own position became awkward. I was glad of the added contacts with China which recognition would bring, but did not want to associate the Centre, or myself, with "China as a cause", a theme taken up by a wide sector of the Australian public and media.

2 Letter, Pierre Ryckmans to Audrey Donnithorne, 14 March 1973.

CHAPTER 14

Life in Canberra, and the Culture Wars: 1969–73

During the year after my arrival, I made some good friends, both in the university community and in the wider society. The Research School of Pacific Affairs shared the Coombs Building with the Research School of Social Sciences. Before long, I came to know Father John Eddy SJ, of the History Department, RSSS. He was a well-regarded contributor to the studies of Australian history which at this time were beginning to multiply, and was a close friend of Manning Clark, who had pioneered the history of Australia as an academic subject and whose student he had been. Father Eddy had joined ANU at around the same time as myself and was a member of the Jesuit community which had only recently established itself in Canberra. He drew together a group of his Catholic friends, including me, from ANU, the public service and other spheres, who met on Sunday evenings in each other's homes, usually at fortnightly intervals; these gatherings were sometimes loosely referred to as the Christian Life Group. Several of the closest friends I made in Canberra came from this group, which included Peter and Doreen Lawler, Oliver and Carmel MacDonagh, Pat and Jean Moran, Jim and Nell Nimmo, Brother Laurie Needham, Mary Newport, Peter and Chantal Curtis and a few others, some joining and leaving according to their presence in Canberra.

Peter Lawler was already a top public servant in the Prime Minister's Department where, in 1966, he had drafted the Cabinet decision that led to the abolition of the White Australia policy. In 1976, he became Secretary (i.e. the permanent head under the Minister) of the Department of Administrative Services, the largest federal government ministry, controlling a multitude of operations, including the federal police. He was knighted in 1981 and, in 1983, appointed Ambassador to Ireland and the Holy See. His wife, Mary Doreen, married him after he had been widowed and left with five young children to whom she was a devoted stepmother; two further children were born to them. Doreen's brother and sister-in-law, Brian and Heather Robinson, sometimes attended these meetings; Heather was very kind to me later when I was ill and often visited me then. Oliver MacDonagh was a distinguished Irish historian who came to ANU a little after me. He and his wife Carmel and their seven children soon became good friends. Jim Nimmo, Secretary of the Federal Department of Housing until his retirement in 1973, and his wife Nell, both rather older than the rest of us, were useful when I was buying a house in 1977 and Jim used his experience to look over my prospective home. Pat Moran, a statistician and an FRS, was one of the few Catholics on the early staff of ANU; his wife Jean was not a Catholic but attended the group meetings. Pat himself tended to be a "*Tablet* Catholic" and I often found myself arguing with him. Mary Newport worked for the Australian Bishops' Conference in Canberra. Father John Eddy himself was a welcome presence in the Coombs Building, sought after for advice by all and sundry far outside the Catholic community. In fact, he used to describe himself as "the casualty officer of the promiscuous society".

One of the advantages of living at University House was the opportunity it gave to meet and get to know many interesting visitors to ANU who stayed there and also of seeing again many academic friends and former associates. It often fell to me to take them around, show them the local sights and introduce them to people, as well as attending lectures and seminars which they gave. These diversions were welcome whether they involved making new friends or giving me the opportunity of getting to know better those with whom I had previously had only a passing acquaintanceship. In 1970, Karl Wittfogel, author of *Oriental Despotism*, and his wife Esther, came for some months and gave a number of lectures and seminars. He had, in his old age, grown passionately and refreshingly anti-Marxist and was particularly friendly to Catholics such as Father John Eddy SJ, and myself. The economist Henry Phelps Brown and his wife were other visitors. Yet another, Shirley Williams (at one time the UK Minister of Education), who had been at Somerville just after me, and whom I had already met on a Sword of the Spirit committee, came to ANU with Bernard Williams, her then husband, a well-known moral philosopher who had once been billed as "the brightest young man in Britain", but who seemed somewhat lacking in stability of character. Their marriage was dissolving while they were in Canberra and later Shirley very reasonably obtained a decree of nullity; I doubt if Bernard ever had much notion of permanence, whether of marriage or of anything else.

Early in 1971, Wu Yuan-li, a long-time academic friend, visited Canberra on his retirement tour at the end of his term as Deputy Assistant Secretary at the Pentagon. An amusing incident during his visit occurred one evening when we were having a drink in the bar at University House. An Australian there, a complete stranger to me, got into conversation, making rather wild accusations against American foreign policy, which I countered with a more muted version. He then turned to my Chinese companion, expecting greater sympathy for his views, and of course completely unaware that he was addressing a senior US government official. Y. L. replied in a very low key, moderate way, suggesting that American policy might not be as wholly black as his interlocutor suggested. Meanwhile, I could hardly contain my mirth at the conversation.

Another very welcome visitor, early in 1971, was Lady Ogilvie, recently retired from St Anne's, Oxford. She suggested that I should put *China's Economic System* in for a DLitt and said that she would help steer me through the process. I should have accepted her very kind offer and later regretted that I did not do so, but at the time my instinctive dislike of degrees kicked in and I turned it down. Later academic visitors in 1971 included S. H. Chou, the author of the standard work on the Chinese inflation of 1937–49, Alan Prest of LSE and his wife Pauline, and three old friends, Jerome Chen, Colin Clark and Maurice Freedman. Jerome was a fellow Sichuanese, whom I had known in England; a historian of modern China who had amassed a mound of information about twentieth century Chinese warlords. He moved from Leeds University to Canada where he spent the rest of his career.

Colin Clark was, of course, always a controversial figure, at the young ANU even more than elsewhere. In its earlier days, ANU, like much of the Australian professional class, was a somewhat WASP (White Anglo-Saxon Protestant) body, de facto if not de jure.[1] True, it recruited some Catholics – Pat Moran for instance – but Pat was willing to disavow currently unpopular church teachings. Another notable Catholic figure in ANU's early days had been the Nobel Prize winner Sir John Eccles, in the Research School of Medicine. He had retired before my arrival and did not seem to have affected the general ethos. Catholic Clark was the most well-known and distinguished Australian economist of his day and would have added prestige to the infant ANU if he had been numbered among its staff. However, the very mention of his name roused ire among the senior economists and others in social science departments, largely because of his failure to keep his religion under wraps.

As well as visitors from outside, living at University House gave me the opportunity of meeting graduate students residing there. One particularly bright young man I can remember was Shimon Cowen, whose name I kept forgetting. Later, his father became Governor General of Australia and then I could always remember the son's name, but by that time Shimon had left ANU. Now he is a distinguished rabbi and the author of an excellent book, *Politics and Universal Ethics*,[2] in which he defends traditional Judaeo-Christian values, or the Noahide Laws, as he denotes them.

---

1 In 1977, for example, ANU's Centre for Continuing Education (the extra-mural branch of the university) discontinued a course on the Philosophy of Aquinas given by a lecturer in the Classics Department of the School of General Studies, a reason privately given to him being that, of the fifty students attending his course, ten were nuns.

2 Connor Court Publishing, 2011.

Early in 1971, the Master of University House circulated a notice that "Members of the House are reminded that children are not permitted in the House, the courtyard or the Fellows' Garden". After talking to other members, most of whom wanted children to be allowed, I decided to do something about it. I wrote asking that the rule should be re-considered: "Even if it is considered necessary to ban them from the Dining Hall and the Bar, that is no reason why we should be deprived of the pleasure of having children around other parts of the House and grounds. The sight – and sound – of children running around has a profoundly humanising effect which an institution such as ours badly needs if it is not to be academic in the most arid sense of that term." I put copies of my letter in the boxes of all other members of the House, appending a note: "If you agree with my letter of protest, please write to the Master or write on the attached copy of my letter 'I agree. Signed ---', or words to that effect, and hand it in to the office." A considerable number of members followed my suggestion. As a result, the rule was relaxed "for an experimental period"; I never heard of it again.

Jane Hawker, the eldest child of my cousins Ilsley and Pat Ingram, was among the youngsters then pioneering the gap year. She bought a round-the-world ticket and spent some time staying with friends in the British Embassy in Washington DC and socialising in high circles before crossing the Pacific, exploring New Zealand and then coming down to the less exalted society of her cousin in Canberra. She based herself with me and later went off to Melbourne and Queensland on her own. This was a period of student demonstrations, about the Vietnam War and other grievances. Jane had never been on a demonstration and felt that she was missing out, so on the next occasion, while in Canberra, she joined one, having carefully decked herself out appropriately. I think she quite enjoyed it but never really got the habit.

I promised that I would drive Jane to the airport when she left Australia, knowing that she planned to fly from Perth. As I had been invited to give a paper at a conference at the University of West Australia during the university break in May 1971, our trip to Perth could be fitted in conveniently. We left in my old Morris 1100, deliberately allowing ourselves a leisurely pace to enjoy the country as we passed through, staying at motels, going by way of Wagga Wagga, Griffith, Barmera, Port Pirie (and driving across some of the Flinders Range with its vineyards) and Ceduna at the eastern end of the Nullabor Desert where we spent two nights, exploring the nearby district. The road across the Nullabor was still dirt, often in bad repair, and the more than 300 miles to Eucla, at the other end, was a hard day's drive, through arid country with little vegetation except some greyish scrub. We took with us, as advised, plenty of water in case of breakdowns (in the traditional manner, I tied a water bag to the front of the car), but there were some rather primitive refreshment stops, although no motels before Eucla. For part of the way, the road ran close to the railway line; elsewhere, the two diverged. From Eucla we drove to Norseman and thence to the old, faded mining town of Kalgoorlie, which we explored before making the final lap of the journey to Perth, having spent eight nights on the way. In Perth, I gave my paper and attended parts of the conference. We went around Perth, a pleasant city, visited Fremantle, its port, and took a trip across the rough channel to the nearby island of Rottnest which is inhabited by large numbers of a peculiar kind of marsupial – quokkas – something between a rat and a squirrel in appearance. We also drove north of Perth to Norcia and saw the abbey and the school for Aboriginal children, founded by Spanish Benedictines in the nineteenth century when the whole area was very wild.

Jane caught her flight from Perth and I set out on the return journey alone. I wanted to see the south-west corner of Western Australia, which we had missed on our journey from Canberra, so I planned to spend the first night at Esperance. I halted at Albany and had a look at the town and then drove on but was stopped by very heavy rain which cut the road. As dusk came down, the number grew of cars blocked on their way and around ten vehicles had gathered. We all spent a cold and uncomfortable night in our vehicles, and at first light one driver, with local knowledge, said he knew a by-road that would take us to a passable highway and went in front to guide the rest of the convoy there. Eventually I reached

Esperance where I enjoyed a hearty breakfast and then drove on to Norseman and an early night's sleep in a motel bed. After that I made good time and got back to Canberra before term began the following Monday.

Towards the end of 1971, I went to Hong Kong for a month's China-watching. My mother had been to England for a hip-replacement operation, followed by convalescence by the sea, and I was in Hong Kong to greet her on her return there. Later I left for a few weeks in England, with an attachment to LSE, where I gave a paper to Peter Wiles's seminar and attended part of a conference on economic development in the USSR and Eastern Europe; I even think I was invited to give a paper at SOAS. A quick visit to Cambridge enabled me to see Barbara E. Ward at Clare Hall and also David Twitchett. It was good to attend the December Chatham House China lunch and get up to date with London thinking about developments in China. I spent Christmas with extended family at Claygate and also caught up with a multitude of godchildren and old friends before returning to Hong Kong and then Canberra.

My health had been taking a downturn and, early in February 1972, I had to enter Canberra Hospital for a hysterectomy and urgent removal of a tumour which turned out to be non-malignant. However, the procedure disabled me for two or three months and it was six months before I had fully regained my strength. During a stay in a nursing home, I was able to watch on television scenes of Nixon's visit to China, then taking place. My colleague, Ruth Daroesman, was very helpful and positioned herself as next of kin while I was in hospital. Patricia Ingram came to Australia during my convalescence when she rightfully thought my need for companionship and help would be greatest. After a stay with me at University House, she drove us to the coast of New South Wales, to a place with the odd name of Tea Gardens, where we spent a week sea-bathing and resting. Eventually my health greatly improved after the operation. Gradually I got back to work, catching up with the backlog of information that never stopped pouring in and which constantly had to be digested and marked up for filing. Keeping up with this torrent of very raw material about China was a perpetual struggle throughout my working life.

Australia proved no haven from the Culture Wars. The successive attacks on first one and then another moral bastion had gathered speed in the 1960s. Within a year or two of my arrival in Australia, demands began to be voiced in different parts of Australia, including the Australian Capital Territory (ACT), for a loosening of the laws against abortion. In February 1971, a local branch of a Catholic men's organisation called a public meeting on the matter which I attended. It was one of the worst-run and most badly-thought-out public meetings I have ever known. Having said that, the organisers must be given credit for having called it at all. The Catholic Women's League should have done so, but was probably too preoccupied with arranging minor social events and too averse to controversy. The platform at the meeting consisted of about five middle-aged laymen in dark suits (and no women) who droned away about abstractions – all praiseworthy and true but not immediately relevant to the crisis facing us of proposed legislation in the Australian National Territory's Assembly.

Around then or a little later – I am now hazy about the timing – a letter appeared in the local paper, the *Canberra Times,* from a colleague whom I did not know, Professor Arthur Burns of the Department of Politics, RSSS, in which he opposed relaxing the abortion laws; I then wrote a letter to the paper supporting him. During the following years, when occasion demanded, I sent similar letters to the press, sometimes responding to contrary letters from colleagues or their spouses. Arthur Burns was not only a political scientist and an academic, he was also a Presbyterian minister and a long-standing member of the ALP, and his wife was an aide to one of the party's leaders. A radical feminist movement was frothing at this time throughout Australia; perhaps it was especially virulent in the ACT because of the highly politicised nature of the capital, where the movement was spearheaded by the Women's Electoral Lobby (WEL). Abortion on demand constituted a major plank of WEL's platform and it was urged on candidates of all parties standing for elected office in the federal or local legislative bodies. WEL drew up an "Emily's List" of women candidates it approved, all of whom supported drastic relaxation of laws against abortion.

Australia is a federal polity. Political parties, while usually national, can vary in tone from one state to another. Local action is all-important to mobilise public opinion or to get, or prevent, something being done, especially for topics such as abortion which come under the jurisdiction of states and territories as well as of the national government. There was an urgent need for a local organisation, on the lines of the Society for the Protection of Unborn Children in Britain, to be set up in Canberra; such bodies were beginning to sprout up in other parts of Australia. Over the next months, discussions took place on this before something was organised finally.

A national election was in the offing and the relaxation of abortion law was on the agenda of many branches of the ALP, notably in ever-trendy Canberra. A group of us decided to set up a local branch of the Right to Life Association. Arthur Burns refused to be president; he was rather eccentric, ill-suited to run anything. He suggested that I should take this role but I turned it down for two reasons – first, I was a newcomer to Australia, and second, we did not want it to be a solely Catholic organization. The original group was almost entirely Catholic except for Burns, and we thought it important that the new body should be headed by a non-Catholic. Eventually we managed to recruit the local Lutheran pastor, Mervyn Stolz, who agreed to take on the job, but could not give it much time; I became vice-president. A public meeting was held in a secular hall to launch the new ACT Right to Life branch and we enrolled several hundred members, though almost all were from the Catholic community. I do not think that Pastor Stolz was able to get active support from a single member of his flock; they were almost all of German origin and had brought with them to Australia the supine attitude to political affairs which in the early twentieth century so sadly characterized their fellows at home.

The local Catholic diocese, headed by Archbishop Thomas Cahill, gave us backing and declared a Right to Life Sunday. An able young Jesuit, Father Paul Duffy, devoted himself to the cause and preached excellent sermons on it. The ACT ALP picked a very pro-abortion candidate for the seat. The Liberal government was tired and the polls predicted its defeat both nationally and locally. Catholics formed around a quarter of the population of the ACT. Their church attendance rate, while not good, was certainly above that of their counterparts in England. Their political affiliation was rather solidly ALP, reflecting both their historical roots as largely the descendants of oppressed Irish immigrants, as well as their economic interests – public servants, benefitting from big government.

Arthur Burns, still a member of the ALP, decided to run against the official party candidate for the ACT seat, labelling himself "Labor against Abortion". As a result, he was expelled from the ALP but, undeterred, he continued his candidacy. I had by then become an Australian citizen; at that date, UK nationals could obtain citizenship by simple registration after two years' residence in Australia, without giving up their UK nationality. Because of the opprobrium Burns was experiencing from colleagues and others, I said I would help him in his campaign, despite my lack of sympathy for the "Labor" side of his platform. In this, I was strengthened by the desire to help the traditional Catholics register their objection to abortion without renouncing their cultural roots. With proportional voting in Australia, it was possible for them to ensure their vote would support a Labor government by giving their second preference to the official Labor man, while registering their objection to the abortion plank in his platform by their first preference being given to Burns who was unlikely to get in; if he did win the seat, he promised he would support Labor on all major matters except abortion. He obtained nearly five per cent of the ACT vote, more than independent candidates usually achieved, but disappointing nevertheless.

The Labor Party won the election, as expected, and Gough Whitlam became Prime Minister. Before long, a Labor MHR (member of the House of Representatives) introduced a bill to make the grounds of legal abortion much wider. It was to be debated on 10 May 1973. The controversy heated up, especially on the campus. The local Right to Life Association of course sprang to action and sympathisers from sister bodies throughout the country arrived in Canberra. Unfortunately, Pastor Stolz was abroad so, as Vice-President, I had to take over. On the evening of 8 May, two days before the bill came up, we held a committee meeting to which leading members visiting Canberra from the sister organisations were invited, to finalise arrangements for the day, including the proposed demonstration in front of Parliament House. The committee, which I was chairing, had a long agenda which we had to get through to ensure that all arrangements were in place for the great day. Some of the visiting members on the committee were rather distinguished – one was the elderly daughter of Joe Lyons, a former much-revered prime minister, and his wife, Dame Enid Lyons, the first woman member of the Australian Parliament and (after her husband's retirement) also the first Australian woman cabinet member. These visitors kept up whispered conversations which disturbed the whole proceedings, yet I felt I could not call them to order; instead, I chided their perfectly innocent and silent neighbours to keep quiet, which anyhow produced the desired result and we completed our work, late and exhausted.

On the day of the debate, things turned out better than we expected. Large crowds gathered on the lawn before Parliament House, mainly of our supporters but with a substantial number of opponents. The police kept the two sides broadly apart, but there was a good deal of interaction which I had to help keep peaceful. An ecumenical service had been arranged at 11 a.m. in St Christopher's Cathedral, so our supporters walked, in straggly groups rather than a procession, to the cathedral, about half a mile away. In the middle of the service, Archbishop Cahill, who was in the sanctuary, came forward and interrupted the sermon to say that the police had given him a message that a bomb was reported to have been placed in the building and that we must all leave immediately (it was just a hoax call by our opponents). So the congregation trundled out, with someone leading with the hymn "Now thank we all our God" and returned to Parliament House to await the vote on the bill. It was soundly defeated. Every single member of the Liberal and Country Party opposition, under the leadership of Malcolm Fraser, voted against it, and together with the more solid of the ALP Catholics, outnumbered the majority of the ALP members. To give Whitlam, the Labor Prime Minister, his due, he told his followers that he expected every one of them to be present and to vote – this meant that wavering Catholics had to face up and vote although some would have preferred to abstain.

It was, of course, only a temporary victory, although that evening it seemed like a foretaste of heaven; but we realised it was unlikely to last. The cultural tempests of the twentieth century before long tore down the defences which centuries of Christian civilisation had tried to maintain to guard the unborn, and young infants, against adult tyranny. It also made it more difficult for the West to protest against wholesale abortion in other parts of the world. Infanticide, especially of girls, had long been traditional in China. With modern medicine, including pre-natal scans, it has become easier to cull unwanted girls before birth. The Chinese Communist government's one-child policy, from 1980, led to government-provided, and often enforced, abortions; parental preference led to these being gender-based. On a less drastic and systematic but still wide scale, the same policies held force in India and in a number of other countries, including among some immigrant communities in the West. In recent decades, most of the abortions done in the world have probably been carried out because the unborn children concerned were girls. The radical feminists demanded "choice" – is this what they wanted?

Nine days after the Bill, I left for Hong Kong and then for the Contemporary China Centre's visit to China, an abrupt switch of focus and effort. My life in the next few months of 1973, travelling in China, the continent of Europe, Britain, North America and Israel, must have chapters of their own.

Visits of more old friends to Canberra brightened life at University House during these years. George Allen's wife Nell had died after a protracted illness not long after his retirement. They were a devoted couple and Nell's death left George devastated. Old colleagues, trying to raise his spirits, suggested that an invitation to Australia might help. In 1973 ANU gladly invited him, and he also visited other Australian universities. His lectures were appreciated and I think he enjoyed his antipodean travels.

As well as visitors to Australia, another advantage of life in Canberra was the intermittent returns, on home postings, of my old friends, Robert and Parvine Helen Merrillees and their two young daughters – Netty (Antoinette), my goddaughter, and her younger sister Dolla (Theodora). In 1969, about a year after I visited them in Cambodia, Bob was moved to the Australian mission at the UN Headquarters in New York, returning to Canberra in 1972 for three years. Then, in swift succession, they went to Beirut and London, coming back to Canberra in 1979. In 1983, Bob was appointed Australian ambassador to Israel and later, after I had left Canberra, to Sweden and then to Greece. After that, he left the diplomatic service and reverted back to his earlier interests, serving for some years as Director of the Cyprus American Archaeological Research Institute before eventual retirement in the French countryside. During their Canberra postings, I saw them when all our heavy schedules permitted. I can remember attending Netty's confirmation, when she read one of the lessons. Before long, the girls transferred from local schools to the French lycée in Canberra. These French schools across the world, controlled from Paris, all teach the same curriculum, so that, on moving to another country, mobile diplomatic children can immediately pick up again at the point they had reached at their previous school. Also, of course, they acquire excellent French in addition to their native language. Before I left Australia to retire in Hong Kong, Netty was already at the University of Sydney where I visited her. She followed her father into the Australian diplomatic service and later married another Australian diplomat, James Larsen, who has served as ambassador in Israel and later in Turkey. Netty took leave from her own career for some years when her three children were young, but then agreed to be available to act as a stop-gap to fill temporary vacancies in Australian missions not too far from where James might be posted; thus, for some weeks, she was Chargée d'Affaires in the Australian Embassy in Berlin and then Counsellor at the embassy in Rome and later Chargée at Nicosia, Cyprus, in the intervals re-joining James in Ankara. Netty's sister, Dolla, went into museum management and, after extensive experience, in 2016 was appointed Director of the Powerhouse Museum in Sydney.

Living in University House was convenient and I was in no hurry to move. However, the property market was rising and, now that I was in a position to put down a deposit on a home, it seemed advisable to do so. I found a small but agreeable house in the inner-city suburb of Red Hill and bought it, with the intention of renting it out until I wanted to live there. Soon afterwards, I heard a government minister, Simon Crean, speak at an ecumenical service. He mentioned that a number of Aboriginals were, for the first time, being appointed to the federal public service, and he appealed to Canberrans to let houses for their use, despite the prevailing prejudice. Afterwards, I spoke to Crean, saying I would gladly let my newly-bought house for this purpose. When I informed my agent, whom I had asked to look after the house, that the tenant was to be an Aboriginal, she had hysterics over the telephone so I told her I would give it to someone else to manage. My new agent, a sensible ex-naval officer, was completely reasonable and everything went smoothly. Before long, I visited my tenant, Graham Emzin, and found he was a thoroughly responsible man, with an English wife and three small children; they were excellent tenants. In any case, my contract was with the Department of Aboriginal Affairs and Canberra landlords consider official bodies as ideal tenants. Eventually, before leaving Australia, I sold the house to the sub-tenants (no longer the Emzins). Graham Emzin later became the owner and licensee of a Queensland hotel, which he had told me was his ambition for the future.

It may have been dealings with the Department of Aboriginal Affairs over the Red Hill house that first brought me into contact with Charles Perkins, a senior official in that department and the first Aboriginal graduate of Sydney University. Like many prominent Aboriginals, he was of mixed race, with white grandfathers and Aboriginal grandmothers. His white wife was a dressmaker, working from home, and I asked her to make me a cotton dress. This brought me to their house where I met his old mother, Mrs Hettie Perkins, the last speaker of the language of the Arrernte Aboriginals. Her son was busy recording her speech. There are several hundred different Aboriginal languages spoken in Australia and this makes language preservation difficult. In 1981 Perkins was appointed Permanent

Secretary of the Department of Aboriginal Affairs, the first Aboriginal to hold such a post. He died in 2000.

My contacts with members of the Aboriginal communities are among my most abiding memories of Australia and I am very thankful to my Aboriginal friends for enlarging my experience of what it means to be human, especially with the close links they sense with a just-past which to us is remote prehistory.

CHAPTER 15

The Australian National University's First China Visit: 1973

The Australian general election in December 1972 changed the situation both for the country and for my Contemporary China Centre. The new government immediately recognised the People's Republic and appointed Stephen Fitzgerald, the Centre's deputy head, as ambassador to Beijing. Before he left, I rubbed in to him that one of his most important duties was to arrange for a visit to China by a delegation from ANU's Contemporary China Centre!

Having settled down in the embassy in Beijing, Stephen came good on my demand and a delegation from our Centre visited China from 28 May to 18 June 1973. I think it was the first such visit by a group from a Western university since 1949. As Head of the Centre, I led the delegation, which consisted of eleven academics (including two graduate students): ten from Australian universities and one from New Zealand. The more senior academics in the group were Eugene Kamenka, Head of the History of Ideas Unit, and his wife, Alice Tay, a Singaporean Chinese in ANU's Law Department; my old friend Ian Adie; another political scientist, Ian Wilson; Alan Thorne, a palaeontologist; Colin MacKerras, whose special interest lay in Chinese theatre; and Enid Bishop, the Head of the Asia Department of the Menzies Library.

The China International Travel Service (CITS), which made the travel and other arrangements for our trip, was part of the Ministry of Foreign Affairs; wherever we went we were accompanied by their staff. A senior official of the CITS headquarters, with interpreters, accompanied our group from Beijing onwards. In each province, he was joined by a member of the provincial branch of the CITS and in each city two or three members of the municipal staff of the CITS were added. Therefore, we were always attended by a considerable retinue.

We crossed from Hong Kong to Shenzhen (then a fishing village) on 28 May 1973 and thence to Guangzhou, where we were taken for a sightseeing trip around the city, with a song and dance performance in the evening. Next day we were shown a commune in Nanhai county and then shops in Guangzhou before leaving on an evening flight to Beijing where we were met at our hotel by Stephen FitzGerald and his wife Gay. Next day we went to Tiananmen Square and the Forbidden City before leaving by train for Shenyang. On this and other trains on which we travelled, a special "soft sleeper" carriage was attached to the train which either we had to ourselves or one or two compartments in it might be occupied by another elite category, the "four-pocket" soldiers of the People's Liberation Army. (Ranks in the Chinese Army were abolished in the Cultural Revolution. However, some soldiers had four pockets on their jackets, others only two.)

In Guangzhou and Beijing our party stayed in "foreigners-only" hotels. In Shenyang, we were lodged for three nights in a palatial government guest house some way out of the city, with no other visitors. One evening there, I wandered out of the compound alone and entered a group of dwellings, perhaps housing staff of a particular factory or other unit. A crowd soon gathered round me, showing exceptional friendliness and warmth, smiling and clapping. They were not forthcoming in conversation but I sensed that perhaps foreigners were seen as a symbol, or even a cause, of the current slight relaxation in policy after the furore of the Cultural Revolution. At Shenyang, we were taken to a couple of large machinery factories about which I had often read. We visited Liaoning University and also the ancient palace and the Manchu tombs – Shenyang, the former Mukden, had been the old Manchu capital. From Shenyang we went, again by train, to Anshan, the greatest early steel centre of the country. There we visited the Anshan Iron and Steel Corporation's huge steel mill and saw a blast furnace (fiercely hot – I wilted after a few minutes and wondered how the workers endured long hours stoking it), a rolling mill and a seamless steel tube plant. Around ten miles from Anshan we were taken to an electric power transformer station where we watched two girls working on live high-tension wires. At the end of the day, it was a relief to visit a hot springs sanatorium where we were able to enjoy a restful bathe. We then left Anshan, again in the soft-sleeper carriage, for the port city of Dalian. Here, for the only time during our visit, we were in a hotel where there were also Chinese guests (apart from Overseas Chinese and staff of the China Travel Service).

At Dalian we visited the port, the Xinghai Park near the sea, and the network of underground air raid shelters in the centre of the city. We also saw the Dalian Locomotive Works and, on a lighter note, sea shell and glassware factories. A visit to the Dalian School for the Deaf and Dumb proved distasteful, at least to myself and some other members of our group. Three children were called in and given acupuncture treatment in front of our party (totalling about twenty persons, including our China Travel Service retinue and a few others). The first, a schoolboy of about thirteen, looked unhappy. The giving of medical treatment before a non-medical audience to a patient in no position to give free consent seemed more than questionable so I walked out, followed a little later by Alice Tay, who was in tears. Dr Kamenka, in my absence, gave the usual speech of thanks at the end, explained our objections, indicating his own agreement with them while making it clear that others in our delegation (some of whom photographed the whole procedure) held contrary views. Some of the staff of the school smiled warmly at me as we left. Our official entourage indicated their annoyance by pinching an article of my underwear drying in my bathroom and returning it to me at what they judged an embarrassing moment as we were leaving to return to Beijing.

At Beijing, we visited the usual magnificent sights – the Temple of Heaven and the Ming Tombs as well as the Great Hall of the People, and also the Zoo. Our visit to Beijing University was one of the highlights of our trip. For this we divided into small groups according to academic disciplines.

From the official Chinese standpoint, of course, the climax of our visit was the interview given us by Zhang Wenjin,[1] an Assistant Deputy Foreign Minister; it was this that distinguished us from a mere group of tourists. The most interesting parts of his discourse were those reflecting on the Soviet Union, whether it or the United States presented the greatest danger to the world: "The Soviet Union...constitutes the greatest danger of expansionism. The Soviet Union is more deceitful because now it is putting out the banner of Socialism and support for people's revolutionary wars. The Soviet Union used to be a socialist country; now a fundamental change has taken place. The Soviet Union said it would help countries, providing arms etc. but really it sends experts to control them ... Unlike the US, the Soviet Union uses more deceitful means to carry out expansionism. Despite the treaty between China and the Soviet Union, the Soviet Union has provoked boundary incidents and has used pressure to control China. The other means it explores is to use revolutionary communist parties and self-styled leftists to carry out subversion, and so-called 'peace and friendship' with India and Iraq which are really military alliances. So China considers the Soviet Union's hegemony more dangerous because its method is more deceitful than that used by the USA."

After this general exposition, Zhang took questions. Three of our international relations specialists asked about relations with India and the Philippines, and about the discussions that were then in progress among South East Asian countries which eventually led to ASEAN. I ventured to ask how severe a threat the Chinese government thought there was of an attack on China by the Soviet Union in the next few years. Zhang replied that relations between the two countries were "rather strained". Border

---

1 Zhang Wenjin, as the senior Chinese Foreign Ministry official in charge of relations with the West, had taken part in the secret talks between Zhou Enlai and Henry Kissinger, the US Secretary of State. He also participated in Zhou's meeting with President Nixon in 1972. From 1978 to 1981 Zhang was Deputy Foreign Minister and from 1982 to 1985 Ambassador to the USA. (Wikipedia)

talks had been going on for three years without any progress being made. The Soviet Union deployed a million troops along the border and was conducting a propaganda campaign against China. On "the possibility of an attack and on what date it would be, China could not judge." Zhang asked us for suggestions for improving Sino-Australian relations and we mentioned more contacts between universities and the possibility of getting a greater number of Chinese publications, especially local newspapers, for our libraries.

Stephen and Gay FitzGerald gave our group a splendid dinner at the historic Chengdu Restaurant. Stephen complained that much of his time was taken up by the internal administration of the new embassy and getting things settled. He said that about ten embassies in Beijing were seriously studying China's internal matters. The dinner was also attended by the Maltese Ambassador to China, Joe Forace, who doubled as Maltese High Commissioner to Australia. Months earlier I had corresponded with him about the possibility of our visit and he put in a good word for us with the Beijing authorities. Malta's relations with China were particularly good at that time and Forace remarked at the dinner that "for the first time in 5,000 years, Malta has a big friend who treats her as an equal", although exactly how, I thought, it would be difficult to say.

Ian Adie and I had a meal with Michael Morgan, Chargé at the British Embassy and I had discussions on economic matters with his colleague John Stern, with Bob Godson of the Canadian Embassy and with Willliam Rope, the Commercial/Economic Officer of the US Liaison Office which had been set up before full diplomatic ties had been established between the USA and Beijing. My old friend Mike Oksenberg was in Beijing with a delegation from the Committee on US-China Relations, and I had a talk with him. I lunched with David Bonavia, then *The Times* correspondent in Beijing, and his wife Judy, whom I already knew in Hong Kong. David, who had worked in Moscow, said it was easier to get things done in China than in the USSR; in Beijing, he could operate without a Chinese assistant while in Moscow he had needed a Russian. The bureaucracy in China was not so overwhelming as in the USSR and, while he was against the whole system, he thought the Chinese ran it better than the Russians. The only unofficial Chinese I was able to meet while in China on this visit was a brother of my former research assistant in London, Tsu-tung Emslie; this brother was a hydraulic engineer teaching in some college in Beijing.

On Sunday, I went to the 9:30 a.m. Mass at Nantang, the sole Catholic church then open in Beijing. The congregation was sparse. The only Chinese present were some elderly women and two men who, I assumed, were officials of the Bureau of Religious Affairs because they stayed until the rest of the congregation had left; when I tried to engage them in conversation, all they said was that they worked in an office. There were quite a number of Africans and a handful of other foreigners. Apart from my visit to Nantang, the only signs of religious life which I observed in Beijing, or anywhere in China at that time, were a number of "Hui", i.e. Moslem, restaurants.

After eight nights in Beijing, we flew to Guangzhou. There we visited Zhongshan University and the Peasants' Institute, and an ivory carving workshop; then we spent a day in Foshan before returning to Hong Kong.

In addition to the official group schedule, several individual members had their own programmes and wrote their own reports. Enid Bishop paid a lengthy visit to the National Library, met senior members of its staff and discussed co-operation with it, such as exchange of duplicates and photocopies and even the secondment of members of its staff to the ANU Library. She also paid similar visits to the libraries of Beijing and Liaoning Universities and of Zhongshan University in Guangzhou. Enid went around as many bookstores as possible, buying publications that ANU lacked and made an arrangement with the Australian Embassy for members of its staff regularly to buy for the ANU Library any new material available only on the domestic market.

Eugene Kamenka called on the Acting Secretary-General of the Chinese Academy of Sciences; a few days later a message arrived from the Academy to ask the Australian Academies of Humanities and of Social Sciences to send specific suggestions for exchanges to the Chinese Academy immediately. We surmised that such action might strengthen groups inside the Chinese Academies which were pressing for normalization of scholarly contacts. Alan Thorne had fruitful meetings with Professor Wu Rukang and his colleagues of the Institute of Vertebrate Palaeontology and Palaeoanthropology of the Chinese Academy of Sciences. Alan visited their institute to learn about their work, which impressed him favourably, and he gave them a seminar on his work in Australia. He was invited to visit them again and, in turn, invited Professor Wu to visit ANU. Colin MacKerras furthered his studies of the Chinese theatre by going to a couple of performances in addition to those put on in the evenings for our whole group, and also by meeting a number of significant people connected with his interests. In contrast, I was not able to make any meaningful professional contact with economists and neither could Alice Tay visit any law courts or meet any legal officials, although she was able to have a useful conversation with two professors of law at Beijing University. The international relations specialists were not able to make contact with the Institute of International Relations.

For myself, one of the most fraught moments on the tour was when someone reported to me that a member of our group, a British graduate student of international relations, had told one of our CITS minders that from the point of view of his own interests, what he would really like to happen during our tour was for the Soviet Union to attack China! After wondering for a moment whether I should ring the British and/or the Australian Embassies, I decided to let it pass. Fortunately, the minders, as I had hoped, apparently decided to treat the young man as a licensed lunatic and overlooked his remark.

In the fourteen-page report on our visit which I wrote for ANU, I noted that it was an achievement that the visit took place at all. Mike Oksenberg, who was in Beijing at the time as a member of a high-level American delegation, said that as far as he knew, no centre of Chinese studies at any US university had yet been able to send such a group.

Our CITS minders were somewhat puzzled by the nature of our group as it became apparent that it included a variety of opinions and differed very much from the groups sponsored by "friendship societies" or consisting of "concerned students" to which they were at that date accustomed. Our head CITS man's initial coolness towards me, and also perhaps to Ian Adie (both travelling on UK passports) may have been coloured by a belief that we were British Foreign Office appointees in the group, a suspicion no doubt confirmed when we both dined with the British Chargé. The CITS man confided to Ian Wilson that it was a pity that Australia still had a feudal relationship with Britain!

The CITS's purpose is dual, covering both hospitality and control. There is a good deal of ambiguity between the two roles. We were entertained in a manner above that to which we were accustomed at home, thus stressing the dignity of our hosts, while at the same time being kept firmly in our place as guests. In pursuance of its dual roles, the CITS minimises (or used to) unscheduled contacts between foreign visitors and local people as well as shielding foreigners from many of the inconveniences of life in China. In all the main cities which we visited, I succeeded in breaking away from supervision at least briefly, to wander around on my own. In Dalian, when I expressed a wish to see the local department store, the local guides seemed deliberately to arrange the programme to prevent this so I insisted on leaving the farewell lunch they gave a bit early and saw the store. I found it probably the best stocked shop (apart from the "friendship stores") that I had seen in China.

However, the general impression I gathered on the trip was that, in terms of post-1949 China, there had been considerable political relaxation. Pictures of Mao and political harangues were reduced from the level I had experienced during my two one-day trips to Guangzhou in 1969 and 1970.

After the China visit and a week in Hong Kong, I took some study leave planned around three conferences at which I gave papers – one in Bavaria at the fine Schloss Reisenburg at the end of June 1973, organized by the German Association of East Asian Studies; the second, the Congress of Orientalists in Paris in July; and the third, a conference on Law and Civil Administration in the Chinese Economy, at Berkeley at the end of August. The first and third were small, well organized gatherings. The Paris Congress, in contrast, was a chaotic shambles, enlivened by the fumings of the thuggish Director of the Moscow Oriental Institute. After the Berkeley conference, I visited a number of other North American centres of China studies including Stanford, Vancouver, Harvard, Columbia, Ann Arbor and Pittsburgh. In between the conferences, and in September, I spent a total of some eight weeks in Britain, attached to LSE as an academic visitor. This interlude enabled me to attend the wedding of Tadjo Szczepanik and Marie-Claire in a beautiful old recusant chapel in Warwickshire. The last part of my study leave was spent in Israel where I had been invited by the Institute of Asian and African Studies of the Hebrew University of Jerusalem and this, coinciding with the outbreak of the Yom Kippur War, must have a chapter to itself.

CHAPTER 16

Interlude – Israel and the
Yom Kippur War: 1973

As head of the ANU's Contemporary China Centre, I thought it my duty to organise protests in Australia, in union with China scholars in various lands, at the refusal of the Soviet Union to allow a Moscow sinologist, Vitaly Rubin, to emigrate to Israel. At that time, the Soviet government was denying such permission to a number of its Jewish citizens, the "refusniks" as they became known. In January 1971, the International Orientalists Congress was held in Canberra, and I went around getting good wishes for Rubin from the chief officers of that body and "big names" in the field of China studies. Having obtained his telephone number, I managed with difficulty to get through to Rubin's flat in Moscow; his line was often blocked. Instead of the informal conversation with him which I would have liked, I felt obliged to direct my words to the Soviet monitors of his calls and just listed the messages of good wishes from the President/Vice President/Secretary etc. of the Orientalists Congress and from Professors X/Y/Z from the universities of this, that and the other. Rubin and his wife were finally allowed to leave for Israel. Sadly, in 1981 he was killed in a road accident in Jerusalem.

As a result of this campaign, I came to know the Israeli diplomats in Canberra. In Hong Kong and at international conferences I had met an intelligent young Jewish China scholar, Eli Joffé, a specialist in Chinese military matters. Around this time, he had moved to Israel and held a position at the Hebrew University in Jerusalem which was building up its Chinese studies. I was invited to break my journey between Australia and London, when on study leave in 1973, and give a seminar at the Hebrew University. This I gladly agreed and so, late on Monday 1 October 1973, I landed at Lod Airport, Tel Aviv. My seminar was scheduled for the next week; the weekend in between included Yom Kippur when, of course, nothing happens in Israel. I did not want my first visit to the Holy Land to be entirely taken up with secular work so I arranged to come a bit early and to spend a few days (at my own expense of course) seeing the holy places in and near Jerusalem and to travel north to Nazareth on the day before Yom Kippur; then on the day after that solemnity to go south to Beersheba before returning to Jerusalem where I would begin the working part of my visit. Hotel bookings I made accordingly.[1]

I took a sherut (a large taxi shared by several passengers – a common mode of transport in Israel) from Tel Aviv to Jerusalem. We went through the Ayalon Valley where heavy fighting had taken place in the 1967 war and during the independence struggle against British forces in 1948 – and also in Joshua's day. We passed the Latrun Trappist Abbey; a Sabra (a Jewish settler born in Israel) girl next to me said that the abbey made excellent wine. Then we wound up to the hill country of Judea; alongside the road lay rusty carcasses of vehicles destroyed in fighting, left there as memorials; then on to Jerusalem.

That evening I visited the Old City, St Anne's Church and crypt and the Via Dolorosa. Making the Way of the Cross with a small group of mainly Mexican pilgrims, led by a Franciscan, we ended in the Church of the Holy Sepulchre. After that, I had supper with a Mexican girl, one of the pilgrim group, in a small eatery, Uncle Moustache's Café, just inside Herod's Gate. Then I telephoned my Hebrew University contacts, Eli Joffé, Martin Rudner and Zvi Schifferin, who invited me to meet them for lunch on Thursday. On Wednesday, I visited Bethlehem and, on the way back from that holy little town, I stopped at Talpiot to call on the cousin of my

1 During my visit to Israel, I kept a diary each day.

old Somerville friend, Esther Unger. She was out but I met her daughter and granddaughter.

Next morning, I went to Bethany before lunching with my friends from the Hebrew University. It was good to see Eli Joffé in his new surroundings. Zvi Schifferin had pioneered Chinese studies in Israel. He was the author of a book on Sun Yat Sen and studied Chinese diplomatic history; he also worked on the role of the military in Guomindang days – part of a general study of the military in politics in East Asia being undertaken in the University. Martin Rudner worked on Malaysia and Indonesia. Avraham Altmann, whom I had not met before, was a historian of pre-war Japan. They showed me the Mount Scopus Campus of the University and the Truman Institute.

On Friday morning, I left Jerusalem for Nazareth, travelling to Tel Aviv by sherut, then changing to another sherut for Haifa where I took a bus to Nazareth. Along the road, motorists stopped to give lifts to soldiers going on leave for Yom Kippur. On the way to Haifa, we passed Mount Carmel and a semi-desert area with sand dunes and tufty grass. The bus to Nazareth became very crowded with people hurriedly travelling home before Yom Kippur began at dusk. After finding my hotel at Nazareth – a Palestinian run establishment, apparently, although I was unable to distinguish between Jews and Palestinians by appearance – I visited the Basilica of the Annunciation, with its breath-taking inscription: "*Verbum caro hic factum est*" ("*Here*, the Word became flesh"). Yom Kippur had already begun and there was no chance of hiring a car to visit Lake Kinneret (Capernaum/Galilee) the next morning, as I would have liked; "You might be stoned," I was told. So on Saturday 6 October in the morning I visited the Basilica again, then the Church of St Joseph, the market and the synagogue-church. I looked for a carpenter's shop in the town and found one – with girlie pictures on the wall. The rocks at Nazareth were whitish, different from the sandy and reddish colours of Judea, and dark juniper trees stood out against them. It was a hot day and, after lunch, I lay down for a short rest. Then I began hearing planes, many of them, flying low over Nazareth. I knew that nothing, but nothing, flies in Israeli skies on Yom

Kippur, so I got up and went downstairs, but could get no information from the hotel staff. I went as I had planned to the 5 p.m. Mass at the Basilica. There were more low-flying planes and an old nun went out of the church to have a good look at them. On my return to the hotel, I found the lights were dimmed and, when I asked the reason, was told obvious lies about a shortage of power. Then there was the noise of distant firing and a loud explosion not very far away, shaking everything. (A couple of days later, I read that FROGs with high-explosive warheads had fallen on Migdal Ha'amek and Yafia, not far off.) From other hotel guests who had radios, I heard reports of a Syrian-Egyptian attack on Israel with fighting on the nearby Golan Heights and that public transport was paralysed. Some Dutch pilgrims were lodged at the hotel and the driver of their bus promised me a seat to return to Jerusalem the next day. The hotel was blacked out with no lights in our bedrooms.

The pilgrim bus left around 8 a.m. Next to me, on the back seat, sat two Israeli girl soldiers to whom the driver had also given lifts. They were quickly re-joining their units and one of them burst into tears. Air activity over Nazareth continued. A splendid view spread out the other side of the Nazareth hills as we descended the steep road to Afula. Beside us stretched irrigated land, including cotton fields; as we drove south, we passed half a dozen tanks going north to the fighting. At around 10 a.m. we reached Sebaste (the ancient Samaria) where we stopped and went around some excavated sites. The next halt was at Jacob's Well, the reputed place where Our Lord spoke to the Samaritan woman. Then we went on to Nablus where we stopped for lunch. On the next stretch of road, between Nablus and Ramallah, we met a continuous stream of military traffic – tank carriers, troop carriers and so forth – pushing north. Several times, when the road narrowed, our bus, and other southbound traffic, had to get to the side of the road to let the military vehicles pass. I remember especially a longish pause at the foot of Mount El Batan and wondered why civilian traffic had not been completely banned from that road so that both lanes could be used for the military – but probably the southbound lane, for logistic reasons, needed to be kept available for urgent use. After the winding mountain road up Mount El Batan, we came down again to the plain, then up again before coming to Bira. Military traffic was pushing northwards the whole time.

Finally, we arrived in Jerusalem about 3:30 p.m. I went to a 5:30 p.m. Latin Mass at St Saviour's parish church in the Old City and walked back to my hotel through dark streets – there were no street lamps but the blackout was not very strict by British war-time standards. In our bedrooms, we were allowed only bedside lamps. Obviously, my seminar was cancelled. No one was interested in East Asia when there was fighting on their doorstep. Also, some of the staff and most of the students of the Hebrew University had been re-called to the army. In Israel students were not admitted to universities until they had fulfilled their military service, three years for men and two for women. After that, they remained reservists until middle aged. Eli Joffé, Israel's only expert on the Chinese military, had been among the first to be re-called. He was asked one question: "What will the Chinese do?" He answered, "Nothing." He was, of course, right; and for the rest of the war, to his intense frustration, he twiddled his thumbs (and listened to the radio) while his students were at the front. Zvi Schifferin telephoned, gave me news about the situation and suggested that I should visit the Israeli and the Rockefeller Museums and Yad Vashem (the Holocaust Museum), which of course I intended to do. However, there were problems because of closures due to staff being called up.

I took time to walk again through the Old City, along the Via Dolorosa and to the Jaffa Gate. I went to Ein Kareem, the birthplace of St John the Baptist, sharing the taxi at first with three young ultra-orthodox youths – long black coats and hats, long hair and rather scruffy – the ultra-orthodox were at that moment almost the only young men around, being exempt from conscription – and later with a woman going to Bayit V'gan. The taxi driver said that the Mea Sharim Ultra-Orthodox types often gave trouble but he approved of those from Bayit V'gan, a religious quarter with new blocks of flats, as being good and reasonable. He himself was of Orthodox Christian Aramaic-speaking parentage and had been driving for thirty-two years. He had become a Catholic on his marriage, at his father-in-law's insistence, "and one cannot find a good wife every day." His wife cared excellently for him and their five children and they got on very well, he said, apart from the fact that he was sometimes impatient when he got home tired from work, but she understood that. Living in Israel presented no problem to his community, he continued, so long as they kept clear of politics. Four of his children were in Catholic schools and one boy in a German Lutheran one.

At Ein Kareem, I visited the Church of St John the Baptist, with blue and white glazed tiles on the walls, the Spring of the Virgin and, on a hill, the Church of the Visitation. Buses and taxis were scarce because of the emergency and I hitched a lift on an Irish pilgrim bus back to Jerusalem. I visited the Cenacle and a room below (now in Jewish hands) which is said to be the scene of the Descent of the Holy Spirit at Pentecost. I went to the Museum of the Holocaust but found it closed. That evening, Martin Rudner rang to say that the Syrians and Egyptians were being routed but that it might take a few more days to end the war.

Since the war began, I had been contacting airlines to enquire about how to get to Hong Kong because all eastward flights from Israel had been cancelled. Martin Rudner, who throughout these fraught days had been very attentive to my situation, picked me up the next morning and we called again at the TWA office in King David's Hotel but to no avail. Then he took me to see the Givat Ram Campus of the Hebrew University and we also visited the Museum of the Holocaust, now re-opened, reviving grim memories of my 1958 visit to Auschwitz. Eli Joffé was able to join Martin and myself and two others for lunch at the American Colony Hotel where naturally we all talked about the war. They thought it would probably strengthen the hawks in Israeli politics. The total size of the Israeli army, including reservists, was said to be around 350,000. For the first thirty hours, the attack was met by the core of professional officers and NCOs and the current conscripts.

That evening, I visited the Church of All Nations at the Mount of Olives and was told that if I came early the next morning, I could go into the Garden of Gethsemane. Next morning I went to the 6 a.m. Mass at the church before the gate of the Garden was opened. I was able to spend some time there, with the eight gnarled old olive trees, the roses, geraniums and other flowers and all the memories held by that hallowed place.

Back at the hotel, Martin rang to say that he and some others would pick me up at 8 p.m. for coffee. Then I made another attempt to get a flight, after which I went to the Museum of Israel where most of the galleries were closed because of staff call-ups; but I saw a gallery of the Canaanite period and a gallery of menorah. I tried the airline office again, without success – all the flights out of Israel seemed to be fully booked. That afternoon I went to the top of the Mount of Olives and visited the Shrine of the Ascension and the Pater Noster Shrine and grotto. Martin Rudner rang to cancel the 8 p.m. coffee because several people were being called up and he himself was expecting to be. Feeling rather desperate at the prospect of being stranded in Israel with most of my local friends disappearing, I rang up the Australian ambassador, Rawdon Dalrymple, who promised to ring me next morning about a flight. He came good and I got a seat on the night of 12 October to Athens whence I flew to Rome and there picked up a flight to Hong Kong.

I landed in Athens very early in the morning with some hours to spare before my flight to Rome, so I hailed a taxi and in the clear light of dawn made a swift circuit of the chief sights, although without time to alight and see them closely. As it has been my only visit to Greece, I am very grateful for the glimpse – it was soothing, too, after the storms of West Asia. Arriving in Hong Kong at last, on 14 October, I went to the Universities Service Centre, the US Consulate and the *Far Eastern Economic Review* and saw a couple of other China-watching contacts, to bring myself up to date with what had been happening outside Israel and its region. I also had dinner twice with my mother, before flying back to Canberra.

Since 1973, unfortunately, I have not been back to Israel and I remain inexpert on the affairs of that region, although on several occasions I have discussed them with those who are more knowledgeable. My instinctive feeling is that, at the base of the strife, lies a problem of identity, specifically of Jewish identity. It is said that there is little if any difference in the DNAs of local Arabs and the Jewish settlers. At the time of the diaspora, after the destruction of the Temple in AD 70, part of the Jewish population is likely to have remained and to have comprised at least some of the ancestors of the present Arab inhabitants. These, surely, should be beneficiaries of the Israeli Law of Return as also should, perhaps, many more of those now living in the lands of the Abrahamic covenant, embracing the "region between the Great River and the Wadi of Egypt".

My own gripe about the Jews is that for nearly two thousand years the Church has been without its natural leaders.

CHAPTER 17

More Culture Warfare, China Studies, Australian Journeyings, Family and Friends: 1973–79

When I returned to Canberra in October 1973, after study leave in Europe, the United States and then Israel (coinciding with the Yom Kippur War) members of the Right to Life Association were discussing the setting up of an NGO to help women experiencing problem pregnancies. We gathered information about similar bodies in other places and then drew up a training programme covering medical, social, legal and other components of the Pregnancy Support Service (PSS) as we named our project. We recruited professionals in these fields to give evening classes which a number of us attended and we brought out our first brochure, with a mission statement which I had drafted. We planned to have a call line operating for two hours every evening on weekdays, manned by a roster of trained volunteers. The greatest problem was to find suitable premises, free or at low cost, for our telephone, volunteer and files, and a place where social workers or others could meet clients. We also had to register the PSS as an NGO and a charity eligible to receive donations. Then we had to make the service known to those who might give us community support – religious bodies, including ethnic chaplaincies (which I went around visiting, drinking red wine with the Catholic Uniate Rite Ukrainians on one evening and vodka with the Russian

Orthodox Ukrainians on the next), welfare and medical agencies, schools and so forth, as well as to advertise the service to the general public.

It was not until around April 1975 that the PSS was able to begin activities. At first, there were few clients who telephoned us. I was on duty one evening a fortnight; for my first seven evenings, I had not a single call except from PSS colleagues, ringing to ask if everything was going all right. Others experienced similar silences. Then, on my eighth evening on duty, a call came from a girl, which made the previous evenings worthwhile. I had a long talk with her and arranged an appointment for her to see one of our professional social worker volunteers the next day, which she did. I do not know the eventual outcome or even who she was. The number of clients grew and, with them, the number of volunteers to help. More training courses were held and, by the end of the year, when my travelling schedule at work made it impossible for me to continue as a PSS counsellor, there were plenty of trained volunteers on the roster. After I moved into my own house, with a self-contained flatlet, I was able, when necessary, to accommodate emergency cases of young women wanting to hide from boyfriends who, in order to avoid child maintenance, were pressuring them to have abortions. RLA and PSS activities gave me a number of good friends in Canberra, including Kathleen Woolf, Beverly Cains, and Joan Apthorp; also, two sisters from Brisbane, Marie-Louise and Janet Uhr. Janet was writing a never-completed thesis on the mediaeval mystic, Julian of Norwich; their father, a Queensland medical man and a leading member of the state's horse-racing community, had worked stalwartly for his fellow prisoners of war in a Japanese camp, for which he was knighted. Later, also through RLA and PSS activities, I became good friends of Erin and Reg Mills, and Rita and Ron Duncan.

These activities also widened my contacts with politicians. Notable among these was Brian Harradine, an Independent senator from Tasmania from 1975 to 2005. After battles with trade union and ALP extremists, Harradine was elected to the Senate as an Independent candidate for Tasmania and held his position from 1975 to 2005, ending up as Father of the Senate. For some years he had an influential role as the swing vote in the Senate. He was always strongly pro-life. I visited him several times in his office in Parliament House and found him a kindly as well as a venerable figure. On one occasion in later years, when I was visiting Canberra from Hong Kong, Senator Harradine called in his like-minded colleague, Senator Bill O'Chee, of Queensland, for me to meet. Senator O'Chee, when elected, was, at twenty-four, the youngest-ever Australian senator, as well as being the first of Chinese extraction. His grandfather had emigrated from Guangdong to Australia, and being asked his name by the immigration officer, indistinctly mumbled, "Ah Chee," to which the official replied, "Very well, Mr O'Chee," and so it remained. Within a few years of arrival, his grandfather prospered, married an Irish-Australian girl in Brisbane's Catholic Cathedral and the grandson was sent to Oxford.

As long as I lived in Canberra I continued to be a member of the Right to Life Association's committee and to take part in its activities; and send occasional letters to the *Canberra Times*. As time went by, we were able to recruit more young members and so I gave it less time, but in the later 1970s, when the ACT Legislative Assembly's Standing Committee on Education and Health launched an inquiry on abortion, I submitted a ten-page memorandum.[1]

This was an era when radical feminism was the current fetish, leading up to International Women's Year in 1975; and for much of the time I was the senior woman academic in the university. A Women's Studies course was instituted and other activities held but I was completely ignored and never consulted. It was clear that the university authorities were not interested in women as such but only in members of the radical sisterhood who would make trouble if their agenda was not accepted. A woman who disagreed with this agenda did not count, was in fact an embarrassment and was sidelined academically. The committee with most power in the Research School of Pacific Studies was the Faculty Board, consisting of heads of departments. It was a moot point if heads of centres, such as my Contemporary China Centre, should be on it, and I never was. However, the day I ceased to be its head and was succeeded by Stephen

1 See the ACT Legislative Assembly's Cornwell Report, July 1977.

FitzGerald, he was immediately put on the board. I was not elected to the Australian Academy of Social Sciences while most others in the field of similar seniority were in it; I was never asked to give the Morrison Lecture (on matters Chinese) nor was I put on the board of the *Australian Journal of Chinese Affairs* which was founded a few years later, in both cases unlike most other China scholars of any standing in the country; nor was I consulted on anything concerning the new-fangled Women's Studies. (Irked, I wrote in without being asked, suggesting it should include a solid chunk of Marian theology.) On the one occasion when I asked permission to accept consultancy work, this was refused, although it was likely to give me an opportunity to get into China at a time when I had only been allowed in for one-night transit visits. When FitzGerald returned from China to take up a professorial fellowship at ANU, he was able to spend a lot of his time building up a consultancy which he later made his full-time occupation. Margaret Thatcher visited ANU when she was UK Minister of Education and was given an official lunch. The university administrators knew I was a friend of hers but did not invite me to it, so I positioned myself in a passage where she would be passing and had a short chat with her. She said to me, "I suppose you will be at the lunch today," to which I had to reply in the negative – all this while ANU was proclaiming its intention to promote the status of women in the university. I was from this time on always conscious of an undercurrent of hostility for not exemplifying the type of "progressive" woman currently in vogue. It was also no help that I did not share the enthusiasm for "New China" which was sweeping Australia at that time.

In July 1974, I gave a paper at a conference in Auckland, New Zealand, my only visit to that country. There was an epidemic of gastric influenza at the time, and I fell a victim to it the night before my paper, which had to be switched to the following day. A very kind and competent Maori room service attendant at my hotel called a doctor to me in the middle of the night. He gave me an effective remedy and then, unbidden, came a second time that night because he was anxious about my blood pressure, finally sending me a remarkably low bill.

After the conference, I was able to stay on for ten days to see more of that beautiful land. I spent two nights at Hamilton, with Marjorie Thompson, the widow of Tom, the second son of my guardians, Hammy and Dora Thompson. After the war, Tom had qualified as a teacher and emigrated to New Zealand, where he died in early middle age of a heart attack. Then I had a brief stay at the hot spring resort of Rotorua; heat from the sun is taken for granted but I found it emotionally comforting to be warmed by Mother Earth. I spent a weekend in Wellington with Pat and Mary Millen, New Zealand diplomats I had known in the Christian Life Group at Canberra. Pat was now Secretary to the New Zealand cabinet and he showed me the Cabinet Room in the "Beehive", their parliament building, just before a cabinet meeting was about to begin. From Wellington, I crossed to the South Island and visited Christchurch where I met Don Donnithorne, an architect, and his wife Dawn. Don had heard of my impending visit to speak at the Auckland conference and wrote, wondering if there might be some family link back in Cornwall. We never found such a link, but I have from time to time corresponded with other Donnithornes in different places, notably with Alan Donnithorne, a conservator of rare books and documents, but with similar results.

Now, in the final years of the Cultural Revolution, rather more publications began coming from China. Also, the Contemporary China Centre had been allotted some positions to fill: the holders would be appointed as well to the appropriate departments in RSPacS, according to their disciplines. Fred Teiwes, an American political scientist, was recruited and in 1974 he became the Centre's deputy head; John Fincher, another China political scientist, was a later addition. Other departments in RSPacS agreed to appoint China specialists if good ones could be found in their disciplines. However, when they had vacancies, it proved impossible to hire suitable candidates. Geographers and anthropologists with China knowledge were particularly difficult to find although I wrote to contacts across the world looking for them.

By this time, I had some graduate students: Kevin Bucknall, who successfully worked for a PhD, and Anton Ikonnikov, the White Russian from Manchuria who had the position of Research Officer and wrote an MA thesis on Chinese mineral resources. Y. S. Chan's collecting forays across China considerably improved the Menzies Library's stock of recent Chinese publications. Day by day I continued to follow Chinese broadcasts and press reports and wrote a number of articles, on China's financial policy for a banking review, on foreign trade as chapters of books brought out in New York and Hamburg and on more general economic topics in various journals, including *The China Quarterly*, where Nicholas Lardy and I conducted a vigorous argument on trends in fiscal control. I also wrote a number of papers for the Australia-China Business Co-operation Committee.

Visitors to ANU in 1974 included Michael Bordeaux of the Keston Institute, whose valiant documenting of the afflictions of Christians in Communist lands I had long admired and contributed to in a very small measure. I was for many years a member of the Advisory Board of Keston's journal but was able to do little to help; for China and other East Asian countries, Britain is not a good listening point. Jerome Chen came once again, this time to give the annual Morrison lecture. John Plamenatz, a Fellow of All Souls, Oxford, and his wife Marjorie were interesting visitors with whom I kept up for some years. Plamenatz, a distinguished political philosopher, had come to England around the time of the First World War as a child refugee from Montenegro where his father had been Foreign Minister. A very special visitor was Father Ladany, staying of course at the Jesuit house in Yarralumla, but giving a seminar at ANU. Eileen Brooke, an old friend from my London days at the Newman Association came, but as a private, not an official visitor; however, she gave a seminar on mental health statistics at an appropriate department of the university. I drove her round bits of the countryside, getting lost on one occasion in a wild part of the bush between Braidwood and the coast.

In November and December 1974, I had four weeks in Hong Kong, China-watching, including attendance at a Marco Polo Club Dinner. The Marco Polo Club was nominally sponsored by some Overseas Chinese brothers from the West Indies, but really controlled by Beijing, to draw

Westerners to a more sympathetic stance towards the regime. It was one of the minor feelers put out, by one side or the other, during these years; an interesting, if curious, occasion, but unsuccessful as a ploy to get me the visa that I wanted for an individual visit to China.

In mid-December, I returned to Canberra and did not take study leave to go to England. I had a lot to do in Australia, both in work and leisure activities, and I planned to keep my study leave until the next year, when I had been invited to some conferences in Europe. This also enabled me to attend the wedding, in January 1975, of two ANU students I had come to know, John Harris and Ruth Picton, in the John XXIII chapel on the campus. They had both grown up in the NSW outback, John at Broken Hill and Ruth in the north of the state. They both, too, had read law at ANU. I introduced them to my friends and solicitors, Jim and Rita O'Connor, in whose firm they later worked, finally becoming partners and then taking it over when the O'Connors retired. John and Ruth brought up a family of six children which I often used to visit.

A few weeks later, my old friend Alex Eckstein and his wife Ruth came to ANU for ten days, covering a weekend Contemporary China Centre seminar at which both he and myself, and others, gave papers. I drove the Ecksteins to the Araluen district near Braidwood, where my colleague David Bensusan-Butt had restored a derelict cottage built by Chinese goldminers in the previous century.

Around this time the infant granddaughter of a school friend of mine at Runton Hill, Sheila Mould, was christened in the John XXIII chapel. Sheila had emigrated with her husband Michael, a motor company executive, to Australia and through a happenstance we had met again. Sheila's son, Jeremy, became a well-known astronomer and was at one time director of the Mt. Stromlo Observatory near Canberra.

Towards the end of 1975, partly covering the Australian summer vacation, I took two and a half months' study leave, planned around two conferences, one in Paris and the other in Puerto Rico, at which I gave papers. I included a few days of holiday en route, in Kuala Lumpur and at Rome. At Kuala Lumpur, I spent two nights with my old friends, Gregory and Margaret Chan. Gregory had risen to be the top judge in the Malaysian armed forces, but he felt his own position, and more important to him, the future of his children, threatened by Malay dominance. So he intended to resign, losing all his pension rights, and migrate if possible to Australia. Fortunately, Al Grassby, at that time Commissioner for Community Relations, whom I approached, proved helpful and the Chan family were given visas. In Rome, I spent two nights and attended an indoor papal audience.

From Rome, I flew to London where, once again, I had academic visitor status at LSE, gave a seminar there and attended a Chatham House China lunch. I also met people connected with the conduct and financing of trade with China, as well as with academics, including Peter Nolan and Michael Yahuda, both then at LSE; with Stuart Schram at SOAS; and officials, including David Wilson, now at the Cabinet Office, who were following Chinese affairs. In addition, I was able to catch up with members of my extended family, godchildren and old friends, spending a night with Mary Douglas, and seeing Lucy Brown, Esther Ehrmann (née Unger), Michael Fogarty, Pen Piercy, now retired to Dorset, and many others. Father John Eddy SJ of ANU was in London and I lunched with him and his confrères at the British Jesuit provincial house at Farm Street. I spent Christmas with my extended family and saw in the 1976 New Year with Pen Piercy in her Dorset cottage.

From London, I went to Hamburg where I gave a lecture at the Institute of Asian Studies. The Director, Dr Draguhn, who had recently visited ANU, took me on an interesting drive around the city, including the docks. Then I went by rail to Münster which I had last seen in ruins in the winter of 1946–7 when I was told it would take until the end of the century to clear the rubble. Now it was rebuilt, a pleasant and prosperous city again. My weekend there was made the more interesting by the fact that my friend from those days, with whom I stayed, Margret Maué, whose first husband died on the Soviet front, was now married to the former city manager, Heinrich Austermann, under whose aegis the Münster miracle had occurred. They had three sons; the eldest was home on leave from his compulsory military service and was talking about life in the army, which was of course then part of the NATO forces facing the Soviets in the Cold War. Suddenly I realised that I was thinking of him and his comrades as being "our army", but that it was in fact the German Army which in two World Wars in the current century had killed members of my family. A profound gratitude overwhelmed me that such a change for the better had come about, at least in Western Europe.

My next stop was Paris, for a conference on Chinese science and technology which was, unusually, being held by the OECD; I gave a paper on the Chinese planning system. In my report to ANU I wrote that this conference was "sensible, informative and down to earth, or at least down to the red mud from bauxite processing, which the Chinese are said to be making into low-grade cement", probably because attendants at the conference "included members of scientific and technical delegations to China and businessmen experienced in dealing with China". I stayed for a night with Marie-Claire Bergère who had a chair at L'Institut National des Langues et Civilisations Orientales and who was working on economic affairs in China between the two world wars. She told me that Jean Chenneaux had given up China studies because he was disgusted with the fall of "the Four" after Mao's death. In Paris, I had dinner with Monna Adie (Besse) who, after a split with Ian apparently occasioned by British tax laws, had returned to Paris where she had just opened an art gallery.

From Paris, I went by train to Geneva where I lunched with my old Somerville friend Cécile Standley (née Offen) who was working at the WHO and then flew, via Madrid, to my next conference at Puerto Rico which was on "China as a Model for Developing Countries" – this was the China then engulfed by the Cultural Revolution. The participants were almost all academic economists. To quote again from my report: "This conference illustrated the susceptibility of American academics to waves of fashion, a trait not unique to the USA but perhaps found there in more acute form than in most places. This generates an overconfidence in what they think they know about a society of which few of them have had first-hand experience and which they implicitly shape in terms of Western categories."

From Puerto Rico I went on, in early February 1976, to Jamaica to spend a few days with an old student from University College London, Claudia Johnson (née Carasco), who was setting up a Science and Technology Unit for the Jamaican National Planning Agency. The Johnsons very kindly drove me over much of that beautiful but, at that time, troubled island. From Jamaica, my return to Australia went by way of Stanford and San Francisco. It was good to see Y. L. Wu again at the Hoover Institute at Stanford, where I gave a paper. Franz Schurmann drove me from Stanford to his home in San Francisco where I stayed with him and his wife Sandy Close; both were friends I'd met many times in Hong Kong. During the drive, Franz astonished me with his torrent of praise for President Nixon, whose foreign policy was to be the subject of his next book. I had regarded Franz as being a rather extreme, but likeable, left winger but, on this topic, he had swung round. The flight across the Pacific I broke at Fiji and Noumea, catching glimpses of those islands, before returning to Canberra in mid-February 1976, in time for the new academic year.

My former Oxford tutor John Hicks (who had since won a Nobel for economics) and his wife Ursula visited ANU for some weeks in March and April 1976. They both gave lectures and seminars and I took them around to see the countryside and local sights such as the splendid open-air fruit market, with covered stalls that was one of Canberra's assets, and, on a weekend, Lake George, a large expanse of flat land near the Canberra-Goulburn road, which filled up with water or went wholly or partially dry, according to rainfall.

During the May vacation 1976, I attended and gave a paper at a conference of the ANZAAS in Hobart which gave me an opportunity to explore a little of Tasmania and also, en route, of Victoria, stopping at Bendigo and Ballarat and then spending a night, and leaving my car, at the home of Michael and Sheila Mould in Frankston before flying to Launceston where I hired another car and drove to Burnie on the north coast of the island. Next day I went southwest to Queenstown on the west coast where I booked a one-day cruise on the wild Franklin and Gordon Rivers. It is the only time I have seen such dense temperate climate forests

– then to Hobart for the conference. While at Hobart, I decided to drive up the nearby Mount Wellington without realising what an ordeal this would be. The ascent of over 4,000 feet, round and round the mountain, made me terribly dizzy but there was no way I could turn around and go back. Once at the top, I had to descend, this time driving at the outer edge of the road, overhanging the precipice. I visited the grim former penal colony near Hobart. Returning to mainland Australia, I spent two days at another conference at Melbourne University before driving back to Canberra to catch up with the pile of China reports and Contemporary China Centre business that had accumulated in my absence.

My cousin, Ilsley Ingram, by now holding a chair in haematology at St Thomas's Medical School, London, visited ANU for a few days in 1976 to give some lectures in its medical school, but his visit was too rushed to show him much of the countryside. In the latter part of 1976, a well-known Chinese painter, Chiang Yee, better known as "The Silent Traveller", spent some months at University House. He was an agreeable presence around the place and at Christmas time gave a number of his friends, including myself, small pictures he had painted. His gift to me, a delightful painting of two pandas with bamboos, hangs in my study in Hong Kong as I write. Around this time, I got to know Augustine Maung Maung, the Burmese Ambassador to Australia, and his wife Clara. He had been a brigadier in the Burmese Army and was taken prisoner by Karen (or possibly other) rebels, militant Christians of the American Baptist persuasion. They threw him into a pit and told him that he could not come out until he agreed to be baptised. He thought it over, accepted their terms and, on his release, betook himself to the nearest Catholic mission and asked for baptism. Augustine and Clara practised their new religion seriously and used to attend Mass daily at St Christopher's Cathedral. When they left Canberra, they asked me to keep an eye on a student-aged daughter in which, I fear, I was not very successful. However, I continued to remain in touch with the parents until Augustine died, and then, for some years more, with Clara.

Meanwhile, the Chinese Cultural Revolution was rolling to its end. During 1976, two events in that country impacted global consciousness.

On 28 July the North China industrial and coal mining centre of Tangshan, a city of around one million people, was destroyed by an earthquake, with a death toll of between 240,000 and 700,000, and possibly more. Foreign press and other observers were kept away, although by chance the Australian Prime Minister, Gough Whitlam, and the Australian ambassador, my erstwhile colleague Stephen FitzGerald, were in the earthquake zone at the time and had a narrow escape. Offers of foreign help poured in but the Chinese government refused them all, even heavy lifting equipment which China then lacked but which the Japanese offered to fly over; as a result, many trapped victims must have died unnecessarily. On behalf of the Contemporary China Centre, I sent a letter of sympathy to the Chinese Embassy in Canberra. A few weeks later, in ominous proximity in time by Chinese notions, came the death of Mao Zedong. As he was the de facto, if not the de jure, head of state, I thought that as Head of our Centre, I should sign the embassy book which I did, showing Mao the respect which Scripture enjoined should be given to Nero. As Chinese tradition dictates, I bowed thrice before the Mao portrait on display, with an unuttered, and perhaps not very confident, prayer in my heart for the repose of the soul of the dead tyrant. It was probably just the standard portrait I had seen countless times before, but that day it seemed to bring out the old peasant in the man and I felt I had been transmigrated to a Chinese country funeral, with white mourning headbands unwrapping and flapping in the wind.

In October 1976, an occasion called the Women of the Year Lunch was held in Canberra[2] (it peregrinated annually around the national and state capitals of Australia), to which I was invited. At my table, I was glad to see an Aboriginal lady with whom I got into conversation. I learned that Mabel Edmund was a member of the Aboriginal and Islander Loans Commission, a body set up by the federal government to provide loans to Aboriginals for home ownership and the setting up of small businesses. This body held meetings in Canberra every month or two and thenceforward, if I was in town when she came, she always had a meal with me at University House

2 Not Sydney, as Mabel Edmund states in her autobiography, *No Regrets*, the University of Queensland Press, 1992, p. 83.

or later, when I had moved, at my own home. This had the good result of inducing me to more ambitious cooking than the usual eggs and bacon or similar that I would eat in the evenings, after a substantial lunch at the university. The previous weekend, I would make a casserole, put it in the freezer, take it out to thaw on the morning of Mabel's visit and then, in the evening, put it into the oven to cook slowly while I drove to fetch her from her motel, which was usually far away.

In November and December 1976, I spent seven weeks in East Asia – four in Hong Kong and three in Japan. In Hong Kong, l made my usual, and expanding, round of contacts. At the University of Hong Kong, I met an Australian lecturer in the Law Department, Roderick O'Brien, who had a special interest in law in the People's Republic, an interest then rare among Western academics.

In Tokyo, I based myself, once again, at the beautiful International House of Japan in Tokyo, except during a conference, when we were all lodged together in a hotel. I gave a paper at a Colloquium on Conflict and Regional Co-operation in Asia. In addition, I spoke at Toho Gakkai (the Institute of Eastern Culture) and to the American Chamber of Commerce.

My old friend, Shinkichi Eto, now Professor of International Relations at Tokyo University, had suggested a number of people in Japan whom I should meet on China matters, in addition to my long-standing contacts. My first visit was to JETRO (Japanese External Trade Research Organisation), a powerful government body. I had an interview with Mr Takahashi of the China division of the Gaimusho (the Ministry of Foreign Affairs). I saw Chuzo Ichiko of Toyo Bunko, one of the world's largest Asian Studies libraries and also a major research institute; and Inuka Nokajima of the (I think, official) International Political and Economic Research Unit. Shigeru Ishikawa of Hitotsubashi University, another old friend, I met again at the Institute for Developing Economies, where I also spoke with Etsuzo Onoue. Professor Ishikawa gave me a magnificent dinner at a French restaurant on the top floor of the then highest building in Tokyo, designed to sway, but not break, during earthquakes. Of course, I also talked with Shinkichi Eto at Tokyo University and visited his home and met his wife Kozuko, the zealous guardian of pets and birds; as he once noted on a Christmas card: "She feeds two kittens, two dogs and dozens of wild birds... in addition to her husband." In August 2005 on the sixtieth anniversary of the bomb on Nagasaki, which he had survived, I telephoned him; fortunately, his health remained all right as did that of his three children and eleven grandchildren. He died in 2007. I also met, once more, Hideo Yamada of Hitotsubashi University, a south-east Asia and Japanese history scholar and had dinner with him and his wife Haruko. Hideo had been a visiting fellow at University College in 1962 and we had shared an office. Later he taught for short spells at the National University of Ireland in Dublin and at the Japanese Centre at Sheffield.

When I visited Sophia University I met, among others, Gregory Clark, the eldest son of my old friend Colin Clark. Richard Rigby was en poste at the Australian Embassy in Tokyo and it was good to be able to see him and Taifang and their eldest daughter Jiajia (Alison) informally, as well as on a visit to the embassy itself. I also talked to Nick Platt of the US Embassy and spoke with a veteran Chinese correspondent in Tokyo, K. C. Lu, who entertained me at the Foreign Correspondents' Club, which had a magnificent view across the city over to Mount Fuji, and I watched that great mountain glow in the setting sun. At the Japan Foundation, I thanked them for funding a visiting scholar to ANU's Contemporary China Centre and discussed the possibility of making a permanent arrangement for such visitors.

I never spent long enough in Japan to make any deep connection with that strange, yet in many ways attractive society. I had always to remind myself that the Japanese were not "Chinese gone wrong". There is a striking contrast between the wholesale and rapid way they adopted the technical side of Western civilization, together with the extraordinary digestion and adaptation of English words into the Japanese language on the one hand, and the determination to maintain their own racial homogeneity on the other. Demographically and economically Japan, perhaps more than any other ancient society, needs large scale immigration, with subsequent efforts to channel newcomers into full participation and integration in national life. However, in Japan any such notion runs up against a colossal psychological barrier. This leads to consideration of the role of the Church in helping to merge peoples and cultures in many parts of the world in many ages. A vision of the unity of the human family must underlie such a role.

Early in 1977, Stephen FitzGerald resigned from the Beijing embassy and returned to ANU as a professorial fellow. It was probably inevitable, and reasonable, that he should take over from me as Head of the Contemporary China Centre, but I was grieved that nothing came of the negotiations which I had begun with the Japan Foundation for it to make continuous placements of Japanese China scholars in the Centre. Two years later, Stephen resigned his ANU position and devoted his time to building up his business consultancy, which flourished. Later, he became for some years head of Goldman Sachs's subsidiary in Australia. This switch from ideological sympathy to disillusionment and then to immersion in business perhaps mirrored that which occurred in China in a wide segment of the people.

At the end of my tenure as Head of the Contemporary China Centre, Wang Gungwu, Director of the Research School of Pacific Studies, wrote to thank me: "The Centre has had an excellent start under your care. My only regret is that we were not able to get all the support we needed for the Centre during your tenure as Head. Despite such difficulties and disappointments, we have come a long way. The Centre has become well-known through your efforts abroad, through its seminars and conferences, through the visitors it has brought to Canberra and through the help and encouragement you have given to make our library one of the best of its kind in the world where contemporary China materials are concerned." The Vice Chancellor, Anthony Low, wrote to me: "The Centre has established itself as the major focus in Australia for academic studies of China. It has most successfully brought together people from different parts of the University who have an interest in China and we are most grateful to you for all the time and energy you have put into its early development."

By May 1977 political fervour in China had softened sufficiently for physical scientists to send delegations abroad; and one from the Chinese Academy of Sciences duly arrived in Canberra and was suitably fêted. However, social studies were still too politically sensitive to permit of foreign contacts.

An interesting and rather amusing event in the first part of 1977 was the plebiscite on the National Song. The rise of republicanism among a sector of Australians had aroused controversy about the National Anthem, which had always been "God Save the Queen". The Labor Government in 1974 commissioned a national opinion survey to determine the preferred song for occasions of national significance, except those of a specifically regal nature, and "Advance Australia Fair" won out. Two years later, the re-elected Liberal Government widened the use of "God Save the Queen" but also conducted a national referendum to choose a song for use on ceremonial occasions when it was desired to mark a separate Australian identity. The two front runners were "Advance Australia Fair" and the traditional "Waltzing Matilda", the personal favourite of the Liberal Prime Minister Malcolm Fraser and which I, too, preferred. However, "Advance Australia Fair" won, it is thought by the votes of non-Anglophone immigrants who did not appreciate the Australian penchant for failed rascals, deriving from the country's days as a penal colony. I never heard the morality of "Waltzing Matilda" raised on this or any other occasion – though making a hero of a suicidal thief might seem doubtful. However, the sentiment that final justification is more likely to come to the broken, finds a deep echo in the harshness of the outback and one that keeps on resounding throughout Australian history.

Jane Ingram, my cousin, was to be married on 30 July 1977 and I had planned to pay a private visit to England for that, before giving a paper at a conference in Taiwan. My mother's health had been declining and in mid-July, while still in Canberra, I had an urgent appeal from her doctor, Don Langford (an old friend of hers, an American missionary in Hong Kong), to take some decisions in respect of her which he did not feel he could take alone. So on 21 July, I flew to Hong Kong where I found my mother was very deranged (perhaps with Alzheimer's, although diagnoses for that were not as common then as later) and not at all able to look after her own affairs. So, with the help and advice of Dr Langford and her pastor, the Rector of St Andrew's Church, Kowloon, Bob Hyatt and his wife Helen, all of whom were very supportive, I was able to appoint someone to have power of attorney for her and then I took her to the Matilda Hospital on the Peak. Dr Langford was anxious that I should find a nursing home in England to which she could be sent as there was nowhere suitable in Hong Kong after she was discharged from hospital; he envisaged there might be a long illness or, at least, period of disability. Apart from Hong Kong, all her friends were in England and I had nowhere to bring her to in Australia, a country where she had never been. As I was planning to return to Hong Kong later that summer, on my way to the conference in Taipei, I would soon be back to see her.

I accompanied my mother in an ambulance, through the newly-opened first under-harbour tunnel in Hong Kong, to the hospital, where I saw her to her bed in a ward. The next day I came again and said goodbye. Her devoted amah, Ah Ho, often came to visit her in the next few days. By that time, my mother was completely deranged and Ah Ho was the only person to whom she would listen or seemed to want to see. Then I took a flight to London where I arrived in time for Jane's wedding. The wedding was beautiful, in the village church at Elmsted, near her parents' first retirement home, Staple Lees on the Sussex Downs. In retrospect, however, the day was clouded. After two children were born and Jane could no longer give Christopher her undivided attention, he proved unfaithful and Jane obtained a divorce.

A few days later, while I was staying with Christopher and Felicity Ingram in Claygate, a telephone call in the middle of the night from the Hyatts told me that my mother had just died. It was a surprise and a shock. The Hyatts had made arrangements for the funeral and they did not think I should return for it. Later that summer, before the Taiwan conference, I spent a few days in Hong Kong, during which I saw the Hyatts and other friends of my mother and sorted out her flat and ensured that provision was made for Ah Ho who had helped my mother so devotedly for years. She was given enough money to build a new house for her family in their village near Guangzhou, in return for which they would look after her for the rest of her days.

The August 1977 Taipei conference on modern Chinese economic history lasted a week, including a two-day tour of the island, taking us south to Tainan and then for a night to a magnificent hostelry in the forests of central Taiwan. Scholars of modern and contemporary China from different lands were invited and had a chance to meet their Taiwanese counterparts and to see what was going on in this other part of the One China. During the sessions, participants were lodged in the Grand Hotel on the outskirts of Taipei, a palatial edifice but not very comfortable. From there, we were taken each day by bus to the conference hall in the city. The conference was funded by the Taiwanese authorities – the still rare tours and other formal jaunts on the Mainland (such as our own in 1973) were likewise, of course, government financed. While realising the biases inherent in such visits on both sides of the Taiwan Straits, those of us who were primarily interested in discovering what was happening in China welcomed all opportunities to try to do so.

After the conference, I stayed on for a couple of days to see something more of Taipei and friends there. Frederick Crook, whom I had met several times in Hong Kong, where he had spent some years in the American Consulate as a knowledgeable expert on Chinese agriculture, was now living in Taipei with his wife Elizabeth and their five children. He had taken extended leave of absence from American government service to answer a call from his religious group, the Mormons, to head their unit in Taiwan of around twenty young American volunteers doing the two-year evangelisation stint which Mormons are expected to undertake. It was interesting to have a glimpse of this group. After they dropped polygamy, the Mormons have zealously followed healthy Christian family principles and have partnered Catholics on anti-abortion and other pro-life issues.

In September 1977, I went from Hong Kong to Jakarta where I stayed for a week with my Canberra colleague Ruth Daroesman in Jakarta, noting changes since my previous visit twenty-five years earlier. After that, I resumed my original plans for study leave in Britain and on the Continent. The Economics Department of LSE once more provided a hospitable base. I was able to attend one of the Chatham House China lunches and meet former colleagues and other London contacts. However, much of my time was spent out of London, visiting and giving papers at other British universities – Edinburgh and Glasgow, where afterwards I spent a weekend with Jack and Maisie Gray in their country village home; Leeds, staying with Brian and Vilma Hook, also in a village outside the city; and Oxford, where I stayed with Francis and Ruth Seton of Nuffield College. I visited George Allen in his retirement flat and at St Antony's met Mark Elvin and Cyril Lin; and Cambridge, where I stayed at Clare Hall, lunched at Newnham and saw Barbara E. Ward and, briefly, Elizabeth Anscombe. A notable growth had taken place on the Continent in studies of contemporary China and I had invitations to visit and give papers in France, Germany and the Netherlands. In Paris, I was invited by Marie-Claire Bergère to lecture at the Institut National des Langues et Civilisations Orientales and spent a night in the flat of my kind hostess. Regretfully, I have never been able to understand the ramifications of the different Parisian units engaged in China studies, nor their links with the various Sorbonnes. In the Netherlands, I visited Erasmus University in Rotterdam where I met Huang Weixin who had written a useful book on water conservancy in China; from there I paid a short visit to Leiden, the first Dutch centre of Chinese studies, but with a primary concentration on language and traditional culture. My visit to Saarbrüken was particularly enjoyable, staying with Jürgen and Marie-Luise Domes, whom I always found congenial. I spent two nights in their house on the mountainside overlooking the city.

In between these visits, I had to catch up with a backlog of radio monitoring reports and other material to be scanned for what I was hoping might be a new edition of my *China's Economic System* which I had already discussed with publishers. Also, I sorted out some of my mother's affairs with her solicitors; my uncle Robert Ingram had died in 1973 and his firm, Crofts, Ingram & Crofts, was being run by his nephew-in-law, Bill Vaughan. Under my grandmother Victoria Ingram's trust, I inherited a small share of her trust funds. I also saw other relatives, godchildren and old friends. I spent several days with Pen Piercy who was now living in the village of Hinton Martell in Dorset where she had created a splendid garden, both flowers and vegetables.

After Christmas 1977, I flew back to Hong Kong for three weeks of China-watching, including a weekend walking round Guangzhou, its lanes and alleyways, reading municipal notices and local newspapers, which foreigners were forbidden to buy but which were pasted on walls. Observing life in Mainland China at first hand made a stimulating change from long-range China-watching.

I returned to Canberra late in January 1978, to clear up various topics for the new edition of *China's Economic System*. My attention in the next few years was particularly on China's financial policy, on investment and on central-provincial economic relations, making use of information and general background gained from interviews in Hong Kong and, later, on the mainland, while writing some more pieces to meet particular requests.

When I had bought the small house in Red Hill a few years previously, I thought that one day I might move there. However, as it was very satisfactorily let to an Aboriginal public servant, I did not want to interfere with that arrangement. I also had more funds now and would have more choice. I looked around and in April 1978 viewed a run-down house, old by Canberra standards,[3] that had been on the market for some time, with an overgrown garden, and apple and other fruit trees in the back yard, together with a swimming pool about thirty feet long and fifteen feet wide and a small pool house. At first, I was rather put off by the pool, fearing it as a responsibility and risk, but realised that safety railings could be installed round it; the price of the house did not seem to be enhanced by the pool. The front garden featured a Western cedar brooding over a

3 The ground lease, like that of all Canberra real estate, for ninety-nine years, dated from 9 December 1954. The house had at one time been owned by Sir William Dunn, a former Secretary of the Department of Foreign Affairs, with whom I corresponded about the house and garden.

lawn and was surrounded by a thick cypress hedge about six feet high, giving privacy to house and garden. At one side of the house towered a tall Californian sequoia pine which someone told me had been planted there by Walter Burley Griffin, the town planner of Canberra. Bushes of lavender and rosemary grew on each side of the front door, wafting a welcoming fragrance. The house was whitewashed with a roof of dull, weathered red tiles and looked pleasing in a quiet way. Half of the house had previously housed the Abraxas Art Gallery and this part, as it stood, was unsuited for residential purposes; probably this, together with the poor state of the property market at the time, had deterred potential buyers. Separate from the house was a garage and also a solidly built windowless brick storehouse which had been used by the gallery for storage of pictures.

I felt the house had possibilities and liked it from the start. My friend, Jim Nimmo, who with his wife were members of our Sunday evening Christian Life Group, and who was a former Director of Housing in the ACT, very kindly went around it with me and he thought it looked all right. I had it professionally surveyed and it was pronounced sound. By the end of May, I had signed the contract and could take possession, although the house was not yet ready for occupation.

Then I made a rough plan of what I wanted done with the half of the house that had to be re-constituted and hired an architect. He made proper plans and agreed to superintend the builder whom I selected from a number of possibilities he suggested; several of these were moderate-sized firms and one was an individual builder, Neville Flynn, to whom, after tenders and interviews, I gave the job on the basis of his lower price. Mr Flynn was an Irishman, rather elderly, small and gnarled, not a man of many words, but good at his trade. As he was a one-man builder, whenever he was called to an urgent job elsewhere, he would leave my less pressing one, sometimes for days. Still, he finished my work in the end, and did it well. On completion, in addition to the five rooms in the part of the house which I already occupied, there was a one-room flatlet with kitchenette and shower room, and another self-contained unit consisting of two bedrooms with a bathroom in between and a living room with its own outside door.

Local laws, I think, precluded me letting these units but they could be used without payment by friends. My section of the house comprised a sitting room and a dining room (which could be combined into one by the lifting of the dividing fixture), my bedroom, bathroom, a study/guest room, and a large kitchen.

There were many other things to be fixed around the house and garden – repainting of various places, a garage door to be fitted, a cover to be bought to prevent the pool being filled with falling leaves, safety railings to be installed to surround it, the large kitchen to be fitted out with a cooker, oven and refrigerator, a washing machine for the small laundry room, a telephone and electric heaters to be installed, curtains to be made and hung, items of furniture to be bought from shops (or at auctions) and delivered at a time when someone would be there. I bought a large pinewood table for the kitchen and had most of my meals (and informal entertaining) on it. At auctions, I bought old chests of drawers and a more elegant table and chairs for the dining room. In fact, both tables were used most often for the spreading out of papers and writing. Thus, if at one time I was writing two different articles, I could use separate tables and avoid confusing the notes of each. In a front room, which I had designated as a study but rarely used as such, I placed a large desk which was one of the few pieces of furniture I had brought from my Kensington flat; but it was used chiefly as an overflow depository of books for which the book shelves were inadequate. This front room had a couch-bed in it and so could accommodate guests, as it soon did my cousin Nicola Ingram. Around this time the Prime Minister's house, The Lodge, was being refurbished and its old furnishings discarded and auctioned. I took advantage of this to buy cheaply a large sofa and two armchairs, all in worn brown leather and very comfortable. The sofa and one armchair added a historic touch to my living room while the other armchair went to the study. Location is of course the deciding factor about any real estate, and on that my house scored well. It was about seven minutes' walk from St Christopher's Cathedral and about five from the Manuka shopping centre. The drive to ANU took around twenty minutes.

There was already a fig tree growing against the wall at the end of the garden, beyond the pool; now I added a vine against another wall, also a mulberry tree (memories of my Uncle Robert's garden at Claygate) and a persimmon. None of these plantings were notably successful – no doubt because I had neither the skills nor the time to care for them. I was fortunate in finding a very agreeable Italian from near Venice – Mrs Res – to give the house a thorough cleaning and thereafter to come to clean it once a week, whether I was there or not. The garden was more than I could manage by myself, so I found a retired gardener who came in for a few hours a week to cut the grass on the lawn and the wide roadside verges on two sides of the house and to keep the rest of the place in a minimal state of tidiness. He was a reliable old man and I got to know him and his family. After a few years, and the death of his wife, he asked if he could work longer in my garden. He said he did not want more money but liked gardening and his own garden was very small. This put me in a quandary. I did not want to spend extra on my garden. If Mr Lawless worked more hours for the same sum, I would be paying less than the minimum wage regulations permitted, yet I wanted to keep him happy. So I told him that I would not stipulate how many hours he should work; he might work for as few or as many as he wanted, and I would pay him a fixed weekly amount. This seemed to suit him well and, after his death, his family thanked me for it.

In July 1978, I was able to move into the house. Alterations to the former gallery were still in progress but that did not affect my living arrangements. The next day, a Saturday, Father John Eddy SJ said Mass in the house where some friends had gathered with me.

Ilsley's younger daughter, Nicola, usually known as Hokey, was now twenty-four and had finished her training as a nurse. She had then volunteered for a Royal Geographical Society expedition to the jungles of Borneo where she was in charge of the health of the participants and had the responsibility of deciding, in the case of injury or illness, whether a helicopter should be summoned to take a patient to hospital. On return to England, she herself went down with hepatitis. After her recovery, by way of convalescence, she came to Canberra, where I now had a house. Hokey arrived in November 1978, just before the Australian long vacation. We decided that after Christmas we would visit parts of the New South Wales and Queensland outback as well as a little of the Queensland coast. Before that, she saw something of the Canberra area, helped plant camellias in my garden, met two of my Aboriginal friends – Mabel Edmund, on one of her regular visits to Canberra for a meeting of the Aboriginal Loans Commission, and Charles Perkins, whose English wife made a dress for her which Hokey still has now, after nearly forty years. Then she met many more of my friends at a huge house-warming party (though held mainly in the garden), for which I thoroughly exploited poor Hokey, whose help was invaluable. She also went off on her own to Sydney and Melbourne to see family friends.

After Christmas, Hokey and I set off in my Ford Escort to Nyngan, and next day Wilcannia, where my Canberra friend, Clare Connell, came to our motel and took us to her family property not far off, which I had already visited on my earlier trip that way in 1971. We were shown stone artefacts, made by Aboriginals, which the Connells often picked up – worked stones, which in Europe would be called prehistoric and, indeed, were so, but in Australia the prehistory in which they were made might be within our own lifetimes. The property was severely affected by drought. We continued to Broken Hill and then backtracked to Wilcannia where we struck north-east to Bourke and spent two nights there. We saw the Mother Teresa Sisters, whom I had met in 1971, and Hokey visited the local clinic where the nurses asked her help in looking at X-rays and with outpatients; the doctors came only occasionally.

From Bourke, we went on to Moree where we celebrated Hokey's twenty-fifth birthday and the following day reached Brisbane, spending three nights there and visiting my Canberra friends, Pastor Mervyn and Sonya Stolz, who were staying at their old home at Benleigh, just south of the city. From Brisbane, we went north along the coast to Bundaberg and its giant pineapple, a statue in honour of a major local product, and there we stayed with family friends of Hokey. We broke off our travels to enjoy four days by the sea at nearby Bargara; then we drove on, through Gladstone, where I wanted to see the large mineral export port, to the next big coastal town, Rockhampton. There we had dinner at the home of my friend Mabel Edmund, meeting her husband Harold (usually called "Digger") and some of their children. Digger was employed at the local meat works.

From Rockhampton we went to Yeppoon, just north on the coast, for a night before striking inland to see something of the Queensland outback. Driving through Blackwater, Emerald, and Alpha, we spent a night at a motel in Barcaldine. We were hoping to go further inland to Longreach but decided to begin our homeward journey southward. The next place where my petrol notes tell me we filled up the car, was at Blackall, around a hundred miles south of Barcaldine and then at Augathella before overnighting at Charleville.

At some stage during that day, between Augathella and Charleville, occurred the only seriously untoward incident on our trip. While I was driving, a red kangaroo suddenly jumped from behind a bush on to the road, just in front of the car. There was no possibility of avoiding it and it was certainly killed. I was a bit rattled but Hokey, fearing that I might lose my nerve, urged me to go straight on, which I did. The radiator had, however, been broken, and before long we were brought to a stop in the middle of nowhere on a very hot day. Fortunately, there was a small-gauge railway line near the road. We sat down close by and hoped a train would come and notice our plight. It was over 40°C in the shade and little shade was offered by the gum trees against which we exhaustedly leaned. We rationed ourselves to a few sips each of our water supply, tried to brush off the multitude of flies and thought we would die. After a couple of hours, a small steam engine puffed along, drawing a few wagons. It stopped on our signal, obeying the chivalry of the bush. We asked the driver to ring the ever-obliging NRMA when he reached a telephone and inform them of our plight and need of rescue. The kind train driver gave us some refreshments, some cans of cold drinks, I remember. Within an hour or so, the NRMA arrived and took us and our car to Charleville, where we spent a very hot night. There, some temporary repairs were made to our vehicle, sufficient to get us back to Canberra, which we did in two days, with a night's stop at

Nyngan. When I went to the NRMA insurance office to claim for damage to the car, the clerk noted the cause of the accident – "hit roo" – as the most routine matter possible, reported to him perhaps a dozen times a day. Hokey stayed for another two or three weeks and left Australia in early February 1979. She remains adventurous and now has been made an Honorary Fellow of the Royal Geographical Society.

By late 1978, the political heat in China had simmered down enough for the Academy of Social Sciences to send a delegation to Australia, and it visited ANU in December. A senior member of the Academy, Professor Luo Yuanzhen, was sitting across the table from me at the meeting we held, and which we began by introducing ourselves. As soon as he heard me say that I was born in Sichuan, Luo rose and came around the table to speak to me, saying that he too was Sichuanese. I told him that I very much wanted to visit our native province; he returned to his side of the table, had a few words to one of the other members of his delegation and returned to me, saying, "It is all arranged – you can go." So it was, but only fourteen months later did I get there.

The exodus of refugees fleeing from the new Communist rulers of South Vietnam had grown hugely in 1978–79 and some of us were urging the Australian government to be generous in accepting them. The government, under Malcolm Fraser, responded quite well. Immigration officials were dispatched to the ramshackle camps near the Malaysian beaches and potential immigrants were registered and then flown to a large camp near Sydney, from which they were dispersed across the country with the help of NGOs and others. In the ACT, an Indo-China Refugee Association (ICRA) was formed; I was for a period on its council. One of ICRA's activities was to hold fund-raising dinners, for which local Vietnamese restaurants cooked the food. One was held in my house, with a buffet meal served to diners (who included the Pro-nuncio, Archbishop Barbarito), crammed into the combined dining and sitting rooms.

I told the parish priest at St Christopher's that I had accommodation to offer refugees, but no time to look after them. However, I would willingly house them if other parishioners would give the needed time and domestic equipment. A parish committee was formed, funds were raised by a special Sunday collection to meet expenses, including the refugees' initial needs; members of the St Vincent de Paul Society inspected my spare accommodation and pronounced it suitable; parish volunteers offered to help the new arrivals, introducing them to shopping in Canberra, to register for social service benefits, to register with a general practitioner for their medical needs, find schools for the children and so forth.

The number of refugees that the government would accept for Australia depended, at least in part, on the speed with which the camp in Sydney was emptied, so we were anxious to take in as many as possible as quickly as possible. Therefore, I suggested that my house, with its two separate spare units, should accommodate a family in the larger two-bedroom and living room unit (with an electric cooker on a table in the living room) and another smaller group, say a mother and a child or two, in the one-room flatlet. Then both groups would register for long-term housing with the ACT Housing Department and wait their turns until more spacious accommodation became available. Someone from the diocese went to the Sydney camp and found an excellent family, parents and four children, the Buis, who arrived in Canberra in July 1979. They were, of course, rather squashed at first but a family who had been living in refugee camps and a beach shack could cope with that.

The Buis are an impressive family. Originally from North Vietnam, well-educated and formerly prosperous, the parents had fled south to escape the Communists. The father, Tam Bui, had been a high school sixth form teacher of Vietnamese history and geography in civilian life, before becoming an officer in the South Vietnamese army and then, on its defeat, spending some years in a harsh penal camp. After his release, he and his wife decided there was no future for the family in Communist Vietnam and that they should attempt to escape and make the dangerous journey to an unknown destination. They thought it best that the family should divide, and leave in two separate groups at different times so that if one got into trouble, they might be able to alert the others to their plight. The first group, Tam and his three sons, Triet, Tri and Quoc, aged about thirteen, ten and three respectively, were caught inside Vietnam and jailed. Tam managed to get a message through to his wife, Hong, who found the necessary Communist palm to grease to secure the release of her husband and sons. These, undeterred, tried again and this time succeeded, reaching the Malaysian coast where they camped by the sea. When the message of their safe arrival there reached Hong, she set out with their daughter Diem. Every day, Tam and the boys would hurry to any new boat that landed, hoping their womenfolk would be on it. Eventually, they arrived and the family was reunited, living off relief rations and any fish they caught until they were moved to a more formal camp where they met the Australian officials who selected them. Those officials can be proud of their choice. All three boys are now medical doctors with specialist qualifications, working in Sydney public hospitals, while the girl is a dentist. Tam and Hong are the happy grandparents of ten.[4]

When the Buis arrived, they knew virtually no English. Six months later, Diem, aged twelve, showed me an essay she had written, without help, on Cretan civilization, for which she had been given full marks. The two elder brothers also did well while the diminutive Quoc, aged four, after a short period at a kindergarten, was able to join his age group in a normal Canberra primary school. The Canberra education authorities, long experienced with immigrant children, ran a six months language school to funnel those of school age into the ordinary system. The Buis' quarters in my house were completely separate from mine, with their own outside entrance, but I tried to see them every day when I was in Canberra, to find out how they were doing. Tam spoke a little French and he and Hong attended an English course, but the parents naturally took rather longer than the children to learn the language. Little Quoc, small for his age but bright, was very shy and would not speak to me although I heard that at school he chatted away happily to his classmates; he shrank back if I touched him. I longed to pick him up and hug him, but had to refrain. After about a year, when he still had not said a word to me, I took unfair

4 At the time of writing, one grandchild is a qualified dentist, one a medical doctor, one an engineer, one a trainee banker, and one a student of dentistry – with five more to go.

advantage of him. I handed round some biscuits and told Quoc that he would not have one until he said, "Please" – and he said the word! I was nervous for the children about the pool, although some could swim, but the parents assured me that it would be all right because they had trained them to be obedient in order to survive the dangers of the journey to Malaysia. Certainly, they gave me no trouble at all, were a constant delight and soon they all could swim. They provided invaluable help when, one Saturday evening, someone – probably a drunk from the nearby Manuka Centre – throwing a cigarette on to my dry hedge, set it alight. Before I had even realized it was burning, the Buis were there with buckets of water and the hose to quench the blaze.

In August 1979, Mrs Do and her two student-aged daughters arrived to stay in my one-room flatlet. The father of the family, a colonel in the old South Vietnamese army, was still in a prison camp but they were hoping that he would be able to join them soon. The wait for a two-bedroom municipal flat for the Do family was not long; fairly soon one was allotted and they left me. Then the Buis were able to spread into the flatlet, which gave the children more space to do their homework. They had to wait longer and it was seventeen months before a four-bedroom house, such as Canberra regulations stipulated for a family of their size, became available. After a year or two in that house, they became almost self-sufficient in vegetables from the produce of their back garden and, when they had learned enough English, Tam got work as a traffic warden and Hong learned computing skills for a job. By the time they had become eligible to do so, they had saved sufficient to put down a deposit to buy their house from the government. Thus, they benefitted from the rise in real estate prices in Canberra over the next few years. When their children began pursuing tertiary studies in Sydney, they bought a house there and sold their Canberra property. In later years, when the children were married and had children of their own, Tam and Hong provided excellent child care facilities for their grandchildren.

In September, I left Canberra for two months' study leave in London, again having visitor's status at LSE where I gave a seminar, and later at Oxford too. I also went for a few days to the University of Bochum, where

Willy Kraus was trying to establish work on Modern China studies and had invited me to lecture. My stay in England enabled me to attend two family weddings, that of Rosalind Ingram to David Talks at the village church in Claygate, and of Mary Vaughan to Hugo Wynn-Williams at the Catholic Holy Redeemer Church, Chelsea. In mid-November, I flew back to Australia, just in time to be present at Roderick O'Brien's ordination to the diaconate.

CHAPTER 18

Back to China on My Own
– In Sichuan Again: 1980

Early in 1980, the invitation finally came from the Chinese Academy of Social Sciences for me to make an individual visit, under its auspices, that was to include Sichuan, Shanghai and Beijing.

Leaving Canberra in mid-April, I spent two and a half weeks in Hong Kong, to catch up with the latest information from the Mainland. The first weekend, I stayed with Barbara E. Ward, the anthropologist, who was on field work from Cambridge, in her flat at the Chinese University in Shatin. Then I moved to what had become my normal haunt in Hong Kong, the three-star Merlin Hotel in Kowloon. As usual, I frequented the Universities Service Centre, and went the rounds of the consulates, press, banks, business houses, missionaries, academics and others. David Wilson was now Political Adviser to the Governor. Over lunch with him, conversation covered the internal complexities in China, especially in the Guangdong bureaucracy and also Australia's attitude to Vietnamese refugees; David asked to be told of anything he could do in this regard. I also had dinner at Victoria House with the Caters; Jack Cater was now Colonial Secretary.

Among missionaries, I saw Father Angelo Lazzarotto and Father Fernando Galbiati of the Italian Fathers of the Pontifical Institute for Foreign Missions (PIME), and Father Ladany and Father Franco Belfiori of the Jesuits. Father Belfiori asked me to take an important letter to one of his confrères in Shanghai, Father Vincent Zhu Hongsheng, who had fairly recently been released after decades in prison and was now living with his brother's family in the former French Concession. I told Father Ladany that I would send him a card from Shanghai. If everything was going well, I would write his name in the usual way, "The Rev L. Ladany SJ"; if things were a bit dicky, I would leave out the "SJ"; if they were bad I would omit the "Rev"; and if very bad, I would just put "Ladany", then the address: Ricci Hall etc.

On arrival by rail at Guangzhou, I was met by representatives of the Chinese Academy of Social Sciences, including Chen Xiaoling, a young woman from the Institute of World Economics, Beijing, my permanent (and agreeable) minder who accompanied me throughout the six weeks of my visit. At each place, she would be supplemented by local minders. I realised that by the time I reached Shanghai (and wanted to visit Father Zhu), I would have had to establish the fact that I was an eccentric who insisted on wandering around on my own, unaccompanied. So, on the next morning, when a car arrived to take me to the Canton Fair, my first port of call, I told my minders that I very much wanted to walk there on my own, to observe the life of the streets. At that time in China, a car was still a great luxury which it was considered odd to refuse.

During my two days in Guangzhou, I met with a group of economists from a number of local tertiary institutions. They confirmed that Guangdong province had a fixed fiscal transfer (tax payment) of one billion yuan per annum to the central government. Fujian, in contrast, received a fixed subsidy of 300,000 yuan from Beijing. They said that in 1979 Guangdong earned eight billion yuan in foreign currency from trade (excluding the Guangdong Fair). When I asked what percentage of these earnings the province was allowed to retain they replied, "Not clear" – the classic way in China at the time for saying that information was classified; this particular item was probably a matter of bitter contention between province and centre. Another controversy devolved around the status of the Municipality of Guangzhou. They obviously wanted their city to be promoted to the same status as cities like Beijing and Shanghai, and not subject to provincial authority. I also visited a commune in Huaxian near Guangzhou; 7,000 city workers lived within its boundaries but were not numbered among the 65,000 commune members. I lunched with John Kamm, who had long been with the American Chamber of Commerce in Hong Kong and was visiting Guangzhou. He later became known as a valiant campaigner for mainland prisoners of conscience and for labour rights in China.

The Shanghai branch of the Academy of Social Sciences had arranged an extensive programme for me, as well as some recreational occasions. On my first day in Shanghai, I was taken on a river trip on the Huangpu River and later in the week to the Jade Temple. I had several formal meetings with groups of academy members, especially from the Institute of Applied Economics, to which I also gave a talk; then a meeting with members of financial and banking bodies and with officials concerned with price control and with enterprise management, with foreign and domestic trade and with raw materials. I visited a commune in Jiading county, a cotton mill, a toothpaste factory, a down garments factory (all, of course, state enterprises), some collective and street enterprises and an industrial exhibition. I also had dinner with the British Petroleum people. On Sunday, I went to Mass at the Cathedral at Ziccawei and saw the Xu Guangqi Garden.

My minders were probably rather glad when I asked for some time to myself, during which I was able to make three visits to Father Vincent Zhu, although no doubt someone tracked my goings and interrogated the poor man afterwards. He lived down a little alley off a street in the former French Concession, in one room with his brother, sister-in-law and their son, a young man in his twenties. The room was partially sub-divided by large furniture, to give Father Zhu a little privacy. After preliminary greetings, explanations and enquiries, I handed him the letter entrusted to me by his confrère Father Belfiori, which I had kept on or close to my person by day and night since leaving Hong Kong. It seemed that he was delaying opening the letter, thinking this discourteous when I had just come. However, I was nervous that the Public Security might suddenly burst in before he had read it, so I urged him to open it at once, which he did. He commented that the letter was indeed important and had come from the Jesuit Father General.

I asked Father Zhu about his experiences over the more than two decades he had spent in prison. He recounted something of the extreme hardships he had undergone – of how he and two other Jesuits were in a small cell that got flooded during heavy rains and that once for weeks the water came up to their waists. Father Zhu spoke of the problems presented by the Government's recently introduced one-child policy. He said that his nephew was soon to get married and that he thought it prudent not to inform him of the Church's teaching on birth regulation because it might be too great a burden in the existing circumstances. However, the young man had come to him saying that his friends had been talking to him about contraception, but that he did not like the idea and asked if the Church had anything to say on the matter.

Father Zhu exuded a sense of serenity and confidence. After recounting his ordeals, he added, "With God's help, it was all easy to get through." I left him feeling I had experienced a whiff of England's penal days. For me, the visit went smoothly and the card I sent Father Ladany from Shanghai was fully addressed.

My Shanghai minders at one stage asked me if there was anything more I would like to do or see in the city. I replied that I would like to meet Bishop Gong Pingmei, the Church-recognised Bishop of Shanghai, who was still in prison at that time. They chided me for this request.

A significant occurrence during my stay in Shanghai in May 1980 was the national celebration of the rehabilitation of Liu Shaoqi, the former number two man in China. Liu oversaw much of the economic recovery of the country after the disasters of the Great Leap of 1958–61 until the beginning of the Cultural Revolution of 1967–76, during which he was overthrown by Mao and died in prison, reportedly in dire conditions. My minder from the Shanghai branch of CASS appeared deeply moved and excused herself from looking after me to attend the local memorial celebration. It signified the beginning of a wider relaxation.

After ten days in Shanghai, I flew to Chengdu for three and a half weeks in Sichuan, being lodged, with my minder, Chen Xiaoling, in the Jinjiang Hotel, the only one where foreigners might stay at that time. This was the first time since 1943 that I had been able to return to my native province and I came with a spirit of both joy and apprehension. That afternoon, after discussing my programme with my hosts, I went out on my own, walking along Renmin St. and down side streets where many small private tailors and dressmakers were sitting at their sewing machines with customers around them. (This betokened a post-Mao relaxation.) Then I went to the Xinhua bookshop, bought some books on law and noticed private traders of vegetables on the road nearby. The back streets looked much the same as I remembered them but I noted one definite improvement in that night-soil containers were now covered, and carried on carts.

I also visited the Catholic church at Pingan Qiao and there met a Father Liu and two laywomen, Mrs Zhou and Mrs Bao; and a layman, Mr Li, whom later I knew as stalwarts of the Catholic Patriotic Association, a body set up by the government to control the Church.

My local hosts, the Sichuan Academy of Social Sciences, had arranged a careful programme for me, including not only professional appointments and general tourist sites but also visits to the places with which I had closest connections. On my first day, we went to the Sichuan Medical College, which now occupied the whole campus of the former West China Union University, where I had studied for a year in 1942–3. I was able to recognize some old buildings and landmarks that remained among the new structures that crowded the grounds. The College's hospital, the former hospital of the West China Union University, remained the leading medical facility in the province, as it still does in the second decade of the following century. Both the Medical University and its hospital were still commonly referred to in Chinese with their old prefix "Huaxi" (West China). Later that day, we visited Du Fu's Thatched Cottage and the Wuhou Temple, where years before I had first met the Redemptorist Fathers. That evening, I was taken to an opera performance. The Academy gave me a splendid banquet which, a few days later, I returned. I must admit that I hate these formal dinners and find them exhausting and not enjoyable.

My working programme in Chengdu included an interview with three officials concerned with agriculture and communes, interviews at the Sichuan Provincial Bureau of Finance, the Sichuan College of Finance and Economics, the Provincial Planning Commission, Economic Commission, Price Commission, Bureau of Statistics, Bureau of Tourism, the Grain Planning Office and the Office of Family Planning; and also at the Economic Research Institute of the Sichuan Academy of Social Sciences. A long and interesting interview with the provincial branch of the People's Bank of China was brightened by meeting one of my former students from the sub-freshmen's English class at Yenching-University-in-Chengdu in 1943, who now worked as a translator at the bank. At the Family Planning Office, I asked if they thought it would be possible to change the firmly established custom of only one child if they wanted to raise birth rates in future. Apparently, I gathered, this consideration did not worry them at all. It is now providing anxiety to the Chinese authorities in the twenty first century.

I visited Sichuan University, the leading tertiary education institution in the province and one of the "key" national universities, benefitting from central government financing. Economics was the only branch of social sciences taught, but the introduction of law, sociology and demography was being considered. A tentative beginning was being made for the university to develop international contacts. I saw a number of international journals and newspapers in the library, which had also been the recipient of the non-medical library holdings of the former WCUU. Fourth-year students were allowed access to foreign books.

In addition, I was taken to see various places of economic activity, including the Sichuan No. 1 Cotton Mill, a measuring tools factory (an enterprise controlled by the central government), the metal exchange, and a couple of agricultural communes within the Municipality of Chengdu. The former practice in enterprises of placing all the stress on raising output was now being shifted to trying to meet market demand; from just fulfilling or surpassing output targets to maximising profit. Life was becoming more complicated for the managers but better for consumers.

On Sunday, I attended the 7:30 a.m. Pentecost Sunday Mass at the Catholic Cathedral in Pingan Qiao, which I had known so well in the early 1940s. All the French clergy had by now of course been gone for nearly thirty years. The congregation comprised around a hundred persons, mostly elderly. The Mass was similar to those I had attended there in the 1940s, with the priest saying the liturgy in Latin silently while the congregation accompanied him with a chant, stopping only for the Consecration. After Mass, I met Father Tang Yuanjia who told me that three priests, in addition to Bishop Li Xiting, lived at the cathedral, but that the bishop and one of the priests had gone to Beijing for meetings. Normally, there were three Masses on Sundays, at 7, 7:30 and 8 a.m. but only two that Sunday because of the bishop's absence. The Sisters were now all working in secular jobs. I also saw the two laywomen of the Patriotic Association whom I had met a few days before. The Church had a few old Latin missals, but no other books. I was told that the Catholic churches at Chongqing and Wanxian had been re-opened and that the Bishop of Wanxian, Duan Yinming, was in Beijing attending the meetings.

That Sunday, I also went to a service at the former Anglican Cathedral at Pifanggai. This had now been turned into a place of worship for all Protestant groups, mixed together in a government sponsored ecumenism. The service, with no apparent liturgy, was taken by a Methodist woman minister and the sermon given by a Baptist pastor, who preached for forty minutes on Martha and Mary, rather favouring Martha! He preached from a desk in front of the Holy Table. Not once, neither in the sermon nor in the rest of the service, was there any mention that it was Whit Sunday: in other words, the cathedral's Anglican past had been obliterated. Later, I was told that six pastors served the church, of whom one was an Anglican, ordained by Bishop C. T. Song in 1955; Bishop Song had died in the 1960s.

From Chengdu, I was taken on an excursion to Guanxian and to the Dujiangyan Dam. This dam dates from 215 BC, in the Warring States period, and for more than two thousand years has provided the Chengdu plain with an effective irrigation system.

Soon after returning to China in 1940, I passed through Guanxian with my parents, on the way to escape the summer heat at a mountain temple on the other side of the river, but had not stopped there. On this occasion in 1980, I was taken to a good viewpoint for the water conservancy scheme and then we walked down to the temple built in honour of Li Bin and his son, the ancient builders of the project. Their statues in the temple had been destroyed in the Cultural Revolution, as had the mountain temple where we had stayed in 1940, but fortunately the main temple had been spared.

On the way back to Chengdu, we saw a partly-completed power station, begun in 1958 as one of the Soviet-sponsored projects of that era but still incomplete when they left, probably at the time of the Sino-Soviet split around 1960. After that, it was reconsidered and abandoned because, I was told, it was thought harmful to the great irrigation system.

After ten days in Chengdu, I was given a tour of five days around other places on the Chengdu plain with which I had connections, but which at that time were as a general rule closed to foreign visitors. The first stop was Guanghan, the county town some thirty miles from Chengdu where my parents lived for over a decade and where I had been based from 1940 to the beginning of 1943. Guanghan county was doing better than most other parts of the province in agriculture and was showcased as an experiment in allowing collective agricultural units to make some of their own decisions on output. There, I was taken to see a production brigade in the town suburbs and I was shown around the town where much new building was in progress. The fine old arch in the park still stood but the others, on the road to Chengdu, which my father had persuaded the local magistrate to spare, had been destroyed, some in the Cultural Revolution, and some for road-widening schemes.

An old friend of mine had been found, and an official accompanied me to his home. The friend was Wang Deren, the youngest son of my father's curate, whom I had last seen in 1943 as a boy of thirteen. Now he had a wife and three children and they were living in what remained of our former house. Like most older buildings I saw, it was in a shocking state of disrepair, the first floor (second floor by Chinese and American reckoning), where I had my bedroom, was now unsafe to enter. The large guihua tree which had stood inside the small courtyard had gone and I was told it had been destroyed in a storm. I asked after Deren's parents and he said they had died, but he assured me that their last days were peaceful.

My official companions and I then went on another twenty miles to Mianyang. For part of the way, the road ran near the Baoji-Chengdu railway and, for the first time in my life, I saw a train in my native province. Agricultural mechanisation was in progress but far from complete; on the way, we saw ploughing by buffaloes but also by tractors, and threshing by hand and by machine. At Mianyang, a much larger city and a prefectural capital, we spent three nights at the government hostel. Mianyang had a lot of new buildings and was being developed into a centre of secret military-related research, although of course I was not told this. Here I had an interesting interview with local officials about the new system of managing state enterprises which was gradually being introduced, forcing their managers to pay attention to market demand instead of just having to reach output targets set by the state.

The following day, we went to Anxian where I had lived until I was four but had never seen since. A small county town on the edge of the plain, with a backdrop of mountains, it had of course changed greatly from my childhood memories. Some new buildings jostled the rather primitive type of housing which I had known. I met the chairman of the *xian* (county) Revolutionary Committee and was given an account of the local economy by the head of the *xian* planning committee. Then I was taken to a production brigade in Zhitong Commune near the town.

At the former mission house, which I visited, the courtyard around which I had furiously driven my tin-can car had been partly covered by a new house while our old home was, like that at Guanghan, in a terrible condition, here also making it dangerous to go upstairs to the second floor. Mrs Yun, aged eighty-five, had been brought to meet me there. Her late husband, a doctor trained at the West China Union University Medical

School, used to be the head of the local Anxian hospital. They were both friends of my parents and Dr Yun was said to have worked with my father in some capacity. One of their daughters was at the Sichuan Medical University in Chengdu, which had taken over the buildings and the role of the former WCUU Medical School. Another daughter was in Beijing while their son taught English in Xinjiang. At the old mission-house I also met Mr Chen Guofu, a postal employee, whose late parents had been Christians and knew my parents.

Next day we went to Mianzhu where I had a great surprise. Wherever I went in the town, untidy throngs of people gathered, lining the streets, running in a completely disorganized manner from all directions, clapping and cheering; it was obviously spontaneous, quite different from formal welcomes which the Chinese authorities are so good at organising. In fact, I felt that the officials were rather embarrassed by what was happening. The townsfolk may have thought that the re-appearance of foreigners meant that the bad days – the Great Leap Forward and the famine, the Cultural Revolution, the incessant campaigns – had passed and that life would become more relaxed. It may, too, have been a tribute to the very few foreigners, a handful of British and French missionaries over thirty years previously, who had ever lived in that small town.

As at every place I visited, at Mianzhu officials gave me briefings on the local economy. I was shown the old Church Missionary Society Hospital just outside the city and spoke to the head doctor in his office. Its glass door still carried, embossed, the Chinese name of Dr John Lechler, who had attended me when I was a child; his Chinese successor was obviously proud to be following in his line. I also saw the former mission church, in a bad state of decay and used as a workshop for making clothes. In rooms attached to the church I met old Mrs Zhang De-en who had lived on the church premises since 1928 and whose late husband had been a cook at the mission. Before they moved to Mianzhu, the Zhangs had also lived at the Anxian mission house where he had cooked for my parents and Mrs Zhang remembered them and me. I was not allowed to visit the former Catholic church, now the office of a geological prospecting team.

The next day, I was taken to the small county town of Santai, my birth place; a rather poor district, but noted for good peanuts – the local officials gave me three packets of the local brand. The town's chief feature was a small, jagged, three-tiered hill which gave the town its name ("three tiers"). On a subsequent visit, a few years later, I found this historic landmark had been levelled, presumably in the cause of modernisation. I saw the former Quaker mission station where I was born. Its small clinic, with only ten beds, had been demolished and replaced by a hospital of 300 beds. Some of the mission residences had been pulled down but one still stood. A kindergarten, I think a successor to one run by the mission, had been expanded. I was allowed to spend a night in the town, although its accommodation, distinctly primitive, was below that which foreigners were usually allowed to occupy. At Santai, as at each of the country areas to which I went, I talked to officials about the local economy and spoke to other people where possible.

After my tour of the country towns, which for me had been charged with emotion, I returned to Chengdu to complete the remaining interviews and visits which had been planned for me. I also gave a talk to members of the Sichuan Academy of Social Sciences. First, I thanked them for the trouble they had taken in arranging my visit and expressed my joy in returning to my native province after so many years away. I knew that in the last three years the economy had improved, but I said that on returning to my *gu xiang* (old home) I must be honest. Sichuan had suffered great neglect in the last thirty years. Much too much had been taken from the farmers. Except for some city people, the province had not shared the growth of, for example, districts near Guangzhou and Shanghai, and certainly not the prosperity of many other parts of East Asia. An observer who was familiar with Sichuan in 1980 and with Taiwan in 1957 had told me that Sichuan's towns were now up to Taiwan's then, but its countryside was not. The province suffered from lack of foreign links. The modern world is very international and, in the West, this is apparent in businesses, universities and cultural life; Sichuan would benefit from more links with the outside world. For modernisation to succeed, economic policies must be freely criticised and debated and this is lacking in China and, as a result, extreme policies have been implemented – I instanced the one-child population policy, more extreme than anywhere else in the world, yet there had been no public criticism. People must be given information on the basis of which they can criticise. The audience seemed to take this well; at least, without objecting.

There was, of course, the inevitable banquet, which I have always found the most disagreeable function in such visits, with excessive amounts of indigestible rich food being piled on to one's plate or bowl, with objections raised if not enough of it is eaten. However, in those days when famine was still a vivid memory, these banquets may have been regarded by the hosts as one of their major perks.

Then, on 12 June 1980, I flew to Beijing for ten days in the capital, where I had interviews at several national level government bodies, whose officials of course were more sophisticated and in touch with the outside world than their local government counterparts in Sichuan. On my first evening in Beijing, I had dinner with Ross Maddock, the Chargé at the Australian Embassy, and the following morning I paid a formal call on my hosts in China, the Institute of Economic Research of the Chinese Academy of Social Sciences.

My working programme in Beijing began with this visit to the Institute of Economic Research, followed, the next day, by an interview at the headquarters of the People's Bank of China. Subsequently, I had meetings at the Ministries of Finance, of Commerce and of Foreign Trade, and at the State Economic Commission; and a joint discussion with members of the Institutes of Agricultural Economics, of Industrial Economics and of Finance and Commerce. I also visited the National Library. At the Australian Embassy its economics specialist, Peter Forsythe, arranged for me to give a lunchtime talk, followed by a discussion, to economic personnel of the embassies of the UK, Canada, Japan, Germany and Belgium. In Beijing, as wherever I went in China, I visited as many bookshops as possible and bought books which I posted back to myself in Canberra, where they duly arrived.

Dinner with Gladys Yang and her husband, Yang Xianyi, of the Foreign Languages Press, gave me my first introduction to the "foreign friends" community in China, that small circle of Western sympathisers with the regime who were well-treated by it so long as they remained compliant and served its purposes. Either on this occasion, or on later visits, I met other members of this rather lonely "friends" community, including Ruth Weiss, whom I already knew from wartime Chengdu. In Beijing, I also spoke with a number of foreign correspondents and businessmen.

My most memorable private occasion in Beijing was the dinner I had at the home of my friend from the Chinese Academy of Social Sciences whom I had met on his visit to ANU a year or two earlier, Luo Yuanzheng and his wife. She told me that she was the daughter of the famed "Christian General" Feng Yuxiang[1] (1882–1948), of whom I had heard from my father and others (although not, I think, from anyone who had known him personally). "So," my hostess said over dinner with tears in her eyes, "you can understand why we wanted to see you." She had certainly preserved her love of her Christian faith but was probably not able ever to practise it openly; it was a moving occasion. In General Feng's last years, he had become close to the Communists and died in 1948 in a mysterious fire on a ship in the Black Sea on his way to the USSR. Luo Yuanzheng told me that he had been with Feng on the ship and could vouch for his death being accidental, contrary to rumours. The Chinese Communists categorised Feng as a "good warlord". His widow became Minister of Health in the People's Republic and his son-in-law, Luo Yuanzheng, had a prestigious job and a high-class flat, allocated by the State Council.

After my visit to Beijing, I flew to Guangzhou for two nights. While there, I attended a meeting, chaired by Professor Sun Ru, Deputy Director of the Guangdong Provincial Research Institute of Philosophy and Sciences, where seven women staff members of the local branches of the People's Bank and the Agricultural Bank answered my questions on matters such

1 Feng had a long and involved military career from the 1920 to the 1940s, switching between different factions on several occasions. In 1914, he was baptised by the Methodist Episcopalians and was zealous in promoting Christianity among his troops, reputedly baptising whole units with a fire hose.

as the allocation of bank loans and rates of interest on deposits and loans, and on the new management system of state enterprises. They told me that in Beijing, Tianjin and Shanghai funds for capital construction were now being given in the form of bank loans (previously, such funds were given just as budgetary grants), but this system had not yet been instituted in Guangdong.

From Guangzhou, I returned to Hong Kong for ten days. To Fathers Belfiori and Ladany I gave news of their confrère in Shanghai; I also spoke to Father Pieraccini and Father Galbiati of the PIMEs. I gave talks to the American Chamber of Commerce, to the Universities Service Centre and to the Department of Economics of the University of Hong Kong, and caught up with my other usual Hong Kong contacts – at the US Consulate, with the Goodstadts, Tim Williams of the Bank of America and others. Then, in early July 1980, I flew back to Canberra, to a weekend including a meeting of the parish refugee committee; a gathering of the Christian Life Group held at St Edmund's College, the base of Brother Laurie Needham, a long-time member of our gathering; and to a splendid Vietnamese dinner with the Bui family, still in my house, a meal doubly welcome because I had not had time to stock up my larder since my return.

CHAPTER 19

Family and Friends, and Another Visit to China: 1980–82

In the course of both work and extra-mural activities, I had opportunities to experience a little of the vast outreaches of Australia. When possible, I tried to travel around by car, to see more of the countryside to which I was particularly drawn, even though my destinations often had to be big cities.

In August 1980, a few weeks after returning to Australia, I went to Adelaide to attend the ordination to the priesthood of Roderick O'Brien whom I had first known when he was a lecturer in law at the University of Hong Kong. The ceremony was held in St Francis Xavier's Cathedral and followed by a number of social gatherings, including some at Roderick's family home. I met his mother and other members of his family and it was a good occasion with general rejoicing at his vocation. Before long, in addition to his parish duties, Father Rod started a special Mass for Chinese Catholics in Adelaide.

The following month, I paid another visit to Adelaide, this time to give a seminar paper at Flinders University, where Victor Funnell was building up a programme of contemporary China studies. From there I drove to Melbourne to talk to a China studies group at one of the universities and to see various other academics and also my second cousin, Janettie McMillan.

Soon after my arrival in Australia, I had contacted the branch of the Ingram family, descended from several children of my great grandfather

Thomas Lewis Ingram, who had gone to Australia in the nineteenth century from The Gambia. I visited Gembrook, a village in the Dandenong ranges where some had settled, opening a small store, still there in 1969 and still bearing the Ingram name, although no members of the family remained nearby. One member, my second cousin Janettie McMillan, I had then met in Melbourne. This time, in 1980 on the way back to Canberra, I stopped at the village of Undera, north of Melbourne, to spend a night with Janettie's daughter, Edith Christoe, and her husband Jim, who farmed there. Edith was at the centre of various activities in the surrounding district, holding, or having held, office in many local societies that bind together scattered country people.

Sometimes, I had occasion to drive to Sydney and on one such trip I visited the grave of my great-great-grandfather on the other side of my family, in Camperdown Cemetery, where James Donnithorne and his daughter Eliza share a large monumental grave. In eighteenth century Cornwall, James's father had been a Warden of the Duke of Cornwall's stannaries, which may have secured young James the entrée to the Prince Regent's circle where, according to family legend, he was reputed to be one of Prinny's wild companions. (Some say the dates are wrong for this.) The legend runs that once, when the Court was trying to clean up Prinny and disband his misbehaving mates, a position was found for James Donnithorne in the East India Company in Calcutta. Be that as it may, James certainly landed up in Calcutta, where he prospered, becoming a Judge and Governor of the Bengal Mint. He married Sarah, daughter of Captain William Bampton RN, whose ship was based in Calcutta and who was a notable navigator. Soon after the arrival of the First Fleet and the founding of the new colony at Sydney, Bampton sailed there and then went north where he charted the Torres Straits, between Australia and New Guinea. He must have reported favourably on what he had seen of Australia because, in due time, his son-in-law decided to retire to Sydney. James Donnithorne acquired a large house in the Sydney suburb of Newtown and made substantial investments in land in New South Wales and Victoria. His daughter Eliza has been reputed by some to be the original for Dickens's Miss Havisham in *Great*

Expectations, but I understand that the weight of evidence is against this. My father remembers that, in his early childhood, some objects, including lace, bequeathed by his great aunt Eliza, arrived at the family home in Twickenham.

To return to 1980, Lady Cowen, wife of the then Governor General Sir Zelman Cowen (the parents of my graduate student friend Shimon Cowen), used to give lunch parties to groups of women, and I was invited to one in August of that year. Thereupon, I bought myself a new dress and drove up to Government House on the appointed day, noticing a prominent left-wing journalist, stomping out a cigarette before alighting from her car, and dressed with seemingly deliberate uncouthness. Lady Cowen was charming and I admired the way she complied both with kosher rules and with customary manners by serving, not coffee but green tea (i.e. without milk), after the meal.

Catholics in Australia were, of course, affected by the long period of theological turbulence, after the Second Vatican Council, in the Catholic Church in Western Europe and in lands colonised by ethnic Westerners. Wildly dissident opinions on faith and morals were voiced by small groups of clergy, religious Sisters and lay people; liturgy in some churches in Australia, particularly in Queensland, was mingled with improvisation; religious teaching in many Catholic schools became woollier and woollier. The aftermath of the Vatican Council, with its emphasis on a larger role for the laity, had been taken by some as a signal that "anything goes". Some bishops lost their nerve and were no longer willing to teach Catholic doctrine and morals clearly, or to see that these were taught clearly by clergy in the parishes and teachers in Catholic schools.[1]

Australians are easy going, but eventually some revolted at this trend.

---

1 During these years, a Catholic lay teacher at a Queensland Catholic school was asked to teach a Year 11 religious education class. "When the Eucharist came up for study, Richard explained the Church's teaching to the students. They were incredulous: most had no idea. One of the students, however, said to Richard, 'You say this is what the Church believes, but that can't be true, because if it was, the Church would never have allowed us to spend a dozen years in Catholic schools without being taught it.' It's pretty hard to counter that logic." See Colin H. Jory's important paper, "Chesterton and the Campion Society: Influences and Perspectives", given at the Chesterton Society

In December 1972, a small group – including a convert from Anglicanism, Father Peter Elliott of Melbourne; Karl Schmude, a university librarian from New South Wales; and Colin Jory, a literary figure and English teacher of Canberra – decided to do something about it by initiating an informal body known as the John XXIII Fellowship. ("Fellowship" was suggested by Colin Jory as an echo of Tolkien's *Lord of the Rings*.) This, as they said, was "unorganised, but not disorganised"; it did not have a paid membership which came about by association rather than by joining, and its only official functions were conferences, normally annual, in one or other of Australia's capitals. These conferences usually had a session at which recent pupils and current sixth formers of Catholic schools, mainly from Queensland, poured out their complaints about the religious teaching and forms of worship they encountered. Father Elliott took a leading part in these conferences and his friend, Father George Pell, also sometimes spoke, and I got to know them both. In 1971 Father Pell had returned to Australia from Oxford where he had been doing a DPhil in church history after being ordained in Rome in 1966. Another friend I made on these occasions was Greg Sheridan of *The Australian*. An organised entity, associated with the Fellowship but independent, was the John XXIII Bookshop Co-operative at Melbourne, which both published and sold books.

The Fellowship traced its intellectual descent, and a core membership, to an earlier body, the Campion Society, founded in Melbourne in 1931. In 1987, the Fellowship's name was changed back to the Campion Fellowship, which had a part, largely through the initiative of Karl Schmude, in giving rise to Campion College, now a flourishing contributor to the intellectual life of Sydney.

I sympathised with the John XXIII Fellowship's purpose but often I was unable to attend the conferences because of absence from the country or other hindrances. However, I managed to get to those in 1982, 1983 and 1984 (two in Sydney and one in Brisbane), and gave talks at them on the Church in China. Among those I got to know at these conferences were a rising Sydney lawyer, John McCarthy, and his wife Christine, who

Conference, 2008, held at Campion College, Sydney.

were to play a major role in Australian Catholic life, John later becoming Australian ambassador to the Holy See from 2012 to 2016. The Fellowship gave me a set of friends, mostly a good bit younger than myself – students and junior professionals and their spouses who in Canberra included John Parsons, the Scarabelottis, the Dunnes, the Jorys, Henry Craft and others, including my old friends, John and Ruth Harris. Also active in the Fellowship, but coming from a rather different background, were Kevin and Beverly Cains. Kevin was a valiant officer of the Public Service Union, which was riven by factional fighting (like many other Australian unions), as extreme left elements battled more moderate members. In course of time, the Fellowship began holding informal local functions. After I moved into my house, meetings and socials were sometimes held there. Occasional retreats took place at local religious communities; in November 1980, for instance, at Blackfriars, the Dominicans' house in Canberra. As a result of all these new links, I got to know other like-minded Catholics, notably Father Paul Stenhouse MSC whose publication *The Annals*, a middlebrow monthly "journal of Catholic culture", has over many years made a stalwart and enriching contribution to the Church in Australia.

The purposely amorphous and unpolitical Fellowship was not directly linked to B. A. (Bob) Santamaria's Movement, but neither was it uninfluenced by it. I had the privilege of getting to know Bob Santamaria on several visits to Melbourne, seeing him at his office and sometimes invited to lunch there, but was never further involved in his direct activities, which I felt were primarily concerned with an era before I came to Australia. At one time, far left-wing forces, especially in the trade unions, had been trying to get a stranglehold on the country and might have succeeded but for the leadership of Santamaria and Archbishop Mannix of Melbourne, in rallying Catholic working people. I think that by the 1970s Bob realised the struggle against Communism, although still important, was no longer the focal point in the perpetual fight between darkness and light; victory in the Cold War was now in sight and the fiercest current battles were in the field of morals in society at large and also in the affirmation of a solid Christian faith in the Catholic community.

A meeting of the Fellowship, which the Pro-Nuncio, Archbishop Barbarito, had kindly agreed to attend, was held at my house, which was near the Nunciature, early in December 1980. Colin Jory had compiled a catalogue of complaints to lay before him of wrongful doctrine being taught at Catholic schools and elsewhere. The Nuncio probably suspected that this would happen and obviously wanted to avoid it, so he immediately launched out on an address of his own, about how after every great council of the church there was a period of conflict and upheaval and this should not cause us anxiety.

Later in December, I went to Taiwan and again read a paper at a conference on China in Taipei, from where I flew to London at my own expense on a private visit, not on study leave, arriving a few days before Christmas 1980 which I spent at Claygate with extended family. At the end of December 1980, I attended the wedding of my goddaughter Clare Corlett to Gavin Oddy at the Catholic Church in Caterham, a happy celebration. After that, I spent a few days in Dorset with Pen Piercy and went on to Oxford where I saw George Allen in his retirement flat, Mark Elvin at St Antony's, John Finnis at University College and lunched with Mike and Rosie Giedroyc. I stayed with my cousins Jane and Chris Hawker in their home in the village of Drayton St Leonard, near Oxford, from where other cousins, Maurice and Jill Ingram, fetched me to spend a weekend with them in Somerset. I also visited my old Aunt Irene, Harold Donnithorne's widow, in Hove, lunched with Tom Ingram in London (he was now pursuing a successful post-Army career as an archivist) and visited his sister and brother-in-law, Esther and Guy Bryan. Mary Davies (née Ingram) and her family I went to see in Bookham.

I met my godson, Dennis Dillsworth, twice, and had dinner with his brother Raymond. Before she died, their mother, my dear friend Jeanne, had begged me to try to persuade Raymond to take back his wife whom he had rejected because, after a tiff when pregnant with their second child, she had suddenly flown back to her family in Freetown, Sierra Leone. Raymond obviously wished to forestall such a conversation, so he also invited another friend, an Indian from Guyana, to our meal together. This friend was a compulsive talker and spoke non-stop through the meal, chiefly recounting enough scandal from his native country to fill many novels. In addition, I visited the Bearcrofts in Barming, the Kays in Wimbledon and Mary Low in Hove, as well as having dinner with David Bensusan-Butt who had retired from ANU and returned to England. Another former academic friend I saw was Peter Wiles, at LSE, where he was approaching retirement. I also visited Keston College in Kent, as I was still hopeful that possibly something similar might be set up somewhere to help Christians in China. After this rather rushed stay in England, I returned for a few days in Hong Kong to catch up on the latest happenings on the Mainland before returning to Canberra just after the Australia Day holiday of 1981.

On returning to Canberra, I began using some of the information collected in China for articles and other publications. In 1981 I brought out, as our Centre's *Contemporary China Paper No. 16*, a booklet entitled *Centre-Provincial Economic Relations in China* followed by an article, 'Control of Investment in China' in the *Australian Journal of Chinese Affairs* early in 1982. However, I was still intending to use most of the material from my last China visit in a new edition of my *China's Economic System*.

Early in 1981, the Buis moved into a municipal house with four bedrooms and so were no longer squashed up in the annex to my house. Unfortunately, they were far away from me, in Belconnen, so I could not see them often. Among the Vietnamese refugees being re-settled were a number of seminarians who, despairing of being able to continue their studies at home, had braved the seas. Two had been provisionally accepted for training by the Archdiocese of Canberra and were now learning English before entering an Australian seminary. They needed accommodation and I was glad to have them in the now empty spare half of my house.

Joseph Tran had captained the boat on which he escaped with, I think, thirty or forty other passengers. They were picked up by a Japan-bound oil tanker. Joseph spent some months in Japan where he made many friends who later corresponded with him, but the Japanese Government would not accept refugees as permanent residents, so he was brought to Australia. The second seminarian, John Baptist Tran (no relation to Joseph), was an older man, a late vocation who was very solicitous of the unaccompanied Vietnamese youths in Canberra who posed a particular problem. One got into trouble and John B. took him under his wing so he, too, came to my house, later becoming a successful chef in a local Vietnamese restaurant. Joseph learned English quickly and well and was in due course ordained for Canberra Archdiocese which, however, would not accept the older John B., for whom language was a greater problem. He refused to be deterred from following his vocation and eventually – I never knew quite how – managed to be sent to England where eventually he was ordained and worked for some time among Vietnamese refugees; on a visit to England, I once attended a crowded Vietnamese language Mass which he celebrated. After some time, Father John B. Tran returned to Canberra where he was then encardinated in that diocese and did good work among the growing Vietnamese community. After he had obtained Australian citizenship, he was given leave by the diocese to spend several months each year in Vietnam, where he was able to bring great help to the local priest-depleted Church. Father Joseph Tran has laboured valiantly in the Diocese of Canberra as a curate, and then as parish priest of Narooma.

After the seminarians left, I had other guests in my house. Professor Tien Ju-kang, a well-known Chinese anthropologist with dissident tendencies, had managed to get out of China with his wife Ruth, and had been invited as a visiting professor to ANU. The Chinese Embassy began paying him unwelcome attention and he became nervous that some harm might befall them. So it was suggested that they should stay in my self-contained flatlet where they would be more hidden than on the campus. They were welcome guests until they left for the United States some weeks later.

The John XXIII Fellowship continued its intermittent activities and, except when I was away from Canberra, I participated and occasionally hosted gatherings, but sometimes problems arose. Once a social occasion was mooted and I was asked if it could be held in my house. At that time, I was in the middle of a work crisis, trying to get down to a long piece of writing, with papers strewn over every available table. I told the person arranging it that I could not attend but they might hold it in my garden, where the pool shed provided facilities, but that they must not come into my house as I did not want to be disturbed while working. Apparently, participants were not informed of this condition. An hour before the gathering was to begin, my doorbell rang and someone outside said that because of transport connections she had to arrive early, and could she come into the house to wait. I spent most of the next hour chatting to her before the others came to begin the social in the garden. Then it began to rain, so they all trooped into the house and sat around the kitchen table, with my papers becoming more chaotic by the minute. It took me a long time before I could regain full concentration on my writing.

In 1981, an occasional member of our Sunday evening group, Gerard Brennan, a judge of the High Court of Australia (and later Chief Justice) invited me to lunch at the High Court and showed me round. He was interested in the law in China and had visited the country. His son, Father Frank Brennan SJ, whom I met several times, became one of the leading Australian Jesuits of his generation; he devoted much time and effort to Aboriginal matters.

Official visitors to ANU in 1981 included my Sichuanese friend in Beijing, Luo Yuanzheng, and also Fei Xiaotong, the foremost Chinese sociologist of his day, on whose works I had drawn. From my personal viewpoint, however, the most memorable visitor on the campus that year was Grace Goodell, an American anthropologist who spent some months as an academic visitor and with whom I have been firm friends ever since. Grace brought her elderly mother, also Grace, with her; they were both solid Catholics as well as most agreeable companions then and on further occasions when our paths crossed; and, often, in the course of innumerable long intercontinental phone calls. At weekends, we went together on drives in the countryside in my rattly old car, very different from the sort of vehicles they must have been accustomed to in the States. The Goodells also attended meetings of the Christian Life Group and got to know some of my friends such as the Lawlers. Grace had carried out a number of overseas field work programmes, including in a village in Iran during the Shah's rule, at the Philippines Rice Research Institute and in Latin America. She followed on with a distinguished career at Johns Hopkins University, DC.

In November 1981, Father Eusebius Arnaiz CSSR, the first Catholic priest I ever met in those far off days of wartime Chengdu, visited Australia and I went to the Redemptorist retreat house at Galong, an easy drive from Canberra, to see him. In the intervening years, I had met him once or twice when he visited England, but this was the last time we were to meet before his death a few years later. Father Arnaiz was now very frail and, at a private Mass where I was the only attendant, he was barely able to get through the liturgy. I owe him a lot, but I do not think he had much understanding of the course of my life. Father Arnaiz wrote an account, in Spanish, of the Sichuan Catholic martyrs under Communism and I asked the Australian Redemptorists if they would publish an English version but have not heard if this was ever done. However, the material he collected was, I think, added to the collection being compiled in Rome on the subject.

Just before Christmas my old friend Pen Piercy (also dating from those Chengdu years), came to Australia for about a month. Some friends of hers, the Rev George Garnsey and his wife, of St Mark's College, Canberra (perhaps the most notable Anglican presence in the capital), came to dinner. Most of Pen's visit was spent showing her something of Australia – Adelaide, Alice Springs, Ayers Rock, Mount Isa, Cairns and Rockhampton. She also went to friends in Melbourne on her own for a few days. Because of time constraints, we travelled by air. After flying to Adelaide, seeing the city and meeting Father Roderick O'Brien for lunch, we hopped on to Alice Springs, Australia's centre point. From there we went to Uluru, the huge sandstone monolith in the Red Desert – then generally known as Ayers Rock – where we passed one night, watching the sun set and, next morning, rise over that gigantic stony outcrop. Pen insisted on climbing to the top early in the morning; I contented myself with following the Psalmist's injunction to "lift up your eyes to the hills". Then we returned to Alice Springs.

Alice Springs is a depressing town, hot, dusty, with river beds, usually dry, stretching through it on which groups, all too often inebriated, of Australia's first people gather, fretting away their time. Wanting a more constructive view of Aboriginal life, we hired a car and drove to St Teresa's Mission where we were shown round by a Marist Brother who was putting the East Aranda language into writing. While waiting for Brother Leo, we chatted to a couple of Aboriginal boys. The elder, Philip, was on holiday from boarding school at Darwin where he was in year ten; he wanted to be a policeman. The younger, James, in year six at St Teresa's, hoped to become a prize boxer. Brother Leo took us round the settlement, now controlled by an elected council which had decided to allow no sale or consumption of alcohol except for beer, twice weekly – it was thought that total prohibition would encourage people to go off to drink elsewhere. We saw a vineyard and a large vegetable garden, producing mainly for self-consumption, with a small portion for sale. Artefacts and works of art were also sold and the settlement had some good artists. Brother Leo said that one great barrier to Aboriginal advancement was that if one person earned a lot, many relatives came and demanded a share, so the successful tended to slack off; it was necessary to strike a balance between Western-type acquisitiveness and their traditional society. He thought that Aboriginal spirituality was similar to that of the Old Testament.

From Alice Springs, we flew to Mount Isa, a copper-mining centre in the midst of the northwest Queensland desert. It was hot, very hot, the hottest I have ever experienced, and very dry; crossing the road was an ordeal, ending with bitumen-dripping shoes. Mount Isa Mines offered an underground tour of their operations; the ever-energetic Pen went on it, but I refrained, thinking I might not survive anything hotter than we were enduring on the surface. From Mount Isa, we took an hour's flight to Cairns, on the Queensland coast, where we stayed four nights, spending one day touring the Atherton Tablelands above Cairns and one day going to Green Island and other parts of the Barrier Reef, having a refreshing swim above the coral. Our final stop was for two nights at Rockhampton where we called on Mabel Edmund before returning to Canberra. Pen left for England the next week.

In February 1982, I went to Brisbane as an examiner for a PhD student. While there, I went to see Colin Clark, now suffering from Parkinson's and seemingly a bit depressed. I told him how much many of us admired him and his work; we thought he would have won a Nobel if not for prejudice because of his stand against the population pessimists, but that he would get the Master's "Well done", which is worth any number of Nobels.

In July 1982, I made another visit back to Sichuan, again at the invitation of the provincial branch of the Chinese Academy of Social Sciences. Before going to the Mainland, I had the usual busy ten days in Hong Kong, going the rounds of the China-watchers and other useful sources of information to get briefed up: to the Universities Service Centre, the Centre for Asian Studies at the University of Hong Kong and the Foreign Correspondents' Club where I heard a talk by Clare Hollingworth, then covering Chinese military affairs. I saw Tim Williams of the Bank of America, lunched with Lee Ngok of the University of Hong Kong and with Leo and Rose Goodstadt and, on the Sunday before I left, with my friend from Oxford days, Patrick Yu and his wife Lucia, at their home. Patrick was in the middle of a successful career at the bar; he had become the first Chinese Crown Counsel in 1951 but turned down offers from three Chief Justices to join the judiciary because of colonial discriminatory terms of employment against locals.

I saw my old Jesuit friends, Father Ladany and Father Belfiori, and Father Fernando Galbiati of PIME who had been writing a thesis under Mark Elvin in England and also propounding the idea of a Catholic University in Hong Kong, an idea which was apparently shot down by local opposition. Father Pieraccini OFM, the Holy See's unofficial representative in Hong Kong at the time, asked me to visit the two remaining legitimate Catholic bishops in Sichuan, Paul Deng Jizhou of Leshan and Matthias Duan Yinming of Wanxian. Fortunately, these two places were among the few in Sichuan then officially open to foreigners. There was an important papal message to pass on to them by word of mouth, which I memorised: "*Summus Pontifex dat permissionem omni episcopo legitimo in Sinis elegendi et consecrandi successorem pro sua diocesi etiam pro alteris diocesis si non adsunt difficultates et dati probitate et solida fide candidati, sub episcopi consecrantis responsibilitate."* (The Supreme Pontiff gives permission to every legitimate bishop in China if not prevented by difficulties to choose and consecrate a successor for his own diocese and for other dioceses if candidates are available with a solid faith and of good life, with the responsibility resting on the bishop performing the consecration.) I was given, for the two bishops, money for Mass offerings, a Bible and a few other books, a cassette tape recorder and some tapes, as well as messages of encouragement and assurance of prayers.

Also, I went to see the Franciscan Missionaries of Mary, whose Sisters I had known in Chengdu in the 1940s and who still had scattered members of their order on the Mainland. They handed me, to give any of their Sisters I should contact, some crucifixes on chains and small figures of Our Lady, both blessed by the Pope, and some relics, tiny fragments of the habit of Blessed Mary Assunta FMM who died in north China at the turn of the last century.

After a day in Guangzhou, I flew to Chengdu on 15 June 1982. The Academy of Social Sciences had no engagements prepared for me until the following week, so I said I would like to go for a long weekend to Leshan, an important prefectural-level city and a well-known tourist centre. I did the usual tourist things there, going on the lake to see the big Buddha statue, visiting the city of Emeishan and the first slopes of Mount Emei. I saw what I could of the local agriculture and the markets and shops in the city.

I had the address of the Catholic church in Leshan but no clear directions of how to get there, and it took some time to discover it down a muddy, winding lane. The old church had been confiscated and turned into the local Communist Party headquarters. When, around 1980, permission was given to re-open a church and the old bishop was released from jail, the Church was allotted, in compensation for its former church buildings in the town centre, a run-down old family compound, including a *tang* (hall) where services could be held, on the fringes of the city.

When I reached the church, the only people on the compound were four elderly, shabbily-dressed Sisters, welcoming, but obviously very nervous of my presence. They told me that the bishop had been summoned to a meeting, accompanied by the seminarian who lived there. They sat me on a stool in the middle of the yard and brought me hot water (the only drink at that time of the Sichuan poor) and, one by one, hurried to where I was sitting, to whisper some words in my ear and then hurry off again. As they spoke to me, the Sisters wiped tears from their eyes. They told me not to believe anything the government said and that, while the local authorities were superficially less oppressive, "in their hearts, they were just the same", and continued to make difficulties. The Sisters affirmed that "in their hearts, the Catholics remained faithful to the Holy Father." They said I was the first foreigner to visit the bishop since his release. In 1981, Bishop Boisguérin, the former Bishop of Yibin, had come to Leshan, but Bishop Deng was away from the city at that time.

One of the four, Sister Mary Rose, aged ninety-three, who had joined the Franciscan Missionaries of Mary in 1917, had been sentenced by the Communist authorities to twenty-one years in a labour camp but released after twelve, probably because of ill health. A magnificent old lady, her memory somewhat affected by her years, she had no front teeth, upper or lower. To her I gave one of the crucifixes and figures of Our Lady and one of the pieces of B. Mary Assunta's habit, that her consoeurs in Hong Kong had sent. I should have liked to take back with me – except that she could not have spared it – one of Sister Mary Rose's tattered garments, in case her Sisters abroad might want, in course of time, to cut that up likewise into small pieces as relics! The other three Sisters, in their seventies, were members of a local order. The Sisters had been teachers and so received a small government pension, while the bishop was also paid a little sum every month. They had just enough to survive, but no more; I could see that the whole compound was dilapidated.

Soon, Seminarian Matthew Luo Duxi returned. He had escorted Bishop Paul Deng Jizhou on foot to the meeting, a mile or so away, to which the government had summoned him; in an hour or so, he would go again to help the old man home. Because of the bishop's age and trouble with a leg, the seminarian probably escorted him everywhere; he also served his morning Mass and looked after him continuously. In Matthew, the old bishop had a most faithful and devoted attendant. Matthew Luo had entered the seminary before the Communist victory; on its closure in the early 1950s, he had been put into enforced agricultural labour, and because of his religious background, disadvantaged by being on the lowest scale of work points, a bitter fate during the famine conditions in 1959–61. He had remained firm in his resolve to follow his vocation and did not marry. When, in December 1979, Bishop Deng was released, the church re-opened and Matthew Luo himself allowed to return, he reported back to the bishop who determined to complete his training privately. A year or two after my visit, the elderly seminarian was ordained. Later, he became the bishop who oversaw the revival of the Diocese of Leshan.

At around 6:30 p.m. the bishop, accompanied by Matthew Luo, arrived home and came to the courtyard to meet me. A slight figure, of natural dignity, with a wisp of beard growing from under his chin, the frail-looking eighty-year-old Bishop Paul Deng said he was in good health, apart from that trouble with a leg. I was then brought a cup of tea, which I feared they could ill afford. I asked to speak to him in the chapel, where I gave him the papal message. He thought about it for a few moments and replied, "*Adsunt difficultates*" – there are difficulties.

The bishop's manner when speaking to me was very nervous. Later, others confirmed that he was nervous by temperament; this must have made his sufferings over the decades all the worse. Bishop Deng told me that his small chapel was the only church open in the diocese, which used to have 13,000 Catholics. In addition to the bishop, he said there remained "three good priests". These three were in the countryside and could occasionally celebrate Mass. The bishop was not allowed to go into the countryside nor even to make sick calls within the city. I passed on to him the messages I had brought from Hong Kong and offered him the Mass stipends, books, a cassette recorder, rosaries and devotional articles, but he refused them all. To make the point still further, he wrote in my notebook "*Si l'on accepte quelque chose de vos mains, il y aura des difficultés pour nous*" ("If anything is accepted from you, there would be trouble for us"). It was hard seeing their poverty and not being able to do anything to alleviate it: I had with me, ready to give the bishop, enough to double his annual income. I asked him what we could do for them and he replied, "Nothing but your prayers."

However, Bishop Deng did have one other request – to be sent the journal of his alma mater in Rome, the College for the Propagation of the Faith, which he said he would be allowed to receive – China has always had great respect for ties between fellow students. The bishop asked me to give his greetings to his former Australian friends at the College. He could not remember their names but said they used to call him "Bravo" and might remember him as Paolo Teng. He had spent twenty-one years in a prison camp and I was the first outsider to see him since his release two years previously. Later I heard, not from him but from the other remaining legitimate bishop in Sichuan province, Duan Yinming of Wanxian, that Bishop Deng had been condemned to death and nearly executed.

I was shown the chapel, capable of seating about a hundred persons on low wooden benches, which had been opened in the traditional *tang*; the Blessed Sacrament was reserved and every morning the bishop celebrated Mass there. On Sunday, I found the congregation to be about forty; on weekdays, about twenty attended. They said that at Christmas 1981 and Easter 1982, around 200 had crowded in, many coming from the countryside. On two of the three days when I was in Leshan, after Mass I was ushered into a small reception room to which the bishop and members of the congregation came. The bishop, while still nervous, was more relaxed than when he had been speaking to me alone. He was obviously on good terms with his flock, engaging them in gentle banter. However, he was always politically on the alert; when someone spoke of current problems with the government, he immediately intervened to say that things were now much better than they had been. I observed that the congregation was predominantly female and none appeared below the age of forty; it was a faithful remnant maintaining the Faith in this outpost, but seemingly destined to die out. However, I left overwhelmed by being able to walk into a decrepit compound in the far reaches of Maoist China and there find a group of people with whom I shared the deepest things in life.

In Chengdu, I had a busy round of interviews with officials at the Bureaus of Finance, of Foreign Trade, of Administration of Industry and Commerce, of Labour and of Census, of the People's Bank and of the Provincial Academy of Social Sciences. As on my previous visit to Sichuan in 1980, I spent a day at Guanghan, where I had lived in the early 1940s and which was now considered a showpiece county, "an experimental point, to get ideas for the province", as my informant told me. Great changes had recently taken place in the agricultural scene there since my visit two years earlier. In 1981, communes and production brigades had been abolished and their former conjoined political and economic roles divided. At least in this part of the country, communes had in course of time been enlarged; their administrative functions were now to be performed by *xiang* (districts) and in the case of production brigades, by village people's committees. Basic decisions, on what to produce and how much, were to be left to the individual farming households, subject to compulsory deliveries of fixed amounts of certain produce (probably grain and vegetable oil). Each *xiang* had an agricultural technical service company, an industrial company and a commercial company. These had co-ordinating roles, especially in the case of agriculture e.g. in setting incentive-driven output targets for the production teams (these had not been abolished) and in the provision of advice and of contracted services, such as ploughing or pest control. Emphasis was being put on developing rural industry. I was given figures for rises in output of grain and vegetable oil. On comparing them with those given me in 1980 in Sichuan, there appeared to be discrepancies, but I had long learned to be sceptical of all statistics in the country.

While in Guanghan, I saw my old friend, Wang Deren and his family, but again in the presence of local officials. However, next evening, when I was back in Chengdu, the Wangs turned up at my hotel. There they poured out a completely different story about the past. During the

Cultural Revolution, Guanghan saw great turbulence. Deren's old parents – my father's onetime curate and his wife – had suffered terribly and, in the end, his mother, whom I had known as a completely unpolitical, devoted wife and mother, was so desperate that she threw herself down the well in the old house where once my family, and now the Wangs, lived. During that time, the Cultural Revolutionaries made a bonfire of Bibles and other religious books at the foot of the guihua tree in the courtyard. The old tree was damaged by the fire and had to be cut down.

From Chengdu, I went by train to Chongqing, spending three nights in the People's Hotel, which combined grandiosity with discomfort to an even greater extent than the hotel in Taipei. I had a meeting with a group from the Chongqing section of the Academy of Social Sciences and then, on 9 July, took a ship down the Yangtse to Wuhan, stopping for a few hours at Wanxian before going through the Gorges. The river was very low, leaving a long climb from the river to Wanxian town; going down, I counted 177 old, irregular, mud and wood steps, and there were no railings to hold. On my way up, I was carrying quite a heavy bag with gifts, felt exhausted and wondered if I should turn around and return to the ship before I slipped and fell. However, I managed to climb on and then a kind fellow climber, seeing my plight, offered to carry my bag. I have never ceased to feel thankful to him as his help enabled me to reach the top and continue to the church, which fortunately was quite near.

Bishop Duan greeted me with warmth and confidence and gladly accepted the money and small gifts I had brought and was happy to receive the messages; the Franciscan relics he would pass on to FMM Sisters in Wuhan. I gave him the papal message which, he said, he had already received shortly before from Father Jean Charbonnier, but he was happy to get it a second time and would now ordain bishops for the vacant sees of the province. Bishop Deng of Leshan had written to him about my visit there, saying that they had had a lot of trouble from the authorities as a result. However, Bishop Duan continued, he thought that more Catholics from abroad should visit Bishop Deng – "the more the better" – because in the long run it would have a good effect. The situation of the Church in

Wanxian, he considered, was the best in the province; there were no notices of the "Patriotic Association" to be seen anywhere on the compound, unlike in Chengdu. (The "Catholic Patriotic Association" is a body set up by the government to control the Church.) Almost every day, the bishop said, someone came to the church to enquire about the Faith. I met Father Song, the parish priest, and Father Zhang and Sister Wu and also Miss Duan, the bishop's sister, who lived at the church.

The bishop sat me down in the courtyard and gave me tea and freshly pressed orange juice, while he talked with me. Bishop Duan, Father Zhang and Sister Wu had been paraded through the streets and jailed during the Cultural Revolution (1967–76). The bishop had for some years been on forced labour at the docks where the other labourers were much younger than him so it was hard for him to keep up with them. Finally, he was allowed to return to his pastoral duties when the church, a very simple building, was re-opened at the end of 1979.

Bishop Duan had studied in Rome in the 1930s and then returned to Wanxian, undertaking parish work and seminary teaching before being ordained bishop in October 1949, the same month as the People's Republic was proclaimed in Beijing. He lived until 2000, having achieved the rare distinction of celebrating the golden jubilee of his episcopal ordination while still administering his diocese. Bishop Duan had a high reputation as a Chinese calligrapher and also as a linguist, fluent in Italian, French and English. He was a magnificent man who helped keep the Church in Sichuan going throughout some of its darkest years and then participated notably in its revival.

The church and compound were old and shabby, without running water, but clean and tidy. In Wanxian, unlike Leshan, the Church occupied its former premises near the centre of the city, with a proper church. A small, well-kept flower garden brightened the middle of the courtyard. While the bishop's household lived in great simplicity compared with anything in the West, there was not the sense of biting poverty I had felt in Leshan. Later, I heard of the stormy days that compound had witnessed, when Bishop Duan had been threatened by Red Guards at the entrance of the Church.

They demanded that he should trample on some pictures of Our Lady; he refused and thought he was going to be killed.

The bishop had wanted to train some young men for the priesthood at the church, but the government stopped it. The only possibility now for training clergy was at a government-sponsored seminary in Beijing which he said was useless: "They would become atheist priests." Some young women in Wanxian were being trained for the religious life but not for any specific order. Bishop Duan was eager for more contacts from abroad and thought that it might be possible to bring Bibles and New Testaments from Hong Kong to Guangdong and post them to Sichuan from there. The relatively relaxed atmosphere at Wanxian could be seen from the fact that the bishop came out on to the street to bid me farewell. Despite all the problems, I left Wanxian feeling assured about the future of the Church in Sichuan.

After Wanxian, the ship went down through the gorges, the towering cliffs on both sides reminding me of that long-ago junk trip in my early childhood. Next morning, we stopped at Yichang, reaching Wuhan the following day. From there, I flew to Guangzhou and thence, by hover ferry to Hong Kong where I spent nearly two weeks.

Visits to Sichuan by outside observers were still not common, so in Hong Kong I was giving as well as getting information as I made the rounds of the Universities Service Centre, the US Consulate, the American Chamber of Commerce, the Hong Kong and the Chartered Banks, and old friends among the community. A lawyer studying the Chinese legal system, Anthony Dicks, was a valuable addition to the usual range of expertise. Once again, I talked with Tim Williams of the Bank of America, Clare Hollingworth of the *Daily Telegraph* and David Bonavia of *The Times*. Leo Goodstadt, by now well-rooted in Hong Kong society, was at various times correspondent for *The Times* and the *Economist*, and a staff member of the *Far Eastern Economic Review*; now, too, Leo had a radio programme on which he grilled local notables.

Also, of course, in Hong Kong I gave news from Sichuan to various missionaries – Father Pieraccini of the Franciscans, Father Lazarotto and

Father F. Galbiati of the PIMEs and Father Ladany and Father Belfiori of the Jesuits – about my visits to the bishops, and I spoke to the Franciscan Missionaries of Mary about Sister Mary Rose of Leshan. Archbishop Dominic Tang of Guangzhou had, after long years of imprisonment, been allowed abroad on health grounds. The announcement of his appointment as Archbishop had infuriated the Chinese government and he was barred from returning. It was good to be able to meet this valiant confessor of the Faith at Xavier House.

When I returned to Canberra late in July 1982, I had to get down to writing and managed to produce five articles and other publications which came out the following year and for which my information from interviews in China and elsewhere was useful. I gave a lunch time talk at ANU on my Sichuan visit and a seminar paper to the Department of Demography on the Chinese Census. I also spoke to the Sunday evening Christian Life Group about the religious side of my trip. My cousin, Faith Page (née Rawlence), and her husband, on a visit to Australia, stayed with me for a few days in October.

I had not thought it would be possible for any of the church people I had met in China to write to me and was surprised and delighted when, in September a letter arrived, in English, from Bishop Duan of Wanxian. He thanked me for my visit and asked me to come again. This was the start of a long correspondence, with at least 155 letters from the bishop in subsequent years. In 1983, I found it possible to get a small booklet through to him by post and I followed this up by gradually sending him more and more books, sometimes with success, but at other times they were returned or confiscated.

At this time, Rebecca Chiu, from Hong Kong, was writing a doctoral thesis at ANU on the early development of the Shenzhen Special Economic Zone. She was in the Department of Geography so I was not involved directly in supervising her but took an interest in her work and later was an examiner for her thesis. She returned home and now has a chair in the University of Hong Kong.

In the late 1970s and 1980s I made other good friends in Canberra. George (Jerzy) Zubrzycki had been recruited by the ANU in its early days and later set up and founded the Department of Sociology in the Research School of Social Sciences, becoming a forceful proponent of multiculturalism rather than immigrant assimilation. He was a native of Cracow and attended the same school and university as the future Pope John Paul II, although they did not meet until the papal visit to Australia of 1973. Zubrzycki had an eventful war – first, in the Polish army and then in the British Special Operations Executive. His wife, Alexandra, a childhood sweetheart who had spent the war in Khazakstan and with whom he was reunited in London, settled well in Canberra where they brought up their four children. I met the Zubryckis many times in the course of university and Catholic life at the ANU and greatly appreciated his social contributions, but I did not get to know them well until my post-retirement visits to Canberra.

Kevin and Margaret Kelly returned to Australia when he retired after being ambassador first to Argentina and then to Portugal. Kevin, in his earlier years, had been close to Cardinal Mannix of Melbourne and was associated with the Catholic movements of those years. The Kellys and their daughters, Anne and Barbara, lived not far from me and were generous in their hospitality, especially in inviting me to several splendid Christmas dinners with the family. Father Eddy introduced me to his sister Mrs Margot Traill and her husband John Traill QC who used his talents to fight legal battles for the pro-life cause. They lived in Sydney where several times I visited them and their six children.

Other new Canberra friends from that period included Bill and Margaret Clifford, both Catholics originally from England. Bill, a member of an old recusant family, was an internationally renowned criminologist and was Director of the Australian Institute of Criminology from 1975 to 1983. He was interested in the Chinese legal scene and I supplied him with information. The Cliffords were keen on the revival of the Latin Mass. After Bill's death in 1986, Margaret devoted herself to this cause. I always enjoyed Latin Masses, as did many of my other friends, especially during that stormy time after the Second Vatican Council when there was much liturgical disorder, and I often attended them, thinking it very desirable that the Latin liturgical tradition should survive. However, while approving of the movement to keep the Latin Mass alive, I never thought of this as a matter of primary importance on which I should spend much time and energy.

Father Ladany wrote urging me to contact a Chinese couple who were to visit Australia. John and Teresa Liu, from Guangzhou, were Catholics who had, before they married, been in the group associated with Bishop Dominic Tang in the early 1950s. The bishop was imprisoned and later both John and Teresa were also incarcerated in prison and labour camps, each for twenty or more years. On their release, both serene and cheerful and ready to get on with life, they met again and then married. Teresa had family in Sydney, and she and her husband visited Australia late in 1982. I got them an invitation to the John XXIII conference, took them there just after Christmas 1982 and then drove them back to Canberra to stay with me for a few days. It was to be the start of a long and much valued friendship that grew after my retirement, a subject which was now beginning to occupy my thoughts.[2]

---

2 John Liu wrote an anonymous account of his experiences: *Inside China – Experiences of a Chinese Catholic 1948–80,* Hong Kong (privately printed).

CHAPTER 20

More China Visits, American and UK Interludes: 1983–84

China was changing rapidly during these years and I had already benefitted, as shown by the fact that I was allowed at least limited entry. The agricultural changes were perhaps the earliest to come. (The urban "spontaneous capitalism", reported intermittently from Shanghai, was no doubt permanently endemic in that metropolis and was nothing new but had continued quietly throughout the Maoist era.) The breakdown of the communes, first reported from the particularly impoverished province of Anhui, began before any government policy change was announced. It originated as a desperate move by hungry collective farm workers and soon led to higher production; this came to the notice of a senior leader and thereupon, post facto, it was affirmed as official policy. I think that several policy changes came about in this way.

In April 1983, I spent a week in Hong Kong catching up with developments in China. This was followed by a holiday in Rome and, after that, a long study-leave first in Oxford with attachments both to St Antony's and Wolfson Colleges and then in the States, primarily at the Harvard Fairbank Centre for Chinese Studies. In the second half of the year, I made another visit to China.

As I was to be away for some months, I lent my house to a young couple, Michael and Sonya Lawler, who were temporarily homeless because Michael's parents, my good friends Peter and Doreen Lawler, were in Dublin for some years where Sir Peter was Australian ambassador, concurrently with holding the same position at the Holy See. Michael was at the time hesitating between taking up law or portrait painting as his career. As a "thank you" on my return, he insisted on painting my portrait.

I had a busy week in Hong Kong during which I gave a seminar paper at the University of Hong Kong's Centre for China Studies and also had an interesting talk with Y. C. Jao, a banking specialist in the Economics Department. China, and its economy, were now in full stream of opening up. Y. C. had lectured at Zhongshan University and had been asked to write a textbook on monetary matters for mainland students which was soon to be published in Beijing. No students from Mainland China had yet enrolled at Hong Kong University because their English was too poor but some junior teaching staff from universities in Guangzhou had come for research and academic exchange. Major changes were under consideration for the Chinese banking system and in the rest of the economy. At the China Department of the Hong Kong Bank, I saw Chris Beckett, who had been in Shanghai about a month earlier and was excited about trends he had seen there: "Shanghai is about to take off ... something interesting is about to happen." He thought that city would be China's high technology area, the place for introducing foreign technology. It was already the training centre for the rest of China with, at any time, about 10,000 young technicians from other parts of the country.

At the American Consulate in Hong Kong, I had a talk with a group of six staff, headed by Dick Williams, the Deputy Consul General. One of the chief topics was the changes taking place in the management system of state enterprises, through which they were given greater incentives by being taxed on profits and then allowed to retain the balance, rather than having to remit all, or almost all, profits to the government. Tim Williams of the Bank of America told me about his recent visit to Hainan where he found the local officials had no notion of how to deal with potential foreign investors; and l saw Dr Fang of the Bank of China. I also spoke with John Dolfin, Director of the Universities Service Centre, who had recently visited Xishuangbanna in South Yunnan and had seen the despoliation of the prime forests there; I discussed with him, too, the future of the USC, which was having difficulty in getting grants from US foundations. Leo Goodstadt was, as ever, an invaluable informant while I found a new contact in George Hicks, a successful commodities dealer with strong scholarly interests in East and South-East Asia. In addition, I spoke with a number of the missionary community including, of course, Father Ladany SJ and Father Lazzarotto and Father F. Galbiati of the PIMEs, and once again saw the indomitable old Archbishop Tang. Around this time, Archbishop Tang visited his great-nephew in Sydney where I met him. In Australia, he said, he discovered "an air of innocence".

In April 1983, from Hong Kong I flew for twelve days' holiday in Rome, staying in the best lodgings I have ever had in the eternal city – at a convent on Borgo Santo Spirito, overlooking St Peter's Square. This time I enjoyed the advantage of introductions from the Pro-Nuncio in Canberra, a ticket for the front row of a Wednesday public audience of John Paul II and also the presence in Rome of two seminarian friends, John Parsons studying at the Venerabile (the Ven. English College) and Brian Harrison at the Nepomeane. The papal audience, in St Peter's Square, was a great and moving experience – getting there early, presenting the ticket at the hatch in the Bernini colonnade and finding my place at the barrier rail an hour or so before the audience began. I tried to chat to those next to me but could find no common language. Then came the amazing instant of holding the hand of the greatest of our contemporaries, now a proclaimed saint.

John Parsons had already gained an excellent knowledge of the city and showed me round. He invited me to the historic English College, one day for Vespers and another day for Mass. Brian Harrison had been accepted by the Diocese of Puerto Rico and had also joined the Oblates of Divine Wisdom, a new congregation that was, I think, still in the process of formation. I visited the Jesuit Curia (headquarters) at 5 Borgo Santo Spirito where the house superior was Father Michael Chu, one of the five (or was it six?) remarkable and heroic Jesuit sons of a saintly mother who were a gift of Shanghai to the Universal Church. (They were distantly related to Father Vincent Chu, the Jesuit whom I had met in Shanghai in 1980.)

The Pro-Nuncio in Canberra had suggested that I should call on Monsignor Ghidoni who ran the China Desk at the Congregation for the Evangelisation of Peoples (better known by its historic name of Propaganda Fide), so one afternoon I went to the fine old building near the Spanish Steps and told the doorman that I wanted to see Mgr Ghidoni. I do not speak Italian, but he indicated that I should go upstairs. I ascended the large stairs and walked through a couple of huge empty salons without seeing a person, and then found a passage off which were offices, but all seemed empty. I went downstairs to the doorman again and gathered that I should come back next morning. I left in some despair, unsurprised that the conversion of the world was proceeding so slowly if it was considered a half-day business. Next day, however, I came back and found Mgr Ghidoni and was impressed by his detailed knowledge of the Church in China and by his assessment of the situation there. Apparently, like his fellow workers, he sensibly took his work home every afternoon where he could get on with it until late in the evening without the interruption of visitors who, like myself, were constantly pouring in from all parts of the world; a good pioneering example of flexible working arrangements. I went to see Father Paul Pang, a Franciscan who had been given a roving commission to work for Overseas Chinese all over the globe and I also visited the Pontifical Council for Culture.

From Rome I flew to London, and thence to Oxford where I was to spend three months of study leave with joint invitations from St Antony's and Wolfson Colleges. I had a beautiful set of rooms at Wolfson, overlooking the Cherwell with its swans but spent most of my time at St Antony's where there was greater involvement with modern China studies including the presence of Cyril Lin and Mark Elvin. St Antony's, of course as ever, hosted an interesting and varied assortment of scholars. I remember a Japanese academic who was writing a life of King Alfred from Anglo-Saxon sources; in Japan, the Anglo-Saxon language seemed to be studied more widely than in England.

In Oxford I gave two lectures and a seminar paper and also saw many old friends including the Parfits who, after leaving Chengdu, had settled there, Norman becoming Oxford's Medical Officer of Health; Father Rodger Charles and other Jesuits at Campion Hall, Peter Hodgson at Corpus Christi College, John Finnis at University College, my former ANU colleague Hedley Bull at Balliol, Elspeth Kennedy at St Hilda's, Lady Ogilvie at St Anne's and the Giedroyc family. I visited Plater Hall, the former Catholic Workers' College, with which I still had links. As usual whenever I visited Oxford, Valerie Jensen (née Corcos), a Somerville contemporary, picked me up and drove me to lunch at her beautiful village home at Wheatley.

It was a great pleasure to have my cousins, Jane and Christopher Hawker, as my guests to a formal dinner at St Antony's. Around this time, Jane's sister Nicola's brother-in-law, Owen Bennett-Jones, about to graduate from LSE, asked if I thought St Antony's would be a good place for him to pursue graduate studies in international relations; I warmly recommended it. I visited other cousins, the Darvill family then living near Oxford, and also Faith and Mike Page at Didcot, on the way, looking up an old friend from Oxford chaplaincy days, David Rogers, who after years working on the staff of the Bodleian Library, was now chronically ill. Another friend from the same time and circle, living in Oxford with impaired health, which had compelled him to leave Quarr Abbey before making his profession, whom I saw again, was Bill Warren, now living in Oxford and hardly able to speak, but still going daily to the Chaplaincy to help in its library. Despite his disability, he managed to complete a DPhil in patristic studies. In London, I gave a talk at a Chatham House China lunch, saw Peter Wiles and Alan Prest at LSE and called at the Sino-British Trade Council and the Great Britain-China Centre. I caught up with many others of my family – lunched with Tom Ingram and with Mary Davies and her family, had dinner with Rosemary and Bill Vaughan, met Rosalind (née Ingram) and David Talks and visited another younger cousin, Philip Ross and, for the first time, met his wife Rosalind. I spent a weekend with my double first cousin Maurice and his family in Somerset where he was struggling with his fish farm. In addition, I saw Johanne Breitenfeld at Nazareth House, Hammersmith where she serenely passed her final years, and Mary Low in Hove. While in London, I met Joanna Bogle; Lucy Brown, with whom I had always kept up since Somerville days; and also Bernard and Teresa Kay and my goddaughters Clare Oddy (née Corlett) and Charlotte Bearcroft and her mother Rosalind, and others. In July, I paid a brief visit to Pen Piercy in Dorset.

After a busy three months in England, at the end of July 1983 I flew to Boston. I had come across a booklet on the work of Catholic philosophers in contemporary Poland by an American-Polish priest, Father F. J. Lescoe[1] which I thought might be of interest to some in China, such as Bishop Duan of Wanzhou, and perhaps also to other Catholics there. After exchanging a few letters with Bishop Duan, I then, as an experiment, slipped a copy of this small publication in the envelope with my next letter to the bishop, hoping it would get through the Chinese censorship, which happily it did. I received a delighted reply from Wanzhou, saying, "I am very happy to know that Poland has developed a new kind of vibrant and viable Christian philosophy." I wrote to Father Lescoe, informing him of the interest that his booklet had aroused from Bishop Duan and asking if on my forthcoming visit to the States, I might discuss with him how the Polish experience of confronting Marxist philosophy might further be channelled to China. Father Lescoe replied by inviting me to visit him in Connecticut where he lived in semi-retirement with his sister, a university professor. So, on arrival in the States, after leaving my heavy suitcase in Boston, I flew to Hartford, Connecticut for a night to meet this learned old priest and his sister before going on the next day to join the Goodells at their home in El Paso, Texas.

Grace Goodell was working at Harvard on a short-term appointment and had efficiently found me lodgings at Rindge House, Cambridge. She had also very kindly invited me to accompany her and her mother and brother Phil on a visit to Mexico, with four days on the way at their pleasant home in El Paso, from which Grace drove me north to New

1 Philosophy Serving Contemporary Needs of the Church (Symposium and Workshop: "Philosophy and the Priest Today", 9–11 Nov. 1979. Catholic University of America Washington, DC) Booklet published by Mariel Publications, New Britain CT.

Mexico to see some of the old Spanish missions, notably Ruidoso and Tularosa, stopping at the little town of Mesilla. The next day we crossed the border to Ciudad Juarez and flew to Mexico City, where we visited the great baroque Metropolitan Cathedral and the market. From there we flew to Guadeloupe and saw the basilica and the shrine, filled with pilgrims. We also visited an old Jesuit mission centre which at one time was a launching point for their missionaries to East Asia; murals depicted the Jesuit martyrs of Japan. Then we went on to Teotihuacan and the grim Aztec pyramids. From there we returned to Mexico City for a couple of days.

Grace and I had a meeting with the Benedictine secretary of the Catholic Migration Council of Mexico whom we quizzed about the present state of the Church in his country. Priests were still fined if they went on to the streets in their clerical collars. He told us that 5 per cent of the places in Catholic schools had to be given free to be filled by the government and that many senior officials sent their children to these schools. The previous president had told the Cardinal Archbishop that he intended to nationalise all Catholic schools and the Cardinal replied that he should not blame him if things went wrong. After that, the President did nothing more about the matter.

I have had very little experience of Spanish culture – later, I was to make a short visit to Spain – but this trip was my first exposure to a Hispanic environment, apart from a busy conference in Puerto Rico in 1975; being escorted round by very gracious companions provided extra pleasure.

On 11 August, I flew to Toronto for a week in Canada, especially to see China scholars connected with the University of Toronto and also to attend parts of an international conference on Chinese philosophy being organized largely by Julia Ching, whom I had first known as Sister Agnes at the Ursuline Convent on the ANU campus when she was studying for a PhD in Asian Studies. She had decided not to take permanent vows in the order but left and launched on an academic career in neo-Confucianism and Chinese religion. A few years later, she married Will Oxtoby, a scholar of comparative religion, and they settled in Toronto where both had chairs.

As it was the long vacation, there were no university activities, apart from the conference, in which to participate; but I was able to see some China scholars, notably Victor Falkenheim, a political scientist who had studied local government in China. He was currently working on a question which particularly interested me as it was affecting the cellular economy on which I had written – the breakdown of control on a territorial basis of the supply of commodities, by the formation of joint ventures straddling regions, and also of new conglomerates, such as Fujian's Mindong Corporation which included both Fujian enterprises and Shanghai suppliers. Victor told me of a graduate student who had been trying to quantify the burgeoning extra-budgetary funds, a phenomenon on which I had written in 1966 as well as in *China's Economic System*; these funds can perhaps be considered the predecessors of the huge sums salted away, in more recent years, in the shadowy local government financial vehicles which have caused Western analysts many headaches. My fellow Sichuanese friend of many years, Jerome Chen, had a post in York University, Toronto and I saw him and also Bill Zhao whom I had known years before when he worked in the Economics Department of the University of Hong Kong.

From Toronto, I went by bus to Hanover where I was picked up by my cousin Margaret Pratt (née Ingram) who took me to their family farm – dairy, with some arable to provide fodder for the cows. This gave me an opportunity to meet her husband Reg for the first time and also their three adopted children; and to get a glimpse of a way of life which I had not known before: a pleasant interlude.

On my return to Rindge House, Cambridge, I went down with a severe bout of arthritis in my hip, one of a few which I suffered around this time. Grace was wonderful in helping me and ensuring I had the treatment I was entitled to at the Harvard Medical Centre. I had noticed a local acupuncture clinic and thought I might take the opportunity to try out that too – but I do not think it made much difference one way or the other.

Things were fairly quiet at Harvard during the long vacation and until term began, so I could catch up on the backlog of China reports which followed me round the world and which had to be read, annotated for cuttings and dispatched back to my research assistant in Canberra. One weekend I bused out to Cheshire, Connecticut, to the Novitiate of the Legionnaires of Christ to visit Chris Streicher, a John XXIII Fellowship friend from Canberra, who was trying his vocation there. This has been my only contact with this curious congregation which has somehow managed to survive its founder's misdeeds. I was impressed with its rigorous asceticism but it was obviously the wrong place for Chris and he left to resume his career as a solicitor in Australia.

One important contact I made at Harvard during the long vacation was Christine Wong, then a young academic at Mt Holyoke College, Mass. I had several long and valuable talks with her. She was interested in many of the same matters in the Chinese economy as myself, including financial relations between the central government and local authorities, the level of administration which controlled different state enterprises, allocation of investment funds, extra-budgetary funds controlled by local authorities and by administrative bodies such as water conservancy or road maintenance concerns. Christine was then facing problems because although all area study programmes were clamouring for economists, few area study economists were yet being employed because appointments were in the hands of economics departments; she herself was making her living teaching "straight" economics. The situation changed radically shortly after my retirement when the upsurge of business opportunities in China led to more funding for university studies of the current Chinese economy in its bewildering complexity. Christine Wong subsequently had a successful career at the World Bank and at Oxford and Melbourne.

The Fairbank Center hosted meetings of the New England China Seminar where I gave a paper and also met a number of scholars from neighbouring places, including Christine Wong, which made up for the lack of anyone at Harvard working in my line. It was useful to talk with Tom Lyons of Dartmouth College who had written a thesis at Cornell on the question of the cellularity of the Chinese economy from 1957 to 1979. He said that from 1976 to 1980, the grain crossing provincial borders in China did not exceed five or six million tons a year, although since then it had probably increased because there had been more zoning for agricultural specialisation. At Harvard, I was able to make some progress with work on Chinese finance and banking, although I was frustrated by the continual changes taking place in China. While at Harvard I gave a talk to the East Asian Legal Studies Program at Harvard Law School. Grace Goodell was a constant source of help and contacts; it was through her that I met Nick Eberstadt whose demographic work I have always admired.

From Cambridge Mass. I visited a number of other universities to give papers and meet China specialists. I spoke at Princeton, Columbia, Cornell, the University of Michigan and the University of Chicago. At Princeton, I saw Lynn White who had recently visited Xinjiang. He reported that at that time there was not too much tension there although there had been some hostile incidents; resentment existed that only a very few people could go to Mecca. Lynn mentioned that the granddaughter of Y. C. Tung, the ship-owner (i.e. the daughter of Tung Chee Hwa, the future first Chief Executive of the Hong Kong SAR) was currently at Princeton, writing a senior undergraduate thesis on what Hong Kong capitalists should do to have their interests realised in the negotiations about the future of Hong Kong. They had their own intelligence network, centred in the Zhejiang-Jiangsu Association premises in Hong Kong.

In New York, early in October, I lunched with the recently widowed Maria London, whom I had met in Hong Kong through Father Ladany. She and her husband, Ivan, also a China-watcher of note, spent long periods in Hong Kong interviewing escapees and others from the Mainland and I had benefitted from discussions with them. Maria told me that Ivan had been baptized before his death. Maria thought that they had both been treated badly, because of their anti-Maoist stance, by other students of China. I also had supper, in their Manhattan apartment, with Mike and Barbara Liccione (née Geach), daughter of Elizabeth Anscombe and Peter Geach.

In Washington DC, in October 1983, I had a long discussion with three officials of the World Bank concerned with China, Edwin Lim, William Byrd and Adrian Wood. They were struggling, as I often was, with financial and other definitions used in China. "International Monetary

Fund definitions are totally useless for China", we agreed. They said there were fierce arguments in the World Bank between China specialists and statistical specialists. Also, they noted the beginning of what was to become a major problem in China's development, that when a state enterprise alienated farm lands, it was obliged to bring in the dispossessed farm households as urban households and give them jobs in the factory that had expropriated their land; sometimes they got jobs without getting urban *hukou* (household registration) and remained as temporary workers in perpetuity. We discussed the large size of China's foreign exchange reserves which they tended to think was unintentional because of gross lack of co-ordination in China: different sets of orders may be given to those who earn foreign exchange on the one hand and to those who spend it, and to those who borrow it.

While in DC, I read a paper to a group of economists at the Johns Hopkins School of Advanced International Studies and had a long discussion with officials of the National Council for US-China Trade which had recently sent a delegation to China on coal gasification; I also spoke with people at the State Department. These talks, like that at the World Bank, were often on the nitty-gritty matters that are all important in any meaningful consideration of the Chinese economy; without them, any study of Chinese economic matters becomes waffle. These significant particulars included, at least at that time, the use of internal foreign exchange rates (differing from official ones) in determining internal trade prices; the pricing of grain transfers between provinces; definitions of budgetary items, especially those with a bearing on military matters; the significance, if any, of frequent re-naming of various government bodies; the power of "paper carriers", sometimes designated as deputy secretaries general, or perhaps staff officers, or even vice-premiers, who controlled the flow of paper and determined what documents and people the leaders saw; the powers of central and local price-fixing organs; the facility, or otherwise, for state enterprises to borrow foreign exchange from the Bank of China – most such things in China are designated state secrets. It was much easier for academics to have meaningful discussions with public servants about these matters and exchange information in the USA than in other countries, largely, of course, because so many more officials worked on them in the States than elsewhere and also because of the greater strength and size there of commercially funded non-state bodies concerned with China, whose staff were in continual contact with their governmental counterparts.

These considerations modified my previous opinions about working in the States, although my friendship with Grace Goodell was probably a stronger factor. Soon after my visit, Grace accepted a chair in the School of Advanced Studies at Johns Hopkins University in Washington DC and, a little time later, when a chair there was advertised in modern Chinese studies, I applied for it and was short-listed. I did not get it and it was probably all for the good. A switch to a new environment and work at this time in my life would have been difficult and it was really a position that should be held by an American who could use, to better purpose, the opportunities it provided for constant contact with and advice to officials of his government.

In mid-October 1983, I made a hurried visit from Harvard to Detroit and then to Chicago. At the University of Michigan at Ann Arbor, I gave a seminar paper and had discussions with Kenneth Lieberthal, a China political scientist (I stayed overnight with him and his wife Jane) and also talked with Bob Dernberger. At the University of Chicago, I spoke at the economics workshop and had a talk with Martin Weil of the National Council for US-China Trade, who studied China's energy matters and with Gale Johnson who had visited China annually for the previous four years.

In Chicago, I also saw the Nobel laureate T. W. Schultz who had always been very encouraging about my work. Earlier in 1983 he had commented warmly about my *China's Economic System* and after my paper in Chicago in October 1983 he wrote: "The contribution you made while you were with us has now gone far beyond the immediate members of the workshop. Most notable is the very favourable response that Professor Ping-ti Ho expressed upon reading your paper. He thought it was one of the best that he had come upon in the area in which he had been trying to get more information. As you might know, Professor Ho is one of our distinguished professors. He asked for five copies so that he could send them to his colleagues and associates ... in China ... Your presentation at the workshop and the discussion that followed and the talks that we had together were for me very rewarding professionally. Would that you were in an office next door so that I could exploit your vast knowledge about China."

Late in October, I said goodbye to the Harvard China Center and to Grace Goodell, who had been doing everything possible to make my time at Harvard as interesting and profitable as possible, and began the journey back to Australia, with many stops on the way. The first stop was at San Francisco where I gave papers at Berkeley and at the University of San Francisco and, at Palo Alto, lunched with Y. L. Wu of Stanford, and Ray Myers. I broke the Pacific flight at Hawaii, to speak at the Honolulu East-West Center. I was still hoping and working to bring out a new edition of my *China's Economic System* and had, in fact, signed a contract for it.

In November 1983, I was back in Canberra, having lost a day to the mid-Pacific date line. The rest of the year was spent catching up with the pile of China radio monitoring reports and press reports waiting for me and on several overdue visits to the dentist. I also gave a talk to the Newman Graduate Society and, just after Christmas, attended the annual conference of the John XXIII Fellowship, at which John and Teresa Liu were again present.

Notable visitors to ANU in the first half of 1984 included an old friend of George Allen, Saburo Okita, the well-known Japanese economist, whom I had met in Japan in 1959; Julian Simon, the American economist and demographer, one of the few writers on population and resources of that time with whom I agreed; and two leading Australian sociologists of religion, Charles Price and Hans Mol who gave a seminar on religious affiliation and social indicators. Oliver Wolters, the China historian whom I had met at Cornell, and his wife Euteen, spent some time at ANU and I was glad to get to know them better. Joseph Cheng of Hong Kong was doing a PhD in political science and I enjoyed meeting him and his wife Grace and their children. My cousin John Ingram and his girlfriend, Julie, later his wife, came to stay with me, which I enjoyed, especially since I had not met Julie before.

In July 1984, I took some study leave and attended a conference at the East-West Centre in Hawaii. The theme of the conference was economic bureaucracies in certain Chinese regions; it was a well-run and stimulating occasion and I welcomed its regional focus. From Honolulu, I flew to Hong Kong where I spent two and a half weeks on my habitual China-watching, followed by seven weeks actually on the Mainland. Among those with whom I spoke in Hong Kong was Richard Conroy who had information about Dukou (later known as Panzhihua) in the southern tip of Sichuan, about which we were beginning to hear rumours at the time – of a big project, hidden in secrecy. He had heard that this development covered around a hundred square kilometres and that a complicated set of minerals had been found there, rare earths as well as iron ore. So it was probable that a plant to produce special hardened steel for military purposes would be set up.

In Hong Kong, I spoke to Ma Lin – who had succeeded my old friend Li Choh Ming as Vice Chancellor of the Chinese University of Hong Kong (CUHK) – about bringing students from Sichuan to his university; so far, the only mainlanders coming had been from the big universities of the east coast. I also saw Kuan Hsin-Chi, whom I had first met at St Antony's, Oxford, and who now had a chair at the Chinese University. He said that the CUHK had formal exchange programmes with Zhongshan University and had also designated three other Mainland universities – Beijing, Fudan and Qinghua – with which relations could be established on a departmental level and exchanges arranged.

In August, I flew to Beijing where my minder for the early part of my visit was Li Bichang, a young man educated at the Foreign Languages Institute of Shanghai and the Collège d'Europe at Brussels; he worked for a government financial consulting firm. He accompanied me to some of the interviews which had been arranged for me and escorted me to a lunch hosted by the head of his consultancy, Xu Yi, in a fine restaurant in Bohai Park. Luo Yuanzheng, my fellow-Sichuanese whom I had first met in Canberra and then at his home in Beijing in 1980, was among the guests. Li Bichang also took me to the Lugouqiao Bridge where the War with Japan had broken out on 7 July 1937. At the US Embassy, I had a long talk with Bill Abnett; among other matters, he gave me information on inter-provincial sales prices for grain, indicating why some provincial-level governments prefer imported grain to that offered by provinces with a surplus. On the Chinese oil industry, I spoke to Mel Searle of the Commercial Department of the American Embassy. An interesting contact made on this visit to Beijing was David Aikman, then of *Time* magazine. An active evangelical Protestant, he later authored the book *Jesus in Beijing*, on the growth of Christianity in China.

Some inkling of the complications and likely future developments in the banking, financial and pricing systems were given me in a number of lengthy interviews with Wang Chuanlun of the Dept. of Finance, People's University, conjointly head of the Department of Economics, University of Shenzhen (whom I had already met in Hong Kong), with Jin Zhonghe, head of the Research Department of the Construction Bank, with Du Lingfeng of the People's University (on central-local financial relations) and with two groups of officials, of three persons each, from the Institute of Fiscal Studies. Raising procurement prices of grain had led to increased grain production. However, the highest prices paid to Chinese growers for grain were still below the cost of imported grain, so I asked why they did not raise the procurement prices to international market levels to increase domestic output further. They replied that time was needed for Chinese farmers to increase output and that fertilizer supply was not enough to meet demand. Also, the rise in grain production had led to storage problems in some places. Prices of inter-provincial grain sales were set somewhere between the lowest state procurement prices paid to farmers for compulsory sales and "negotiated prices" which were the highest prices paid for above-quota production; sometimes they were at a higher price than for retail sales. The four specialist banks – the Bank of China, the Industrial and Commercial Bank, the Construction Bank and the Agricultural Bank – were directly under the State Council; however, they were also under the "guidance", but not the leadership, of the People's Bank. To complicate matters further, the Construction Bank, while its administration was directly under the State Council, for the purpose of grants and loans it was under the "guidance" of the Ministry of Finance (but currently, it was giving no grants, only loans).

It was evident that in the spheres of finance, pricing and banking, the system was in a state of flux. Until the economic administration of the country was more settled, a new edition of my *China's Economic System* would be impossible to write and then it would take some years to complete. In three years I would reach the compulsory retirement age and after that I would not have the research assistance and other requirements for work. In any case, I was longing to retire and had only postponed it because of departmental politics – I thought I should continue to fight for the department to remain focused on area studies despite the interests of its new head.

From Beijing, I flew to Shanghai for a week. I briefly attended a conference on Nantong, a Yangtze estuary port which forms part of the greater Shanghai district.

I was asked to give a talk to a group of nine economists from the Shanghai Economic Research Centre headed by Tao Zuji. I spoke of the ring of large cities around the Pacific which were developing on rather similar lines, economically and culturally – San Francisco, Los Angeles, Vancouver, Honolulu, Sydney, Hong Kong and, perhaps, Tokyo. In these cities, even in 1984 Hong Kong, manufacturing was becoming relatively less important and the service industries were rising – commerce and finance, the knowledge industry, tourism, education and culture. An international Pacific culture was growing up in these cities, less so in Tokyo but even there more than in the past; race and nationality were becoming less significant. Hong Kong showed the benefits of informal international contacts and relations and also the importance of the rule of law, freedom for individuals and enterprises, low taxation and the non-interference of government in business. In the discussion that followed, they spoke of the "Delta Economic Zone", a term which they said was replacing the "Shanghai Economic Zone". The Delta Economic Zone was not an administrative body but a co-ordinating one, a loose organization for combining efforts within the delta area for developing its resources. The question had arisen of whether Shanghai should help interior provinces raise the efficiency of processing their own raw materials or whether Shanghai itself should continue to process them. I suggested that if prices were free, this question would easily be decided. They thought it would be wasteful for interior provinces to process their local raw materials. Shanghai must, they said, retain its traditional industries but also develop new ones. They were keen that Shanghai, and China as a whole, should become more internationally minded but they were less eager to reduce differentiation between different parts of China. In Shanghai, I also talked with American and Australian consular officials, with David Donaldson, manager of the Chartered Bank, and a number of others.

From Shanghai, I flew to Chongqing and thence, next day, to Wanxian, landing at one of the most primitive airports I have seen – on a plateau among the mountains above the city and an hour or two's journey from it. Only a handful of flights took off or landed there every week and only to Chongqing, Chengdu and perhaps, Wuhan. A perilously steep and narrow road connected the airport to Wanxian far below. On a couple of later trips to Wanxian, I again went by air. Once, the airport bus stalled and nearly slid off an icy patch of ground overhanging a steep cliff; we had to jump out quickly and stand shivering for a couple of hours until a replacement bus arrived; then, having missed our flight, we spent the night in the nearby village. Finally, I stopped flying to Wanxian and decided that the river, or later, a circuitous bus route, was safer.

In 1984 Wanxian and Leshan were still the only two country places in Sichuan open to foreign visitors and I was anxious to see something of the Wanxian region, much poorer than the rich Chengdu plain. From Wanxian, foreigners were permitted to go on only a few designated tours in the neighbouring district, tours operated by China Travel Service, and were forbidden to travel independently on their own. I asked which tour would give me the best opportunity to see something of the local agriculture and was told that it would be the one to the old temple in Yunyang county, and that I might invite Bishop Duan to accompany me. This was a great advantage as he was very knowledgeable about the district. China Travel Service provided a car, driver and guide. We crossed the river by ferry and drove for some hours along a country road, in bad condition but under repair. The countryside was much poorer than the Chengdu plain. We stopped at a local market and then went on to the famous old temple honouring Zhang Fei of the Three Kingdoms era (AD 222–280), which we visited. Parts of the complex were in danger of slipping into the river. A few years later, when the level of the water was being raised by the construction of the Yangtze Dam, the whole temple was dismantled and taken, stone and tile by stone and tile, to a higher site where it was re-erected to provide a major tourist attraction. We lunched at the temple and then crossed the river again to reach the port town of Yunyang, the next stop down river from Wanxian. It was on the same side of the river as Wanxian, but with no road connection.

I was shocked to see the poverty of Yunyang, with buildings left unrepaired for half a century. The bishop, whose movements around his diocese were still limited by the authorities, had never been able to visit Yunyang since his episcopal ordination in October 1949, although there was a church there about which he had had no news in the intervening years. I was happy to be able to provide him with an occasion for visiting it. The old church building was decrepit, like the rest of the town. Former parishioners had taken it over, living there and guarding it. When the bishop came in and introduced himself, an old man got up and threw himself at his feet, weeping. The Catholics had sometimes gathered together for prayer but had no other services for decades. The town, including the church, never saw any repairs because before long, it was scheduled to be covered by the waters of the lake formed by the dam, which was already under discussion. Eventually, a new Yunyang arose above the future lake and it included a new Catholic church built with funds raised by our appeal, launched in Hong Kong.

In August and September 1984, during my nine days in Wanxian, I was able to have a number of long conversations with Bishop Duan in addition to my professional programme of talks with local officials and visits that were arranged for me. He asked me to tell people outside China that "we are very devoted to the Holy See and that we pray for the Pope every day." The catechism printed in Beijing made no mention of the Pope, "but we teach this secretly to catechumens". The so-called bishop's oath, which the government demanded from those about to be ordained bishops, did not mention the Pope or the Holy See but only the Vatican. The bishops and clergy understood the difference but fortunately the government did not. The ordaining bishop is ordered by the government to ask the priest to be ordained, "Are you willing to break off all relations with the Vatican?" The only relations that could exist with "the Vatican" were diplomatic relations with the Pope as Sovereign of the Vatican City State; since such relations did not exist with China, there were none that could be broken off. This was quite different from breaking off spiritual relations with the Bishop of Rome. In any case, when Bishop Duan, after receiving authorisation from the Holy See, ordained Bishop Liu of Chongqing, he had left out the "all" from the oath and they both agreed to make the mental reservation that they meant only political and economic relations (which also did not exist). The omission was noticed and criticised by the "Patriotics". Before consecrating Bishop Liu, Bishop Duan privately told the Chongqing Catholics (who of course did not know he had received papal permission), that he had not separated himself from the Holy Father, but was not in contact with him.

The Bishop told me that there were about 500 Catholics in the city of Wanxian, mainly women at home, reflecting the lesser political pressure on women and on those not in jobs. On Sundays, there was an attendance of about 200 at each of the three Masses. School pupils were forbidden to come to church. Priests in the city were not allowed to go out of town without permission nor might they celebrate Mass in Catholic homes in the countryside. For the great feasts, country Catholics came in large numbers. In 1983, 700 attended at Christmas, including pagans, standing outside the church. With the change from collective to private farming, people were freer to come to church.

In March 1983, a seminary was opened in Chengdu to train priests for the provinces of Sichuan, Yunnan and Guizhou. Bishop Duan did not have confidence in the seminary and said it was under the government. He thought the four-year course much too short, considering the poor background of the students. In Wanxian, an appeal was made to Catholic families in the countryside for candidates with a secondary school education who wanted to enter the seminary. They came to the city, staying in the bishop's compound for a month, being taught catechism. These young men had seldom or never before attended Mass or seen a Bible. Then they would be baptised and make their First Communion – if they had been baptised secretly in infancy there would be no record – and, if the bishop deemed them suitable, sent forthwith to Chengdu to take the entrance exam for the seminary in catechism, history, geography, Chinese literature and politics. Last year there were three candidates from Wanxian of whom only one passed the entrance exam; he was now a seminarian. Bishop Duan said there were a lot of young women in his diocese who wanted to become Sisters but the government would not allow him to open a novitiate.

Bishop Duan told me that the reversion to family farming, since around 1980, continued to bring a great improvement to rural life. Country people now had enough to eat although they were still very poor, with little cash; but those near towns could take advantage of the free markets to sell produce. However, the growing prosperity of the coastal regions of China was much publicised and made Wanxian people jealous. Great pressure was being used to enforce the one-child policy and in Sichuan there were compulsory abortions and forced sterilisations. The bishop had spoken to government officials about natural family planning and they liked the idea but thought it would not work among uneducated people. (I knew that Drs John and Lyn Billings had disproved this in India and elsewhere and contacted them on my return to Australia.) The local government had asked the bishop to get a Catholic hospital for Wanxian and the bishop gave me a written request for this to take to potential donors. The hospital never in fact materialised (it was found that religious hospitals built in China under the Communists were, on completion, soon taken over by the government), but it could have been a centre for teaching natural family planning.

Plans for the Three Gorges Project, a huge Yangtze River Hydro-Electric scheme, had recently been announced, with Wanxian – at the western edge of the Gorges – as its operational base. This would involve linking the city by rail to the line at Daxian. Part of the city of Wanxian would be submerged although at that time it seemed that the church would remain at the edge of the proposed great lake.

It may have been in the course of this visit that the old bishop told me that he was "adopting" me as a younger sister and would call me *mei mei* (younger sister), and that I should call him *ge ge* (elder brother). Matthias Duan was warm and outgoing, putting people at ease, although sometimes impatient with those he thought stupid.

From Wanxian, I went to Chongqing and thence to Chengdu where the Sichuan Academy of Social Sciences had arranged interviews for me with some of their own staff. The Academy's Tang Hongjian spoke to me of the switch of labour from agriculture to industry and other sectors which had begun in 1978 and was gathering pace, although as yet not so fast in Sichuan as in the coastal provinces. With other staff of the Academy, I had interviews about Sichuan's foreign trade and on capital construction in the province. Another Academy economist spoke to me about Chongqing's position in the Sichuan economy. That municipality was in the process of detaching itself from the province. For example, it was not dependent on Sichuan for foreign exchange but controlled its own. Soon afterwards, Chongqing was officially separated from Sichuan and became a city directly under the central government, like Beijing, Shanghai and Tianjin. Wanxian Prefecture then became part of the Municipality of Chongqing and no longer part of Sichuan province. Daxian Prefecture, however, which had been in Wanxian Diocese, remained in Sichuan. Wanxian's name was changed to Wanzhou which was in accordance with its administrative status.

This had repercussions for the Church. For reasons of control, the Chinese government does not permit dioceses to straddle provincial borders.

Daxian Prefecture was thereupon transferred, by government decree, to the Diocese of Nanchong. Bishop Duan was a native of Daxian and he grieved that his home district was no longer part of his diocese. The Holy See does not recognize the alterations to Catholic diocesan boundaries made unilaterally by the Chinese government, but in practice, local dioceses have to accept them on a de facto basis. The Church, however, is not primarily concerned with territory but with people, so this is not nearly as important to it as the appointment of bishops.

In Chengdu, I visited the new seminary which had been opened, in the cathedral compound, since my last visit. I went to the chapel, where about a dozen seminarians were praying. While I was there, some came and some went, but there were never less than about a dozen; their demeanour was devout. Then I spoke to the dean, Father Chen Shizhong of whom Bishop Duan had spoken well. He told me that in this first year, the seminary had thirty-four students, mostly eighteen to twenty-five years old; the oldest was twenty-seven. Any older students would study privately. The seminary library comprised a handful of old books, locked in a bookcase.

From Chengdu, I went for two days to Leshan where I was taken to see evidence of the new economic reforms, including some of the new "rich farmers" who had been able to profit from permission to become "specialised households", concentrating on a cash crop such as fruit. One householder wanted to set up a factory to produce pig feed and was told he would be allowed to employ as many workers as he wanted in it, even a couple of hundred.

Early in 1984, Bishop Deng of Leshan had been severely ill. When news of his illness reached Hong Kong, Father Pieraccini obtained from Rome a card written to the old bishop in Pope John Paul's own hand at Easter. I was given this card to take to Bishop Deng. In the only moments I had alone with the bishop and the newly ordained Father Matthew Luo, I produced this card and handed it to him. He looked at it for a short time and then, obviously frightened, gave it back to me, indicating that I should not show it to Father Luo who was at the other side of the room. At that moment, someone else came into the room and I had no other opportunity to speak to the bishop privately.

Economically, the return to family farming had led to a great rise in living standards in both country and town, especially in rich farming districts such as Leshan where natural conditions are much better than around Wanxian. I formed the impression that Bishop Deng's household were now better fed and had more of the necessities – though not the comforts – of life. Old Sister Mary Rose turned up for Mass in a newish cotton jacket. Once more, I tried to give the bishop some money, but again he refused, saying that they were much better off than formerly. The Pope's card was returned to Father Pieraccini.

The great event in the Church in Leshan since my visit in 1982 had been the ordination of Father Luo at the age of sixty-four. Apart from him and the bishop, the diocese had three other priests and also five students at the seminary. Four churches had been, or were about to be, opened in other places in the diocese.

While in Sichuan, I was also allowed another visit to Guanghan, my former home town, and to meet the Wang family once more; and to have another interview with a local official about that county's economy.

In the restaurant at the Jinjiang Hotel at Chengdu, I had for several days observed a close group of four people, seemingly of one family and not Han Chinese, at a nearby table. A young woman, in a local-style blue serge suit, was accompanied by two older men, also in quite good but obviously local clothing and, with them, another man in a smartly tailored foreign looking suit. I found some excuse to chat to the young woman, who knew a little Chinese and was friendly. She was Tibetan, named Jiong An, and the three others were her uncles. Two had come with her from Ganze in the Tibetan part of Sichuan and the third uncle, the smart-suited one, lived in Switzerland. He spoke German and Chinese and had visited the Tibetan settlements in India where he knew the Terings, the headmaster of the Tibetan school at Mussoorie and his wife, whom I had met when I visited my aunt Tina Ingram there in 1967. He had previously come back to China several times. The whole party was about to leave for Beijing for National

Day (1 October) celebrations and the Swiss uncle would attend meetings there. I surmised that he was one of the Tibetans who liaised between the Dalai Lama and the Chinese. Jiong An was twenty-nine and was a student at a school in Ganze in which her father was a teacher; an elder sister was in Tokyo, working in electronics. Jiong An spoke, but did not write, Chinese, and asked an uncle to write her name and address in that language for me.

Jiong An came for a walk with me along Renmin Lu and we also chatted together on other occasions. As they seemed to be on reasonable terms with the Chinese authorities, I asked if any of the family were Party members. Jiong An said no, adding that few Tibetans belong to the Party. She herself was religious and prayed every day to the Tibetan saints; she said that she knew of a Catholic saint of whom she was very fond, but had forgotten her name; it was a woman with a child in her arms. I said, "Maliya?" (the Chinese for Mary) and she said, "Yes, yes, Maliya. I am very fond of her." Jiong An warmly invited me to visit her home in Ganze and said she would take me to Lhasa and be my interpreter. Afterwards, we corresponded a little. She wrote me two letters, again urging me to visit her, and also sent some cards; I wrote and sent Christmas cards and pictures of Our Lady.

Chengdu had now become the starting point for Western tourist trips to Tibet. That September, I came across a couple from London, Helen Zarod and Martyn Hall, who had hastily returned from Tibet where Helen had nearly died of altitude sickness and Martyn had just in time got her on a plane to return to Chengdu, where she was making a recovery.

I spent October 1984 in Hong Kong, at the Centre for Asian Studies of Hong Kong University and gave a seminar on my recent visit to China. As usual, I had talks with academics there and at the Chinese University and with consular officials, business people and missionaries. I also wrote, for the Holy See, a report on my visit to which I received a very gracious reply, saying that the Holy Father had been informed of my visit and sent his appreciation and blessing.

The draft agreement on the Sino-British Joint Declaration on the future of Hong had just been signed so it was a particularly interesting time to be in the colony. Many of my friends there were in the forefront of public discussion on the issues involved. The inevitability of the step was generally acknowledged but it was met with more apprehension than rejoicing. Emigration of business and professional people from Hong Kong to Canada and other lands accelerated. The rise in Hong Kong property prices temporarily halted and even reversed a bit, from which I benefitted a few months later.

Since at least the 1970s, Father Ladany had been thinking about a project for large scale translation of books for China. In 1981, I had discussed this with Michael Kelly SJ, at that time a Jesuit scholastic in Hong Kong, and with Father Bernard Chu SJ, the Jesuit Provincial for the Chinese Apostolate, to whom in October 1981 I sent a long memo on the topic. I had also talked to my contacts in Rome about this. In December 1984 Father Ladany wrote a memo setting out his ideas on the subject. "When China turned to the West in the beginning of this century," he wrote, "she learnt from the West a materialistic outlook on life ... This way of thinking ... has brought a lot of harm to China. It was thought that only matter, only material progress, counts. This destroyed the normal human virtues and instilled hatred instead of love, vengeance instead of forgiveness and led to the exploitation of man in a totalitarian system. It is therefore important that the total inner core of human civilisation should be widespread and the thinking of the nation transformed. ... That is why one has to try to bring into China books which can strengthen the spiritual forces of the nation. This is also a preparation for introducing the Christian way of thinking. ... one has to convert public opinion, as a preparation of the soil for Christianity."

Early in November 1984, I returned to Canberra to sort out my papers and my future. I had a wonderful Christmas lunch with Kevin and Margaret Kelly and their daughters and then, at the end of the year, I attended the annual John XXIII Fellowship conference and turned my thoughts to retirement.

CHAPTER 21

Retirement to Hong Kong: 1985

At the beginning of 1985, I was already sixty-two and eligible to retire on a reduced pension or work for another three years until the age of compulsory retirement. My dislike of the institutional side of university life had not diminished with the decades, the strain of keeping up year after year with the mass of raw news material coming in from China day by day was increasingly burdensome and mentally draining, and I felt I was getting stale. Also, now that China was more accessible, I wanted to be able to go in and out from a nearby base. In short, I wanted to retire in Hong Kong.

Years previously, I had discussed retiring to Hong Kong with my old friend the anthropologist Barbara E. Ward, and we agreed it would suit us both admirably. She could continue her studies on fishing villages and, for her husband, Stephen Morris, also an anthropologist, it would be a good base for his research in Borneo. For me, Hong Kong was in some way my home town – both my parents had lived there for the last parts of their lives and were now buried in the Colonial Cemetery. The trouble was that the price of property had risen and getting a place to live would be costly. Barbara, alas, died in 1983. Real estate prices had, however, dipped somewhat, probably with the signing, in October 1984, of the agreement on the ending of Hong Kong's colonial status in 1997, so the idea of retiring to Hong Kong became more thinkable. The glimpses of Catholic life in my native province of Sichuan and the possibility of helping the old bishops, and perhaps assisting the publication of religious literature in Hong Kong, while also carrying on with research on the Chinese economy: all this attracted me.

Those were what might be called the "pull" factors, drawing me to Hong Kong. The "push" factors, propelling me to leave ANU, had grown. Apart from Wang Gungwu, none of the other Directors of RSPacS under whom I worked had a first-hand understanding of the demands of China studies, although Anthony Low, Director from 1973 to 1975 and later Vice Chancellor, was always sympathetic. Gungwu, of course, both knew and felt the problems and distress engulfing modern China studies and while he was at ANU and later, when he was Vice-Chancellor of the University of Hong Kong, my relations with him and with his wife, Margaret, were warm. This was helpful while I was head of the Contemporary China Centre but he was unable to persuade other departments in the School to appoint China specialists.

In 1980, Heinz Arndt, the head of our department, had retired, although he still retained an office elsewhere on campus and continued his research on the economics of Indonesia. A few years earlier, he had secured a chair in the department for a friend of his, Max Corden, who had made his name for work on the theory of trade protection but told Arndt that he wanted to switch to applied area studies. Heinz was eager for him to take over as head of department on his own retirement. When the chair was advertised, as it had to be – although I knew it was virtually decided in advance – I sent in an application, saying that I realised that I was unsuited to be head of the department, which had a high concentration of work on Indonesia, but I contended that there should be a second chair in the department for the economic studies of China. In this, I was encouraged by letters from my referees in reply to my request to give their names. Shigeru Ishikawa of Hitotsubishi University wrote: "I consider you are naturally entitled to be a successor of Professor Arndt's chair", while Jürgen Domes of the University of Saarbrücken replied, "I am quite astonished that a scholar of your calibre and international standing did not get a chair a decade ago."

My application for a chair was turned down and Max Corden was appointed as the sole professor in the department. After his appointment, however, Max gave up his previous intention of working on area studies, and continued with theoretical work on international trade. This might have been foreseen considering how difficult the switch would have been to someone in middle life – he was already in his fifties. Arndt, who had enthusiastically schemed for Corden's appointment, now turned violently against him, personally as well as professionally, to the extent that they were hardly on speaking terms. I got on all right with Corden, while considering him inappropriate for our department.

In 1977, the RSPacS had set up a School Review Committee to which I sent a memo. In March 1984, a Review Committee of the Contemporary China Centre followed, to which I also made a submission. After Steve FitzGerald's resignation, the headship of the Centre was held from 1979 to 1983 by Ian F. H. Wilson, a political scientist in ANU's School of General Studies and thereafter by the then Director of RSPacS, who was not a China scholar.

In March 1984, before leaving for China, I wrote to the new committee, sending also the submission I had made to the School review committee in 1977, to which it was a natural appendage. In 1977, I had recommended that the School should be re-organised on regional lines instead of by disciplinary departments. Now I repeated this refrain with special reference to contemporary China studies: "The attempt to assimilate research on Contemporary China with that of the disciplinary departments of the RSPacS has failed. Departments [other than Far Eastern History] have seldom appointed China specialists to positions – especially tenured positions. Michael Lindsay and I have been the only two contemporary China specialists ever to hold tenured positions in RSPacS outside the Department of Far Eastern History. We have both felt the atmosphere uncongenial and have not fitted well into our respective departments. No doubt this may be because of personal factors and we may both be considered difficult. However, this is in the nature of China specialists, through a process of self-selection, aggravated by attempts to force us into disciplinary moulds which are inappropriate to our work … [I recommend that] all the China specialists in RSPacS [at least those outside the Department of Far Eastern History] should be put together in the CCC which should then be elevated to departmental status ... Those disciplinary departments which have not appointed China specialists should – when their next vacancy occurs – have taken from them the resources for the China specialists they have failed to appoint and those resources should be allotted to the CCC ... that some will permit this only over their dead bodies may help to create the necessary vacancies! ... A practical example of the way this disciplinary structure of the School hampers my own work is seen in the cases of three potential students ... All would seem to be capable of doing good research on China's economy but none are qualified, on the criteria laid down by the Economics Department, to be PhD students in the Department. In other words, the disciplinary criteria are irrelevant to most work on the Chinese economy – so arrangements have had to be made for these students to be enrolled in the Asian Studies Faculty. Then, as I have now been made a member of this Faculty, I will be able to supervise them." Requests for opinions had been made by the Committee to others outside ANU. I sent a copy of my submission to Bob Beveridge of Monash University who wrote to the Committee chairman to say he agreed with me.

Later, I made an oral submission to the Committee. I spoke of the stranglehold of disciplines, choking out regional studies. In the RSPacS Economics Department, three positions were now occupied by economists not working on the region and whose work could more appropriately fit into one of the other two economics departments in the University – that of RSSS or of the School of General Studies.

Students of Chinese society were also disadvantaged by other factors – those outside the field failed to realise the problems caused by the scale of work on China; it is acceptable for a scholar to specialise on the economy, politics, history etc. of a single country of e.g. Western Europe and it is assumed by university administrators and others that the equivalent studies of China are comparable whereas they demand much more in both time and resources. This panders to the Western illusion of China being a monolithic whole. China should be thought of as a continent.

The demands of language study, especially of Chinese or Japanese, were not recognized by those who were primarily oriented to academic disciplines. Throughout RSPacS language study had been neglected. Connected with this had been the failure to allow enough time for PhD programmes in Chinese studies; in the US, these might take five or six years, including a couple of years of language study of which at least one must be spent in a Chinese environment. Even when the importance of language had been accepted, there had often been an idea that regional studies equalled a discipline plus an appropriate language, omitting another vital factor – how things happen in a different cultural and physical environment. A neglect of this had led to colossal errors in recent studies of modern China. For example, the sense of obligation for words, thoughts and deeds to correspond is weaker in China than in cultures of a Judaeo-Christian background. Western left-wing intellectuals entered Chinese studies in the expectation of associating with their fellow believers, assuming that professed Chinese Marxists believed Marxism in the manner that "belief" is traditionally meant in the West. When they found this belief was much shallower, their disillusionment was bitter.

The authorities of ANU and RSPacS lacked the will to promote modern Chinese studies. As head of the Contemporary China Centre for its first six and a half years, I was not given the necessary authority to fight for it and to get resources for it because I was not on the right committees; this also meant that I might be uninformed about what was happening and how decisions were being made. I had frequently asked to be put on Faculty Board, the decision-making body in the School, and was always told that this was being considered. Then, immediately I had been succeeded by Steve FitzGerald as head of the CCC, the Centre's head was put on Faculty Board.

The Committee's report came out in 1984 while I was away in China. It rejected my proposed changes: "The proposal that the Centre be transferred into a fully-fledged multi-disciplinary Department of Contemporary China Studies has been considered ... It was rejected on the grounds that it would require additional resources far in excess of what it would be realistic to aim at, and imply reorganization of the School on an area rather than a discipline basis which would be unlikely to command sufficient support in the near future."

In 1983, I had applied once again for a personal chair – several departments in the two research schools in the Coombs Building had more than one professor, and a chair would automatically give me a place on Faculty Board and a greater say in what happened to our department and the CCC. Also, I felt I had earned one, as those I asked for a reference emphatically implied. However, this request was turned down. I had thought a further application might be boosted if I was given an Oxford DLitt and so in 1983 dispatched an application to Oxford, but without any of the preliminary work on the ground which Lady Ogilvie had apparently thought advisable when she offered to undertake the task for me. For a long time, I heard nothing and then in December 1984 received a handwritten letter from the Chairman of the Oxford Social Studies Board saying, "The Social Studies Board decided not to award you the degree of DLitt. I am extremely sorry however both about the decision and about the inordinate time it has taken us to reach it – though this was the result not of our negligence but of the fact that the decision was very finely balanced."

This was, of course, a disappointment, but it was also in a way quite a relief and a closure. I had done all I could to preserve our department's concentration on area studies and now I would not have to stay on but could turn my attention to retirement. I had no great intellectual esteem for anyone, if anyone there then was, at Oxford at that time, in my own field, and therefore their poor opinion of my work was not a severe blow. This may have shown arrogance on my part but in my years of frequenting circles of young academic China-watchers in Hong Kong, I had come across few from British universities. There was Anthony Dicks, who was intelligently carving out for himself a niche in Chinese law, but not many others.

Therefore, early in February 1985, I informed ANU that I intended to retire, with effect from 2 October. Around this time another all too frequent circular from the university administrators demanded a report on work done. I replied: "In 1981 I signed a contract with C. Hurst & Co. of London to write a sequel to my *China's Economic System*. I gathered a lot of material and wrote a chapter and a half. However, these chapters were out of date before I had finished them. From what I have heard in interviews in China, the rate of institutional change is likely to continue equally fast in the next few years. I have therefore concluded that the book cannot be written, at least in the foreseeable future. I have also come to the conclusion that Hong Kong is the only place from which the rapid changes in the Chinese economy can reasonably be studied. So I have decided to retire ... and move to Hong Kong. My most solid work in the past year has been on the economy of Sichuan province and I hope to continue work on this subject in the belief that it is at the provincial level that the most significant research needs to be done at present." I listed ten articles and chapters of edited books which I had authored from 1981 to 1984, plus articles in the London *Times* and the *Wall Street Journal* and a twelve-page critique of the World Bank Report on China which I had written in response to a request from Sir John Crawford; a paper I wrote for a conference in 1984 was included in the conference proceedings and I was currently preparing three papers for conferences to be held in 1985. Having sent in my resignation, I felt bold enough to add: "I would like to put it on record, after experience of universities in four continents over the last forty-two years, that I have found it much more unpleasant to be a woman in a university since the rise of the so-called 'women's movement'. During my university life I have suffered little, if at all, from 'male chauvinism' but, in recent years, have felt constantly threatened by hostility from radical feminists. No notice appears to be taken by the University of the views on matters affecting women held by women in the University who are not radical feminists."

I had some papers to finish and other pieces of research to follow up and wanted to make arrangements with the University of Hong Kong for research facilities after my retirement so in mid-March I went to Hong Kong for a round of information gathering there, seeing my usual contacts and participating in discussions at the Universities Service Centre and the University of Hong Kong and elsewhere. I talked with H. C. Kuan and Joseph Cheng, both of whom I had first met as graduate students abroad. Now back home, they were in the early stages of outstanding careers in local universities. Among expatriates, I spoke to Clare Hollingworth, Leo Goodstadt, and Anthony Dicks and his wife Vicky. HKU offered to give me an honorary research position after my retirement and also expressed willingness to house my extensive files. (NB These, if still extant, would be of little value now except to show how research had to be done in that pre-digital age.) This took a load off my mind as my files would not fit into any small Hong Kong flat. I went across the border for a couple of days to visit Shenzhen and Zhuhai, then fast-growing new cities. I also saw a number of missionaries and Archbishop Tang.

On previous visits to Hong Kong, I had already decided the block where, if possible, I would like to find a flat – Kingsfield Tower, a newish corner building opposite the University across one street, and opposite St Anthony's Church across another. The actual finding and purchase of a flat in that block turned out to be surprisingly quick and easy, hardly deflecting me from my normal Hong Kong China-watching pursuits, thanks to the help of Margaret Chan, wife of my old friend Gregory.

After Gregory Chan resigned from his position as chief judge of the Malaysian armed forces, he moved to Australia where he and his family settled at Perth. He was unable to find a suitable legal job there, so as soon as the children were old enough to be left and the family had all obtained Australian citizenship, he took a position as a magistrate in Hong Kong while Margaret worked there in a real estate agency. Margaret's agency covered another part of Hong Kong Island to that where I wished to be, but she knew how to get things done in Hong Kong property matters and also, of course, she spoke Cantonese, so she was a great help. It happened to be on 19 March, the Feast of St Joseph, whom I had also invoked to find a place to live, that Margaret came with me to Kingsfield Tower, the block I had in mind, and asked the doorman if any flat in the block was on sale. He said no, but added that on the eighteenth floor there was a family which was soon emigrating. We went up and found that the owners were out but would be back that evening so we went again then. The Pangs showed us round the flat, which had three bedrooms, two bathrooms and a largish (for Hong Kong) living room, with lots of built-in cupboards and some book shelving. They said they were soon leaving, with their three children, for Canada and wanted to sell it. Mr Pang was one of several brothers who had held a family council at which it was decided that one of the family should emigrate to Canada and get citizenship before Hong Kong's handover, so if things went badly, he would be able to help the rest of the family to leave. The flat owner exported handbags to Canada and knew the country, so it was decided he should be the one to go. I asked how much they wanted for the flat, and they said HK$860,000, including a car space. Mrs Chan indicated to me that that was all right and, as it was within my price range, I agreed on the spot. The next day, we all met at the office of their solicitor, and signed an agreement and I put down the necessary deposit. I got a bridging loan from the bank for the rest, because I had not yet sold my Canberra house. The Pangs seemed happy to have sold the flat so quickly and without paying an agency fee, and so was I at the swift and hassle-free purchase. I took it as a sign that my decision to move to Hong Kong had been right and was grateful both to St Joseph and to Margaret Chan.

John and Teresa Liu were now back in Hong Kong but on a precarious basis. They had no proper place to live and were more or less camping in a warehouse; they did not have long term visas or jobs. I now had a flat in the colony but would not be moving there until October and even then, would not need the whole flat to myself, so I asked the Lius if they would like to share the flat, which they agreed. Because of the discomfort of their existing accommodation, they were eager to move in as soon as I had possession of it in late April, bringing in their bed even before the hot water heater and washing machine and other items had arrived. This was convenient for me as they would be there to receive equipment and furnishings as these were delivered to the flat, while I continued with my professional programme, staying at HKU's guesthouse, Robert Black College. John and Teresa both found jobs – John, helping with Father Ladany's China News Analysis and Teresa as a secretary to their old friend and mentor, Archbishop Dominic Tang.

The Pangs had left in the flat some old furniture which was not worth selling or taking to Canada. This included a dining table and six chairs which I gladly kept, having resolved not to try to replicate the rather more elegant style of the furnishings of my Canberra home. An old television set was also left in the flat, so for the first time in my life I became a somewhat reluctant owner of one. There were also a number of built-in wardrobes, cupboards and drawers and I bought the minimum of new furniture. The flat has never been re-decorated, and by now (2018) it has become rather shabby. However, it has suited me well, and the others who have lived in it too, throughout the now more than thirty years I have been here.

While in Hong Kong a friend of mine, Dorothy Lee, a retired teacher, took me to one of the centres for Vietnamese refugees, Jubilee Camp, near Tuen Mun. In a disused industrial building, hundreds, perhaps thousands, of people had been crowded. Mainly women and children, they often had only one or two double bunk beds for a family, in a large room with many more people. Despite everything, they seemed remarkably cheerful. Probably, they were relieved that they had survived the most perilous phase of their lives, escaping on fragile boats from Vietnam. Now they had shelter, food, medical care and hope for a better future when they would be settled in some recipient country. NGOs were doing what was possible to provide some rudimentary education for the children with a little English teaching for the adults.

On my return to Canberra early in May 1985, I had to finish the papers for some forthcoming conferences, including one for an ANU conference on religion in communist China. I also had to clear up and dispatch a huge collection of files and decide what to do with my professional library in my university office which, with purchases in Hong Kong and the Mainland, had grown quite large and was often drawn on by others – not only Gough Whitlam! The Australian National Library lacked a number of my Chinese books and I offered to donate these to it. Australian tax laws provided that the value of gifts to the National Library could be set against tax, so the library had the books valued and I received tax relief. Quite a number of English language economics books which I did not want to take to Hong Kong remained, so I put up a notice telling anyone who wished to come and help themselves to them.

A visitor to ANU in June was Mary Somers Heidhuis, whom I had known when I met her parents in Washington DC in 1967 when she was a shy child. Now, as a specialist on South East Asia, she came as a visitor to RSPacS and l was glad to see how she had developed into a very competent professional. In July, I drove to Brisbane for a conference and on the return journey visited the University of New South Wales at Armidale, where I stayed for a night with my friends Karl (the UNSW Librarian) and Virginia Schmude and the next day looked in on David and Delene Michalk at Orange. David had been in charge of an Australian agricultural aid project in Hainan. Another conference in the same month was that, held at ANU, on Religion in Communist Countries, at which l gave a paper on Religion in China since 1949. I concluded that "religious policy in China is a good indicator of the degree of intensity or relaxation in the political atmosphere at any time or place. Chinese authorities consider anything outside their direct control in religious matters riskier than in commerce, industry and finance. Therefore, policy towards religion reflects with some sensitivity the prevailing attitude of officialdom to the world outside China and also its degree of nervousness or self-confidence about its own security at home." After the conference, a meeting took place of the Australian branch of the Keston Institute for the Study of Religion in Communist Lands. In August, Keston organised a conference in Adelaide, to which I went and spoke. From Adelaide l drove to Melbourne where I had an appointment to see Bob Santamaria at his office. I also took the opportunity to visit some other old friends, including the Adies and the Moulds, to say goodbye before leaving Australia.

Years before, the John XXIII Fellowship had sponsored Brian Harrison to study in a Roman seminary after he had been thrown out of Sydney Seminary at Manly for challenging the heterodox theology of its teaching. In June 1985, he was ordained in St Peter's, Rome by Pope John Paul II and had been accepted to work in the Diocese of Puerto Rico. Before beginning there, Father Harrison returned to Australia for what was perhaps rather a triumphalist victory tour. One Sunday that June, he celebrated a Mass of Thanksgiving in Sydney, followed by a social gathering. Tony Abbott

– later Prime Minister of Australia – who, if I remember rightly, had also left Manly Seminary under a somewhat similar cloud – was among those present. A week later, Father Harrison visited Canberra where the local members of the Fellowship entertained him and he called on the Internuncio.

I booked a flight to Hong Kong for 25 October and was anxious to sell my Canberra house before then so as to clear my bank bridging loan. The house was put up for auction, but not a single bid was made and when I left Australia, it still had not been sold. I left it in the hands of an agent, saying he could use his judgement so long as he consulted me before reducing the price below my stipulated minimum. He found a buyer at my minimum price, but at the settlement date, the would-be buyer did not put up the deposit, so the deal fell through. Just at that time, my agent was approached by another client, who was eager to buy the house and, to make sure, offered AU$2,000 above my minimum, so it was sold. Not until some time afterwards did I discover that the purchasers were old friends of mine, John Connors, a prominent local surgeon and his wife Patricia who, with their children now flown the nest, wanted to downsize their previous home.

In my mind was the thought that when I was too old and infirm to do anything useful in Hong Kong, I would return to Australia. So I bought a small unit in a new development just east of Manuka shopping centre and south of St Christopher's Cathedral and furnished it with items from my house. Then I arranged for it to be let on leases of not more than six months at a time.

I have to admit that I am no good at watching commercial entertainment. It bores me and I keep on thinking how much better use I could be making of the time if I were elsewhere. Also, I seem incapable of remembering the various characters, or following a plot on stage or screen. Before leaving Australia, however, I thought I must go at least once to some performance at the Sydney Opera House, which often is used abroad as an icon for Australia. So I arranged a two-day visit to Sydney, the first evening dining with the widowed Margot Traill and her children at their home in St Ives. John had died in 1983 after a long illness, leaving Margot with six children, some still quite young. Margot's brother, Father John Eddy, visited them as often as he could, providing a father figure for his five nieces and their brother. The next day I met Lucy Denley for dinner and a performance (typically, I have forgotten what it was) at the Opera House.

Another event, at the end of my tenure at ANU, was the requiem for Anton Przybylski, an astronomer from Poland, who had been a constant, but quiet presence at Mass on and near the campus and also supported the Right to Life Association. I never knew him well but always held him in high esteem. His PhD was the first degree that ANU ever awarded and Przybylski's Star is named after him.

Soon after my retirement, Wang Gungwu and Margaret gave a fine farewell dinner for me as did many others of my friends, so the last days of my time in Canberra were spent in a flurry of kind hospitality. A couple of weeks before leaving, I went to my last meeting of the Christian Life Group which had meant much to me down the years; it was held at Xavier House, hosted by Father John Eddy. I was present at the AGM of the Pregnancy Support Service, which was going strong. On the anniversary of John Paul II's election, I went to a reception at the Nunciature. Before leaving Canberra, I sold my old car to a graduate student and have never driven again. Then, on 25 October 1985, I flew to Hong Kong.

The years after my retirement have been the happiest and most significant part of my life, for which my previous work and experience was just a preparation. I have written up my activities during these years in considerable detail to provide a quarry for those in China who, at some future time, may want to write the history of their dioceses or parishes. However, publication or other wide dissemination at the present time might endanger persons and communities I have visited and must wait until the Peace of the Church comes to China.

CHAPTER 22

Interim Final Chapter

Reticence is currently a much-underrated quality. I admit to reticence in matters of personal relationships. Self-expression was often seen as a great virtue of the twentieth century, with its suppression supposedly leading to inhibitions, which are presumed always to be harmful. This disregards the possibility that some inhibitions may be desirable, indeed essential to civilised life. In fact, reticence may also be an indirect form of self-expression. This may account for what may appear to be gaps in my biography. At various times, I certainly felt a strong attachment to some of my male friends, more perhaps than they reciprocated, but it never went far. In all cases, they later found much more appropriate matches and I realised both how unsuited we would have been and thankful that nothing came of it. Perhaps I desired primarily the security of a home of my own which I had lacked for most of my childhood. Certainly, I would have loved a home filled with lively children, preferably in the country or with a rather wild garden attached. Always I resolved that if I married, I would, if possible, immediately give up my job, at least for a time, with relief at having found a more important vocation.

However, as the years went by, it became apparent that this was not the way I was being led. So instead of children of my own, I appreciated and loved any youngsters I happened to meet, either casually as short-term friends or in a longer-term relationship as young relatives, godchildren or children of friends. In an age when children have been regarded as burdens, or even as socially reprehensible, I have tried to show that I consider them as important to me in their own right and that I enjoy their company. Young cousins and godchildren[1] (a dozen – or thirteen? or fourteen? – depending on how many unofficial godchildren are included) have a special place in my affections. In young children, the *"imago Dei"* shines brightly – though evidence of original sin can also blossom quite early! In later years, my cousins of younger generations, and also my godchildren, have been very kind, keeping in touch with and, when possible, visiting their ageing and eccentric relative across the globe.

Radical feminism, in the older generation of my family and then further afield, especially in Australia, cast a shadow over my life and is something which I have, throughout my days, felt to be persecuting me. In more "conspiracy theory" moods, I might surmise that the feminist movement is just a giant macho plot to make women do even more of the world's work than they have always done. For my generation in Britain, however, there was also a realisation that being a woman meant having escaped the possibility of being killed on the beaches of Normandy, in the deserts of North Africa or the jungles of Burma.

Of course, a distinction must be made between pragmatic feminism and the ideological type. The tragedies suffered by women in parts of the world subject to little Christian influence – polygamy, female infanticide, the scorn of widows, genital mutilation and so forth – must be opposed. Also, there will always, in the course of history, be shifts in the division of labour between genders as new technologies or changing resources alter the way in which mankind (yes, let us keep in use the old Anglo-Saxon word – as Churchill said, in the English language, man embraces woman) earns its livelihood and brings up its young. The industrial revolution and subsequent technological and organisational changes brought about a major such shift, taking out of the individual household many of the most skilled and interesting tasks – educational, medical, musical, artistic and managerial as well as manual – which had previously filled much of the time

---

1 Pope Francis's *Amoris Laetitia*, when discussing the "wider family" (Section 187, pp. 142–3) makes no mention of godparents, a disappointing omission.

and attention of women, especially those of the more prosperous classes. This left a vacuum, often filled with trivia, and this led to frustration and resentment. For this reason, feminism arose among the better off. Working class women did not protest at gender discrimination excluding them from mining or curtailing the hours they might work in factories. Florence Nightingale, before finding her great vocation, pined for "some regular occupation, for something worth doing, instead of frittering time away on useless trifles."[2]

An even deeper reason for frustration and resentment was a failure to give sufficient appreciation to what have been the core tasks of the home and, indeed of the whole human race, throughout time: the birth, nurture and upbringing of the next generation and the spiritual and psychological, as well as the physical, sustenance of all family members. The skills, concentration and perseverance needed for these pursuits were, and still are, grievously underrated and considered of a much lower order than the professional, technical or manual qualifications of the money-earning family breadwinners. (Incidentally, my friend and one-time mentor, Colin Clark, raised eyebrows when once he calculated that the contribution made to the national income by the average housewife, if properly assessed, was greater than that of the average wage of male manual workers.) Possibly, one way of boosting the esteem of homemaking as an occupation might be to make allowance for time thus spent when assigning grades on promotion scales, by those later transferring to paid jobs. Another way would be to provide similar benefits to families choosing parental home care for small children, to the subsidies given for outside care facilities and similarly, with safeguards, for home schooling. In any case, the economic cost of parents staying at home can now be lessened or obliterated by online home economic activities, including a good deal of the blossoming "gig" economy, which should be encouraged.

The scope of activities open to women in at least some parts of the ancient world can be seen in the final chapter of the scriptural Book of Proverbs, attributed to "Solomon, son of David, King of Israel", in the

2 Roy Strong, *Story of Britain*. Pimlico Edition, 1998, p. 436.

encomium on "The Perfect Wife". This paragon is skilled in manufacturing and commerce: "She is always busy with wool and flax ... she makes her own quilts ... she weaves linen sheets and sells them, she supplies the merchant with sashes"; "She is like a merchant vessel bringing her food from far away". In fashion design, "She is dressed in fine linen and purple" (clothes could not in those days be bought ready-made, nor fashions learned from Paris or *Vogue*). The lady deals in real estate and agricultural investment too: "She sets her mind on a field, then she buys it; with what her hands have earned she plants a vineyard". She is not neglectful of the future but is well insured against its uncertainties: "She is clothed in strength and dignity, she can laugh at the days to come". Neither is our heroine ignorant of the arts of public relations (and did she have a hand in her own write-up?) or of oratory: "Her husband is respected at the city gates ... when she opens her mouth, she does so wisely". She is a philanthropist who "holds out her hand to the poor, she opens her arms to the needy" and also a good educator: "On her tongue is kindly instruction", and as she raises her children well, "her sons stand up and proclaim her blessed".[3] This "Perfect Wife" is no reclusive *purdahnasheen*.

The lack of esteem for the traditionally feminine tasks of the homemaker, which probably intensified in the West (especially in Protestant societies, perhaps less so in Catholic lands such as Italy and Poland) from the industrial revolution onwards, should have been the main complaint of feminists. Connected with this, reasonable demands rightly arose that, as one skilled occupation after another was transferred from the home to outside agencies by technical, organisational and managerial developments, the women who from time immemorial had been undertaking these tasks, should be allowed to continue to do them, but in the new environments to which the work had moved.

This part of the demands of the feminists, the pragmatic side of the movement, was justified. The social friction engendered by major occupational shifts should be minimised and harmony fostered. Instead, an ideological debate often ensued in which women claimed an age-old

3 Book of Proverbs chapter 31 verses 10–31 (quotations taken from *The Jerusalem Bible*).

victimisation, giving rise to a gender conflict. Victimhood is apt to do immense damage to whoever claims it because it diminishes the perceived scope of free will, responsibility and self-reliance. Specifically, it has been drummed into successive generations of young women that education was denied girls in the past. Traditionally, in most families of course, the upbringing of children would have included a one-on-one training of girls by their mothers (or perhaps by older sisters or aunts), and boys by their fathers (or other elders) in the skills that would be needed by adults in families of their type. Usually, for girls, this would be those for necessary tasks which can most easily be combined with the breastfeeding and care of young children (an essential job for each generation if the human race is to survive), such as cooking, the making, washing and repair of clothes and the cleanliness of the household, together with the raising of poultry and such small animals – in China including pigs – as could be kept near the home. Jobs demanding absence from the home, including trades which might more successfully be carried out where a lot of people gathered, as well as those in which greater physical strength is an advantage, such as the carrying of goods (an unpleasant and dull job, which absorbed a large share of the male labour force – as well as some of the female – in pre-industrial times) or metal and wood work, were more likely to be male-dominated; fathers would teach them to their sons as required in their individual circumstances. This individual parental teaching probably declined greatly in the course of the industrial revolution, especially that of boys, which would have been a reason for priority being given to the institutional education of boys over that of girls as literacy became more important for the new manual jobs in which men had to earn a living. For girls, domestic service provided a secure paid livelihood as well as a training for the future care of a home. The links it made between social classes must not be forgotten. As the general standard of living rose in the nineteenth and twentieth centuries, many future housewives must have learned from the homes in which they were employed, the possibilities open for more comfortable lifestyles when their own family incomes rose.

In many families, mothers continued conscientiously to teach domestic skills and, even more importantly, the general management of the home, to their daughters, even if the sons now learned from their fathers, by way of domestic skills, little but the art of carving a joint of meat; and even this was lost when joints went out of fashion, perhaps because of smaller families. In other cases, families assumed homemaking skills would be covered by domestic science taught girls at school, or even in domestic training colleges later. As I found, these classes might be useless. In any case, the differing circumstances surrounding home meals and home care and that in school classes, makes it difficult to transfer skills easily from one to the other. Sometimes, including with me, this home training was missing and this meant that, despite all the talk of improvement in women's education, many girls were getting far less of one important component of education than their counterparts in former generations.

My mother had never acquired many of the small-scale domestic skills. Her youth was divided between India and her parental homes in England – at Brighton, then Tunbridge Wells and, from around 1910, at Wimbledon, all of which were well-staffed. India would have provided her with an understanding of the over-riding responsibilities of running a household where modern facilities such as health care were lacking. This benefitted her later in Sichuan when improvisation was necessary and she showed considerable ability in this, as when she had to set up a field hospital during local military skirmishes; and later, in Hong Kong, when she established a home for destitute old ladies.[4] But there was a deeper misunderstanding of the role of the homemaker, a role that covers much more than material and managerial skills and encompasses social, psychological and spiritual dimensions. Protestant evangelicalism was a Christianity without Mary. For my mother, "God's Work" consisted of being a missionary in the public sense, speaking at meetings, teaching the Gospel to classes or individuals, or doing works of mercy in a religious setting. She scorned the idea of being a housewife – this was a private

---

4 For this, and for her work among refugees in resettlement blocks, Gladys was awarded the MBE by the Hong Kong colonial government.

activity, not in her view "God's Work". I think my father had more understanding of the importance of his parental role than did my mother and this, as well as a yearning for Cornwall, might have led him to accept the Falmouth parish offered him in 1936 had it not been for Gladys's strong opposition. My parents' mutual relationship was primarily that of colleagues in missionary work rather than as partners in homemaking and this confused my own position in the family.

It is the importance attributed to Mary, because of the Incarnation, that conveys the primary significance of the homemaker in human society and in human history. Her acceptance of the Motherhood of the Incarnate Word: the years of His quiet upbringing and nurture and the care of the home, as refugees in Egypt and then at Nazareth during His childhood, His adolescence and life as a young adult; all these have had a far greater importance for the human race than the work of any pope, bishop, statesman, philosopher, writer, inventor or philanthropist.

Only in recent years, when among old papers I found my father's account of his conversion, have I come to realise the continuity between my father's spiritual development, from his attendance at the Edinburgh Conference in 1910 with its stress on Christian unity, and my own. For this unity to manifest itself, because of Christ's Incarnation, something more solid and visible is needed than the ecclesial longings of the early ecumenical movement.

Christ did not write a book but founded a community. Within this community books were written about His life and teaching and about the early life of the Church and some letters of its first leaders collected. Over the centuries, the community assessed these books[5] and, with the promised guidance of the Holy Spirit, its leadership decided which should be in the canon of those written under divine inspiration. When disputes over the interpretation of these writings arose, it was the leadership – the Magisterium – of the community which decided the matter.

---

5 This process can be observed in e.g. *Eusebius: The History of the Church* (which I have recently been reading) where, writing in the 4th century, the author mentions ongoing disputes about the acceptance of various epistles and part of the book of Revelation.

My spiritual life has always been humdrum and ordinary, nothing spectacular, but finding in prayer and the sacraments the strength to carry on. Life may sometimes have seemed tedious, day after day. Middle age, especially, drags on for so long and I remembered Ronnie Knox's warning in sermons, of the *accidie* (boredom) of middle life being a greater danger than the temptations of youth. My favourite spiritual reading, after the Scriptures, is that very simple book, Brother Lawrence's *Practice of the Presence of God*. As long as I am conscious of His Presence, I am content and do not look for further emotional excitement.

As my life span lengthens, I have felt a growing realisation of the responsibility that old age brings to try to interpret earlier times to the present. Our age is one of enforced toleration of diversity among contemporaries, whether within our own society or in strange societies worldwide (except towards those contemporaries who fail to adapt with chameleonic efficiency to current political correctness). This is accompanied by a scorn of diversity between historical time zones and a feeling of immense superiority to our fellow human beings of past centuries.

One of the benefits of the classical studies of any ancient civilisation, including Scriptural study, is the respect entailed and instilled for a pre-industrial society. Even in practical matters, those days were in some ways superior to ours. Imagine, at the present time, a couple with a baby, on the spur of the moment, deciding to travel on foot or by donkey, and apparently being able to do so peacefully, from Bethlehem to Egypt, perhaps via the Gaza Strip, without visas or foreign exchange arrangements (although the Holy Family would have had, safely tucked away, those easily portable, easily divisible and highly valuable gifts, providentially just brought by the Magi). Then think of Saul of Tarsus walking on the road from Jerusalem to Damascus – try it today (2018)! Much earlier, Abraham and his kin, with large flocks of livestock as well as caravans containing children, the elderly and others, meandered across West Asia from (what is now) Iraq, through present-day Syria, Israel, Palestine and, some generations later, entered Egypt. Today, the tribe would have been decimated or corralled into refugee camps on the way.

Much scorn is shown today to the reticence of past generations on sexual matters, but the benefits of modern laxity in this sphere is not obvious. Old-fashioned reticence enabled most of the young to grow up in a healthier environment than at present. Nowadays a single well-placed academic article in a prestigious journal can set off a campaign to overthrow millennia-old moral teaching without regard for tradition – tradition being the instinct for giving a vote to past generations. Perhaps deep studies, which I have not come across, have already been made of the epidemiology of ideas. The speedy spread of youth radicalism in the mid-1960s is an example. It was not just coincidence that the Red Guards were terrorising China around the time of the student unrest in Western Europe and North America. The succession of campaigns for laxity in laws governing divorce, then contraception and abortion, then homosexuality and same-sex marriage, and then euthanasia, seems unstoppable except, if continued, by extinction through natural selection, by means of demographic decline in societies where such practices are usual. The Church can, and should, proclaim the moral law but is unable to enforce it. The Creator, however, can do so, working through His Law of Natural Selection. The Laws of evolution will prove much stronger than statutory laws, whether permissive or prohibitive. The permissive society is a cul-de-sac: it has no future.

Every person's life is lived against the background of world events and intertwined movements. The decline of the British Empire, the demographic collapse of the West, the Second World War, the Cold War, Britain's changeable, wavering ties in the latter twentieth and early twenty-first centuries with Europe and the old Empire: all these have formed the backdrop to my own slow pilgrimage. Most prominent has been the turbulent history of China, the land of my birth, followed by its economic upswing in the latter part of my life and its prospective demographic decline in future years. More comments on this may fall within the final volume of my memoirs which, I hope, I will be given the strength to complete but which it may not be possible to publish or circulate, for the sake of friends in China, until long after my death.

My personal life and my academic writings have both spanned China before and after 1949. Sometimes, newcomers to the Chinese scene think that, whatever else may be said about the Communists, the post-1949 government may at least claim that it, at last, raised the labouring masses of the country to post-industrial standards of living. A closer study, however, suggests that what delayed and impeded such a development was, first, the Japanese invasion of 1937 and then, the introduction of the Communist economic and political models after 1949. In 1936, China seemed a nation of hope. Early in 1937, the British Commercial Counsellor at Shanghai reported "that Chinese private interests can adapt themselves to modern economic needs is shown by the growth of a number of enterprises ... the outstanding feature (sc. of China's economic life at that time) ... is the increasing, justified confidence which the Chinese themselves as well as the world at large have in the future of this country, a confidence based on the remarkable growth of stability achieved in recent years and the improved political, financial and economic conduct of affairs – government and private."[6] Indeed, it may have been apprehension at China's growing economic might which prompted Japanese aggression. The Communist victory in 1949, ending the devastating civil war, led to a marked improvement in the next few years but this was stymied in 1958–9 by the absurd excesses of the Great Leap Forward, resulting in the Mao famine of 1959–61 in which 30 million or more people may have died in China. This was followed by a few years of recovery under the influence of Liu Shaoqi before the Cultural Revolution of 1967–76 crashed down on the intellectual and cultural life of the country as well as on its economy.

These events, resulting first from Japanese aggression and then from Communist rule, effectively postponed China's modernisation until the 1980s. An informant, familiar with both Taiwan in 1957 and Sichuan in 1980, told me that by the latter year Sichuan's towns had reached the

6 United Kingdom, Department of Overseas Trade, Report on Economic and Commercial Conditions in China 1937 (quoted on pp. 28–9 of G. C. Allen and Audrey Donnithorne, *Western Enterprise in Far Eastern Economic Development: China and Japan,* Allen & Unwin, London, 1954).

level of Taiwan's in 1957, but its rural areas had not caught up similarly. The communist regime, like the Japanese invasion of China, had been an impeding factor, not an agent of progress. Repairing the damage done was slow. The most long-lasting harm inflicted on China by the Communists may have been the One-Child Policy which will need generations to assuage. Those who envisage a brilliant twenty-first century for China should look at Japan now. The legacy of mutual suspicion and distrust engendered by the regime, too, will take long to dissipate. Radical political ideas, such as those generating the Great Leap and the Cultural Revolution, can spread like wildfire, thanks to modern communications, while constructive economic and social policies are far harder and slower to implement. Above all, the moral fundaments of society, especially family life, can only gradually be rebuilt.

Meanwhile, there are a number of other problems related to China on which I should like to comment. The first must be a question of definition. What is China? The government in Beijing always assumes China is primarily a nation state. But that, surely, is to demean China which, in my view, is first and foremost a civilisation – a civilisation which certainly encompasses and enfolds a nation state but which is much greater in time and space and concept than that nation state. A modern nation state is a cut and dried entity, with boundaries. "Greater China" may also cover the Chinese diaspora, considerably increased in recent decades, rooted in Chinese civilisation but scattered worldwide. In time as well as in space, Chinese civilisation does not have the same boundaries as the nation state of China. It is now known that early China was multipolar (or that there were at that time several Chinas?), with many early centres of civilisation developing in different parts of what is now called China. The old idea that Chinese civilisation grew out of one centre in the Yellow River basin must be discarded as discoveries have shown that, in other parts of present day China, early centres of culture existed contemporaneously with the Yellow River civilisation, these separate centres gradually coalescing. For example, the archaeological discoveries at Sanxingdui in Sichuan, with which my father was associated, show the high level of culture attained by Shu in early times.

Always at the back of my mind, in studying China, has been the question of how far, in fact, is China (the nation state) governable, by any regime or system of rule. The answer to this may lie in the old Chinese proverb, that governing a large country is like cooking a small fish – it should not be overdone. This was best followed by those honouring, if not always following, the political philosophy of *wu wei er xing*,[7] sometimes translated as "masterly inactivity", that of the ruler setting the tone for officials and people to follow, but not doing much else. Of course, it presupposes strong family structures as the primary and rather independent units of society.

The old legend told to illustrate this principle is that of an emperor who, travelling one day's journey from his capital, came across a prosperous farmer ploughing a field, enjoying all the benefits of peaceful rule, yet who had never even heard of the emperor or his government, so light had been their exactions. *Wu wei er xing*, however, is fundamentally different from the concept of laissez faire. Laissez faire assumes an abnegation of responsibility by the government (leaving it to the market – or whatever – to decide) while *wu wei er xing* involves a continuing obligation of the rulers to set an example. A stark contrast is also glaring between this and all modern political models, whether of the Western welfare state or still more of the Communist. It also contrasts with the Greek ideal of the positive, ennobling effect of participation in the civic life of a *polis*. The clash between the contrasting views of China and Greece is something I find hard to resolve but I suspect a solution may lie in the concept of "the common good". The harmonious resolution of this intellectual conflict will have to await the realisation of the Kingdom of God, which – if any human comparison is possible – might be envisaged both as the culmination of *wu wei er xing* and also as an ideal *polis,* the City of God, the new Jerusalem.

---

7 *Wu wei er xing* was the phrase I remember hearing in lectures at WCUU in Chengdu in the 1940s, but it has been pointed out to me that in Daoist literature, *wu wei er wei* is generally used while the version *wu wei er zhi* has also been instanced. The general meaning, however, is the same: governing by example, but not trying to micro-manage.

Man's fallen nature is the reason why *wu wei er xing* has proven impractical and why active government became necessary. This can be acclaimed as a *felix culpa* by necessitating the *polis* as a method of re-education of sinful humanity. However, the opposite has too often been the case, with the depravation of political authority reaching new depths in Stalin's Soviet Union, Hitler's Germany and Mao's China. But human stubbornness goes both ways; tyrants soon find it working against them, usually because they wish to do too much. Despite, or as a result of, fierce campaigns on numerous policies, China's Communist government controls the country chiefly in the sense that if it perceives something that it thinks must be suppressed or done at any one point of time or in a particular place, or that superficial wide compliance with a policy must be evident for a period, it can probably secure the enforcement of its writ, though at the likely expense of having less vigour left for some other task which therefore is unfulfilled. The one-child policy may be cited to contradict this. In the countryside, the campaign was often savage, but in many places seemingly intermittent or not comprehensive, as instanced by examples of multi-child families and rumours of non-reporting of girl births. In urban areas, in most parts of the world, easy and cheap access to contraceptives seems sufficient to reduce birth rates to well below replacement level without coercion, although, in Chinese cities, work units and street committees played important roles in this. When policies ride on waves of societal opinion, as did in China the youth movements of the late 1960s, or from the 1980s, population control movements in urban areas, the Chinese authorities could surf the waves. It is more doubtful if they will be able, if they so wish, to reverse strong demographic trends. The governments of the world are apt to confuse the birth rate with the bank rate and to think that both can be switched around at will. Blanket, long-term systematic implementation of policies is elusive – the government has over-cooked the fish.

Cultural continuity and traditional values are, at the time of writing, being trumpeted by China's political leader, who simultaneously reiterates his Party's atheism. Yet surely, one of the most traditional of China's concepts is that of "Tian" – Heaven – sensed as the overriding and beneficent power in the universe. Nor, at any time in Chinese history, has a fiercer attack been made on traditional values and historic physical structures than that carried out, in the Cultural Revolution, through the instrumentality of the Communist Party or its offshoots.

Another matter concerning China that has dogged the latter part of my life – the distinction, and confusion, between the underground and above-ground Christians, especially Catholics in China – is not unconnected with the question of the significance of words in China which I discussed in the final chapter of my *China's Economic System* and which I repeat here: "The Chinese have a sophisticated attitude to outward expression of opinion ... words are regarded as symbolic counters, to be moved about the chessboard of life in order to produce the desired effect. This leads to reservations and subtleties of expression and action which need to be interpreted within the framework of the Chinese environment and which a stranger might not understand. There commonly lacks the sense of an obligation for words and beliefs, or words and actions, to correspond. While this phenomenon is certainly present in other cultures, it is not normally so strong as in China. It has the result that outward compliance is easily obtained but that an individual's or a group's 'public face' must not be taken as an indication of its 'private face'. Thus, conformity though easily won is apt to remain superficial ... sabotage need be none the less effective for being done in silence. Indeed, the more contrary to central government orders that local cadres are acting, the more loudly they may give verbal support to those orders."[8] In the second (as yet unpublishable) part of my memoirs, I hope to take up this line of thought again.

My own sentiment is that overmuch attention has been given, by observers of China, to formal definitions and wording in political and social contexts. Sometimes, situations are best left as accepted ambiguities, such, for example, as the "two Chinas". As applied to religious matters, formal diplomatic relations might not necessarily benefit the Catholic Church, which might then lose its advantage among the Chinese people of

8 Donnithorne, *China's Economic System*, pp. 508–9.

being seen as at odds with a despised and disliked regime. The resumption of diplomatic relations between China and the Holy See will probably come eventually, but in God's good time, in this millennium or the next. Also, we must bear in mind that, perhaps, the greatest long-term danger to the Church in China may come not from government oppression, but from government patronage and that, as in the fourth century West, the switch from one to the other might arrive with surprising speed. Such a development would be facilitated by any concession made by the Holy See to allow the Chinese government a role in the appointment of bishops. Meanwhile, the Church must continue to pursue its mission at ground level in the haziness of our mortal view. Clarity may be necessary in certain areas of law and in natural sciences, but is sometimes best neglected, or at least not unduly worried about, in social and political – and, sometimes, with discretion, even in religious – matters.[9]

I often wish that the monsignori in the Secretariat of State, instead of spending time and effort on trying to re-establish diplomatic links with the Chinese government, would go out to the streets of Rome and look for any Chinese tourists who seem bewildered and offer to show them round the sights. On one of my last visits to Rome, in the 1990s, I noticed two young Chinese near St Peter's, looking puzzled and consulting their guide book. I went up to them and, after their surprise that I addressed them in Chinese, asking if they would like to be shown round the basilica, they gladly agreed. Later, they gave me the address of their family firm in Shanghai where, a year or so afterwards, I called on them. There are now more opportunities to share the knowledge of the Incarnation with Chinese abroad rather than worrying over what the Church is unable to do in their homeland, although we should also try our best to help the local Church there. Let us remember that on the birthday of the Church, when the Holy Spirit descended on that prayerful gathering of believers, their immediate reaction was not to discuss how to deal with Caesar in the imperial capital, but to go out into the streets around them to speak

---

9 The United Kingdom had good de facto relations with the Holy See long before it had formal diplomatic ties, which were not fully restored until 1982.

both to the locals and to the visitors from overseas who were thronging the city.[10]

Most of the material in the account of my retirement years, to be published later, will be taken from reports I made of visits to Catholic dioceses on the Mainland, chiefly in Sichuan, Guizhou and Yunnan, during the years from 1986 until 1997, when I was expelled from the Mainland and had to cease visiting those areas. These chapters, in which I quote extensively from the reports I sent to interested parties in Hong Kong, Rome, Germany, France and elsewhere, I envisage primarily as a quarry from which those who may in future be writing the histories of their dioceses in China, can mine raw materials, to supplement local information. In addition, I include chapters on our publication project, Shengming Yiyi Publications, which provided religious literature in simplified characters for the Mainland and on the Association for International Teaching, Educational and Curriculum Exchange (AITECE), an organization primarily for sending teachers to China. The years after 1997, when I could no longer travel on the Mainland, due at first to visa refusal and then to infirmity, are dealt with more summarily, but cover continued co-operation on projects, especially in the new towns of the Three Gorges area, with the re-building of churches after the Sichuan earthquake of 2008 and also working with Hong Kong colleagues who could travel more freely. Growing contact with Mainlanders coming to Hong Kong or passing through to further destinations has helped me keep in touch with Sichuan and the rest of southwest China where my heart still lies. As years pass and frailty increases, there is less to say, except to ask my friends to remember China, and me too, in their prayers both now and after my departure from this vale of exile.

---

10 Acts of the Apostles, Chapter 2.

Vyvyan H. Donnithorne, 1960

Vyvyan H. Donnithorne, 1966

Appendix:
V. H. Donnithorne's Account of His Conversion

These notes were written by Vyvyan Henry Donnithorne after he had settled in Kowloon, Hong Kong, in 1953. They have been lightly edited and typed by his daughter Audrey from his handwritten manuscript. His use of old spellings of Chinese place names has been retained.

Archdeacon V. H. Donnithorne

Conversion

After leaving school at sixteen, V. H. Donnithorne studied engineering at the University of London College of Engineering. Then he became an engineer in London, becoming technical manager for a company manufacturing X-ray apparatus for hospitals all over the UK. During these years the constant insistence of the teachers and text books on the sole adequacy of physical "science" and the universality of the "laws of matter", and consequent emphasis on man's entire self-dependence, gradually obliterated early childhood faith. He therefore arrived at the age of twenty-three already an agnostic and strongly contemptuous of what he considered the "unscientific" Christian faith. In that year, 1909, at the age of twenty-three, he was sent by his company on a business tour of Scotland and northern England, with instructions to visit hospitals and doctors who were contemplating installing an X-ray department, and providing them with advice and estimates. These were the earlier premier days of radiology, when the apparatus was extremely primitive compared to the present elaborate installations. In this tour, he did quite well in the way of drumming up orders for his firm. His last call on this tour of business was on the general hospital at Penrith, in Cumberland. Penrith is the change station for Keswick, in the Lake District, where the Keswick Convention was at that time in session. Having made this last call, and finished his work on Friday evening, he decided to continue along the branch line for the few miles to Keswick, and spend the week-end in the enjoyment of the beauties of the Lake District, instead of spending it in London. When he arrived at Keswick, the Convention was in progress and he put up for the week-end at the house of a relative, where all of the other house-party had come to attend the Convention. Here he was very much out of his element; all the house party were enthusiastic Christians, all carried Bibles wherever they went; and all the conversation was about religion. Out of courtesy to his hosts, more than anything else, he agreed to go with them to some of the tent meetings. The first he attended was the great Missionary Meeting on the Saturday morning. What he saw and heard on that occasion made an ineffaceable impression. This was the first time he had ever come across evangelical Christianity in its true form. He was immediately struck by the huge text over the platform, that read: "ALL ONE IN CHRIST JESUS". Hitherto he had thought of the Christian Church – as he had seen it – as a medley of antagonistic and fiercely competing sects. But *these* people were different. They were "all one"; that was undeniable; they *loved* each other, even when their denominations were different; it was with reluctance that they separated again; then, they were certainly *happy*, and had a light in their faces. Clearly all these people had "something" – and "something" which was very desirable. *Where* did they get it *from*, and *how* did they get it? It must be from the *Book* they always carried about with them and from which they could not be parted!

So he made a first decision: as soon as he got back to London, he would start to read this Book himself, and ascertain whether perhaps there *was* something in it after all! His college lecturers and professors had poured scorn upon the Bible as a source of *truth*; nobody believed in *that* book now, they said; it was only a collection of old wives' fables! But to these people at Keswick, and to the platform speakers, it was something more than that! When he was free by himself again, he would empty his mind of old prejudices and read this book with a new purpose.

On Monday evening V. H. Donnithorne was back in London, reported on his tour, and back to his home in Queen's Gate, South Kensington. That evening he opened the Bible and began to read the Gospels. But he still realised he was bitterly prejudiced against the possibility of any "revelation", except that which could be demonstrated by aid of the test-tube and chemical balance. Therefore, in an attempt to empty his mind of accepted prejudices, before he began his reading, he would pray a little prayer, quite sincerely and with humility: "O God – if there is a God, which I do not know at present – show me if Jesus Christ is our Saviour or not; and if you do show me that He is, I promise to serve Him." That was all he knew, and all he did; but each evening after the days' work in the engineering office, he would read the Gospels until bedtime and pray the same prayer. And after a few days, the Book began to grip him. Someone was speaking from it and making demands from it. Bit by bit, he yielded ground, and let the Book grip him. Jesus, especially, was inexplicable. His words were penetrating, and came from one who *knew*. He was a phenomenon which no test-tube, or chemical balance, or telescope could explain! It was Revelation of a Person, not "investigation" of a phenomenon. Three weeks after leaving Keswick he had found certainty and truth in Christ as Saviour.

Call to Mission Field, and educational preparation

Immediately, he felt a compulsion to express his new faith in Christian service. Within a fortnight of his conversion, he had discovered the Cambridge University Mission to Bermondsey, working by means of Christian boys' clubs amongst desperately needy and ignorant boys in the darkest slums of London's East End. There he found the real Gospel in energetic action. The mission was carried on by keen evangelical undergraduates from Cambridge; the Gospel was preached with power and reliance upon Scriptural truth; and conversions were seen almost every week. Here he served in the Gospel for three years, working in the City every day and spending every week-end in the Bermondsey slums with his boys.[1] He was invited to form a troop of Boy Scouts for the boys; and this he did, forming the first Bermondsey Boy Scout Troop and becoming the Scoutmaster. This Boys' Club was his first – and best – theological training school. Here he worked under the encouragement and supervision of the very godly and evangelical Director, the Rev Harold Salmon. Mr Salmon was himself a Cambridge graduate, and had been frustrated by ill-health from his early ambition to serve his Lord in the mission field, but had never lost his early missionary enthusiasm. Very soon after commencing work in this club under Harold Salmon, V. H. Donnithorne himself found a movement in his heart tugging him towards the mission field. As he was at this time securely settled in a business career in the engineering field this urge towards the mission field seemed preposterous and absurd; and so said all his relatives to whom he broached the idea. But, nevertheless, the idea persisted and grew stronger and stronger. Somehow, he must get this matter settled. About this time, he obtained news that there was to be something called a missionary conference to be held in Edinburgh in January 1910. (This was, of course, the great Edinburgh Conference of 1910, from which so much sprang, the beginning of missionary comity in the mission field.) Getting leave from his firm, he went up to Edinburgh, and presented himself at the Assembly Hall at the opening date – only to find that the meetings were open only to "delegates" from the mission churches who were bearers of the certified badge! Here was a dilemma indeed; he had come all the way up from London to find out whether there was really any sense in this "missionary business" or not and he could not get admission to the meetings! At his hotel in Prince St. he had met a fellow guest at table, who seemed to be connected in some way with this missionary conference. To him he applied and stated his grievance. His friend was no less a person

1 Note by A. G. Donnithorne: V. H. Donnithorne continued his association with the Bermondsey centre while at Cambridge from 1911 to 1914 but presumably spent less time there then.

than Mr D. E. Hoste, Director of the China Inland Mission at the time. Mr Hoste looked at him a minute and then said: "Well, would you be willing to be an usher?" Accordingly, an usher's badge was pinned on to him and he was able to attend all the sessions to show the delegates their allotted seats. At this famous conference, he received a more definite call: to the mission field; and not only to the mission field, but to the field of China in particular. For at these meetings he made firm friends with the young leader of the Chinese delegation, a young man called Wang Quincey. Now the "call" had become so clear and insistent that something had to be done about it. Therefore, he sold out of his engineering business, and went back to college to prepare himself for a missionary career. This time it was Cambridge University, not London, because there the evangelical faith had taken hold more strongly than anywhere else, and there was a very strong missionary fervour in the CICCU (Cambridge Inter-Collegiate Christian Union). Also, Cambridge had that year decided to put on a Chinese Tripos (course for honours degree). He therefore took the entrance exam and became an undergraduate of Clare College, taking the tripos course in Chinese classical language. The Chinese Tripos turned out to be a very searching course of studies, comprising not only the main books of the Chinese classics, the books of Confucius and of Mencius, but also the History of China from the beginnings to the Sun Yat Sen Revolution; and the history of the Far East.

After three years, he graduated, and obtained his degree of MA; that was the fatal year of 1914; therefore, the next three years were spent in the army, on active service first as a private soldier in the Royal Fusiliers and then as an officer in the Royal Hampshire Regiment. A severe leg wound sustained in the Battle of Loos at the beginning of 1916 caused him to be invalided out of the army; so he was able to return to Cambridge for post-graduate study, and studied theology at the evangelical college of Ridley Hall. Eventually, having graduated in theology at the end of 1919, the war having ended, he was able to take up again his missionary ambition. Bishop Cassels, one of the "Cambridge Seven", who was bishop of the Anglican church in Szechuan province, was in great need of a man to come out and take charge of the university students' hostel in Chengtu, and for this purpose he came to Cambridge and appealed to the CICCU for such a man. Hearing that V. H. Donnithorne was preparing for China, and reading the Chinese tripos, the bishop interviewed him in his rooms on King's Parade, with the result that V. H. Donnithorne was definitely booked to come to Chengtu for this post.

He was married on 19 September 1919 to Gladys, daughter of T. Lewis Ingram of the Middle Temple, and sailed for China in November; and made the long journey up the Yangtse River by Chinese junk in four months. The board of missionaries in the field, in whose hands the local administration of the mission lay, saw the need of the vast population of the country districts, in a population of 70 million, in a province the size of the whole of France, as paramount to the need even of the students in Chengtu, and after two years of language study, and the passing of the prescribed exam, he was appointed to pioneer evangelistic work in the large frontier city of Anhsien, in west Szechuan. This was the largest missionary district in the west China mission, and comprised not only the main station in the city of Anhsien, but also seven other city outstations, each with a church and a Chinese pastor, and each distant a whole day's walk from the home base. Also, a visit had to be paid at least once a year to the furthest outstation of Mowchow, the city on the border between China and Tibet, and a month's hard travel away. He was still suffering from the broken left leg and although crutches had been discarded, he was obliged to walk still with two sticks. As each outstation had to be visited at least once a month, and Communion administered, all this meant a vast amount of foot-slogging, for there were only narrow mud roads, and no motor vehicles; and carrying-chairs, with three men, were exorbitantly expensive. There was nothing for it therefore but to walk on foot, on the rough mountainous roads, from outstation to outstation, and then to walk back. But one compensation grew out of this exhausting routine of foot-slogging, which was that, in the course of many years of such work, the bad leg steadily regained strength, till when he left the western province more than forty years later, the bad leg had become just as strong as the good one.

In 1925 occurred the unfortunate "May 30th Affair" in Shanghai, when Chinese students clashed with police, with the result that all over China there were anti-British risings. In August that year, Mr and Mrs Donnithorne had gone to the mountains for a cool retreat in the middle of that very hot summer, when they were surprised in their retreat cottage by an array of Chinese robbers, who seized them and their little daughter Audrey, two years old; tied them up and hurried them off to their robbers' stronghold in the heart of the mountains, where they were held for a month while the robbers tried fruitlessly to extract ransom money.

Two years later, all British missionaries in the country were advised to leave their stations and assemble in Shanghai. Returning to England in 1927, V. H. Donnithorne returned to Cambridge University for the third time, this time as Chaplain of Downing College, the leading science college.

On returning to the field in 1929, he was appointed first the Secretary of the Western China mission, and later as Archdeacon of the West Szechuan Diocese, remaining in the position, under a Chinese bishop, Bishop Song, until the "Liberation", when the Communist forces overran China and overthrew the government in 1949. Mr and Mrs Donnithorne then settled in Kowloon to carry out relief work for the Chinese refugees.

Index

Abnett, Bill 376
Adie, W. A. C. 'Ian' 177, 278, 282, 285, 397
Adie, Monna (née Besse) 303, 397
Aikman, David 376
Allen, George C. 131–2, 134, 143–6, 162, 170–1, 174, 178, 18–2, 187, 192, 211, 229, 246, 274, 313, 344, 374
Alley, Rewi 75
Altmann, Avraham 289
Anscombe, Elizabeth see Geach, Elizabeth
Armstrong, Hilary 123
Anxian 5, 10–14, 333–4
Apthorp, Joan 296
Aris, Ungku 136
Arnaiz, Rev. Eusebius 80, 348
Arndt, Heinz 194, 246, 388–9
Auschwitz 154–5, 292
Austermann, Heinrich 302
Avery, Ellen 97
Avis, Patricia 117

Baker, Hugh 177
Bampton, Capt. William 340
Barbarito, Archbishop 320, 344
Barclay, Gurney 28–9, 33, 61
Barley, Ronald 225–7
Bartlett, Marion (née Phillips) 50–1
Barlow, Colin 246
Bearcroft, Peter 116, 220, 345
Bearcroft, Rosalind (née Chamberlain) 116, 125, 220, 345, 367

Becker, Jasper 181
Beckett, Chris 363
Beipei 83, 120, 198
Belfiori, Rev. Franco 325, 327, 338, 350, 359
Bell, Coral 178, 260
Bennett-Jones, Nicola (née Ingram) 204, 217, 316–17, 366
Bennett-Jones, Owen 366
Bensusan-Butt, David 246, 301, 345
Berezina, Julia 155
Bergère, Marie-Claire 303, 313
Bergoglio, Jorge (Pope Francis) 160
Berry, Sir James 24
Berry, Lady Mabel (née Ingram) 16, 21, 24–5
Beveridge, Bob 250, 390
Bijvoet, Astrid 201
Bijvoet, Hanny 118, 200–1
Billings, John 381
Billings, Lyn 381
Bishop, Enid 278, 283
Blacker, Carlos 117
Blacker, Carmen 117
Blau, Gerda 211
Blunden, Edmund 157
Blythe, W. L. 178
Bogle, Joanna 367
Boisguèrin, Bishop 352
Bonavia, David 282, 358
Bonython, John 249
Bordeaux, Michael 300
Bowley, Marian 131, 197

Bowman, Phyllis 238
Bown, Lalage 116
Boynton, Lucy 77
Brandauer, Frederick 187
Brandauer, Marie 187
Braye-Yuen (Uen), Germaine 81, 96
Breitenfeld, Elisabeth 215
Breitenfeld, Hubert 175, 215
Breitenfeld, Johanne 214–15, 367
Breitenfeld, Norma 175
Breitenfeld, Walburga 215
Breitenfeld, Walter 214
Brennan, Rev. Frank 347
Brennan, Sir Gerard 347
Brooke, Eileen 50, 192, 225, 300
Brown, Capt. H. 94
Brown, Isobel see Crook, Isobel
Brown, Lucy 118, 302, 367
Brus, Włodzimiers 149
Bryan, Derek 75
Bryan, Esther (née Ingram) 42, 121–2, 344
Bryan, Guy 42, 122, 344
Bryan, Hong-ying (née Liao) 75
Bucknall, Kevin 178, 299
Bui, Diem 322
Bui, Hong 322–3
Bui, Quoc 321–3
Bui, Tam 321–3
Bui, Tri 321
Bui, Triet 321
Bull, Hedley 260, 366
Burns, Arthur 270–2
Buxton, Jacqueline 29, 175
Buxton, Martin 29, 146, 175–6
Byrd, William 371

Cahill, Archbishop Thomas 271, 273
Cains, Beverly 296, 343
Cains, Kevin 343
Calcutta 83–4, 86–8, 340
Canberra 45, 50, 102, 141, 147, 180, 194, 196–7, 236, 242, 244–5, 247–51, 254–5, 257, 259, 262–5,

267–9, 271–6, 287, 293, 295–7, 299, 301, 304–6, 309–10, 312, 314–15, 317–19, 321–3, 325, 336, 338, 340, 342–3, 345–6, 348–9, 359–61, 364–5, 370, 374, 376, 386, 395–6, 398–9
Cantlie, Sir James 93
Cantlie, Lieut.-Col. Kenneth 93
Carstens, Patricia 216
Cassels, Bishop William 4–5, 421
Cater, Jack 189, 194, 325
Cater, Peggy 189, 325
Chamberlain, Rosalind see Bearcroft, Rosalind
Chan, Flora 261
Chan, Gregory 199–200, 301–2, 394
Chan, Margaret 200, 302, 394–5
Chan, Y. S. 260, 300
Charles, Rev. Rodger 366
Chen, Guofu 334
Chen, Jerome 177, 266, 300, 369
Chen Xiaoling 326, 329
Cheng, Grace 374
Cheng, Joseph 374, 393
Chengdu 5, 58, 64–7, 69–70, 73–82, 84–5, 96, 98, 129, 135, 167, 174, 186, 200, 206, 255, 329–35, 337, 348, 351, 355–7, 366, 378, 379, 381–5
Chesneaux, Jean 259
Chey, Jocelyn 260
Chiang Kai-shek, Madame 94
Chiang, Yee 305
Ching, Julia see Oxtoby, Julia
Chinnery, J. 177
Chiu, Rebecca 359
Chongqing 14, 58, 62, 64, 74, 83, 85–6, 92, 120, 198, 233, 331, 356, 378, 380, 382
Chou, Eric 178
Chou, S. H. 266
Chmielewski, Janusz 165–6, 184
Christoe, Edith 340
Christoe, Jim 340
Chu, Rev. Bernard 386

Chu, Rev. Michael 364
Church Missionary Society 3, 14, 28, 39, 41, 43, 46–8, 61, 63, 70, 83, 334
Churchill, Winston 46, 49, 94, 99, 102, 401
Chuzo, Ichiko 307
Cirillo, Rev. R. 228–30
Clark, Colin 146, 210, 236, 266, 308, 350, 402
Clark, Gregory 308
Clark, Manning 263
Clifford, Bill 360
Clifford, Margaret 360
Close, Alexandra 'Sandy' 304
Coonan, Rev. John 212, 234
Connelly, Matthew 211
Conroy, Richard 375
Coombs, H. C. 'Nugget' 245
Corcos, Valerie 117, 366
Corden, Max 388–9
Corlett, Ann (née Nicholson) 132, 220
Corlett, Wilfred 131–2, 220
Cowen, Lady 341
Cowen, Rabbi Shimon 266, 341
Cowen, Sir Zelman 341
Cox, Jnr. Cmdr. Cecily 93
Craft, Henry 343
Crane, Rev. Paul 123, 210
Crawford, Sir John 242, 245, 393
Crofts, Anthony 100
Crofts, John 25, 27, 218
Crofts, Maud (née Ingram) 16, 21, 24–5, 27, 55, 100, 121, 218
Crofts, Rosemary see Vaughan, Rosemary
de Crombrugghe, Dom Albéric 81, 186
Crook, David 75
Crook, Elizabeth 312
Crook, Frederick 312
Crook, Isobel (née Brown) 75
Curtis, Chantal 263
Curtis, Peter 263

Dalton, Hugh 124

Dargan, Rev. Herbert 233
Daroesman, Ruth 247, 269, 312
Darvill, Hilary (née Reay-Smith) 124, 366
Darvill, John 366
Davies, Mary (née Ingram) 344, 366
Dawe, Jeanette 117
Delhi 4, 16, 20–1, 53, 87–8, 155–6, 163, 173–4, 190–2
Deng, Bishop Paul Jizhou 350, 352–4, 356, 383–4
Denley, Lucy 399
Denmark 74
Dernberger, Bob 373
Deutscher, Isaac 177
Dicks, Anthony 358, 392, 394
Dicks, Vicky 394
Dikötter, Frank 181
Dillsworth, Dennis 204, 219, 344
Dillsworth, Dilmot 204, 219
Dillsworth, Jeanne 204, 219–20, 344
Dillsworth, Raymond 344
Dingle, John 215
Dingle, Monica 215
Dolciani, Mary 220
Dolfin, John 159, 363
Domes, Jürgen 258, 313, 388
Domes, Marie-Luise 313
Donaldson, David 378
Donnithorne, Alan 299
Donnithorne, Dawn 299
Donnithorne, Don 299
Donnithorne, Edith see Rawlence, Edith
Donnithorne, Gladys (née Ingram) 4–5, 21, 406, 422
Donnithorne, Harold 24, 344
Donnithorne, Harriet 23
Donnithorne, Irene 344
Donnithorne, James 340
Donnithorne, Lilian (née Ingram) 24, 45, 121
Donnithorne, Sarah (née Bampton) 340
Donnithorne, Stuart 26–7

Donnithorne, Archdeacon Vyvyan H.
3–5, 24, 27, 67, 417
Douglas, Dame Mary 234, 302
Draguhn, Werner 302
Drew, W. 177
Drewnowski, Jadwiga 149
Drewnowski, Jan 149
Duan, Bishop Matthias Yinming 331,
350, 354, 356–9, 367, 379–83
Duffy, Rev. Paul 271
Duncan, Rita 296
Duncan, Ron 296
Duncanson, Dennis 178
Dunn, Sir William 314
Dyer, Teresa see Kay, Teresa

Eccles, Sir John 266
Eckstein, Alex 301
Eckstein, Ruth 301
Eddy, Rev. John 263–5, 302, 317, 360,
399
Edmund, Harold 'Digger' 319
Edmund, Mabel 306–7, 318–19, 349
Ellegiers, Daniel 258
Elkisch, F. 215
Elliott, Bishop Peter 342
Elvin, Mark 177, 313, 344, 350, 365
Elwes, Monsignor Valentine 113
Emslie, Tsu-tung 133, 167–8, 170, 176,
188, 283
Eto, Kozuko 308
Eto, Shinkichi 162, 259, 307

Fairbank, John 186
Falkenheim, Victor 369
Farrer, Rev. Austin 95, 110
Feeney, Margaret 232
Fei, Xiaotong 347
Feng, Yuxiang 'The Christian General'
337
Fincher, John 299
Finnis, John 344, 366
FitzGerald, Gay 279, 282
FitzGerald, Stephen 259–60, 262, 279,

282, 297–8, 306, 309, 389, 391
Flynn, Neville 315
Foot, Philippa 110
Forace, Joe 282
Forsythe, Peter 336
Fox, Rev. Roger 192
Freedman, Maurice 147, 152, 177, 193,
266
Funnell, Victor 4, 147, 177, 250, 339
Fuzhou 46

Gaitskell, Hugh 131–2
Galbiati, Rev. Fernando 325, 338, 350,
359, 364
Gambia 4, 17, 19, 22, 340
Ganshin, G. A. 164, 172
Garnett, Sister Margaret 'Peggy' 37
Garnsey, Rev. George 348
Gaussen, Helen see Peacocke, Helen
Gaussen, Horace 44–5
Gaussen, Louise (née Ingram) 44–5
Geach, Barbara see Liccione, Barbara
Geach, Elizabeth (née Anscombe) 118,
313, 371
Geach, Peter 371
Gedda, Luigi 211
Ghidoni, Monsignor 365
Giedroyc, Michal 'Mike' 161, 344, 366
Giedroyc, Rosie 161, 344, 366
Gittings, John 177
Glunin 164, 172–3
Godfrey, Archbishop 210
Godson, Bob 282
Goodell, Grace 347, 367–9, 371, 373–4
Goodstadt, Leo F. 194, 338, 350, 358,
364, 394
Goodstadt, Rose 338, 350
Gong (Kung), Archbishop Pingmei 328
Gonzi, Archbishop 230
Graham, David C. 67
Grassby, Al 302
Gray, Jack 177, 313
Gray, Maisie 313
Guanghan (Hanchow) 58, 60, 62–70,

79, 120, 332–3, 355–6, 384
Guillermaz, General J. 196
Gurgaon 20, 53, 156, 173

Hague, Sir Douglas 131–2
Haiphong 57
Halifax, Lord 94
Han, Su-yin 194
Hanchow *see* Guanghan
Harradine, Brian 296–7
Harris, John 301, 343
Harris, Ruth (née Picton) 301, 343
Harrison, Rev. Brian 364, 397–8
Hawker, Jane (née Ingram) 217, 267–8,
    310–11, 344, 366
Heidhuis, Mary Somers 397
Hicks, George 364
Hicks, Sir John 112, 304
Hicks, Lady Ursula 112
Hill, Roland 214–15
Ho, Ping-ti 373
Hodgson, Peter 222, 366
Hogan, Sir Michael 207
Holland, William 'Bill' 178, 187
Hollingworth, Clare 350, 358, 394
Honey, P. J. 177
Hook, Brian 313
Hook, Vilma 313
Hoste, Rev. D. E. 4, 421
Hoyle, Molly 126
Howard, John 255
Hsia, Ronald 156, 177
Hsieh, Chiao-Min 177
Hsu, Bishop Francis C. P. 117–18
Hu, Ruth 64
Huang Weixin 313
Huck, Arthur 178, 250
Hunkin, Bishop 43, 52
Hunter, Kay 216
Hyatt, Helen 311
Hyatt, Rev. Bob 311

Ichiko, Chuzo 307

Ikonnikov, Anton 261, 299
Ingram, Esther *see* Bryan, Esther
Ingram, Evangeline 'Tina' 21, 25, 41, 94,
    104, 190–1, 384
Ingram, Geoffrey 187, 216
Ingram, George 25–6, 87, 192
Ingram, Gladys *see* Donnithorne, Gladys
Ingram, Helen 'Nell' 17, 21, 25
Ingram, Ilsley (G. I. C. Ingram) 25–6,
    33, 47, 49, 101, 127, 204, 217, 267,
    305, 317
Ingram, James 18–19
Ingram, Jane *see* Hawker, Jane
Ingram, Jill 217, 344
Ingram, John 374
Ingram, Julie 374–5
Ingram, Lilian *see* Donnithorne, Lilian
Ingram, Louise *see* Gaussen, Louise
Ingram, Loveday (née Donnithorne)
    16, 24
Ingram, Mabel *see* Berry, Lady Mabel
Ingram, Margaret *see* Pratt, Margaret
Ingram, Mary *see* Davies, Mary
Ingram, Maurice 217–18, 344, 366
Ingram, Nicola *see* Bennett-Jones, Nicola
Ingram, Patricia (née Forbes Irving) 49,
    127, 217, 269
Ingram, Philippa 101
Ingram, Robert 16, 21, 25, 99, 187,
    190–1, 216–18, 231, 313, 317
Ingram, Rosalind *see* Talks, Rosalind
Ingram, Ruby *see* Pitt, Ruby
Ingram, Tesa 101
Ingram, Dr Thomas L. 4, 19
Ingram, Thomas L. of The Gambia 22,
    340
Ingram, Tom 26, 100–1, 205, 344, 366
Ingram, Victoria (née Skinner) 4, 18–20,
    60, 121, 314
Ishikawa, Shigeru 162, 259, 307, 388

Jansens, Rev. 210
Jao, Y. C. 363

Jin Zhonghe 376
Jiong An 384–5
Joffé, Eli 287–9, 291–2
John XXIII Fellowship 342, 346, 370, 374, 386, 397
Johnson, Claudia (née Carasco) 216, 304
Johnson, Gale 373
Johnson, Monsignor Vernon 113–14
Jones, J. R. 160
de Jonghe, Archbishop G. 137, 208
Jory, Colin H. 342–4
Joy, Rev. Patrick 206–7, 210, 233

Kamm, John 327
Kamenka, Alice (née Tay) 278, 280, 284
Kamenka, Eugene 278, 280, 283
Kay, Bernard 116, 159, 189, 197, 367
Kay, Teresa (née Dyer) 116, 135, 159, 197, 367
Kawashima, Toyono 163
Kawashima, Yoshio 163
Kelly, Rev. Edward 'Ned' 233
Kelly, Kevin 360, 386
Kelly, Margaret 360, 386
Kelly, Philippa 261
Kennedy, Elspeth 116, 366
Kent, Bruce 234–5
Kessler, Cécile (née Offen) 116, 303
Kierkegaard, Soren 81
Kirby, Stuart 156, 174
Kielt, Rev. James 232
Kiwanuka, Benedicto 203–4, 224
Kloskowska, Antonina 'Tola' 148–9, 152, 165
Knox, Monsignor Ronald 'Ronnie' 113, 407
Kramer, Olga 195
Kraus, Willy 324
Kuan, Hsin-Chi 375, 393
Kung, H. H. 77
Kunming 57–8, 64, 73–4, 76, 86

Ladany, Rev. Laszlo 160, 232–3, 300, 325–6, 328, 338, 350, 359, 361, 364,

371, 386, 395
Lai, David 177
Lal, Parshadi 18–19, 156, 173
Langford, Rev. Graham 82, 200
Lapwood, Nancy 75
Lapwood, Ralph 75
Lardy, Nicholas 300
Larsen, Antoinette 'Netty' (née Merrillees) 275
Larsen, James 275
Lattimore, Owen 177–9
Łatyk, Maria 172
Law, Kathleen 215
Lawler, Lady Doreen 263–4, 363
Lawler, Michael 362–3
Lawler, Sir Peter 45, 263–4, 363
Lawler, Sonya 362
Lazzarotto, Rev. Angelo 325, 364
Lee, Dorothy 396
Lechler, John 14, 205, 334
Lescoe, Rev. F. J. 367
de Lestapis, Rev. S. 236–7
Lewis, John 186
Leys, Simon see Ryckmans, Pierre
Li, Bichang 375–6
Li, Choh Ming 375
Li, Bishop Xiting 331
Liao, Grace 59
Liao, Hong-ying 75
Liccione, Barbara (née Geach) 371
Liccione, Mike 371
Lieberthal, Jane 373
Lieberthal, Kenneth 373
Liechti, Elisabeth 33
Lim, Edwin 371
Lin, Cyril 313, 365
Lindsay, Michael (Lord Lindsay of Birker) 98, 174, 184, 389
Lindsay, Xiaoli 174, 184
Liu, Bishop Xianru of Chengdu 329
Liu, John 361, 374, 395
Liu, Shaoqi 181, 328, 409
Liu, Teresa 361, 374, 395
London, Ivan 371

London, Maria 371
Low, Anthony 309, 388
Low, Mary 113–14, 199, 204, 345, 367
Lubbock, Georgette (née Ashmead-
 Bartlett) 100
Luo, Chongshu 72–3
Luo, Wenyu 72
Luo, Bishop Matthew Duxi 352
Luo, Yuanzheng 320, 337, 347, 375
Lupton, Colina (née MacDougall) 174,
 178
Lupton, Geoffrey 174
Lutley, Rev. Bertie 79
Lutley, Martha 79
Lyons, Sir Joseph 273
Lyons, Dame Enid 273
Lyons, Tom 370

McCarthy, Christine 342
McCarthy, John 342
McClement, Monsignor Frederick
 202–3, 212
McCormack, Rev. A. 236
Macdermott, George 251
MacDonagh, Carmel 263–4
MacDonagh, Oliver 263–4
Macdonald, Mary 110
MacDougall, Colina see Lupton, Colina
Macedonski, Alexander 166
MacFarquhar, Sir Alexander 156
MacFarquhar, Lady 156
MacFarquhar, Roderick 156
McIver, James 177
MacKerras, Colin 278, 284
MacKisack, May 108
Mackinnon, Donald 110
McMillan, Janettie 339–40
Mah, Feng-Hwa 178
Makower, Helen 127, 200
Manchukuo see Manchuria
Manchuria (Manchukuo) 46, 71, 74, 94,
 162, 179, 300
Marcel, Gabriel 114
Maritain, Jacques 78, 86

Marshall, John 236
Marshall, Peter 258
Martin, Anne 117
Maude, Christopher 127
Maué, Margret 122, 124, 302
Maung, Augustine Maung 305
Maung, Clara 305
Maurice, Michael 127
Maxwell, Bishop Alec 56–7
Mazumdar, Dipak 132, 156
Mei, Tsu-Tung see Emslie, Tsu-tung
Mei, Yi-Chi 76
Mei, Yi-Pao 76, 167
Melbourne 178, 247–8, 250, 267, 305,
 318, 339–40, 342–3, 348, 360, 370,
 397
van Melckebeke, Bishop Carl 137
Merrillees, Parvine Helen (née Razavi)
 89, 189, 220, 275
Merrillees, Robert 189, 220, 275
Mianyang 5, 14, 333
Mianzhu 5–6, 9–11, 14, 334
Michalk, David 397
Michalk, Delene 397
Millen, Pat 299
Millen, Mary 299
Mills, Erin 296
Mills, Reg 296
Mintoff, Anne 229–31
Mintoff, Rev. Dennis 228–9
Mintoff, Dom 228–30
Mintoff, Joan 229–31
Mintoff, Moyra (née Bentinck) 229–31
Miyashita, Tadao 163
Milward, Rev. Peter 163
Mitchell, Capt. W. 93
Mol, Hans 374
Molgaard, Margaret 73–4
Molgaard, Val 73–4
Montgomery, Lieut.-Col. Brian 91
Moran, Jean 263–4
Moran, Pat 263–4, 266
Morgan, Michael 282
Morris, Barbara E. (née Ward) 177, 189,

269, 313, 325, 387
Morris, Stephen 387
Mortimer, Rachel 31
Mortimer, Reginald 31
Mould, Michael 301, 304, 397
Mould, Sheila 301, 304, 397
Moule, Ernest C. H. 46, 48, 51, 69
Moule, Josephine 48, 50
Mowll, Bishop Howard 6, 12
Munthe-Kaas, Harald 174, 177
Murphey, Rhoads 178
Murphy, Richard 117
Myers, Archbishop 96
Myers, Ray 374
Myrdal, Alva 211
Myrdal, Gunnar 211

Needham, Joseph 179–80
Needham, Rev. Brother Lawrence
    'Laurie' 263, 338
Nehru, R. K. 190
Newport, Mary 263–4
Nicholson, Ann see Corlett, Ann
Nimmo, Jim 263–4, 315
Nimmo, Nell 263–4, 315
Nokajima, Inuka 307
Nolan, Peter 302
Nove, Alec 146–7, 179
Nowicki, Jozef 149, 152, 165

Oddy, Clare (née Corlett) 220, 344, 367
Oddy, Gavin 344
Ogilvie, Sir Frederick 129
Ogilvie, Lady Mary 95, 126, 265, 366,
    392
Olçomendy, Bishop 206
Okita, Saburo 162, 374
Okozaki, Ayakoto 162
Oksenberg, Michel 'Mike' 259, 282, 284
O'Brien, Rev. Roderick 307, 324, 339,
    348
O'Chee, Bill 297
O'Connor, Jim 301
O'Connor, Rita 301

O'Neill, Rev. Michael 232
O'Sullivan, Richard 222
Onoue, Etsuzo 307
Oxtoby, Julia (née Ching) 368
Oxtoby, Will 368

Page, Faith (née Rawlence) 359, 366
Page, Mike 359, 366
Pajecka 172
Palliser, Sir Michael 221
Pang, Rev. Paul 365
Paranjpe, V. V. 155
Parfit, Jessie 79, 366
Parfit, Norman 79, 366
Parsons, Rev. John 343–4
Paul, Margaret (née Ramsey) 132
Peacocke, Bishop Cuthbert 'Cip' 44–5
Peacocke, Helen (née Gaussen) 44–5
Pell, Rev. George (now Cardinal) 342
Perkins, Charles 276, 318
Perkins, Dwight 186, 259
Petre, Ann 122
Phelps Brown, Henry 265
Phillips, A. W. H. 'Bill' 257
Phillips, Cyril 170–1
Phillips, Marion see Bartlett, Marion
Picton, Ruth see Harris, Ruth
Piercy, Lady Mary 98
Piercy, Penelope 73, 77–8, 95, 98, 110,
    121, 126–7, 200, 302, 314, 344, 348,
    367
Piercy, Priscilla 127
Piercy, William (Lord Piercy of Burford)
    98
Pitt, Joy see Ross, Joy
Pitt, Marcelle see Reay-Smith, Marcelle
Pitt, Philip 124
Pitt, Ruby (neé Ingram) 124
Plamenatz, John 300
Plamenatz, Marjorie 300
Plater, Teresa 153–4
Platt, Nick 308
Plimsoll, Sir James 255
Pollak, Marzena 148, 175, 182, 196

Poplai, S. L. 190
Pratt, Margaret (née Ingram) 369
Pressnell, Leslie 132
Price, Charles 374
Prest, Alan 266, 366
Prest, Pauline 266
Prout, Margaret Fisher 41
Przbylski, Anton 399

Quan, Phan 222

Rawlence, Duncan 45, 47
Rawlence, Edith (née Donnithorne) 24, 45
Rawlence, Faith see Page, Faith
Rawlence, Jenefer see White, Jenefer
Rawlence, Patrick 101
Rawlence, Roger 100
Raymond, Aubrey 178
Razavi, Dorothy 96
Razavi, Parvine Helen see Merrillees, Parvine Helen
Reay-Smith, Jack 124–5
Reay-Smith, Marcelle (née Pitt 124–5)
Reader, Eleanor 52
Regis, Sister Maria 162
Reid, Billy 253
Rey, Helena 151–3, 196
Rey, Krysztof 148–50, 152, 165, 172, 175, 184, 196
Rhys Williams, Elspeth 238
Richman, Barry 186
Ride, Lindsay 158
Rigby, Harry 247
Rigby, Norma 247
Rigby, Richard 247, 308
Rigby, Tai-fang 247, 308
Robbins, Lionel (Baron Robbins of Clare Market) 235
Roberts, Margaret see Thatcher, Margaret
Roberts, Niall 225
Robinson, Brian 264
Robinson, Heather 264

Robinson, Joan 168, 180–1
Rogers, David 366
Rope, William 282
Ross, Joy (née Pitt) 124–5
Ross, Philip 125, 366
Ross, Ronald 125
Roth, Cecil 113
Rouchouse, Bishop Jacques 80
Roy, Andy 69
Rubin, Vitaly 287
Rudner, Martin 288–9, 292–3
Ruhlmann, Lois 196
Ruhlmann, Robert 196
Russell, Betty 96
Ryckmans, Pierre 247, 261–2
Ryckmans, Han-fang 247

St John, Janet (née Thompson) 29, 31–4, 36, 43, 55, 101, 206
Salmon, Rev. Harold 420
Salvation Army 17, 20, 25
Santai (Tongchuan) 5, 335
Santamaria, B. A. 'Bob' 343, 397
Sanxingdui (Three Star Knoll), Guanghan 67, 410
Sapieha, Cardinal 154
Scarabelotti, Gary 343
Schapiro, Leonard 146–7
Schifferin, Zvi 288–9, 291
Schmude, Karl 342, 397
Schmude, Virginia 397
Scott Thomson, Gladys 101, 179
Schram, Stuart 177, 302
Schurmann, Franz 304
Schultz, T. W. 373
Searle, Mel 376
Sebes, Rev. Joseph 185
Seton, Francis 313
Seton, Ruth 313
Shanghai 5, 14–15, 69, 71, 85, 134, 160, 195, 261, 325–9, 335, 338, 362–5, 369, 375, 377–8, 382, 409, 414, 423
Sheridan, Greg 342
Shilcock, Grace 36

Shilcock, Joan 36
Sichuan (Szechuan) 3–5, 13–14, 29, 36,
   46, 51, 54–8, 60–6, 68–72, 74, 76,
   79–81, 83, 120, 146–7, 155, 186–7,
   198, 205, 320, 325, 329–30, 334–6,
   348, 350, 352, 354–5, 357–9, 375,
   378, 381–2, 384, 387, 393, 405,
   409–10, 415
Sikorski, Gen. Władysław 90
Silcock, Arnold 135
Silcock, Tom 135, 194
Simon, Harry 250
Simon, Julian 211, 374
Skinner, Col. James 20, 156, 191
Skinner, George 19
Skinner, Michael 191
Skinner, Rosie 192
Skinner, Victoria see Ingram, Victoria
Sladkovski, M. I. 155
Slawinski, Roman 182
Slocombe, Canon 103
Smith, Rev. Earnshaw 'Annie' 44
Soegijapranota, Bishop Albertus 208
Song, Bishop C. T. 79, 331, 357, 423
Spencer, Anthony 225, 228, 236
Spraos, John 132
van der Sprenkel, Sybille 177
Standley, Cécile see Kessler, Cécile
Stenhouse, Rev. Paul 343
Stern, John 282
Stolz, Rev. Mervyn 271–2, 318
Stonier, Alfred 131–2
Storrs, Major Jack 91, 93, 102
Straits Trading Co. 136
Streicher, Chris 370
Stuart, Leighton 76
Sturmey, Stanley 132
Sucharchuk 155
Sun Ru 337
Sun Yat Sen 72, 93, 289, 421
Sundrum 246
Sutherland, Lucy 111
Swiezawski, Stefan 153–4
Szczepanik, Ann 156–7

Szczepanik, Edward 156–7, 174, 224
Szechuan see Sichuan

Talks, Rev. David 324, 366
Talks, Rosalind (née Ingram) 324, 366
Takahashi 307
Tan, Dato Sir Cheng-Lock 136
Tan Ek Khoo 135
Tang, Archbishop Dominic 359, 361,
   364, 394–5
Tang, Rev. Yuanjia 331
Tao, Col. 67
Tao Zuji 377
Tay, Alice see Kamenka, Alice
Taylor Smith, Bishop John 44
Teh, Huey-Beng 190
Teiwes, Fred 299
Thatcher, Margaret (née Roberts) 110,
   115, 120, 132, 199, 298
Thompson, David 29, 36, 100, 206
Thompson, Dora (née Watney) 29,
   31–33, 36, 45, 61, 206, 299
Thompson, Rev. Hamlet 'Hammy'
   29–31, 34, 45, 54, 205–6, 299
Thompson, Janet see St John, Janet
Thompson, John 29, 36, 101, 205
Thompson, Marjorie 205, 299
Thompson, Tom 29, 36, 101, 205, 299
Thorne, Alan 278, 284
Tien, Ju-kang 346
Tien, Ruth 346
Tongchuan see Santai
Topley, Kenneth 194
Topley, Margery 194
Tout, Herbert 131
Traill, John 360, 398
Traill, Margot 360, 398
Tran, Rev. John Baptist 345–6
Tran, Rev. Joseph 345–6
Tretiak, Dan 174
Tretiak, Lois 174
Trevelyan, Mary 203
Trevor, Capt. Ivor 93

Tung, Chee Hwa 371
Turowicz, Jerzy 153
Twitchett, David 269

Uhr, Janet 296
Uhr, Marie-Louise 296
Unger, Esther (née Ehrmann) 116, 289, 302

Varga, Rev. Andrew 233
Vaughan, Dame Janet 109, 119, 126
Vaughan, Rosemary (née Crofts) 218, 366
Vaughan, William 'Bill' 218, 314, 366
Velasco, Bishop Juan 233
Vernon Harcourt, Janet 39
Vetch, Henri 157, 250
Vogel, Ezra 186
Vokinger, Hans 125

Wałensa, Lech 157, 224
Waller, Derek 177
Wang, Chuanlun 376
Wang, Deren 332–3, 355–6
Wang, Gungwu 247, 309, 388, 399
Wang, Jingwei 92
Wang, Margaret 388, 399
Wang, Rev., of Guanghan 63–4
Ward, Barbara E. see Morris, Barbara E.
Warren, R. W. 'Bill' 366
Watney, Lily 33
Watt, Rev. F. J. 5
Wee, Anne 190
Weil, Martin 373
Weiss, Ruth 75, 337
Wheeler, Col. 177
White, Barbara Sue 195
White, Jenefer (née Rawlence) 102
White, Lynn 195, 371
White, Rev. Victor 114
Whitaker, Ann 116
Whiteside, Rev. R. A. 5
Whitlam, Gough 242, 255, 260, 262,

272–3, 306, 396
Wightman, Phyllis (née Ticciati) 112, 116
Wilberforce, William 3
Wiles, Peter 147, 177, 258, 269, 345, 366
Williams, Dick 363
Williams, Shirley (Baroness Williams of Crosby) 265
Williams, Bernard 265
Williams, Tim 338, 350, 358, 363
Wilson, David 156, 194, 259, 302, 325
Wilson, Dick 177
Wilson, Ian 278, 285, 389
Winnington, Alan 175–6
Wittfogel, Esther 265
Wittfogel, Karl 265
Wolters, Euteen 374
Wolters, Oliver 374
Wong, Christine 370
Wong, Ellen Hee-Aik 190
Wong, John Chiu-Hon 133, 177
Wong, Lin-Ken 185
Wong, Quincy 3
Wood, Adrian 371
Woodruff, Douglas 214, 235
Woolf, Kathleen 296
Woolgar, Rev. Daniel 95–6
World Bank 185, 370–2, 393
Woytyła, Karol (Pope John Paul II) 154, 360, 383, 397
Wren, Lieut.-Col. 91
Wright, Margaret 50
Wu, Rukang 284
Wu, Yuan-Li (Y. L.) 185, 265, 304, 374
Wynn-Williams, Hugo 218, 324
Wynn-Williams, Mary (née Vaughan) 218, 324

Xian 70
Xindu 70
Xu, Yi 375

Yang, Gladys 337
Yang, Jisheng 181

Yang, Xianyi 337
Yahuda, Michael 178, 302
Yakovev, A. G. 172
Yamada, Haruko 308
Yamada, Hideo 162, 308
Yu, Archbishop Bin 85, 233
Yu, Lucia 350
Yu, Margaret 158
Yu, Patrick S. S. 117–18, 158, 350
Yu, Xiguang 181

Zakrzewski, Edward 166
Zarod, Helen 385
Zhang, De-en 334
Zhang, Rev. Zhiyu 357
Zhang, Wenjin 281–2
Zhao, Bill 369
Zhou, Rev. Brother Peter 187
Zhu, Rev. Vincent Hongsheng 326–8
Zubrzycki, Alexandra 360
Zubrzycki, Jerzy 'George' 360

Lightning Source UK Ltd.
Milton Keynes UK
UKHW010033170820
368169UK00014B/146